A851087167

D1799568

Civil Society, Capitalism
and the State

Civil Society, Capitalism and the State

Part 2 of The Liberal Socialism of
Thomas Hill Green

imprint-academic.com

Published in the UK by
Imprint Academic, PO Box 200, Exeter EX5 5YX, UK

Distributed in the USA by
Ingram Book Company,
One Ingram Blvd., La Vergne, TN 37086, USA

ISBN 9781845402147

A CIP catalogue record for this book is available from the
British Library and US Library of Congress

'There are some people, I know, who think that we have only to sit still, and Reform will come of itself. There is a game one sees children playing at, in which one says to the other, "Open your mouth and shut your eyes, and see what will come to your great surprise." (Laughter and cheers.) So they think — these good, easy souls — that if we only shut our eyes close enough, and open our mouths wide enough, the cherries will drop in through some unseen beneficence of the governing class.'
T.H. Green, public meeting of the Oxford Reform Club, 25 March 1867 (Works, vol. 5, p. 227)

'If we wish to investigate the best constitution appropriately, we must first decide what is the most desirable life; for if we do not know that, the best constitution is also bound to elude us.'
Aristotle, Politics, Book 7, section 1

'But the effect of her being on those around her was incalculably diffusive: for the growing good of the world is partly dependent on unhistoric acts; and that things are not so ill with you and me as they might have been, is half owing to the number who lived faithfully a hidden life, and rest in unvisited tombs.'
George Eliot, Middlemarch, the closing paragraph.

'Let the flag of England be dragged through the dirt rather than sixpence be added to the taxes which weigh on the poor.'
T.H. Green, quoted in Nettleship, Memoir, pp. xx–xxi

Contents

Part 2 of *The Liberal Socialism of Thomas Hill Green*

Preface

Civil Society, Capitalism and the State is the second and final part of *The Liberal Socialism of Thomas Hill Green*. The first part was published in 2010, with the title *The Metaphysics of Self-realisation and Freedom*. Together, these books come to around a quarter of a million words and deal with all aspects of Green's philosophical system, excluding his logic, analysing particularly his metaphysical, ethical, social, political and economic thought. *The Liberal Socialism of Thomas Hill Green* as a whole presupposes the truth of the quotation from Aristotle which opened this book: 'If we wish to investigate the best constitution appropriately, we must first decide what is the most desirable life; for if we do not know that, the best constitution is also bound to elude us.'[1] Green's friend and colleague William Lambert Newman remembered Green speaking of this passage 'in terms of high approval'.[2] Even those readers with only the most rudimentary knowledge of Green's thought should not be surprised by this fact. Green was influenced deeply by Aristotle, and he insists repeatedly that in order to assess the value of any particular society, political system or economy, one must decide to what extent it enables human beings to lead their best life.

Green's perfectionism has worried many people. Some have argued that it implies a form of personal essentialism, such that Green believes human beings are at their best when they live in accordance with their 'true' concrete human nature. More to the point, many critics impute to Green the belief that individuals should be forced, by the state, say, or by 'society', to live in a particular way because that is their 'vocation' as human beings. This might cause concern because the critic rejects essentialism, or because she holds that, even though there is a 'best' way for humans to live, no one should be forced to live it.

Among other things, *Civil Society* seeks to allay these fears. It argues that, although Green does believe human beings have an underlying human nature which they should work to realise in their lives, as a universal nature it is made up of a rather abstract set of potential needs and capacities. Only when individuals live in societies that allow them to act in ways that, as individuals, they find valuable will each of them be able to construct lives that they find valuable. Importantly, it is argued in this book that, for Green,

---

[1]   Aristotle, *Politics,* trans. T.A. Sinclair, rev. T.J. Saunders (Harmondsworth: Penguin, 1957), Book 7, §1.
[2]   William Lambert Newman, 'Recollection', in Colin Tyler, ed., 'Recollections Regarding Thomas Hill Green', *Collingwood and British Idealism Studies*, 14:2 (2008), 27.

each individual should tailor her own life to herself, and that ultimately only she can judge whether a particular way of life expresses her true nature. *Civil Society* explores the ways in which Green theorises the preconditions of such a life: in what sort of society should the individual live in order to be able to arrive at well-informed and conscientious judgements regarding the particular life that is best for her? It establishes why Green believes the individual should work to ensure the good functioning of the social institutions she values; in Green's terms, why she should promote the common good. Yet, *Civil Society* also establishes at great length that, for Green, this enquiry cannot be a purely theoretical activity. In fact, it shows that he believes ultimately it is an activity that infuses our inherently practical daily lives. Green shows the ways in which, as George Eliot puts it, 'that things are not so ill with you and me as they might have been, is half owing to the number who lived faithfully a hidden life, and rest in unvisited tombs'.[3]

The irreducibly practical nature of the individual's construction of her own good life has implications for the method it is appropriate to use when interpreting Green. Whereas most chapters of *Metaphysics* were almost exclusively philosophical, *Civil Society* contains a lot more history. One can only really understand Green's arguments regarding the nature of the modern state and sovereignty, of rights, duties and obligations, of civil disobedience, education and the economy if one understands something about the context in which he was writing. All thoughts are thoughts of real individuals in determinate contexts (you and I, here and now), and understanding those contexts is particularly important if one wants to understand correctly their thoughts on society, politics and the economy.[4] In this regard, the speeches, letters and parliamentary evidence collected by Peter Nicholson in the fifth volume of Green's *Works* become profoundly significant. One cannot properly understand Green's philosophical writings in these applied areas unless one takes account of these records of his practical interventions in the issues of his day. This is merely one more debt that scholars of British idealism and British political thought more generally, owe to Peter.

I have been very conscious throughout writing *Civil Society* that people who are interested in Green's social, political and economic thought might not be that concerned about his metaphysics of the will, and might wish to be able to read this book without reading the first one. Consequently, while this book builds on the argument of the first, I have done my best to enable people who have not read *Metaphysics* to understand the argument of *Civil*

---

3   George Eliot, 'Middlemarch', in her *Works*, 20 vols. (New York: Jensen Society, 1910), vol. 11, p. 237.

4   For the methodological background, see Colin Tyler, 'Performativity and the Intellectual Historian's Re-enactment of Written Works', *Journal of the Philosophy of History*, 3:2 (2009), 167–86.

Society. Obviously, the nuances of my interpretation of Green can be gleaned only by reading both books. For that reason, at various points I cite specific passages in *Metaphysics* that shed light on specific arguments in *Civil Society*.

Civil Society is based loosely on the final four chapters and conclusion of my very first book, *Thomas Hill Green (1836–1882) and the Philosophical Foundations of Politics*.[5] Even though the latter received very pleasing reviews, I have treated its text as a very rough draft. I have reworked thoroughly every page, significantly extended each section, restructured and redivided chapters with no regard for the arrangement of the original text. The resulting book is nearly twice as long as the original. I have altered radically many of the core arguments in light of the research I and others have carried out since 1997, not least by bringing out much more carefully and thoroughly what I see as the constructivist elements of Green's theory. The most fundamental shift is that I now read Green as primarily a socialist, although one with important liberal concerns. Taken together, these changes are so extensive and radical that *Civil Society* constitutes a new book.

I am very pleased to thank Peter Nicholson for his continuing advice and criticism as editor of Imprint Academic's series *British Idealist Studies: T.H. Green*. Once again, Peter has been generous and careful with his comments, saving me from many errors along the way. I continue to owe him a huge personal debt. I am also pleased to thank Keith Sutherland, Graham Horswell and, formerly, Anthony Freeman for their assistance and great patience as publishers. I wish to thank the Master and Fellows of Balliol College, Oxford for their permission to consult and quote from their holdings of Green's papers. I wish to thank also the Principal and Fellows of St John's College, Oxford, for their hospitality during my time as a Visiting Scholar with them in the summer of 2007. This book has benefitted very significantly from the life of the Centre for Idealism and the New Liberalism at the University of Hull, of which I am Joint Director with my friend and colleague, Jim Connelly. In this regard, in addition to Jim, I am also pleased to thank Matt Beech, Richard Bellamy, David Boucher, Thom Brooks, Glenn Burgess, Jon Cruddas, Alberto de Sanctis, Maria Dimova-Cookson, Owen Fellows, Michael Freeden, Janusz Grygienc, Stéphane Guy, John Horton, Louise W. Knight, Simon Lee, Sean Magee, Bill Mander, Catherine Marshall, Sue Mendus, John Morrow, Noël O'Sullivan, Adrian Paylor, Jean-Paul Rosaye, Avital Simhony, Hanno Terao, Emily Thomas, Geoffrey Thomas, Andrew Vincent and Dave Weinstein. I wish to thank the staff of the Brynmor Jones Library at the University of Hull especially Richard Bayliss, who continue to make the research process even more pleasant than it would be otherwise, through their friendly and efficient assistance. Thanks

---

5   Colin Tyler, *Thomas Hill Green (1836–1882) and the Philosophical Foundations of Politics: An internal critique* (Lampeter and Lewiston, NY: Edwin Mellen, 1997).

go to some of those friends at Hull whom I have not already mentioned: Sophie Appleton, Claire Hairsine, Justin Morris, Philip Norton and Richard Woodward. They have all contributed to this book in one way or another, although without taking on any responsibility for its remaining errors.

Finally, as always my greatest thanks and love go to Pip my wife and Lucy our cat. Pip has endured too many conversations about Green and British idealism, and Lucy has received nothing like the attention she deserves and demands (she is far more than what D.G. Ritchie calls a 'quasi-person'). My life would be much less rich without Lucy and completely meaningless without Pip. This book is dedicated to my mum Edna and my brother Will, as well as to the memory of my dad Bill.

Colin Tyler
4 July 2012

Abbreviations

References within this book are given in the following format: §[chapter].[section]

References to my *Metaphysics of Self-realisation and Freedom* (Exeter and Charlottesville, VA: Imprint Academic, 2010) are given in the following format: MSF §[chapter].[section]

Where the notes reference both this book and MSF, the former are distinguished by the letters: 'CS'.

Items referenced by section number are listed below followed by an asterisk. All other references are to page numbers. The following abbreviations are also used below:

(GW [volume]:[page or section]) = R.L. Nettleship and Peter P. Nicholson, eds., *Works of Thomas Hill Green*, 5 vols. (Bristol: Thoemmes, 1997).
Nettleship, 'Memoir' = Richard Lewis Nettleship, 'Memoir' (GW 3:xi-clxi).

Writings of Thomas Hill Green

'Aristotle': 'Philosophy of Aristotle' (GW 3:46-91).
DSF: 'On the Different Senses of "Freedom" as Applied to Will and the Moral Progress of Man', in T.H. Green, *Lectures on the Principles of Political Obligation, and other writings*, ed. Paul Harris and John Morrow (Cambridge: Cambridge University Press, 1986), pp. 228-49.*
'Elementary': 'Two Lectures on "The Elementary School System of England"' (GW 3:413-55).
'English Revolution': 'Four Lectures on the English Commonwealth' (GW 3:277-364).
'Faith': 'Faith: Address on 2 Corinthians v. 7' (GW 3:253-76).
FC: 'Force of Circumstances' (GW 3:3-10).
'Grading': 'Lecture on the Grading of Secondary Schools' (GW 3:387-412).
'Hume I': 'Introductions to Hume's "Treatise of Human Nature": I. General Introduction' (GW 1:1-299).*
'Hume II': 'Introduction to the Moral Part of Hume's "Treatise"' (GW 1:301-71).*
IPR: 'Review of J. Caird, "Introduction to the Philosophy of Religion"' (GW 3:138-46).
'Kant': 'Lectures on the Philosophy of Kant' (GW 2:2-155).*
'Legislative interference': 'Legislative interference in moral matters', in Green, *Political Obligation* (Harris and Morrow), pp. 306-9.

'Lewes I': 'Mr. Lewes' Account of Experience' (GW 1:442–70).*

'Lewes II': 'Mr. Lewes' Account of the Social Medium' (GW 1:471–520).*

LLFC: 'Lecture on "Liberal Legislation and Freedom of Contract"', in Green, *Political Obligation* (Harris and Morrow), pp. 194–212.

LMPP: 'Lectures on Moral and Political Philosophy [1867]' (GW 5:108–82).

'Logic': 'Lectures on Logic' (GW 2:157–366).*

'Loyalty': 'Loyalty', in Green, *Political Obligation* (Harris and Morrow), pp. 304–06.

'Moral Philosophy': 'Notes on Moral Philosophy', in Green, *Political Obligation* (Harris and Morrow), pp. 310–33.*

'Oxford High School': 'Lecture on "The Work to be Done by the New Oxford High School for Boys"', (GW 3:456–76).

PE: Prolegomena to Ethics (GW 4).*

'Pleasure': '*Pleasure* as the Chief Good', in Colin Tyler, ed., *Unpublished Manuscripts in British Idealism: Political philosophy, theology and social thought*, 2 vols. (London and New York: Thoemmes Continuum, 2005; Exeter and Charlottesville, VA: Imprint Academic, 2008), vol. 1, pp. 82–87.

'Pol. Econ.': 'Notes on ancient and modern political economy', in Green, *Political Obligation* (Harris and Morrow), pp. 313–17.*

'Popular Philosophy': 'Popular Philosophy in its Relation to Life' (GW 3:92–125).

PPO: 'Lectures on the Principles of Political Obligation', in Green, *Political Obligation* (Harris and Morrow), pp. 13–193.*

'Rudiments': 'Rudiments of "The Philosophy of Aristotle" and related texts', in Colin Tyler, ed., *Unpublished Manuscripts in British Idealism: Political philosophy, theology and social thought*, 2 vols. (London and New York: Thoemmes Continuum, 2005; Exeter and Charlottesville, VA: Imprint Academic, 2008), vol. 1, pp. 1–13.

'Sittlichkeit': 'Metaphysic of Ethics, Moral Psychology, Sociology or the Science of Sittlichkeit', in Colin Tyler, ed., *Unpublished Manuscripts in British Idealism: Political philosophy, theology and social thought*, 2 vols. (London and New York: Thoemmes Continuum, 2005; Exeter and Charlottesville, VA: Imprint Academic, 2008), vol. 1, pp. 14–71.

'Spencer I': 'Mr. Spencer on the Relation of Subject and Object' (GW 1:373–409).*

'Spencer II': 'Mr. Spencer on the Independence of Matter' (GW 1:410–41).*

'Watson': 'Review of J Watson, "Kant and his English Critics"' (GW 3:147–58).

WG: 'Witness of God': Address on 1 Corinthians v. 7, 8' (GW 3:230–52).

'Works of Fiction': 'The Value and Influence of Works of Fiction in Modern Times' (GW 3:20–45).

From Metaphysics to Practical Philosophy

Introduction: Green's Intertwining of Philosophy and Practice

The guiding aim of Thomas Hill Green's writings and public life was to help to foster a society in which every sane adult lived as an active citizen of an enriching society whose fundamental meanings and values she freely endorsed. While Green recognised that concrete world-views would vary between societies, he held that every good society would share certain fundamental features. Not only would every individual be a citizen but all citizens would be treated equally. Equal treatment required equal status, something that in turn required everyone to be accorded broadly equal access to social opportunities and resources, irrespective of their gender and race. Class-distinctions would be destroyed, even if social functions continued to be differentiated. As citizens, every individual would act in accordance with her own conscientious judgement regarding what was required of her personally and how society should be organised collectively. At the same time, the individual would appreciate the need to act responsibly and in proper recognition of the value of existing social norms. Nevertheless, where the individual judged that conventional norms tended to hinder the self-realisation of herself and her fellow citizens, she should seek to change those norms. Wherever possible the individual should seek to bring this change about within conventional structures and processes, and with the minimum level of disturbance to the remaining social, economic and political structures. Nonetheless, there were circumstances in which dissent, civil disobedience and rebellion were not merely the individual's right but her positive duty. At the extreme, it might be the individual's duty to engage in violent conflict and even revolution, as happened during the Italian upheavals of the 1850s and 1860s, and the 1861–65 American civil war. Unusually for an Oxford man, in the last instance Green supported earnestly the North's fight against slavery.

Given that Green's ultimate goal was essentially practical, it is unfortunate that he presented his philosophical justification of this position in such an obscure manner. It is not that Green was incapable of writing or speaking well, as his popular lectures and speeches demonstrate. His 'Lecture on Liberal Legislation and Freedom of Contract', for example, is a wonderful piece of oratory which still manages to convey complex philosophical ideas in a clear, coherent and engaging manner.[1] Nevertheless, in his philosophical and theological writings, Green prioritises precise and exhaustive analysis over immediate clarity. One of the main problems is his tendency to construct sentences as if he were a late-eighteenth or nineteenth century German idealist such as Immanuel Kant or Georg W.F. Hegel. The central paradox of Green's career was captured eloquently in 1911 by Henry W. Nevinson (1856–1941), a radical journalist and sometime resident of Toynbee Hall, an institution itself inspired by the writings of Green and his pupil Arnold Toynbee. Writing about Oxford in the 1860s and 1870s, Nevinson observed: 'and there was Green, wrestling with incomprehensible utterance, but more incomprehensible in his recognition of working people's existence'.[2]

Even though Green's philosophical and theological works tend to be obscure, his practical commitments and practical influence were very well-known to those with whom he had personal contact and to those who read about him, whether in the works of his philosophical followers or in the reminiscences and memoirs of the substantial number of practical people with whom he came into contact (see MSF §1.II).[3] Yet, as often happens to major figures, the reputations of Green and those whom he influenced came under sustained attack from the next generation of philosophers and polit-

---

[1] LLFC *passim*.

[2] Henry W. Nevinson, 'The Oxford Mood' (originally from *The Nation*, 18 March 1911), as reprinted in his *Visions and Memories*, ed. Evelyn Sharp (London: Oxford University Press, 1944), p. 120. The 'Oxford Mood' is Nevinson's review of Edward Bagnall Poulton, *John Viriamu Jones and other Oxford Memories* (London: Longmans, 1911). Nevinson probably drew on his own direct knowledge of Green, as although Poulton mentions Green twice (pp. 71, 178n1, both times admiringly), neither occasion anticipates Nevinson's comments. Thirteen years later, Nevinson referred to Green in rather less inspiring terms: 'As the gravest philosopher I have known—Thomas Hill Green of Oxford—once said, "We must go grimly on our way".' Henry W. Nevinson, '*Aurea Legenda* – The Joy of Miracle' (originally from *The Rationalist Annual*, 1924), reprinted in Nevinson, *Visions and Memories*, p. 96.

[3] The most illuminating discussions of this influence are Denys P. Leighton, *The Greenian Moment: T.H. Green, religion and political argument in Victorian Britain* (Exeter and Charlottesville, VA: Imprint Academic, 2004); Nettleship, 'Memoir'; and Melvin Richter, *The Politics of Conscience: T.H. Green and his age* (London: Weidenfeld and Nicolson, 1964).

ical figures (see MSF §2.II). That the distortion of Green's guiding aspirations could be severe is indicated by the deeply misplaced assessment presented by the Labour Party grandee and socialist intellectual Richard Crossman (1907–74). 'The British idealists mark an important stage of development', Crossman wrote in 1939, ' – the divorce between political theory and political practice in this country'.

> 'While the problems of imperialism, Home Rule, and trade union rights dominated practical politics, Oxford witnessed the growth of a philosophy too sublime to relate itself to such mundane matters. Flourishing between 1870 and 1914, its advocates elaborated a system of *metapolitics* by which they demonstrated the place occupied by the State in the essential nature of things.'[4]

As the more astute of Crossman's political contemporaries such as William Beveridge appreciated, British idealists including Sidney Ball, Bernard Bosanquet, Edward Caird, John Caird, Sir Henry Jones, David George Ritchie, Arnold Toynbee and Green himself devoted much of their lives to practical social activism and social reform, the guiding principles of which they articulated in their respective philosophical writings.[5] Contrary to Crossman's unfortunately-all-too-conventional allegations, in reality one is far more likely to find socially and politically active members among the

---

[4] R.H.S. Crossman, 'British Political Thought in the European Tradition', in J.P. Mayer in cooperation with R.H.S. Crossman, P. Kecskemeti, C.J.S. Sprigge and E. Kohn-Bramstedt, *Political Thought: The European tradition* (London: J.M. Dent, 1939), p. 197. For a more measured statement, see Mark Bevir, *The Making of British Socialism* (Princeton and Oxford: Princeton University Press, 2011), pp. 230–33.

[5] William Beveridge, *Power and Influence* (London: Hodder and Stoughton, 1953), pp. 9, 21, 33–34. On Beveridge's involvement with Toynbee Hall, see *ibid.*, pp. 15–28. José Harris greatly overstates the non-pragmatic, deeply metaphysical approach to philosophy and social reform in her assessment of Beveridge's debt to Edward Caird (José Harris, *William Beveridge: A biography* (Oxford: Clarendon, 1977), pp. 41–43). Consider, for example, the following passage from an address that Caird gave at the inauguration of the Civic Society of Glasgow at the time of Beveridge's matriculation at Oxford: 'men are coming to see more and more clearly that there is no royal road to social welfare, no simple "open sesame" which will enable us to unlock all the complex and intricate problems of modern life. Man is after all the most puzzling of beings to himself, and the question what effect any institution or any measure to relieve his wants or draw forth his powers, any plan for helping, educating, or giving even amusement to him, will have upon a class or community of men, whether it will really aid or hinder them in the long run, is not to be settled except by the most careful watching of experience and the most thorough analysis of it and reflexion upon its bearings.' Edward Caird, *The Present State of the Controversy between Individualism and Socialism* (Glasgow: James MacLehose, 1897), p. 4. The passage is typical of the British idealists named above.

British idealists than among any other post-1789 philosophical movement. (The nineteenth-century utilitarians are possibly the only serious rivals.)

Crossman and many others had lost sight of the fact that Green had spoken passionately in favour of local democracy and the extension of the franchise not least in the run-up to the 1867 Reform Act, worked for the admission of women to higher education and the easing of the costs on the poor of attending the University of Oxford. He worked hard for temperance reform and took a great interest in the rise of the trade union movement, appearing on union platforms in the 1860s and 1870s (see §10.IV below). Finally, he died at the relatively young age of 45 years, a few months after being re-elected as a local councillor in Oxford. Far from seeing these practical issues as being too 'mundane' to be worthy of his attention as Crossman alleges, these and a great many other efforts to 'live a useful life' earned Green significant respect not merely from the progressive elements at Oxford, but also from the ordinary inhabitants of the town, around two thousand of whom lined his funeral route on 29 March 1882.[6] As has been noted already, Green's philosophical position and his practical activities were inseparable. His friend and former pupil David George Ritchie emphasised this point in a well-known passage.

> '[Green's] philosophical thinking was to him no mere exercise of intellectual ingenuity, but provided the basis of his conduct and influenced the details of his actions to an extent very rare even amongst those whom we consider the most conscientious of men. He neither despised the small matters of local politics, nor forgot the wider interests of mankind. He went straight from the declaration of the poll, when he was elected a town councillor, to lecture on *The Critique of Pure Reason*. He was robbed of his sleep by thinking about the Eastern Question, and dreading lest the country should be driven, by motives "of which perhaps a diffused desire for excitement has been the most innocent," into what he regarded as an indefensible and unrighteous war. His strong opinions on the liquor traffic were in his mind directly connected with his conception of the ethical end and the nature of rights.'[7]

Green's interlinking of theory and practice is a recurring theme of this book. *Civil Society, Capitalism and the State* is the second and final part of *The Liberal Socialism of Thomas Hill Green*. The first part was published in 2010, with the

---

6   On his deathbed, Green reminded his wife Charlotte that she should 'lead a useful life' (recorded in letter from Benjamin Jowett to C.M. Symonds, 8 June 1893, in Evelyn Abbott and Lewis Campbell, eds., *The Life and Letters of Benjamin Jowett, M.A.*, 2 vols. (London: John Murray, 1897), vol. 2, p. 470); see also Peter Nicholson, 'Introduction' (GW 5:xv–xxxi); on Green's funeral, see John Prest, 'The Death and Funeral of T.H. Green', in John Prest, ed., *Balliol College Annual Record 1998*, (privately printed, 1998) pp. 23–25.

7   David George Ritchie, *The Principles of State Interference: Four essays on the political philosophy of Mr. Herbert Spencer, J.S. Mill, and T.H. Green*, third edition (London: Swan Sonnenschein, 1902 [1891]), pp. 131–32, quoting PPO 165.

title of *The Metaphysics of Self-realisation and Freedom*. Together, these books develop and defend a new reading of T.H. Green's philosophical system and its associated practical commitments. They argue that almost all previous scholars have misunderstood key features of Green's broader system, not least his theories of the will and the eternal consciousness. Moreover, they show that scholars have misconceived the fundamental character of Green's social and political thought, frequently assuming that it is most illuminating to read him as at root a liberal rather than a socialist.

As becomes clearer below (§1.II–III), *Metaphysics* established that Green bases his thought on the claim that each individual is constituted partly by the same abstract human nature, the numerous contours of which she is driven innately to express in determinate form as an active, coherent and intrinsically-valuable personality. It was shown that Green ascribes intrinsic value only to the individual person and that he believes that one can have a solid faith in the existence of God (called more usually the 'spiritual prin-ciple' and, a very few times, the 'eternal consciousness') only to the extent that one bases that faith on an even-more solid and logically prior acknow-ledgement of the fundamental reality of the individual. He argues that the animal aspects of human existence should be transformed into the indiv-idual's self-conscious virtues, via a process of sublimation and self-control. In this way, the individual can realise her true good by living a life of true freedom: that is, an intrinsically valuable life which she chooses freely to live and which she judges conscientiously to be intrinsically valuable for her to live given her concrete personality and specific talents. In terms of contem-porary philosophical debates, Green was shown to develop a form of cultur-ally-sensitive virtue ethics. Finally, *Metaphysics* established that Green's ethics is neither purely consequentialist nor purely deontological, and that, contrary to the allegations of some contemporary scholars, Green combines elements of both Kantianism and romanticism at the heart of his philo-sophical system.

The present book extends this analysis, firstly, by establishing that ultim-ately Green values social and political institutions only to the extent that they enable individuals to develop the best in themselves, something that he calls their respective determinate true goods. He is sceptical regarding the trends in his day of conceiving of society in organic terms and of under-standing human improvement as the outcome of some sort of allegedly inevitable social evolution. Society will only improve where individuals work to help it improve. The guiding ideal of Green's social theory is a society of self-directed virtuous individuals choosing freely to work for the common good of their community and the realisation of their own respect-ive talents. Nevertheless, he is very conscious of the immense obstacles that an individual can face: poverty, ignorance, substance abuse especially alcoholism, legal and political exclusion, arbitrary power, and so on. It is the individual's duty to fight to remove such obstacles from their own lives and the lives of their fellows, and, where the task is beyond individuals, it is the state's role to do so. He argues that moral rights and duties are socially-acknowledged claims, and that legal rights and obligations are legally-embodied powers and requirements. Those rights, duties and obligations deserve our obedience to the extent that they form systems of claims which sustain a public environment in which individuals can develop themselves. Yet, the individual remains under a positive duty to try to reform any elements which, in her own conscientious judgement, do not serve this end and which could be revised given the individual's particular circumstances. Green goes so far as to argue that, in extreme cases, the individual can be under a positive duty to engage in violent revolution. While Green believes capitalism can facilitate individual self-realisation, he is very conscious of the need for peasants and workers to assert themselves through cooperative movements and trade union activities, rather than relying on poor relief and other patronising and ultimately conservative systems of state-provided benefits.

The remainder of this chapter provides greater detail regarding the main line of argument found in *Metaphysics*. Hopefully, this will help to jog the memories of those who have been kind enough to have already read this first part of *The Liberal Socialism of Thomas Hill Green* while providing a brief background for those who have not.

II

Green's Purpose and Philosophical Method

Chapter one of *Metaphysics* reconstructs Green's reasons for rejecting the generally-centralist forms of mid-Victorian socialism in favour of a variant of cooperative republicanism, a position which anticipated closely the 'liberal socialism' of the likes of L.T. Hobhouse. It is noted that scholars such as Vincent Knapp have seen Green's political thought as being far closer to a complacent form of liberalism than to socialism, while James Kloppenberg and others have read Green as a socialist, even though he believed that a properly reformed capitalism could help to realise personal freedom.[8] The interpretation defended in *Metaphysics* and the present book accords best with this second position. *Metaphysics* highlights Green's reputation among his friends and followers as a socialist. As J.A. Symonds, Green's brother-in-law, observed in a letter to his sister Charlotte, 'Personally I may say that he

---

8   Vincent J. Knapp, 'T.H. Green on the Exorability of Property', *Agora*, 1 (1969), 63. James T. Kloppenberg, *Uncertain Victory: Social democracy and progressivism in European and American thought* (New York and Oxford: Oxford University Press, 1986), p. 147.

inducted me into the philosophy of democracy and socialism'.[9] Symonds observed a little later that Green had the 'faculty of feeling by a kind of penetrative instinct that modern society had ripened to a point at which the principles of democracy and society had to be accepted as actualities'.[10] Symonds's remark is profoundly significant for a number of reasons, and not least because it points towards the relationship between Green's method and his politics.

With this thought in mind, chapter two of *Metaphysics* considers one of the most inadequately researched subjects in the previous scholarship on Green: the nature and range of his intellectual debts. It is established that, in addition to his generally recognised if often over-emphasised debts to G.W.F. Hegel, Green drew heavily on philosophers such as Aristotle, Thomas Carlyle, Johann G. Fichte, Immanuel Kant and R.H. Lotze, political theorists such as Giuseppe Mazzini, and most significantly elements of the romantic tradition, not least the works of William Wordsworth and Johann W. Goethe. Recovering Green's wider intellectual context is shown to shed significant new light on the much-vexed question of Green's relationship to socialism. Indeed, throughout this analysis the underlying goal is to establish that Green's writings reveal their real depths and implications when he is read as a liberal socialist, with liberal socialism itself being conceived in the following terms, defended by L.T. Hobhouse.

> 'If… there be such a thing as a Liberal Socialism… it must clearly fulfil two conditions. In the first place, it must be democratic. It must come from below, not from above. Or rather, it must emerge from the efforts of society as a whole to secure a fuller measure of justice, and a better organization of mutual aid. It must engage the efforts and respond to the genuine desires not of a handful of superior beings, but of great masses of men. And, secondly, and for that very reason, it must make its account with the human individual. It must give the average man free play in the personal life for which he really cares. It must be founded on liberty, and must make not for the suppression but for the development of personality.'[11]

Metaphysics shows that ultimately Green's philosophy aims to understand the self and its actions in the world. Hence, after section 27, the term 'self'

---

9   Letter from John Addington Symonds to Charlotte Byron Green, 3 November 1886, quoted in John Addington Symonds, *The Letters*, 3 vols., eds. Herbert M. Schueller and Robert L. Peters (Detroit, MI: Wayne State University Press, 1969), vol. 3, p. 176.

10   Letter from Symonds to C.B. Green, 3 November 1886, in Symonds, *Letters*, vol. 3, p. 176.

11   Leonard T. Hobhouse, *Liberalism* (London: Williams and Norgate, n.d. [1911]), pp. 172–73. For the contrast between Green's liberal socialism and John Stuart Mill's elitist model, see Colin Tyler, 'Elitism and Anti-elitism in Nineteenth Century British Political Thought', *History of European Ideas*, 32 (August 2006), 345–55, especially 345–51.

appears on almost every page of Green's most important philosophical work, *Prolegomena to Ethics* (1883). The self had long been a central concept in Green's philosophy by the time he started to write the *Prolegomena* some-time in 1878, something that one might expect of a philosophical idealist. He rejects the conception of the self as a substance which exists prior to its activities: the Greenian self is formed through its interactions with other selves and through self-reflection.[12] Moreover, Green rejects Hume's bundle theory, whereby the self is merely a 'succession' of ideas and impressions: the Greenian self conceives of itself necessarily as a being existing in time, and possesses the capacity to critically assess its own ideas and feelings from a point outside of the flux of its sensations, emotions and beliefs.[13] The Greenian self is the harmonisation of 'the desires, feelings, and thoughts of the individual man' in the latter's character or personality (these final two terms are synonymous for Green).[14] The individual's self can be understood as having faculties of Desire, Intellect, Will and self-consciousness, but these faculties exist and the self they constitute has a being and identity only to the extent—and only in the manner—that they structure an interrelated content of concrete desires, ideas, plans and activities.[15] It is this content which arises through the individual's continual interactions with other persons, and which finds some degree of stable expression through the structures of known worlds that are shared with other persons. Green encapsulates the fundamentals of his position as follows in the *Prolegomena*: 'We can only know' the self, he writes, 'by a reflection on it which is its own action; by analysis of the expression it has given to itself in language, literature, and the institutions of human life; and by consideration of what that must be which has thus expressed itself.'[16]

Chapter three of *Metaphysics* begins to reconstruct and analyse this con-ception of the self and the implications that Green draws from it. The chap-ter starts by exploring Green's often-underappreciated early article on 'The Philosophy of Aristotle' (1866), wherein he criticises Plato for resting con-tented with a purely abstract form of philosophical analysis. He believes that by conceiving of knowledge of abstract universals (the 'Forms') as the term-inus of philosophical endeavour, Plato fails to appreciate that 'the mere universal is a shell to be filled up by particular attributes'.[17] Against Plato, Green argues that when executed successfully the 'ideal theory' builds 'again that which it destroyed, and the sensible thing becomes, as such, the

---

12   'Hume I' 7.
13   'Hume I' 319.
14   PE 99.
15   PE 115–53.
16   PE 100.
17   'Aristotle' 56.

determinate subject of properties'.[18] That said, Green does start from the same point as many other philosophers in the broadly idealist tradition, including Plato, Kant and Hegel: philosophy should begin to discover knowledge and morality by trying to understand the world around it. Counterfactually, one cannot begin by withdrawing from the established features of that world. In other words, philosophy should commence with a transcendental analysis of experience, rather than by attempting to evade the realities of the world via a rationalist retreat into radical doubt regarding the evidence of the senses.

Consequently, Green's own philosophical investigation starts with the 'disentanglement of that which is implicit in the language, knowledge, and acts of men'.[19] Peter Nicholson has suggested that one should conceive of this first stage of Green's philosophical method as what David Ritchie described as Green's 'critical metaphysics'.[20] On this view, 'To discover the *a priori* element in knowledge, *i.e.*, that element which, though known to us only in connection with sense-experience, cannot be dependent upon sense-experience for its validity, is the business of [this first critical stage of] a philosophical theory of knowledge'.[21] Green employs two techniques of critical metaphysics. One is a process of introspection whereby the critical metaphysician identifies those intuitions that he holds regarding the fixed truths of the world: that is, the propositions that he holds initially unreflectively but which subsequently he finds he cannot reject even after careful reflection. The conviction that humans know things about the world is one such intuition for Green, as is the conviction that ultimately all true propositions will form one complete and harmonious system. These intuitions extend into the normative realm as well. For example, Green intuits that the fundamental sources of the value of the individual are her abilities and drives to realise certain eudaimonic and rational capacities, and that all individuals should be treated as being of equal intrinsic worth. Green holds that even though these intuitions are historically-located, nevertheless they are also held to be true by the modern introspective critical metaphysician. One finds something very like this claim in other philosophers of course, not least Kant, Hegel and Rawls. The other technique of critical metaphysics employed by Green is that of propositional and conceptual analysis: in other words, the testing of the clarity and coherence of conventionally-employed concepts and propositions. The critical metaphysician should use both of these tech-

---

18 'Aristotle' 57.

19 'Aristotle' 64.

20 Peter P. Nicholson, 'Green's "Eternal Consciousness"', in Maria Dimova-Cookson and W.J. Mander, eds., *T.H. Green: Ethics, metaphysics and political philosophy* (Oxford: Clarendon, 2006), pp. 147–48.

21 David George Ritchie, 'Origin and Validity', in his *Darwinism and Hegel, and other philosophical studies* (London: Swan Sonnenschein, 1893), p. 14.

niques (the intuitional and the analytic) to identify the *a priori* elements in knowledge. Critical metaphysics does not stand alone, however. In fact, in Ritchie's terms, Green holds the analysis of critical metaphysics to be a prelude to the synthesis of 'speculative metaphysics', which attempts to explain experience as a whole using the conceptual categories and principles arrived at through critical analysis. In other words, once the critical metaphysician has discovered the fixed points of experience, the speculative metaphysician has to accept these elements as proven, and then develop an interpretation of them which respects their core features while relating them to each other in an internally-consistent and clear fashion. Knowledge claims are justified to the extent that the speculative metaphysician achieves this goal, and truth is a function of the clarity and coherence of the resulting system.[22] As new experiences arise constantly, '*this* Metaphysics can never be complete'.[23]

This dual-stage philosophical method rests on certain key assumptions. The first is the Kantian claim that not only is knowledge possible but that individuals do actually know things (that is, they hold true beliefs and have good reasons for holding those beliefs to be true). The second assumption is that certain elements of experience should be treated as fixed points, in the sense that they should be conceived as *a priori* facts to be discovered by the critical metaphysician. The third core assumption of Green's philosophical method is clear from the preceding point: namely, that when understood correctly and related properly to one another, true propositions form an internally-consistent and complete network or system.[24] Gaps and inconsistencies within this system imply either that the critical metaphysician has missed or misunderstood certain key *a priori* elements of experience, or that the speculative metaphysician has failed to relate these elements correctly. The final causes of gaps and inconsistencies are the imperfections of the phenomena (including the social practices and institutions) analysed by the critical metaphysician.

Like almost every other philosopher then, Green assumes that the world is ultimately coherent, and hence that any incoherence in our conception of it is a sign of error. (Indeed, this is an assumption made by almost all non-philosophers as well.) Yet, Green acknowledges that, given the multitude of inconsistencies and omissions in our understanding of the real world, the assumption of the systematic character of true propositions must be in part merely a working hypothesis. Nevertheless, the assumption of the ultimate unity of truth has a firmer status than this for Green, in that he sees it as a

---

[22] On coherence theories of truth such as Green's, see Harold H. Joachim, *The Nature of Truth* (Oxford: Clarendon, 1906), chapter III.

[23] Ritchie, 'Origin', p. 14.

[24] PE 32.

postulate that is entailed by every individual's instinctive belief than knowledge is possible.[25] In fact, he goes still further, pointing to the constructed character of 'true' propositions, claiming at one point that: 'we only find unity in the world because we have an idea that it is there, an idea which we direct our powers to realize.'[26]

Metaphysics argues that the individual's innate and often unconscious assumption of the ultimate harmony of all true propositions transforms the gaining of knowledge from a process of discovery into one of constructing hypotheses to be tested, not least in the light of the implications of our future experiences. This process can be characterised as an example of what Stendhal called 'crystallisation': 'a mental process which draws from everything that happens new proofs of the perfection of the loved one' (see MSF §§2.IV, 3.II, 3.IV).[27] In the present context, the 'loved one' is the system of true propositions. Indeed, Green himself frames the point in these terms: he writes that in attempting to understand the world better, the individual's mind is akin to the person captivated by 'the idea, let us say, of winning the love of a woman', an idea which 'evokes the effort of the lover to realise the idea'.[28] The love metaphor is deeply significant, indicating as it does Green's probable source for this and several other aspects of his theory of mind: Aristotle's theory of the 'prime mover' (see MSF §4.II).[29] Reading this profoundly significant aspect of Green's system in this Aristotelian way helps to counter many of the misunderstandings that continue to plague interpretations of what many judge to be the core concept of his theory of mind: the eternal consciousness. As is indicated in the next section, *Metaphysics* takes issue with the personification of the eternal consciousness, something which *Metaphysics* argues is a process of nominalisation that has had fundamental and harmful effects on previous interpretations of Green's philosophy.

III

The Eternal Consciousness and the Separateness of Personalities

Chapter four of *Metaphysics* turns to this single most controversial aspect of Green's philosophical system, which goes by a great many names in the *Prolegomena* although usually scholars refer to it by one of the names that Green uses least often: the 'eternal consciousness'. (The popularity of the phrase in the secondary literature is itself a potentially thought-provoking

---

25 It comes through very clearly, for example, in PE 10, 13–15.
26 PE 149.
27 Stendhal, *Love*, trans. G. Sale and S. Sale (Harmondsworth: Penguin, 1975), p. 45.
28 PE 134.
29 Aristotle, 'Metaphysics', in his *Metaphysics, X–XIV, Oeconomica, Magna Moralia*, trans. Hugh Tredennick and G. Cyril Armstrong (Cambridge, MA, and London: Loeb, 1935), Book XII, §vii.

fact for those historians of philosophy who are interested in the reception of texts, given that Green uses the phrase 'eternal consciousness' only in the *Prolegomena* and even then only in eight paragraphs, the first being para-graph 67 and the last paragraph 115.)[30] Critics have tended to be particularly scathing of what they see as Green's personification of the eternal conscious-ness: his claim that the human capacity to gain knowledge is possible only if one assumes that God communicates truth to the individual. While develop-ing an interpretation of the eternal consciousness that could be acceptable to atheists, *Metaphysics* acknowledges that, unfortunately, scholars have not imported this personification into Green's texts. It argues that in order to understand why Green styles individual minds as 'vehicles' for the eternal consciousness, one must first appreciate certain of his other beliefs. Some of these beliefs have already been noted above. Green holds it to be a fact: that individual human beings can know things about one and the same world (they can hold true beliefs regarding that world); that such knowledge can be true only to the extent that it is systematic; that the only world about which humans can ever know anything is the world as it exists 'for us' as beings with consciousnesses constituted by structures of propositions (the knowable world is a 'world of experience'); and that individuals can never gain a perfect understanding of that world. It is in order to reconcile these various complex propositions that Green posits the existence of a single, per-fect consciousness of which individual consciousnesses 'partake' (on his also greatly misinterpreted use of this and similar words, see MSF §4.II). Green claims that

> 'The true account of… [knowledge] is held to be that the concrete whole, which may be described indifferently as an eternal intelligence realised in the related facts of the world, or as a system of related facts rendered possible by such an intelligence, partially and gradually reproduces itself in us.'[31]

In this way, Green conceives of the eternal consciousness as God, a divine person existing in part in separation from individual human beings while at the same time exercising its agency immanently within them.

It is argued in *Metaphysics* that there is no logical necessity to personify the eternal consciousness, and consequently no philosophical necessity to equate the eternal consciousness with God. Instead, at most the eternal con-sciousness must be a projected ideal of a perfect individual consciousness: that is, the consciousness of an individual human being that understands the fundamental principles of the world as a coherent whole (that is, in a com-plete and internally-consistent manner). In short, the eternal consciousness is Green's absolute idealist rendering of Kant's 'transcendental unity of apper-

---

30   The phrase 'eternal consciousness' occurs only in the following paragraphs: PE 67, 72–74, 82, 83, 95, 115.
31   PE 36.

ception'.[32] I am not aware that the German equivalent of the phrase the 'eternal consciousness' is ever found in Kant. Nevertheless, in certain important writings, Kant does ascribe to 'nature' an agency very like that which Green ascribes to the 'spiritual principle in nature' (or eternal consciousness).[33] Green's phrase is found however in the writings of a rather different philosopher who predates Green: Søren Kierkegaard. Even though Green never mentions Kierkegaard, it is striking that they share a profound belief in the individual's existential craving for the agency of an 'eternal consciousness'. For example, near the beginning of *Fear and Trembling* (1843) Kierkegaard writes the following.

> 'If there were no eternal consciousness in a man, if at the bottom of everything there were only a wild ferment, a power that twisting in dark passions produced everything that is great or inconsequential; if an unfathomable, insatiable emptiness lay hid beneath everything, what would life be but despair? If it were thus, if there were no sacred bond uniting mankind,… if the human race passed through the world as… the wind through the desert, a thoughtless and fruitless whim,… — how empty and devoid of comfort would life be! But for that reason it is not so…'[34]

For both Green and Kierkegaard then, we posit the existence of an 'eternal consciousness' in order to avoid what both of them feel to be the desperate conclusion that we live in a world that lacks any objective purpose or meaning.

Metaphysics establishes that accepting Green's personification of the eternal consciousness is a contingent feature of his philosophy not a necessary one, weakens radically the main criticism that has been levelled against his thought: that his system reduces individual persons (you and I, here and

---

[32] Immanuel Kant, *Critique of Pure Reason*, trans. Norman Kemp Smith (London: MacMillan, 1929), pp. 135–61 (A 106–130, and B 129–46).

[33] Immanuel Kant, 'The Idea for a Universal History with a Cosmopolitan Purpose', in his *Political Writings*, second edition, ed. Hans Reiss (Cambridge: Cambridge University Press, 1991), pp. 41–53; Immanuel Kant, *Critique of Judgement*, trans. J.C. Meredith (Oxford: Clarendon, 1952 [originally published 1790]), Part 2, pp. 150–63 (Prussian Academy edition pp. 475–85). See also Colin Tyler, *Idealist Political Philosophy: Pluralism and conflict in the absolute idealist tradition* (London: Continuum, 2006), pp. 6–9.

[34] Søren Kierkegaard, *Fear and Trembling*, trans. Alastair Hannay (London: Penguin, 2005 [originally published 1843]), p. 14. In his *Philosophical Fragments, or a Fragment of Philosophy* which appeared the next year, Kierkegaard sought to answer the questions, 'Is an historical point of departure possible for an eternal consciousness; how can such a point of departure have any other than a mere historical interest; is it possible to base an eternal happiness upon historical knowledge?' Søren Kierkegaard, *Philosophical Fragments or A Fragment of Philosophy*, second edition (Princeton, NY: Princeton University Press, 1962 [first edition 1932] [originally published 1844]), p. iii.

now) to epiphenomena, mere shadows of a single, mystical yet more real personality. In other words, acknowledging the contingency of Green's personification of the spiritual principle undermines the widespread belief that his philosophy entails we derive the reality of individual persons from a belief that they are mere adjuncts of God. In fact, Green himself is emphatic in rejecting precisely such an allegation: 'It is only because we are consciously objects to ourselves, that we can conceive a world as an object to a single mind, and thus as a connected whole'.[35] Moreover, spiritual development is 'unintelligible' unless it means the improvement of the personalities of individual human beings.

> 'The spiritual progress of mankind is thus an unmeaning phrase, unless it means a progress *of* personal character and *to* personal character – a progress of which feeling, thinking, and willing subjects are the agents and sustainers, and of which each step is a fuller realisation of the capacities of such subjects. It is simply unintelligible unless understood to be in the direction of more perfect forms of personal life.'[36]

In many ways, the most fundamental claim defended in *Metaphysics* is that Green adds nothing to his philosophy by personifying the eternal consciousness. The latter should be understood only as the abstract potentials or capacities that constitute a shared 'human nature', a notion which Green himself invokes habitually in his mature writings. This conclusion is significant for various reasons, not least because its truth is a fundamental assumption of much of the remainder of my interpretation of Green's social and political thought.

IV

Self-construction and True Freedom

Chapter five of *Metaphysics* establishes that Green holds every individual to be driven to act self-consciously in a world that she understands fully (see MSF chapter 5). Doing so is a precondition of living a 'free life': that is, a life lived 'according to the motions of… [one's] own will'.[37] Drawing on a romantic tradition that owes so much to Aristotle and others, Green conceives of the substantive aspects of human capacities as modified forms of ancient Greek virtues, especially those expressed in Socratic rationality and Aristotelian eudaimonia (MSF §§7.II, 8.III). Central here is the development of the conceptions of the virtues of wisdom, temperance, courage and justice, from which 'Christendom' derived 'its moral categories, its forms of practical judgment'.[38] Historical change has played a vital role in this regard.

---

[35]   PE 182.
[36]   PE 185.
[37]   PPO 151.
[38]   PE 250.

Over generations, individuals' social contexts and personal reflections have together determined the precise manifestations of these virtues and hence of the concrete capacities that they have expressed. More than this, given the general progress since the time of the ancient Greeks and the early Christians, Green conceives contemporary ethics as representing 'not merely ... a new theory about virtue, but... a higher order of virtue itself'.[39] These requirements develop only through the interactions of the particularised personal consciousnesses and consciences of historically-situated individuals. Crucially:

> 'Such a requirement is implied in the conception of the unity of virtue, as determined by one idea of practical good which was to be the conscious spring of the perfectly virtuous life—an idea of it as consisting in some intrinsic excellence, some full realisation of the capabilities, of the thinking and willing soul.'[40]

This neo-Aristotelian requirement articulates a 'demand of the moral nature' of human beings, and brings out another core ethical requirement: namely, 'the conviction that every form of real goodness must rest on a will to be good, which has no object but its own fulfilment'.[41] Green emphasises the profound influence of this ancient Greek principle on Christian theology and life, and philosophically on Kantian ethics.[42]

The possibility of self-satisfaction separates the individual human being from the animal, and action that seeks self-satisfaction is 'distinctively human' (MSF §5.III).[43] In fact, reflecting the further influence of Aristotle's notion of the prime mover, Green argues that every individual is driven by an inherent need to seek self-satisfaction. Moreover, he conceives of this drive as constituting the individual's effort to secure her 'positive' or 'true' freedom: that is, the activity in which she chooses to pursue an end that her conscience presents as being objectively valuable.[44] Here, Green combines insights from Christian (especially Pauline) thought and Kantianism.[45] In the Fichtean terms often adopted by Green, this is the individual's highest 'vocation' (see MSF §2.III).[46] For Green, to the extent that the individual achieves

---

[39] PE 251.

[40] PE 251.

[41] PE 251.

[42] PE 251–32.

[43] PE 91.

[44] See, for example, PE 83–91.

[45] '[For Kant,] Freedom... in this sense of a determination by a reason which constitutes the agent's conception of himself as an absolute end or giver of law, must belong to an act if it is to be morally good.' 'Kant' 89.

[46] Green presents this drive explicitly as the individual's 'vocation' at PE 164, 173, 176, 197, 237, 240, 250, 285, 353.

this ideal condition, she embodies her human nature in a concrete form and so is truly free.

Even though Green conceives human development in spiritual terms, he argues that the first stage in the process of improvement is constituted by the individual's transformation of her pre-reflective, inchoate, often unconscious and chaotic 'animal' impulses into the comprehended determinate desires of a self-conscious human being (MSF §5.IV). He develops this point most clearly in the very important fragment extracted from the manuscript of the *Prolegomena* that was published subsequently as 'On the Different Senses of "Freedom" as Applied to Will and the Moral Progress of Man'.

> 'In order to any approach to this satisfaction of itself the self-realising principle… must overcome the "natural impulses," not in the sense of either extinguishing them or denying them an object, but in the sense of fusing them with those higher interests, which have human perfection in some of its forms for their object. Some approach to this fusion we may notice in all good men; not merely in those in whom all natural passions, love, anger, pride, ambition, are enlisted in the service of some great public cause, but in those with whom such passions are all governed by some such commonplace idea as that of educating a family.'[47]

It is important to emphasise this point because scholars have neglected the fact that, in developing his theory of mind and self-realisation in the late 1870s and early 1880s, Green draws on the then-contemporary theories of the unconscious and its emanation that were being discussed by the likes of Herbert Spencer and G.H. Lewes, and that he anticipates Sigmund Freud's theory of sublimation (MSF §5.IV). It is suggested in *Metaphysics* that this aspect of Green's theory could and probably did provide some comfort to his friend J.A. Symonds, who for many years struggled to come to terms with his homosexuality.

The process of transforming 'animal' impulses into distinctively human desires, and eventually into the individual's will, requires the individual to orientate correctly her critical reflections on her beliefs regarding the world and morality, something that she should do with reference to her conception of an ideal system of meanings and values. This is an instance of what was called above the process of 'crystallisation'. The individual constructs her own determinate orientating ideal partly by reflecting on the standards of personal excellence that inform her society's practices and institutions, partly from her own conscience, and partly from her often rather less choate sense of ultimate values that currently her conscience fails to articulate clearly and which her society fails to recognise in its fundamental structure and guiding principles.[48] Unfortunately but unsurprisingly, the resulting

---

[47]   DSF 21.
[48]   PE 187–89.

ideal will be always partly inchoate, incomplete and inconsistent. Consequently, the individual will always be prone to moral perplexity and error. For that reason, she will always feel frustrated by her innate drive to act well (MSF §§6.III–IV). In fact, Green is emphatic that this sort of personal conscientious struggle must remain the highest state that humans can ever achieve in this world.

The unavoidable nature of this ambiguity influences Green's attitude to personal responsibility, making him tolerant of all genuine attempts to act well, even where ultimately such efforts prove to be either ineffective or fundamentally misguided. He holds that it is only when individuals are conscious of their desires and choose either to act on or to suppress them, that they should be praised or blamed. This claim is problematic for Green however, because, *Metaphysics* argues, he presents two incompatible theories of agency (MSF §§6.V–VIII). The first is called the 'self-interventionist' model in *Metaphysics*, in that it conceives of personal agency as entailing the possibility that the individual can choose whether or not to act in a certain way. Green's second theory leaves no room for such choice, as it is a form of 'spiritual determinism': the individual's actions emanate from the interaction of her particular determinate character with her particular determinate circumstances. Even though her character has been formed by the interaction of her abstract human potentials and her past experiences and is in a sense who she is, without the possibility of deciding not to act otherwise than how she is actually does, it seems counter-intuitive (to me at least) to hold her responsible for her actions. The individual simply performs the actions that necessarily result from the interactions of her character and her circumstances.

Chapters seven and eight of *Metaphysics* consider a number of related issues in light of the preceding analysis. Chapter seven examines the rarely understood relationship between Green's theory of personality and utilitarianism. It returns to the point that the motions of the individual's will can take her in a number of directions. Satisfying some of her preferences will bring her great pleasure for a long time while other pleasures will be more short-lived. Yet, no matter how long these pleasures last, they always tend to fade, eventually leaving the individual with pleasant memories at best, but no real development of her character or situation. The life of pleasure-seeking can never bring the individual a deep and lasting sense of fulfilment (also see MSF §7.III). Green places huge significance on the distinction between the feelings of pleasure on the one hand, and those of fulfilment, or as he more usually calls them, 'self-satisfaction' on the other. Self-satisfaction can arise for the individual only as a consequence of realising her higher capacities.

Chapter eight of *Metaphysics* establishes that scholars such as John Skorupski are incorrect when they claim that Green prioritises (interpersonal) morality so highly that he ignores the self-referential aesthetic facets of a normal human life (MSF §8.IV). Green is far too heavily influenced by the romantic tradition to neglect the fact that it is intrinsically valuable to develop one's own 'spiritual' capacities. In a similar vein, G.E. Moore is incorrect when he claimed that Green believes desiring an object or state of affairs makes that thing good (MSF §8.IV). Instead, Green sees the desire as, at most, a *sign* of the 'goodness' of an object or state of affairs. It is established also that Green's ethical theory manages to combine both consequentialist and deontological elements (MSF §8.V). As a result, one should resist the attempts of scholars such as Avital Simhony and David Weinstein to place in him either one of these camps to the exclusion of the other.

Metaphysics helps one to see that, although Green's guiding aspiration is to develop a coherent philosophical system, his ultimate hope is not narrowly intellectual or academic. As R.L. Nettleship rightly observed, Green wants to develop a 'working theory of life'.[49] Nettleship might well have had in mind what is called in German a *'Weltanschauung'* which translates in English as a 'world outlook', something that Roger Scruton defines as: 'A general conception of the world, in which beliefs, values and metaphysical presuppositions are all woven together so as to instil the world with significance, and facilitate the transition from thought to action.'[50] *Metaphysics* establishes also that Green founds his normative thought on the notion of human development, and insists that such development is not inevitable and in fact can occur only in and for individual persons. For example, he regards it as meaningless to claim that human development occurs in nations understood as corporate entities or in some 'collective Humanity'.[51] This is a normative as well as an ontological claim: the only development that is intrinsically value is the realisation of the higher capacities of real individual human beings in the contingent and changing circumstances of their daily lives.

V

The Structure of the Present Book

Green's emphasis on the intersubjective nature of personal identity-formation leads him to argue that individual self-realisation entails — indeed, seems to be reduced to — individual service to a common good. Indeed, in his *Lectures on the Principles of Political Obligation*, he goes so far as to claim that the individual's 'right to free life' 'can only be grounded on the capacity,

---

[49] Richard Lewis Nettleship, 'Professor T.H. Green. In memoriam', *Contemporary Review,* 61 (January–June 1882), 862.

[50] Roger Scruton, *The Palgrave MacMillan Dictionary of Political Thought*, third edition (Houndsmill: Palgrave MacMillan, 2007), p. 733.

[51] PE 182–85.

which belongs to the human nature, for freely fulfilling some function in the social organism.⁵² This and related claims are explored at length in the present book. With L.T. Hobhouse's conception of liberal socialism in mind (quoted in §1.II), chapter two examines Green's theory of the relationships obtaining between social practices and the individual's true good. It rejects the claim of Avital Simhony and others that Green's social theory is a form of organicism, even though Green's social theory is relational. The chapter explores the ways in which Green's practical philosophy both is perspectival and endorses value pluralism, even if his metaphysics aspires to an 'absolute' viewpoint and a form of internally-differentiated value monism. Chapter three analyses Green's theory of the common good, emphasising the fact that he did not value all determinate common goods equally. It considers the non-competitiveness of the common good, as well as the degree to which individuals are required to be selfless, and the justificatory role played by considerations of social justice in Green's social thought. Chapter three also considers the implications of Green's perspectivalism in this regard.

Chapter four reconstructs Green's theory of the social reformer placing particular emphasis on the positive role he ascribes to personal alienation, before analysing his theory of social criticism. The chapter then considers Green's response to perplexities of conscience, before turning to his implicit invocations of Hegel's 'cunning of reason' and spiritual determinism at certain points in his analysis. Chapter five considers the roles played by progress and education in Green's theory, comparing his position to that of Giuseppe Mazzini, whom he admired greatly. Chapter six analyses the place of recognition in Green's theories of moral rights and duties on the one hand, and legal rights and obligations on the other. It examines his alternative to the natural rights tradition of Rousseau, Spinoza and others, before exploring this alternative in greater depth by comparing it to that of J.G. Fichte. It considers the limits of Green's ethical position by asking which entities does it preclude from the possession of rights, and concludes by examining the theory of punishment which Green sees as a necessary facet of any coherent theory of rights.

Chapter seven turns to Green's conceptions of sovereignty, the sovereign and the state. It begins by highlighting the striking but previously-overlooked similarities between Green's position and that defended by Constructivist and English School international relations theorists. The chapter moves on to consider the theoretical and practical factors relating to the determination of appropriate state action, before reflecting on the problems caused for practical reason by the inherent limitations of political philosophy. Chapter eight develops this analysis by turning to Green's writings on democratic participation, cultural diversity and conscientious civil diss-

---

⁵² PPO 155.

ent. Together with final two chapters, chapters seven and eight develop the claim made in the earlier chapters, that Green's guiding ideal is the development of self-assertive, conscientious individual citizens.

Chapter nine examines the most fundamental principles of Green's political economy. It begins by establishing that, contrary to the allegation of C.B. MacPherson and his followers, Green bases his political economy squarely on self-realisation and makes no appeal to utilitarian principles. The chapter shows that Green supports capitalism because it can embody the mechanisms of free exchange, and only supports capitalism to the extent that it embodies those mechanisms. The chapter concludes by considering possible criticisms of the most fundamental principles of Green's political economy. Throughout, Green insists that the practical implications of these principles are the result of the interaction of those principles with the actual circumstances obtaining in concrete times and places. With this mind, chapter ten turns to Green's practical political economy. Starting with a brief analysis of his proto-New Liberal position on bequest and inheritance, the discussion turns to Green's position on land reform, illuminating it via a comparison with J.K. Galbraith's subsequent analysis of the market system and the technostructure. Next, it is shown that Green gives only grudging support to both state-run and charitable welfare schemes, because he sees them as at best stop-gaps which are necessary in lieu of vibrant trade union and cooperative movements. His guiding ideal is the creation of those participatory movements. Their existence would allow the dismantling of schemes in which individuals are treated as passive recipients of welfare, rather than as active citizens who have secured fair treatment through their own collective self-assertion. This aspect of Green's political economy is developed via a comparison with the radical republicanism of Giuseppe Mazzini. Finally, a series of comparisons of his position with those of Friedrich Engels, L.T. Hobhouse, Karl Marx, William Morris, Robert Owen, R.H. Tawney and Arnold Toynbee are used to draw out the nuances of Green's liberal socialism. The concluding chapter draws together the main lines of argument developed in the course of both this book and the previous one, to establish that Green is indeed best understood as a liberal socialist of the type later defended by Hobhouse.

Social Practices
and the True Good

'Our ultimate standard of worth is an ideal of personal *worth. All other values are relative to value for, of, or in a person.'*[1]

I

Introduction

Green locates the supreme value of individual human beings in their capacity to live as self-directing and self-creating 'spiritual' agents. He argues that collective practices and institutions derive whatever value they have from helping individuals to realise this ultimate personal good. More formally, collective institutions and practices are valuable only to the extent that they constitute and sustain an environment for action in which individuals have a reasonable chance of developing and leading their own freely-endorsed and enriching lives. The next three chapters analyse the understanding of the relationship between the individual and her society that underpins Green's theory, focusing on his theories of the common good, conscientious agency and social criticism. It is established that these theories form the heart of his defence of the individual against harmful and illegitimate interference by groups, institutions and other individuals.

This chapter begins by sketching Green's conception of the true good in §2.II, before examining Green's rejection of the organic metaphor in social theory in §2.III, and then in §2.IV analysing Green's relational social ontology in order to establish the need for a sympathetic social context in which the true good can become a determinate principle of our daily lives. §2.V considers the often-misunderstood relationship between Green's value theory and value pluralism. §2.VI summarises the argument thus far.

It is important to enter one brief caveat before proceeding. It was established in MSF chapter six that Green adopts two incompatible theories of the will which are differentiated in large part by the issue of voluntarism. This ambiguity does not create any problems for the present chapter as every-

---

[1]   PE 184.

thing that follows here obtains whether or not the will is capable of being directed voluntaristically. There are problems for his theory of conscientious agency however, as becomes evident in chapter four.

II

Green's Conception of the True Good

As was shown at length in MSF and in summary in the previous chapter, Green conceived of the individual as a spiritual being: a being born with capacities for rational thought, eudaimonic development and virtuous action, capacities to which the individual herself feels drawn to give concrete, self-conscious and iterative expression in her personal character and daily life. Here, Green builds on the philosophies of Kant, Aristotle and others: a self-conscious and rational being can possess a feeling of true self-satisfaction only to the extent that she acts in ways that are not merely wise, self-disciplined, courageous and just, but which also conform to the categorical imperative to respect humanity, whether the latter is located in herself or in another person (MSF §§7.II–III, 8.II, 8.V).[2] Counterfactually, individuals feel alienated from themselves to the extent that they do not seek to act in these ways, and for this reason. To the extent that the individual's practice is guided by her efforts to realise her higher capacities in a rational form, she expresses an 'eternal or distinctively human consciousness', and performs 'distinctively human actions' (MSF chapter five).[3] Moreover, through her interactions with others she tends to help sustain a 'distinctively human society'.[4]

Moreover, it was established in MSF (§7.IV) that Green holds that once the individual achieves this state of self-realisation, she achieves her 'true good'. It was shown also that Green conceives the true good to be that activity or state of character which brings 'abiding satisfaction' to the individual's 'abiding self'.[5] In Geoffrey Thomas's words, here '"true" has the force at once of genuine as opposed to false or spurious, and of ultimate as opposed to derivative or conditional'.[6] Unfortunately, Green refers to the true good as both (i) a state of character, and (ii) the practical expression of that character in determinate circumstances (MSF §7.V). Despite the resulting ambiguities within Green's theory of the true good, his position can be expressed more formally as the following series of propositions.[7]

---

2   PE 192–98.
3   PE 83, 87, 88, 91, 132, 390.
4   PE 126.
5   DSF 1; PE 158, 234.
6   Geoffrey Thomas, *Moral Philosophy of T.H. Green* (Oxford: Clarendon Press, 1987), p. 247. See PE 171, 191.
7   First stated at MSF 155–56.

1.   The individual should act out of a good will;

2.   A will is good to the extent that it seeks the attainment of objects which the individual believes to be intrinsically or inherently valuable, and does so in a manner that can be willed as a universal law;

3.   Ultimately the realisation of distinctively human capacities in the 'world of practice' is the most valuable object for a human being;

4.   An agent has a good character to the extent that she is motivated primarily to realise her own eudaimonic capacities and those of her fellows, and does so in a manner that can be willed as a universal law;

5.   The agent attains her true good to the extent that the actions issuing from her personality achieve this primary goal.

MSF also analysed at some length the relationships between Green's conception of the true good, personality and contemporary virtue ethics (MSF §§7.I–II, 8.III). He was shown to hold that the individual realises her true good to the extent that she expresses in her daily life a coherent personality which embodies concretely her 'distinctively human capacities' ('personal excellence, moral and intellectual') and with which she identifies freely.[8] In this way, Green conceives the true good to be a historically-sensitive form of Aristotelian eudaimonia which is being modified continually in light of the Kantian imperative to embody and respect rational agency as such. Given the limitations of the individual's animal nature (her inescapable physicality and the attendant limitations of her self-awareness and reasoning abilities) the true good is an always-unattainable ideal of personal flourishing. Nevertheless, the individual always tends to feel driven to engage freely and habitually in actions that she believes constitute the 'full exercise or realisation of the soul's faculties in accordance with its proper excellence, which… [is] an excellence of thought, speculative and practical'.[9] As the individual's own guiding ideal, her conception of her ultimate true good is realised in part as her internalised arrangement of 'virtues and excellences', especially her own concrete conceptions of fortitude, temperance, self-denial and justice.[10] The individual's formulation of these virtues is central here. Even though the ancient Greeks gave the original authoritative statement of such virtues and excellences and their interrelationships, their theories were inherently time-bound. The conceptions of the virtues have developed over subsequent generations, to the point that, for example, whereas the Greeks associated fortitude solely with the warrior, Green argues that by the 1870s courage can be understood just as appropriately as a virtue of those who

---

[8]   PE 355.

[9]   PE 254.

[10]   PE 355.

dedicate themselves 'to the service of the sick, the ignorant and the debased'.[11]

Even though we all fall short of our ideals, no one can be forced by others to flourish. In part, this is because the individual can flourish only if she follows her personal judgement about the features and intrinsic worth of her true good: each of us can only flourish when we freely endorse our own conception of the various ideals that guide our respective lives. One can also not be forced to develop because human flourishing is individuated in another sense: a life that is good for one person need not be good for another. This second source of individuation has profound implications for Green's theory of the well-ordered society, as will become evident below. These implications stem from the fact that Green conceives the true good to be a hypothetical and always underspecified ideal, an ideal that exists for each of us only once we have exercised our own respective capacities of personal judgement in light of our own respective personal socialisation and circumstances. In other words and in the terms that it was developed throughout MSF and so far in the present book, the individual's conception of her own best life arises from her own iterative attempts to arrive at a concrete conception of 'the idea—the conviction of there being such as thing' as 'the unconditional good'.[12] It is an ideal 'we only find… because we have an idea that it is there, an idea which we direct our powers to realise', just as we do in regard to our conviction that the world of experience is underlain by a 'unity' (or rather harmony) of clear and rationally-interrelated principles.[13] This 'finding' is the result of a process that I have labelled 'crystallisation',[14] which accords with Kant's notion of a 'practico-dogmatic principle of transition to this ideal of perfection'.[15] In short, Green argues that every individual posits her own hypothetical ideal of a true good, and she posits it so as to motivate and guide her iterative attempts to act well in the world.

Given this analysis of the individual's 'progressive determination of the idea of the [highest possible] end' of human action, it is relatively easy to establish the error in the frequently-made allegation that Green's justification of the moral or (more properly because less restricted) 'true' good is circular.[16] I will concentrate here on John Plamenatz's formulation as it is the

---

11 PE 258.

12 PE 195.

13 PE 149.

14 MSF 38, 52, 83–84, 93, 107,146–48, 183–86.

15 Immanuel Kant, 'What Real Progress has Metaphysics Made in Germany Since the Time of Leibniz and Wolff?', in his *Theoretical Philosophy after 1781*, ed. H. Allison and P. Heath, trans. Peter Heath (Cambridge: Cambridge University Press, 2001), p. 394 (Prussian Academy edition 20:307).

16 PE 241. For the allegation of circularity, see E.F. Carritt, *Morals and Politics: Theories of their relation from Hobbes and Spinoza to Marx and Bosanquet* (Oxford:

most coherent formulation of this charge that currently exists Plamenatz's case centres on the following passage from the *Prolegomena*.

> 'As... [the individual's] true good is or would be... [his will and reason's] complete realisation, so his goodness is proportionate to his habitual responsiveness to the idea of there being such a true good... In other words, it consists in the direction of the will to objects determined for it by this idea.'[17]

On the strength of this passage, Plamenatz claims that

> 'Green... equates the goodness of the individual with *the complete realization* of certain of his capacities, and also with a *responsiveness to the idea* that such a realization would be good. It follows from this that a man's capacities are completely *realized* when he is *responsive to the idea* that such a realization would be good.'[18]

Turning to the interpretation first, such a theory is indeed circular. Yet, it is a misreading of Green. In fact, it is clearly a misreading of the passage Plamenatz quotes from the *Prolegomena*. Certainly, Green does distinguish the 'true good' from 'goodness', but obviously he does not do so in the way that Plamenatz alleges. Green equates the true good with the complete actualisation in the individual's personality of her highest rational and eudaimonic potentials, whereas the agent's 'goodness' is her actual (and probably imperfect) embodiment of these potentials. Indeed, not even Plamenatz is satisfied with his initial attack. He considers an alternative way of interpreting the passage from the *Prolegomena* quoted above.

> '[As] Green thinks that some goods are not true goods, he must mean that they are not really goods at all, in the sense that all statements made about them asserting that they possess the property of being good would be false. If he does not mean this, he means nothing, for this is the only possible meaning of his words.'[19]

It is vital to distinguish 'good' understood as 'possessing intrinsic worth' from 'a good' understood as 'an object desired by an agent'. The agent's good qua intrinsic worth may not be found through her goods qua desired

---

Clarendon Press, 1935), p. 132; E.F. Carritt, *Ethical and Political Thinking* (Oxford: Clarendon Press, 1947), pp. 46–48; H.D. Lewis, 'Does the Good Will Define its Own Content? – a study of T.H. Green's *Prolegomena to Ethics*', in his *Freedom and History* (London: George Allen and Unwin, 1962); John P. Plamenatz, *Consent, Freedom, and Political Obligation* (London: Oxford University Press, 1938), pp.65–68; see also Jerome B. Schneewind, *Sidgwick's Ethics and Victorian Moral Philosophy* (Oxford: Clarendon Press, 1977), pp.408–11; Michael Freeden, *The New Liberalism: An ideology of social reform*, reprinted with corrections (Oxford: Clarendon Press, 1986 [1978]), p. 57. Cacoullos argues against Plamenatz (Ann R. Cacoullos, *Thomas Hill Green: Philosopher of rights* (New York: Twayne, 1974), pp. 127–29).

[17] PE 180, quoted in Plamenatz, *Consent*, p. 65, Plamenatz's editing and clarification.
[18] Plamenatz, *Consent*, p. 66, italics in original.
[19] Plamenatz, *Consent*, pp. 66–67.

objects: witness Green's own alcoholic brother, Charles Dickens' Ebenezer Scrooge, or Esau selling his 'birthright for a mess of pottage'.[20] Plamenatz's perplexity originates in part from Green's use of one term to refer to two concepts. Yet, he is far from being alone in using the 'good' in both senses.[21] As with contemporary philosophers such as John Rawls, Green's meaning is usually fairly clear from the context. It is also clear that his justification of the true good is not circular.

Plamenatz objects also that Green cannot explain which comes first, persons or the true good, and that, consequently, Green's theory is unsustainable.[22] In fact, primarily this objection expresses a doubt regarding the coherence of Green's theory of socialisation rather than the nature of the true good as such. The objection fails to appreciate the coherence and complexity of Green's position. It will be demonstrated in the next section that Green regards personality and social forms as being necessarily interrelated. Individuals are born with the capacity to conceive of and, once they have been socialised, to live according to an idea of a true good. Plamenatz's objection fails to appreciate this.

In spite of such counter-arguments regarding Green's ethical theory, many scholars have remained uneasy. A significant number of them have claimed that Green presents an organic conception of society. More often than not, they have alleged that he defends a form of monolithic homogeneous social holism and, in terms of logic rather intention, authoritarianism.[23] The next section establishes that although Green rejects social holism and organicism, he does defend a relational social ontology. Furthermore, it will be established in subsequent chapters that Green's social ontology does not lend any more support to authoritarianism than do many forms of liberalism.

---

20 For Esau, see PE 96–98.
21 See, for example, John Rawls, *A Theory of Justice*, revised edition (Oxford: Oxford University Press, 1999), §§60–68; and, more broadly, Jerrold J. Katz, 'Semantic Theory and the Meaning of "Good"', *Journal of Philosophy*, 61:23 (10 December 1964), 739–66; Geoffrey Sampson, 'Good', *Linguistic Inquiry*, 1:2 (April 1970), 257–60.
22 Plamenatz, *Consent*, p. 68.
23 For example, Isaiah Berlin, 'Introduction', in his *Four Essays on Liberty* (Oxford: Oxford University Press, 1969), pp. lx–lxii. For trenchant and effective rebuttals of Berlin, see W.J. Mander, *British Idealism: A history* (Oxford: Oxford University Press, 2011), pp. 241–43.

III

The Dangers of Imposing an Organic Metaphor
onto Green's Social Ontology

Green argues that the individual could not realise her true good herself were she to live alone in the world. This is not to say that humans live together solely to realise their higher capacities, of course. Initially, human beings form societies simply to facilitate the satisfaction of their material needs. Even as societies become wealthier, securing one's material interests is a motive which is never totally absent from human action.[24] Moreover, all recorded societies have had some division of labour, and these sub-groupings have tended to interrelate to form a series of interconnected social networks.[25] Green defends this type of social division of labour on the grounds that it can ease harmonious social interaction and so promote personal material interests.[26] Dividing labour in this way tends to increase productive efficiency and reduces competition for scarce social resources. Moreover, specialisation allows the individual to pursue her dominant personal interests more effectively by providing the context of a series of social networks which together can provide for the satisfaction of her other desires. In this way, a social division of labour can both help the individual to develop herself and to stabilize her society, at the same time as enabling her to concentrate her efforts in specific areas of work. By thus limiting the 'scope' of her 'personal interests',[27] the individual is brought to rely on help from other individuals, and stable societies tend to arise.

These are pragmatic reasons for humans to form groups, and as such they constitute purely self-interested yet still significant senses in which personal autonomy is 'a power which each man exercises through the help or security given him by his fellow-men, and which he in turn helps to secure for them'.[28] Yet, Green insists that individuals do not feel obligated to perpetuate social structures simply because a well-functioning society allows individuals to satisfy more of their material desires more efficiently and more safely.[29] More significantly, security of material provisions is a precondition for spiritual growth. As Green writes, 'Until life has been so organised as to afford some regular relief from the pressure of animal wants,

---

24 PE 281; PPO 124–28 *passim*. Cacoullos misses this point (Cacoullos, *Thomas Hill Green*, p. 123).

25 PE 190.

26 There are several classic discussions of this point of which Green would have been aware. For example, Plato, *Republic*, 369–72; Aristotle, *Politics*, 1252a24–1253a39; David Hume, *A Treatise of Human Nature*, ed. L.A. Selby-Bigge, second edition, rev. P.H. Nidditch (Oxford: Clarendon, 1978 [1888]), pp. 534–49.

27 PE 191.

28 LLFC 199.

29 PE 242; PPO 113–36 *passim*.

an interest in what Aristotle calls ['living well', or 'well-being'], as distinct
from [merely 'living'], cannot emerge'.[30] In fact, as soon as the means of
satisfying the agent's material needs have been secured in a society, there
arises in the individual the idea of a permanently better life: a 'haunting
human sense of some supreme good', in the words of Newman Smyth (see
chapters nine and ten below).[31]

Green understands it to be a necessary feature of human life that individuals require socialisation if they are to be able to conceive of a world of
actions and ways of life that possess intrinsic or ultimate worth.[32] In W.J.
Mander's words, 'this transform[s] the seemingly individualistic doctrine of
self-satisfaction into something almost directly its opposite'.[33] Individuals
tend to value the societies of which they are members to the extent that they
believe them to embody such a world. In other words, an individual tends to
value the society in which she lives to the extent that she believes it to be an
enriching, well-ordered and 'complex organisation of life, with laws and
institutions, with relationships, courtesies, and charities, with arts and
graces through which the perfection is to be attained'.[34] This claim gives
Green's moral and political philosophy much of its distinctive flavour. Consequently, it is important to reflect more closely on the social ontology
underpinning it.[35]

Much of the secondary literature characterises Green as a social organicist.[36] Avital Simhony argues that one can understand almost all British

---

30 PE 240.

31 Newman Smyth, *Christian Ethics*, second edition (Edinburgh: T. and T. Clark,
    1893), p. 21.

32 For example, PE 324; PPO 2; 'Moral Philosophy' *passim*.

33 Mander, *British Idealism*, p. 204.

34 DSF 23.

35 At least one commentator is unclear about Green's theory (Cacoullos, *Thomas Hill
    Green*, pp. 72–85 *passim*).

36 For instance, Leonard T. Hobhouse, *Metaphysical Theory of the State: A criticism*
    (London: George Allen and Unwin, 1918), pp. 96, 118; Harold J. Laski, 'Leaders of
    Collectivist Thought', in H. Grisewood, ed., *Ideas and Beliefs of the Victorians: An
    historic reevaluation of the Victorian age* (London: Sylvan, 1949), *passim*; John Bowle,
    Politics and Opinion in the Nineteenth Century: An historical introduction (Oxford:
    Arden, 1954), pp. 224, 254, 297; Michael St John Packe, *The Life of John Stuart Mill*
    (London: Secker and Warburg, 1954), p. 403; Melvin Richter, *The Politics of
    Conscience: T.H. Green and his age* (London: Weidenfeld and Nicolson, 1964), pp.
    202–05, 224–25; Harold R.G. Greaves, *The Foundations of Political Theory*, second
    edition (London: G. Bell, 1966 [1958]), p. 19; Berlin, 'Introduction', p. xlix(n);
    Isaiah Berlin, 'Two Concepts of Liberty', in his *Four Essays*, pp. 133n1, 150; J.
    Kemp, 'T.H. Green and the Ethics of Self-realisation', in G.N.A. Vesey, ed., *Reason
    and Reality: Royal Institute of Philosophy Lectures, Volume Five, 1970–1971* (London:
    MacMillan, 1972), pp. 236–37; Bernard J. Diggs, ed., *State, Justice and Common
    Good: An introduction to social and political philosophy* (Glenview, IL: Foresman,

idealist social theories (including Green's) properly only if one distinguishes three types of social ontology. The first, atomistic individualism, rests on the 'ontological primacy of the individual', and conceives social groups to be simply aggregates of atomistic individuals. The second, holistic organicism, conceives of the 'social whole' rather mysteriously, as being 'somehow more real than individual human beings involved in it'.[37] These are well-known alternatives and I will not comment on them further for the moment.[38] Simhony contends that, with the possible exception of Bernard Bosanquet, all the British idealists adopt a third approach which she labels 'relational organicism'.[39] This social ontology has three 'salient features'.[40] Firstly, it conceives of the mutual interdependence of whole and parts as being 'non-

---

1974), p. 26; Nalini Pant, *Theory of Rights: T.H. Green, Bosanquet, Spencer and Laski* (Varanasi: Vishwavidyalaya Prakashan, 1977), pp. 27–28; Gerald F. Gaus, *The Modern Liberal Theory of Man* (Beckenham: Croom Helm, 1983), pp. 68, 82–85; W.H. Greenleaf, *The British Political Tradition, Volume Two: The ideological heritage* (London: Methuen, 1983), pp. 29, 124–42; Howard Kainz, *Democracy East and West: A philosophical overview* (London: MacMillan, 1984), pp. 56, 58; R.A.D. Grant, 'Defenders of the State', in G.H.R. Parkinson, ed., *An Encyclopaedia of Philosophy* (London: Routledge, 1988), pp. 701–02; Gerald F. Gaus, 'Green, Bernard Bosanquet and the Philosophy of Coherence', in C.L. Ten, ed., *Routledge History of Philosophy, Volume VII, The Nineteenth Century* (London: Routledge, 1994), pp. 440–45. Cacoullos is one of the few commentators to deny that Green is an organicist (Cacoullos, *Thomas Hill Green*, p. 14). On the wider debate, see H.J. McCloskey, 'The State as an Organism, as a Person, and as an End in Itself', *Philosophical Review*, 72 (1963), 306–26; Mander, *British Idealism*, p. 229.

[37] Avital Simhony, 'Idealist Organicism: Beyond holism and individualism', *History of Political Thought*, 10:3 (1989), 515.

[38] One might see Jeremy Bentham and Giuseppe Mazzini as exemplars of the respective positions. 'The community is a fictitious *body*, composed of the individual persons who are considered as constituting as it were its *members*. The interest of the community then is, what? – the sum of the interests of the several members who compose it.' Jeremy Bentham, *Introduction to the Principles of Morals and Legislation*, edited by J.H. Burns and H.L.A. Hart (Oxford: Clarendon Press, 1996), chapter 1, section 4. 'We have begun to suspect, not only that there is upon the earth something greater, more holy, more divine than the individual – namely, Humanity – the collective being always living, learning, advancing toward God, of which we are but the instruments; but that it is alone from the summit of this collective idea, from the conception of the Universal Mind, "of which," as Emerson says, "each individual man is one more incarnation," that we can derive our mission, the rule of our life, the aim of our societies.' Giuseppe Mazzini, 'On the Genius and Tendency of the Writings of Thomas Carlyle' [1843], in his *Life and Writings,* ed. Emilie Ashurst, 6 vols., second edition (London: Smith, Elder, 1891), vol. 4, pp. 73–74.

[39] On Bosanquet, see Colin Tyler, *Idealist Political Philosophy: Pluralism and conflict in the absolute idealist tradition* (London and New York: Continuum, 2006), chapters 4 and 5.

[40] Simhony, 'Idealist Organicism', 520–22.

reductive': society is not simply an aggregate of ontologically discrete members, and yet these members cannot be reduced to mere adjuncts of an intrinsically-valuable collective entity such as the 'Nation' or 'Humanity'. Secondly, both the whole and its parts are mutually-constituting.[41] In this regard, Simhony quotes F.H. Bradley: 'the social whole "cannot live *except* in its many members. Just so each of the members is alive but *not apart* from the whole which lives *in it*".'[42] The third 'salient feature' of relational organicism reconciles the first two claims.

> 'The constitutive elements are, respectively, unity and difference (social structure and human agency, respectively) which, deprived of their respective absolute independence of each other, make up the third view of society — relational organicism — but not in mere conjunction, rather in their mutual interdependence.'[43]

Rather than being three separate features of one social ontology as Simhony claims, these are simply three perspectives on the same point. For Simhony's relational organicist, the individual derives her concrete sense of personal identity from the ways in which she relates to other individuals as agents iteratively in practice.

Yet, great caution is needed here. In fact, even though the organic metaphor dominated much mid- and late-Victorian social thought, not least that of Herbert Spencer and G.H. Lewes, it exerted its greatest influence over the British idealist social thought only after Green's death in March 1882.[44] Even careful and sympathetic scholars such as Simhony (and myself in the first edition of this book) have failed to take account of the fact that Green himself reserves the terms 'organism' and 'organic' almost exclusively for the 'physiological' sphere: the 'animal', 'physical' and 'material' world.[45]

---

41 See also D.C. Phillips, 'Organicism in the Late Nineteenth and Earlier Twentieth Centuries', *Journal of the History of Ideas*, 31 (1970), 413, 418–20.

42 Simhony, 'Idealist Organicism', 521, quoting Francis H. Bradley, *Ethical Studies*, second edition (Oxford: Clarendon Press, 1927), p. 79, Simhony's emphasis.

43 Simhony, 'Idealist Organicism', 522.

44 See Henry Jones, 'The Social Organism', in Andrew Seth and R.B. Haldane, eds., *Essays in Philosophical Criticism*, with a preface by Edward Caird (London: Longmans, Green and Co., 1883), pp. 187–213.

45 See Colin Tyler, *Thomas Hill Green and the Philosophical Foundations of Politics: An internal critique* (Lampeter: Edwin Mellen, 1997), chapter 3 ('Relational Organicism and the Common Good'). Excluding the passages cited already and his critique of G.H. Lewes' theory of the 'social medium' ('Lewes II' 9–129), Green uses organic terms in 'Hume I' 7, 12, 15, 16, 18, 24, 29, 51, 58, 62, 106, 157, 169, 177, 181, 188, 197, 247, 283, 284, 307, 309, 345; 'Hume II' 3, 37; 'Spencer I' 5, 6, 14; 'Spencer II' 37, 47, 63; 'Lewes I' 65, 66, 67, 72, 80–81, 83–84, 88–90; PE 15, 50, 60, 62, 67–68, 70–74 *passim*, 77, 79, 80, 82–85 *passim*, 89, 99, 115, 119, 175, 177, 187, 250, 273, 293, 327, 352; 'Logic' 7, 11, 15, 21, 28, 50, 53, 54; DSF 10; 'Works of Fiction' 24; 'Aristotle' 82.

Organic 'processes' are carried out by 'nervous' and 'mechanical structures', which serve the 'natural' 'functions' of 'sentience' and the like. Green refers to the 'social organism' in one footnote in 'On the Different Senses of "Freedom"…' and six sections of *The Lectures on the Principles of Political Obligation*.[46] In the latter work, he invokes the notion of the 'social organicism' twice in his discussion of the 'right to life and liberty', positing (before rejecting as meaningless) a hypothetical transnational society founded upon the 'conception of all men as forming one society in which each individual has some service to render, one organism in which each has a function to fulfil'.[47] He does argue that the 'right to free life' 'can only be grounded on the capacity, which belongs to the human nature, for freely fulfilling some function in the social organism'.[48] Occasionally in the *Prolegomena*, Green uses the term 'organic' in the sense of 'denoting or characterized by a harmonious relationship between the elements of a whole', yet he does so without implying that society should be conceived as an organism.[49] At times, he uses the word 'organ' in the sense of 'agent': for example, 'As a man and a citizen, indeed, it is his function to serve as… [the] organ [of the 'aspiration after perfection of conduct']; to give effect to it in his own conduct, to assist in communicating it to others'.[50] Nevertheless, very rarely indeed does he come close to characterising society as an organism. At one point he argues that 'it is human society as a whole that we must look upon as the organism in which the capacities of the human soul are unfolded'.[51] Yet, he writes this when arguing that to assess a society's worth one should not focus upon merely the most spiritually-advanced members of society; in addition, one should consider the extent to which the development of any particular subgroup is made possible only by existence of oppressive social conditions for others. Even here, Green remains focused on the free individual rather than some unified social whole: ontologically, the 'organism' is 'essentially a society of self-determined persons', and 'There can be no progress of society which is not a development of capacities on the part of persons composing it, considered as ends in themselves'.[52] It is for this reason that Green criticises the use of the organic metaphor in social and political theory. He writes the following in *Political Obligation*.

> '[For the natural scientist] Life does not reside in any of the organs of life or in any or all of the processes of material change through which these pass… It is a function or end which they realise according to a plan or idea which deter-

---

[46] DSF 10, 11n; PPO 125–26, 130, 141, 154–55.

[47] PPO 154.

[48] PPO 155.

[49] *Oxford English Dictionary*. PE 5, 70–74, 83, 231, 250, 327, 352.

[50] PE 327.

[51] PE 273; see also PE 352.

[52] PE 273.

mines their existence before they exist and survives their disappearance. If it were held, then, that the state were an organised community in the same sense in which a living body is, of which the members at once contribute to the function called life and are made what they are by that function, according to an idea of which there is no consciousness on their part, we should only be following the analogy of the established method of interpreting nature.'[53]

Immediately, Green rejects this organic social ontology because 'it represents the state as a purely natural, not at all a moral, organism'.[54] Understood in this way, the organic metaphor implies that individuals are merely 'organs' for the realisation of the good of something else, namely a social whole. Not simply this, but thus understood individuals fulfil this role unwittingly. As such, social organicism denies the intrinsic worth of individual members as well as leaving individuals with no room for self-directed moral action. Green argues that an organic social whole could not possess any intrinsic moral worth because, in these ways, it would fail to be a moral entity. In short, Green invokes the organic metaphor only very rarely in his social and political theory, and when he considers it in any depth he expresses grave doubts as to its ability to articulate the core features of a worthwhile human community.

Green does acknowledge very significant links between the 'human organism and the social medium in which it lives'.[55] Yet, as was established in MSF (§5.IV) in every such instance he is at great pains to emphasise the profound transformations that must occur before the individual's 'organic' qualities can attain any true value. In fact, such transformations are so fundamental that what begins as 'organic' eventually takes on a wholly 'spiritual' character. Ultimately, this is the only manner in which the 'organic' is significant for Green: as a 'medium' for the 'spiritual' (sc. the eudaimonic and the rational) and the abiding satisfaction that spiritual self-realisation can bring.[56] Green encapsulates his position clearly in 'On the Different Senses of "Freedom"...'

'In order to [make] any approach to this satisfaction of itself, the self-realising principle... must overcome the "natural impulses", not in the sense of either extinguishing them or denying them an object, but in the sense of fusing them with those higher interests, which have human perfection in some of its forms for their object. Some approach to this fusion we may notice in all good men, not merely in those in whom all natural passions—love, anger, pride, ambition—are enlisted in the service of some great public cause, but in those

---

[53] PPO 125.
[54] PPO 126.
[55] PE 5; see also PE 83, 231.
[56] PE 177.

with whom such passions are all governed by some such commonplace idea as that of educating a family.'[57]

Only individuals can possess intrinsic worth because only individuals can be self-determined agents who seek to realise goals whose attainment the agents judge to be categorically required of them. Social practices and the society they constitute derive whatever worth they possess from the worth of the individuals by whom they are 'brought into being and sustained'.[58] Social forms 'take a character, which does not belong to them as merely natural, [but rather] from agencies [that are] distinctively human'.[59]

Failing to recognise this fact—as one does by invoking the organic meta-phor—runs the danger of implying that Green believes a well-ordered society is one in which individuals perform roles which help the social mechanism to function and reproduce itself, and, crucially, that the worth of the individual's actions is derived from the fact that those actions help this extra-personal system to function and reproduce itself. Whether relational or holistic, organic readings tend to support the claim that Green believes that one can only properly assess the individual's true good, true freedom and social practices by referring to the impersonal meta-perspective of society conceived as a single, integrated mechanism. As has been established in this section, this is precisely the vision of the social world that Green rejects. Instead, he holds that societies exist only as well-informed, intellectually-careful individual members interpret them, and there is no more authorit-ative judgement of their worth than the conscientious judgements of their individual members. As will become clear below, Green holds that any one society can be viewed in any number of ways from any number of perspec-tives, and a society is well-ordered to the extent that it allows the different voices of agents situated in these various perspectives to be heard in multi-faceted, iterative public debates. His concerns regarding the organic meta-phor are, in other words, the flip-side of his defences of both social egalit-arianism and democratic inclusion, as well as educational reform (see §5.V, as well as chapters eight and nine).

IV

Green's Relational Social Ontology

While it is misleading to characterise Green's social theory as a form of organicism, Simhony and others are correct when they argue that Green places relational distinctively human (sc. 'spiritual') agency at the centre of his theory of the good life. As was established in MSF (§§6.I–IV) Green holds, firstly, that the truly good life can be lived only self-consciously and

---

[57] DSF 21. Thanks to Sean Magee for locating the passage.

[58] PPO 126.

[59] PPO 126.

so must be known, and, secondly, that the individual can know the meanings, values and contours of her personality and life only to the extent that
those meanings, values and contours have determinate content and practical
efficacy. More than this however, following Aristotle, Fichte, Hegel and
others, Green holds that such knowledge is possible only when the individual can experience herself as an object: only then does the individual gain
the distance from herself required for self-awareness and hence critical self-
reflection. The most obvious way in which the individual can start to understand herself as an object is through her experiences of the ways in which
other people relate to her. Consequently, Green writes: 'Some practical
recognition of personality by another, of an "I" by a "Thou" and a "Thou"
by an "I," is necessary to any practical consciousness of [personality], to any
such consciousness of it as can express itself in act.'[60] Practice cannot be
replaced by mere contemplation or abstract theorising, because individuals
sustain more textured relationships with one another through more defin-
itely and effectively mutual and ongoing participation in shared practices.
Moreover, practical interaction tends to draw on and hence partially reveal
the presently-unarticulated elements of the individual's personality, more
effectively than can the necessarily more articulated activities of contemplation and abstract theorising.

The practices in which individuals gain a sense of the nature and significance of their respective personalities are sustained by this mutual and iter-

---

[60] PE 190. Brink's succinct discussion of Aristotle is helpful here (David O. Brink,
Perfectionism and the Common Good: Themes in the philosophy of T.H. Green (Oxford:
Clarendon Press, 2003), §§XVI–XVII. Brink notes that there are similar discussions
of Aristotle in Green's manuscripts (Brink, *Perfectionism*, p. 44n20). In a passage
from Hegel's *Encyclopaedia of the Philosophical Sciences* which Green records in his
manuscripts, Hegel emphasises the individual's related need for subjective self-
awareness of her particularity: 'Just as light is the manifestation of itself and its
Other, darkness, and can manifest itself only by manifesting that Other, so too the
"I" is manifest to itself only in so far as its Other is manifest to it in the shape of
something independent of it.' Georg W.F. Hegel, *The Philosophy of Mind: Part
Three of the Encyclopaedia of the Philosophical Sciences (1830)*, trans. William Wallace
and A.V. Miller (Oxford: Clarendon Press, 1970), §413z. This is a complete translation of one of the two passages from this work which Green quotes in German
in MS6b, T.H. Green Papers, Balliol College Oxford. The German reads: 'Wie das
Licht die Manifesation seiner selbst und seines Anderen, des *Dunklen*, ist und sich
nur dadich offenbaren, kann daß es jenes Andere offenbart, so ist auch das Ich
nur insofern sich selber offenbar, als ihm sein Anderes in der Gestalt eines von
ihm Unabhängigen offenbar wird.' MS6b, emphasis in original. In the *Philosophical Propaedeutic* (an unpublished translation of which survives among the T.H.
Green Papers), Hegel contends that a 'Self-Consciousness which is for another is
not for it a mere object but is its other self... It beholds in the other its own self.'
Georg W.F. Hegel, *Philosophical Propaedeutic*, trans. A.V. Miller, ed. Michael
George and Andrew Vincent (Oxford: Basil Blackwell, 1986), p. 61.

ative participation. The more concrete the various activities of the participants in these acts of practical recognition, the more concrete will tend to be
their respective senses of personal identity. The more fully developed the
capacities of the participants (the I and its various Thou's), the more complex and multidimensional tend to be the relationships between them.

Green uses the example of language to develop his understanding of the
relationships in which the individual stands to her various practical contexts. He notes that there is no way in which an agent can avoid the need to
possess a language.[61] In fact, he claims that the individual's experiences
within the linguistic structure into which she is born, grows and acts, are the
most basic and influential stimuli on the development of her personality.
Yet, language and the individual's life in its wider forms are not self-
sustaining. They are framed with reference to shared 'institutions and
arrangements of life, social requirements and expectations, [and] conventional awards of praise and blame'.[62] In that a language makes sense only in
the context of an understanding of such practices and institutions, the
individual's determinate capacities for agency are necessarily socially-
conditioned, then. Consequently, Green observes that,

> 'social life is to personality what language is to thought. Language pre-
> supposes thought as a capacity, but in us the capacity of thought is only
> actualised in language. So human society presupposes persons in capacity —
> subjects capable each of conceiving himself and the bettering of his life as an
> end to himself — but it is only in the intercourse of men, each recognised by
> each as an end, not merely a means, and thus as having reciprocal claims, that
> the capacity is actualised and that we really live as persons.'[63]

When claiming that 'social life is to personality what language is to thought',
Green does not mean that these are merely analogous relationships. Rather,
they are two instances of the same relationship and, indeed, two aspects of
the same process of identity-formation. Social life, personality, language and
thought condition one another, they are what they are in their concrete part-
icularities because of the interactions of which they are all necessary elements. Suppress or alter one and you tend to suppress or alter the other
three.

In a crucial sense, every individual's personality is 'derived from a common dwelling-place with its associations, from common memories, traditions and customs, and from the common ways of feeling and thinking
which a common language and still more a common literature embodies'.[64]
As the complex particularised instantiation of a system of meanings and

---

[61] 'Kant' 71.
[62] PE 279.
[63] PE 183.
[64] PPO 123.

values, the individual's personality is a living and hence changing network of epistemic, aesthetic and moral concepts which initially are instilled in her through the necessarily social processes of 'inheritance and education'.[65] In these ways, the individual's linguistically-framed interactions are both conditioning factors in the development of personality and the media through which are framed the social institutions that are preconditions of that development.[66] Green observes in his unpublished manuscripts that it is,

> 'Quite true that individual man neither is, nor conceives himself as, anything apart from relations to others. Such relationships make up the reality of the man's self, but it is only as centred in his self-consciousness that they are what they are... All that individual is or has is derived from that society in which he lives, but *it is derived to that* individual.'[67]

Yet, even though external influences are necessary elements in the formation of all determinate agents, individuals are not perfectly malleable, and so are not solely created by such influences.[68] Human beings are not born as Lockean tabula rasa.[69] Identity-formation and social interaction are reciprocal processes that give practical expression to the meanings and values with which the individual identifies herself and her well-being, which are in turn partial expressions of her always partially inchoate conception of her underlying human nature. Moreover, given human imperfection, to some extent these meanings and values must be always partially distorted expressions of that nature.[70] Green's position is incompatible, then, with the claim that an individual is properly understood as a 'subject position'.[71] In other words, for Green the individual cannot be merely 'a site constituted' by social forces (see MSF §1.III).

'Human nature' or the 'human spirit' finds practical expression through socially-derived systems of meanings and values, then. Indeed, as should be clear from MSF and what has been argued so far in this book, Green's philosophical system is founded upon his analysis of the complex of practical interrelationships between the abstract human spirit and determinate human lives with their specific beliefs and values, and between these determinate human lives and their particular social environments.[72] It should be evident also that these expressive processes are driven ultimately by the

---

[65] DSF 23.

[66] DSF 24; 'Kant' 107–10 *passim*.

[67] MS23, T.H. Green Papers, Balliol College, Oxford (Green's contractions have been silently expanded).

[68] Green criticises G.H. Lewes at length on this point ('Lewes II' esp. 93).

[69] 'Hume I' 9–16, 19.

[70] PE 180, 232.

[71] Chantal Mouffe, 'Towards a Liberal Socialism', in her *Return of the Political* (London and New York: Verso, 1993), p. 7.

[72] PE 205; PPO 38–39.

individual's innate requirement to satisfy her higher needs in practice and to give practical expression to her higher capacities. Counterfactually, these processes are not driven inherently by the social systems of meanings and values that give content to these needs and capacities. It is only as the individual interprets and uses them that these systems have significance for her. They are the material she uses to answer deeper, inescapable drives of her human nature.

The needs and capacities which the individual is driven to manifest include her need to express both her conception of what she could be at her best (which might be called her projected ideal personality), and her consciousness of and drive to live in conformity with a principle which she feels best accords with that projected ideal personality.[73] In the terms used earlier, she tends to use this projected ideal when she crystallises her personality. In practice, such crystallisation tends to work through both intrasubjective and intersubjective processes, and to do so iteratively. In other words, it requires the individual to complete and reconcile her own meanings and values as well as to develop attitudes to the meanings and values of others with whom she interacts. In this way, she can develop more satisfying conceptions of her own true goods and a more successful strategy for realising them in her daily life. Green summarises much of his theory in the following passage from the *Prolegomena*.

> 'The idea of the good, according to this view, is an idea, if the expression may be allowed, which gradually creates its own filling. It is not an idea like that of any pleasure, which a man retains from an experience that he has had and would like to have again. It is an idea to which nothing that has happened to us or that we can find in existence corresponds, but which sets us upon causing certain things to happen, upon bringing certain things into existence. Acting in us, to begin with, as a demand which is ignorant of what will satisfy itself, it only arrives at a more definite consciousness of its own nature and tendency through reflection on its own creations — on habits and institutions and modes of life which, as a demand not reflected upon, it has brought into being.'[74]

That Green conceptualises the development of individual personality using his social theory helps him to identify the source of our sense of the authority of the meanings and values internalised by the individual. He does this by emphasising the reliance of the individual's meanings and values on the perceived 'objectivity' of socially-validated meanings and values. This quality of perceived objectivity facilitates personal agency by helping to stabilise

---

[73] John MacCunn, *Six Radical Thinkers: Bentham, J.S. Mill, Cobden, Carlyle, Mazzini and T.H. Green* (London: Edward Arnold, 1907), pp. 240–45; George H. Sabine, *A History of Political Theory*, rev. T.L. Thorson (Hindsale: Dryden, 1973), p. 672.

[74] PE 241. See Maria Dimova-Cookson, *T.H. Green's Moral and Political Philosophy: A phenomenological perspective* (Houndsmill: Palgrave, 2001), p. 96.

both the individual's sense of personal identity and the worlds of practice in which she conceives herself to be able to act. Yet, throughout Green's writings on social ontology, he is at pains to emphasise society's perspectival character. As he observes in *Political Obligation*, intrinsically-valuable action is that 'determined by an idea on the part of the agent, by his conception of an end or function'.[75] This perspectivalism plays a pivotal role in Green's social theory as it means that, ultimately, each individual has to judge for herself whether any particular socially-validated meaning, value, practice or institution truly is 'objectively' authoritative, and, if it is, then in what ways and to what extent. It will become evident in chapters three and four that Green's perspectivalism has profound implications for his often greatly misunderstood theory of the common good and his largely ignored theory of social criticism.

V

Value Pluralism and the True Good

Before concluding this analysis of Green's conception of the relationship between the true good and social practice, it is necessary to consider Isaiah Berlin's very influential assertion that certain ultimate values inevitably conflict with each other, and his claim that 'That we cannot have everything is a necessary, not a contingent truth'.[76] Berlin's claims have been widely accepted, yet they appear to contradict Green's contention that a core criterion for judging whether ultimate values had been fully realised is the extent to which they form a harmonious and complete system of concepts and practices.[77] Exploring this dispute between Berlin and Green marks the transition to the discussion of Green's theory of the common good in the next two chapters.

---

75 PPO 126.
76 Berlin, 'Two Concepts', 170.
77 Berlin, 'Two Concepts', 167–75; W.G. de Burgh, *From Morality to Religion* (London: MacDonald and Evans, 1938), p. 210; H.D. Lewis, 'The Individualism of T.H. Green', in his *Freedom and History*, pp. 90–104 *passim*; H.D. Lewis, 'T.H. Green and Rousseau', in his *Freedom and History*, pp. 129–30; Gerald G. MacCallum jnr, 'Berlin on the Compatibility of Values, Ideals, and "Ends"', *Ethics* 77 (1966–67), 139–45; Kemp, 'T.H. Green and The Ethics of Self-realisation', 238, 239; John Gray, 'On Negative and Positive Liberty', in Z.A. Pelczynski and John Gray, eds., *Conceptions of Liberty in Political Philosophy* (London: Athlone Press, 1984), pp. 321–48; Ben Wempe, *T.H. Green's Theory of Positive Freedom: From metaphysics to positive freedom* (Exeter and Charlottesville, VA: Imprint Academic, 2004), pp. 211–19 *passim*; Richard Bellamy, 'T.H. Green and the Morality of Victorian Liberalism', in Richard Bellamy, ed., *Victorian Liberalism: Nineteenth century political thought and practice* (London: Routledge, 1990), p. 140; Peter P. Nicholson, *The Political Philosophy of the British Idealists: Selected studies* (Cambridge: Cambridge University Press, 1990), pp. 125–26, 270n15. PE 322–29 *passim*, 251–52.

Berlin sketches two main justifications for value pluralism. Firstly, the belief that ultimately there is only one fully coherent metaphysical order of values has been 'responsible for the slaughter of individuals on the altars of the great historical ideals'.[78] Clearly, this suggests a merely pragmatic reason for believing in value pluralism, and in itself it has no truly philosophical purchase. Green might well accept that there is a very good pragmatic case for not treating value pluralism as a 'permanent' truth. Secondly, Berlin assumes that the current prevalence of value pluralism in itself does much to discredit an allegedly monistic view such as Green's.[79] Yet, why should the fact that values conflict here and now establish it is 'a necessary, and not a contingent truth'[80] that they always will? Indeed, Green himself emphasises that, at present, we experience continual and profound conflicts between values, in precisely the same manner that Berlin argues.[81] Green accepts that this might always be the case, and that, from any perspective available to human beings, actual normative standards might always be imperfect.

Berlin calls his own approach, rather misleadingly, an 'empirical view of politics', and he argues that Green holds a 'metaphysical' view.[82] Yet, both approaches presuppose the truth of various metaphysical and empirical claims. There can be no final proof of the relative superiority of either approach that, ultimately, does not simply beg the question of which one is correct. Nevertheless, as has just been done in regard to Berlin, one should consider the reasons Green offers for his claim that each individual should seek to create a harmonious system of ultimate values, given the ample evidence of conflicting values in our present world. Why should one believe that, ultimately, all values form a fully coherent system in the manner which Berlin and others so strenuously and famously deny?

Green's position is logically entailed by his ontology of human existence. It will be remembered from MSF §§3.II and 4.II in particular that for Green human beings are driven to create harmony in their worlds of knowledge and practice. As he writes in the *Prolegomena*, 'we only find unity in the world because we have an idea that it is there, an idea which we direct our powers to realise'.[83] Our need to seek to do so is a 'demand' of the rational

---

78 Berlin, 'Two Concepts', 167.

79 Berlin, 'Two Concepts', 171–72.

80 Berlin, 'Two Concepts', 170.

81 PE 321–28.

82 These labels are misleading because every empirical judgement must rest upon some metaphysical presuppositions, no matter how vague and confused they are, and no matter how little the person making the judgement attends to them (if indeed she does so at all). Similarly, Green's metaphysical theory is an empirical judgement in the sense that it is derived from an analysis of experience.

83 PE 149.

facet of human nature.[84] This is the guiding principle of Green's critical and speculative metaphysics (MSF §3.II). Ultimately then, he believes incompatible meanings and values to be evidence of imperfection because incoherence is evidence of imperfection. The belief that self-contradiction is a sure sign of error is a necessary presupposition of our conviction that we know things about the world, and as such it is a fact whose truth the philosopher should treat as indisputable (MSF pp. 38–39).[85] Consequently, every individual feels driven to seek to conceive her world through the lens of a fully complete and coherent system of meanings and values which she believes to be true.

In short, Green accepts fully that individuals are condemned to imperfection here and now and, as will become clear in subsequent chapters, probably forever, and to that crucial extent his position accords with that of Berlin.[86] Moreover, the individual experiences a constant drive to give practical expression to her idea of the true good. Green argues that, as a result, the 'special features of the object in which the true good is sought will vary in different ages and with different persons, according to circumstances and idiosyncrasy'.[87] This means that even philosophers are 'unable to say anything' regarding the universal features of the individual's 'ultimate well-being' except 'that it must be the complete fulfilment of our capabilities'.[88] Given the unalterable conditions of human life, there will always be some degree of possibly quite violent and sustained conflict between ultimate values held by real individuals, and between those values and the lives those individuals live on a daily basis. It is for this reason that Green himself is a principled pragmatist in his practical political activities, something that will become particularly evident below, in chapter ten. Green could agree with Berlin that, 'To demand more than… [value pluralism] is perhaps a deep and incurable metaphysical need; but to allow it to determine one's practice is a symptom of an equally deep, and more dangerous, moral and political immaturity'.[89] Yet, it bears stating once again that the unavoidability of human imperfection does not undermine Green's ethical and political thought. Indeed, if individuals were not imperfect, there would be no need for either morality or politics.

---

84 PPO 137.
85 PE 252.
86 PE 183.
87 PE 239.
88 PE 239. Implicitly, Mander (*British Idealism*, pp. 242–43) denies this.
89 Berlin, 'Two Concepts', 172.

VI

Conclusion

The different strands of Green's derivation of the true good can now be brought together. Green argues that social interaction can only occur between persons who possess certain potentials which have intrinsic spiritual value. Given that all social relationships presuppose the agency of those between whom the relationships exist, any interaction which fails to fully recognise this agency, such as that which occurs between a master and a slave, must be imperfect for humans.[90] Consequently, ultimately it must be unsatisfying, given the demands for coherence that are inherent within human nature. Hence, social relationships can be truly satisfying only to the extent that they embody self-conscious, full and mutual practical respect between persons.[91]

The fact that humans are imperfect expressions of their highest nature means that no one individual can become all that she believes she could become. No one individual can realise perfectly every one of what she understands to be her truly human potentials.[92] Nevertheless, in a vibrant and diverse society, the individual is far more likely to become aware of other values and virtues than the ones which she exercises at present. In this way, a diverse society benefits all of its members.[93] As Green's observes in his manuscripts: 'Rational life is not a uniformity, but a harmony. Manifold in unity.'[94] Less abstractly, it will be established in the next chapter that Green believes what is needed is a culture of cooperation for mutual improvement. Such a culture will be one in which each member helps her fellows to make the best of themselves: to realise her true good and so become truly free. It will be shown, that for Green, in Joseph Raz's phrase, the common good is an 'inherent public good'.[95] An egalitarian culture of mutual service is too ephemeral and fragile to be directly created or maintained, just as one cannot directly create an atmosphere at a party or in a theatre. Yet, in spite of this fact, this 'multi-stranded creation' (in Mander's words) can be encouraged indirectly.[96] Each citizen performing her particular duties for duty's sake encourages others to do the same and so tends

---

[90] PE 176.

[91] PE 245, 270; LLFC 199–200.

[92] PE 183, 191, 256, 273, 286, 309, 377; see Gaus, *Modern Liberal Theory*, pp. 54–74 *passim*; Nicholson, *Political Philosophy*, p. 271n18.

[93] Gaus, *Modern Liberal Theory*, pp. 19–21; Nicholson, *Political Philosophy*, p. 126; Gaus, 'T.H. Green, Bernard Bosanquet and the Philosophy of Coherence', 418–20.

[94] 'Rudiments', 4.

[95] Joseph Raz, *The Morality of Freedom* (Oxford: Clarendon Press, 1986), p. 187; see also Richard Bellamy, 'T.H. Green, J.S. Mill, and Isaiah Berlin', in his *Victorian Liberalism*, p. 283.

[96] Mander, *British Idealism*, p. 206.

both to promote and to manifest Green's conception of a eudaimonically-enriching kingdom of ends. The more valuable common goods are those which more adequately give practical recognition and respect to agents as persons. Nevertheless, human imperfection does make the kingdom of ends 'admittedly only an ideal'.[97] With this fact in mind, chapter four explores the conception of active citizenship entailed by Green's social theory and the common good.

[97] Immanuel Kant, 'Groundwork of The Metaphysics of Morals' (1785), in his *Practical Philosophy*, trans. and ed. Mary J. Gregor (Cambridge: Cambridge University Press, 1996), p. 83 (Prussian Academy Edition 4:433).

The Common Good

I

Introduction

One of the main difficulties for Green in deciding on clear and effective ways to serve one's community, is the inherent ambiguity in his model of the relationships between concrete individuals and their concrete communities. This ambiguity is reflected in the diverse interpretations that one finds in the scholarly literature. Nevertheless, some readings of Green's position are more plausible than others. Clearly, Dante Germino is deeply mistaken to regard it as 'doubtful that [Green] possessed any real concept of community at all. His "independent," self-governing man is ultimately too absorbed in his own personal problems and possessions to become fully involved with those of others'.[1] Green is emphatic that an individual is only properly self-governing when she seeks freely to help others. In other words, he holds that she finds her abiding satisfaction in the attainment of 'a good not private to the man himself, but good for him as a member of a community'.[2] Similarly, Kenneth R. Hoover's claim that for Green 'the communal remains in the abstract world of consciousness, rather than in the real world of political behaviour' is also unsupportable.[3] Rather, as James T. Kloppenberg puts it, Green's ethics 'begins and ends in praxis'.[4] This intrinsically practical turn reflects the Aristotelian elements of Green's position: an individual can be truly good only to the extent that her actions are motivated by the desire to act well, something that makes each of her ethically-motivated actions not merely instrumentally-valuable but also 'an end in itself'.[5]

---

[1]   Dante Germino, *Machiavelli to Marx: Modern western political thought* (Chicago and London: University of Chicago Press, 1972), pp. 269–70.

[2]   PE 232.

[3]   Kenneth R. Hoover, 'Liberalism and the Idealist Philosophy of Thomas Hill Green', *Western Political Quarterly*, 26 (1973), 562; see also Michael Freeden, *The New Liberalism: An ideology of social reform,* reprinted with corrections (Oxford: Clarendon Press, 1986 [1978]), p. 57.

[4]   James T. Kloppenberg, *Uncertain Victory: Social democracy and progressivism in European and American thought* (New York and Oxford: Oxford University Press, 1986), p. 142.

[5]   Aristotle, *Ethics*, Book 6, §ii (11392b2).

In line with this fact, it was established in chapter two that Green's moral and political thought is founded upon his conception of human nature and the social theory that it underpins. This dependence came out clearly in Green's use of the idea of the true good, which he characterises as that personal good which actualises the individual's highest nature. Actualising one's nature fully is the only object whose attainment will bring an abiding satisfaction to a human being.[6] It was shown that the individual's highest nature can only be present within the world 'subjectively' as her determinate capacity for action and 'objectively' as social norms, practices and institutions. The agent feels an inherent drive to express in practice her presently only partly choate conception of her highest capacities.[7] It is only when the individual participates freely in enriching social practices and institutions that her internally-complex capacity for agency can receive the determinate content, self-awareness and orientation that are necessary for the individual to be able to take advantage of opportunities for meaningful self-expression and self-development.[8] Without a sympathetic social context, the agent is merely an 'empty shell', and so is incapable of acting autonomously and morally. Indeed, properly speaking she could not act at all. In this way, Green follows Aristotle in arguing that an individual without a suitable social environment can be at best a poor and stunted expression of her highest nature.[9] Given the individual's inherent drive for self-realisation, she could never attain her true good nor could she gain permanent satisfaction of her abiding self.

Clearly, Green's social theory is not a form of atomistic individualism: the agent must live according to forms of life which are, or arise out of, 'inherited' social practices. She has limited powers to step beyond her inherited social forms, something that entails a denial of the ontological primacy of the individual.[10] That said, while one should be more cautious than scholars such as Michael Freeden regarding the alleged predominance of the individualistic elements of Green's thought, chapter two established that Green is not a social holist.[11] There is after all a significant sense in which, for him, the individual is the primary unit of analysis in his metaphysics of knowledge, his theory of the will and his conception of morality. Relatedly, it was shown that Green defends a similarly 'relational' social ontology.

---

6   PE 171.
7   DSF 1.
8   PPO 2–5.
9   Aristotle, *The Politics*, Book I, §ii (1252a24–1253a39).
10   Avital Simhony, 'Idealist Organicism: Beyond holism and individualism', *History of Political Thought*, 12:3 (1991), 515.
11   Freeden, *The New Liberalism*, pp. 58–60 *passim*; see also Rudolf Metz, *A Hundred Years of British Philosophy* (London: George Allen and Unwin, 1938), p. 283.

The next step in Green's social theory is his move to a notion of the common good. The latter is one of the most controversial and dangerously misunderstood aspects of his philosophical system. It has led many scholars to describe Green as confused, as reducing the individual to a mere adjunct of society, as blindly conservative, as valorising the state, and many other such things. All of these criticisms are rebutted in the remainder of this book. The present chapter begins an analysis of Green's conception of the common good, something that is continued in chapter four. §3.II examines the derivation and philosophical structure of Green's conception of the common good. §3.III focuses this analysis onto the relationship between common good, moral freedom and Green's eudaimonic kingdom of ends. The latter is achieved by exploring the intellectual provenance of Green's theory of the common good, concentrating particularly on his reactions to relevant aspects of the thought of Rousseau, Kant and Aristotle. §3.IV defends Green's claim that there is a significant sense in which the common good is non-competitive. §3.V asks whether Green requires the conscientious citizen to be completely selfless. §3.VI explores Green's defence of the common good on grounds of social justice. §3.VII draws out some of the most significant implications of Green's perspectivalism for his theory of the common good. §3.VIII summarises the argument of the present chapter, highlighting the further issues raised by Green's theory of the common good, issues that are pursued more fully in chapter four.

II

The Philosophical Derivation of the Common Good

Green claims that an individual can understand and commit herself to 'an idea of something absolutely desirable' or 'a supreme good' only to the extent that she believes that ideal to be one of the guiding normative principles of her society, or, as Green puts it, to be part of the guiding 'system of social requirements and expectations, of which each would seem to have reference to a definite social need'.[12] In other words, Green argues that a supreme good can exist for an individual only if she believes that (i) she can achieve it by interacting with other members of her society, (ii) via determinate social practices or refinements of those practices, and (iii) that gaining that good would be beneficial for every other member as well as herself.[13] It is with this thought in mind that Green defines 'true' or 'positive' freedom as

> 'a positive power or capacity of doing or enjoying something worth doing or enjoying, and that, too, something that we do or enjoy in common with others. We mean by it a power which each man exercises through the help or

---

[12] PE 199.

[13] PE 199.

security given by his fellow-men, and which he in turn helps to secure for them... [It is] in other words, the liberation of the powers of all men equally for contributions to a common good.'[14]

As Richard Bellamy has put it, Green conceives of the 'common good' as 'a set of common meanings about what are worthwhile goals of freedom and of how they should be shared'.[15]

Green himself acknowledges that, initially at least, his 'suggestion' that the individual's true freedom and supreme good must be found in actions directed at serving a common good might appear rather 'extravagant'.[16] In order to see that it is not as strange as it first seems, one should reflect more carefully on the meaning of Green's claim, and then on the justifications that he offers for it. These things will be done in this section, before Green's theory of the common good is analysed in light of his remarks regarding three of his most significant intellectual forebears: Jean-Jacques Rousseau, Immanuel Kant and Aristotle.

In the abstract, Green's conception of the common good has three facets. It is an ideal that the individual (i) seeks self-consciously in cooperation with her fellows,[17] (ii) believes it is right to pursue, and (iii) understands as being of equal intrinsic worth (but not necessarily pleasurable) for all members of her society.[18] Green argues that such a concept of 'a common good' is entailed by the concept of 'a community': 'Some sort of community, founded on such unity of self-consciousness, on such capacity for a common idea of permanent good, must be presupposed in any groupings of men from which the society that we know can have been developed.'[19] Straight away, it might appear that Green reduces personal freedom merely to serving socially-specified needs and goals. That he does not do so becomes clear when one considers the justifications Green offers for his claim that a true good not only is but must be a common good.[20] I.M. Greengarten identifies four.

---

14 LLFC 199, 200.

15 Richard Bellamy, 'T.H. Green, J.S. Mill, and Isaiah Berlin on the Nature of Liberty and Liberalism', in H. Gross and R. Harrison, eds., *Jurisprudence: Cambridge Essays* (Oxford: Clarendon Press, 1992), p. 284.

16 PE 199.

17 PE 199.

18 For example, PE 200–01; 'Kant' 123.

19 PE 202.

20 I.M. Greengarten, *Thomas Hill Green and the Development of Liberal-Democratic Thought* (Toronto: University of Toronto Press, 1981), pp. 37–39. Many of these claims are noticed by other scholars: W.J. Mander, *British Idealism: A history* (Oxford: Oxford University Press, 2011), pp. 204–08; Dimova-Cookson mixes them in her *T.H. Green's Moral and Political Philosophy: A phenomenological perspective* (Houndsmill: Palgrave, 2001), chapter three, while Brink presents a more systematic account in David O. Brink, *Perfectionism and the Common Good: Themes in the philosophy of T.H. Green* (Oxford: Clarendon Press, 2003), §§XIV–XXII *passim*.

Firstly, the individual's true good is shared with other individuals because they share a common human nature. Secondly, the individual can gain a permanent satisfaction for her highest nature only by meeting the needs of a collective trans-generational entity that will survive her.[21] Thirdly, an individual's animal nature leads her to feel a purely altruistic concern for the well-being of others. Fourthly, an individual can conceive of a true good only through her intellectual and practical recognition of the determinate true goods of other persons.

To what extent can each of these arguments justify Green's claim that an individual can realise her personal true good only by pursuing a common good? The first argument identified by Greengarten fails miserably.[22] The mere fact of sharing an abstract human nature tells one little. For example, if one were to hold the dominant element of our shared human nature to be a drive for dominance over others, then ultimately every person should attempt to prevent others from attaining their personal good, rather than attempting to realise a common good. ('Ultimately' because there may well be contingent reasons for the individual to help others to realise their own personal goods, even if, at some point, the individual's drive for dominance will lead them to renege on such schemes of enlightened self-interest.) The second line of argument which Greengarten identifies in Green is that the true good must be a common good because pursuing an inherently collective object is the only way in which an individual 'can sustain himself in that thought of his own permanence to which the thought of permanent well-being is correlative'.[23] Many nationalists have propagated versions of this claim, and it retains great emotional appeal for many people.[24] Indeed, it was a core belief for Giuseppe Mazzini, whom Green admired greatly. Yet, the idea that an individual can gain permanent self-satisfaction by projecting

---

Sidgwick and others struggle but ultimately fail to understand Green's justification of this crucial move. Henry Sidgwick, *Lectures on the Ethics of T.H. Green, Mr. Herbert Spencer, and J. Martineau*, ed. E.E. Constance Jones (London: MacMillan, 1907), pp. 56–59, 76–79; Kloppenberg, *Uncertain Victory*, pp. 128–32; Ann R. Cacoullos, *Thomas Hill Green: Philosopher of rights* (New York: Twayne, 1974), pp. 72–85 *passim*, 120–22, 133–44 *passim*. Against this view, see W.H. Fairbrother, *The Philosophy of Thomas Hill Green* (London: Methuen, 1896), pp. 171–79, 183–84; and — to a certain extent — Gerald F. Gaus, *Modern Liberal Theory of Man* (Beckenham: Croom Helm, 1983), pp. 61–63.

[21] See also John MacCunn, *Six Radical Thinkers: Bentham, J.S. Mill, Cobden, Carlyle, Mazzini, and T.H. Green* (London: Edward Arnold, 1907), pp. 234–35; Amal K. Mukhopadhyay, *The Ethics of Obedience: A study of the philosophy of T.H. Green* (Calcutta: World Private, 1967), pp. 60–61.

[22] PE 377. Compare with Mukhopadhyay, *Ethics of Obedience*, pp. 58–60.

[23] PE 232. See also PE 229–32, 246.

[24] See Paul Gilbert, *The Philosophy of Nationalism* (Boulder, CO: Westview, 1998), chapter nine.

into her own present self-image a belief in her group's existence beyond her own death is a fiction that will motivate an individual only to the extent that she is willing to delude herself that groups are homogeneous, trans-generational agents with their own corporate personalities. Consequently, the idea does not seem strong enough to give significant support to Green's claim that the individual's true good must be a common good, and indeed it is something that elsewhere Green denies explicitly and at length (§4.II).[25] To the extent that Green relies on these first two justifications then, at best his theory of the common good fails to convince, and at worst it contradicts core elements of the remainder of his philosophical system.

Green offers a third, slightly more convincing, justification for his claim that the individual's true good is a common good. He argues that the human being is the sort of animal that cares naturally for her fellows, and that this instinctive feeling is transformed into a concern for the common good when it is reconceived in relation to her nature as a social being: 'out of sympathies of animal origin, through their presence in a self-conscious soul, there arise interests as of a person in persons'.[26] There are problems with this justification too however, not least because usually Green denies the normative force of purely instinctive animal drives. Only when the individual uses her reason to sublimate her animal sympathies do the latter possess any true value. (This previously greatly underappreciated point was examined in depth in MSF, chapter 5.)

Fortunately, this third justification is merely a poorly-expressed version of a fourth, rather more successful, Greenian justification identified by Greengarten: an individual can gain an enriching sense of her own personality and worth only to the extent that she acknowledges the intrinsic spiritual worth of all other persons with whom she interacts, because only to the extent that she does so can she form a definite conception of possible objects or states of being the attainment of which realise her higher capacities.[27] This justification builds on Green's theory of the intersubjective formation of personalities and their goods which was analysed in §2.IV.[28] It owes much to

25 PE 183–87.
26 PE 201; see PE 200–01.
27 PE 200–01.
28 Also see W.G. de Burgh, *From Morality to Religion* (London: MacDonald and Evans, 1938), pp. 265–66; George H. Sabine, *History of Political Theory*, re. T.L. Thorson (Hindale: Dryden, 1973), pp. 659–60; Charles M. Sherover, ed., *The Development of the Democratic Idea: Readings from Pericles to the present* (New York: Mentor, 1974 [1968]), pp. 304–08 *passim*; Andrew Vincent and Raymond Plant, *Philosophy, Politics and Citizenship: The life and thought of the British idealists* (Oxford: Basil Blackwell, 1984), pp. 22–23, 26–27; Avital Simhony, 'T.H. Green: The common good society', *History of Political Thought*, 14:3 (1993), 225–47; Avital Simhony, 'T.H. Green's Complex Liberalism: Between liberalism and communitarianism', in Avital Simhony and David Weinstein, eds., *The New Liberalism:*

Rousseau's conception of the 'general will', an idea which Green regards as the most important and powerful idea in Rousseau's social and political thought. Indeed, Green links the general will explicitly to his own social ontology when he defines the general will as 'an impartial and disinterested will for the common good'[29] and as the 'impalpable congeries of the hopes and fears of a people bound together by common interests and sympathy'.[30]

Critics have alleged that the general will and the common good are hopelessly vague and even mystical concepts.[31] For example, John Horton has described Green's common good as deeply 'conceptually confused': 'Goods can be common in the sense that different people hold the same things to be valuable but they are not common in the sense that one person's good is the same as that of another.'[32] Horton surveys a number of different senses in which one might call goods 'common'. He starts with the example of health, which can be a 'common good' in the sense that most people wish to be healthy, yet this shared desire does not make it a logical truth that one individual can be healthy only if all other members of her community are so. Horton himself recognises this is not the sense in which Green holds the true

---

Reconciling liberty and communitarianism (Cambridge: Cambridge University Press, 2001), pp. 69–91.

29 PPO 69. For Green's related objections to Rousseau's use of the social contract idiom see PPO 116. For two differing views of the relationships between Rousseau, Green and the general will, see John H. Muirhead, 'Recent Criticism of the Idealist Theory of the General Will', *Mind,* 33 (1924): no. 130, 166–75, no. 131, 233–41, no. 132, 361–68; and D.H. Monro, 'Green, Rousseau, and the Culture Pattern', *Philosophy,* 26:99 (1951), 347–57. The former focuses upon the British idealists, including Green. 'Popular Philosophy', 113–17 *passim,* 122–24 *passim*; PPO 77; see Avital Simhony, 'On Forcing Individuals to be Free: T.H. Green's liberal theory of positive freedom', *Political Studies,* 49 (1991), 312–15 *passim.*

30 PPO 86.

31 The classic work here is Jacob Talmon, *The Origins of Totalitarian Democracy* (London: Secker and Warburg, 1952), but the claim has become ubiquitous among certain groups of scholars.

32 John Horton, *Political Obligation* (London: MacMillan, 1992), pp. 75, 76. This attack is made also by E.F. Carritt, *The Theory of Morals: An introduction to ethical philosophy* (London: Oxford University Press, 1928), pp. 61–64; John Plamenatz, *Consent, Freedom, and Political Obligation* (London: Oxford University Press, 1938), pp. 29–33, 68–73; H.A. Prichard, *Moral Obligation: Essays and lectures* (Oxford: Clarendon Press, 1949), pp. 69–74; and Melvin Richter, *The Politics of Conscience: T.H. Green and his age* (London: Weidenfeld and Nicolson, 1964), pp. 254–59 *passim* as well. Also, see Cacoullos, *Thomas Hill Green,* pp. 123–44 *passim.* For a reaction to Prichard specific formulation of this objection, see Peter P. Nicholson, *Political Philosophy of the British Idealists: Selected studies* (Cambridge: Cambridge University Press, 1990), pp. 64–67. Prichard's objection to Green's derivation of the common good is supported by Monson, 'Prichard, Green, and Moral Obligation', 81–86. On Plamenatz's attack, see Mukhopadhyay, *Ethics of Obedience,* pp. 93–99 *passim.*

good to be a common good. Next, there can be 'public goods' in the economic sense: their provision is either conceptually or, more usually, merely practically, non-excludable and non-rival. One person's consumption does not noticeably affect the potential consumption of another and the public good cannot be provided for one person without it being provided for another, *ceteris paribus*. Street-lighting and clean air are frequently cited as examples here. Again, Horton recognises that this is not the sense in which Green uses the term 'common good'. For Green, the common good, like the general will, is *necessarily* common. It is part of its very nature that it must be pursued by people as members of a group or, more specifically, as members of a community. For Green then, 'any apparent conflict between personal interest and the common good', as Horton notes, 'must be illusory—the claim becomes a metaphysical one'.[33] Yet, Horton sees this as a claim 'with some potentially sinister implications'. In short, Horton alleges that, as with Rousseau's general will, Green's common good runs the risk of justifying the community or state 'forcing' the individual 'to be free', under certain plausible circumstances.[34]

Such hostile interpretations have been bolstered by the related claim that Green's social theory presupposes, in the words of Isaiah Berlin, a 'metaphysical doctrine of the two selves—the individual streams versus the social river in which they should be merged, a dualistic fallacy used too often to support a variety of despotisms'.[35] Similarly, Michael St. John Packe has alleged that Green believes a 'man had no significance apart from the group or society of which he happened to be a part'.[36] From this, Packe concludes that, by the 1870s, the 'era of the beehive state was dawning, and the freedom of the individual was going out of fashion'.[37]

---

[33] Horton, *Political Obligation*, p. 76.

[34] Jean-Jacques Rousseau, *The Social Contract*, trans. M. Cranston (Harmondsworth: Penguin, 1968), Book 1, chapter 7 (p. 64).

[35] Isaiah Berlin, 'Introduction', in his *Four Essays on Liberty* (Oxford: Oxford University Press, 1969), p. xlix(*n*).

[36] Michael St John Packe, *The Life of John Stuart Mill* (London: Secker and Warburg, 1954), p. 403.

[37] Packe, *Mill*, p. 526n8. One finds other similar interpretations of Green: George H. Sabine, 'The Social Origin of Absolute Idealism', *Journal of Philosophy, Psychology and Scientific Methods*, 12:7 (1915), 174–77 (but not Sabine, *History of Political Theory*, p. 638); Y.L Chin, *The Political Theory of Thomas Hill Green* (New York: W. Dray, 1920), pp. 155–58; Harold J. Laski, 'Leaders of Collectivist Thought', in H. Grisewood, ed., *The Ideas and Beliefs of the Victorians: An historic reevaluation of the Victorian age* (London: Sylvan, 1949), pp. 417–22 *passim*; Adam B. Ulam, *The Philosophical Foundations of English Socialism* (Cambridge, MA: Harvard University Press, 1951), pp. 38–39, 69; Richter, *Politics of Conscience*, pp. 202–05, 224–25, 255–59; Harold R.G. Greaves, *The Foundations of Political Theory*, second edition (London: G. Bell, 1966 [1958]), p. 19; Germino, *Machiavelli to Marx*, pp. 266–67; J.

At times, Green does indeed seem to flirt with collectivism. For example, in a speech to the Oxford Auxiliary of the UK Alliance on 24 November 1874, he advocates fighting for stronger liquor legislation through the use of 'a great social resolution which would be called the tyranny of the majority'.[38] In fact, he invokes this sort of argument frequently in his speeches, especially when addressing issues of temperance and land reform, and not least when attacking the Conservative Party, something he did throughout his life.[39] Moreover, in the *Prolegomena* he portrays the ideal community as the embodiment of the 'idea of a society of free and law-abiding persons, each his own master yet each his brother's keeper'.[40] Even if Green is merely being polemical in these cases, they do give ammunition to those who wish to portray him as a dangerous collectivist.

Unsurprisingly, contemporary philosophers have continued to attack positions such as the one Horton, Berlin and Packe attribute to Green. Ronald Dworkin, for example, has condemned that 'baroque metaphysics which holds that communities are fundamental entities in the universe and that individual human beings are only abstractions and illusions'.[41] It is ironic in the present context then that Dworkin himself has defended a social ontology that invokes the concepts of the common good and the general will, even if Dworkin himself fails to acknowledge the coincidence of view. He gives the following example of what he calls his 'practice view of social integration'.

> 'An orchestra has a collective life not because it is ontologically more fundamental than its members, but in virtue of their practices and attitudes. The musicians recognize a personified unit of agency in which they no longer

---

Kemp, 'T.H. Green and Ethics of Self-realisation', in G.N.A. Vesey, ed., *Reason and Reality: Royal Institute of Philosophy Lectures, Volume Five, 1970–71* (London: MacMillan, 1972), pp. 236–37; W.H. Greenleaf, *The British Political Tradition, Volume Two: The ideological heritage* (London: Methuen, 1983), pp. 29, 124–42; Noël O'Sullivan, *The Problem of Political Obligation* (New York: Garland, 1987), pp. 182–83.

[38] T.H. Green's speech to the Oxford Auxiliary of the UK Alliance, 24 November 1874, as reported in the *Oxford Chronicle*, 28 November 1874 (GW 5:245).

[39] See, for example, Green's speeches to the Oxford Reform League, 25 March 1867, reported in the *Oxford Chronicle* on 30 March 1867 (GW 5:226–32); the Oxford Auxiliary of the UK Alliance, 7 February 1877, reported in the *Oxford Chronicle* on the 19 February 1877 (GW 5:291–92); public conference of the UK Alliance, reported in the *Oxford Chronicle* on 4 February 1882 (GW 5:386–93); Oxford Liberal Associations, 7 March 1882, reported in the *Oxford Chronicle* on 18 March 1882 (GW 5:393–401). See also PPO 118.

[40] PE 271.

[41] Ronald Dworkin, *Sovereign Virtue: The theory and practice of equality* (Cambridge, MA: Harvard University Press, 2000), p. 225. This link to Dworkin is noted also in Mander, *British Idealism*, p. 206n.

figure as individuals but as components; the community's collective life consists in the activities they treat as constituting its collective life... An integrated community has interests and concerns of its own — its own life to lead. Integration and community are genuine phenomena,... on the practice view. But on that view they are created by and embedded in attitudes and practices, and do not precede them.'[42]

Notice that Dworkin's practice view is far more demanding than a straight-forward theory of social embeddedness such as was set out in the previous chapter. Dworkin's musicians do not merely conceive and execute their plans of action using concepts and practices found within a conventional hermeneutic framework. More controversially than this, they direct all their efforts to serving the good of the orchestra as an irreducibly collective entity.

The 'common good' or 'practice view' of social integration is not necessarily oppressive. For example, it would seem excessive to see most orchestras as oppressively collectivist enterprises (certainly, Dworkin does not believe most of them to be so). (North Korean orchestras might be exceptions here.) One of the main reasons for questioning the good judgement (or indeed good faith) of someone who objected that they are, could be traced to the aims being served by the orchestra (the creation of complex music of certain types) and the presumption that the performers could leave the orchestra if they so wished. By accepting the rules of the orchestra, the players are able to engage in its unique practices, practices which they value, and, if they remain performers for a sufficient length of time, to develop talents and qualities that would otherwise have remained latent. The underlying thought is that, if the orchestra was not to be organised in accordance with Green's common good social theory (a.k.a. Dworkin's practice view of social integration), then it would not be possible for individuals to play certain types of music. (Similarly, audiences would be unable to have a certain type of aesthetic experience.) In more general terms, denying individuals opportunities to engage in certain practices denies them the chance to develop and exercise the associated skills and talents and to have certain sorts of experiences. After a certain point, such restrictions become so extensive that it becomes impossible for the individual to enrich her life in certain ways.

Green applies this argument to many aspects of his analysis of human life. He points out that serving the common good of a society of free and equal citizens facilitates the creation of certain goods or states of affairs that are central to what it is to be a fully-realised human being.[43] For example, for a free society to exist, it is not sufficient merely that any one individual feels that she can express her opinions and associate with others, without being

---

[42]　Dworkin, *Sovereign Virtue*, p. 226.
[43]　For example, PE 199–205 *passim* but the claim is ubiquitous.

punished for so doing. A free society exists only to the extent that every member of the community recognises that such freedoms of self-expression and association are assured for all, or at least that these freedoms are assured within wide boundaries that are determined by clear and known laws which are enforced by formally-authorised and commonly-endorsed bodies. In other words, a free society is created by the general will that members benefit from a wide, generally acknowledged and effective protection of speech and association, protection which precludes arbitrary interference with members' abilities to express themselves and associate with whomever they wish. The common good of living within a free society is founded upon a general will understood, in contemporary republican terms, as the will to live a collective life free from, and without fear of, 'arbitrary interference' in (or 'domination' over) members' speech and association.[44] To the extent that this common good receives continuing active endorsement and support by all its members, the free society exists. To the extent that this common good does not do so, a free society does not exist.

Green develops the civil and political ramifications of this view in ways that are far more radical than one finds in many contemporary republicans.[45] As a social egalitarian and democrat, Green argues that it is not sufficient for an enlightened minority to seek to impose the rules of a free society on the majority, nor for a passive or powerless majority to endorse the idea of a free society without seeking to instantiate the practices of that society through their daily interactions.[46] By taking part in, say, public meetings and voluntary associations, by voting, or by playing one's role as a member of a non-oppressive family, the individual helps to sustain a free society, to develop and exercise the requisite skills and talents, and to have the associated experiences. In short, Green insists that it is only when every individual enjoys both formally and in practice the rights of citizenship and seeks to fulfil her duties as a citizen of an internally-differentiated society that a free, enriching society exists.[47]

The preceding statement of Green's theory can be summarised more formally as follows. The general will is the will which the individual enacts when she seeks to promote or sustain the common good of her society. The fundamental principles of a free society form the basis of a valuable common

---

[44] Philip Pettit, *Republicanism: A theory of freedom and government* (Oxford: Oxford University Press, 1997), chapters 7 and 8.

[45] For a detailed analysis of the relationship between contemporary republicanism and Green's civil and political thought, see my 'Contesting the Common Good: T.H. Green and contemporary republicanism', in M. Dimova-Cookson and W.J. Mander, eds., *T.H. Green: Ethics, metaphysics and political philosophy* (Oxford: Clarendon Press, 2006), chapter 11.

[46] PPO 13, 19.

[47] PPO 141.

good, in that when individuals interact iteratively with each other within social frameworks founded upon principles of the type outlined above, they instantiate a way of life that is intrinsically valuable and otherwise unattainable. On a much smaller scale, Green's social theory helps us to understand a vibrant orchestra or even a successful university seminar. More significantly here, the analysis can be extended to ways of life beyond the core institutions of a free society such as a Greenian eudaimonic kingdom of ends, an ideal which includes but it is more complex than a free society.

III

Common Goods, Moral Freedom and Green's Eudaimonic 'Kingdom of Ends'

It is possible to deepen this analysis by considering Green's intellectual debts in greater depth. For Aristotle, Rousseau, Kant, Green and effectively Dworkin, a well-functioning society must be based upon a 'common *ego,...* life and... will.'[48] This common good is given substance as a determinate culture, conceived as a shared, vibrant and relatively harmonious network of fairly determinate meanings and values. These meanings and values condition the identities of the members of the relevant society. To the extent that individuals identify with and endorse such cultures (such fundamental meanings and values), they enact a general will by serving a common good. This is significant because by honouring the general will of a free well-ordered society, Rousseau argues, the individual sustains the civil conditions which facilitate her life of 'moral freedom', 'which alone makes man the master of himself; for to be governed by appetite alone is slavery, while obedience to a law one prescribes to oneself is freedom'.[49] Similarly, Green observes in his 'Lecture on Liberal Legislation and Freedom of Contract', that the 'noblest savage' must submit herself to social restraint as 'the first step towards the full exercise of the faculties with which man is endowed'.[50] The participants' respective endorsement of shared social principles grounds the authority of their collective enterprise, then. The rules governing the participant's behaviour are grounded in reasons that carry intrinsic weight for her. This is another way of stating that in seeking to further a common good of a group with which she freely identifies herself, the agent is acting in a manner that reflects her own ultimate meanings and values. In this sense, she is truly or positively free.

Famously, Rousseau's conception of moral freedom was reworked as one of Kant's most powerful ethical concepts: the categorical imperative. For Kant, the core of the individual is found in her capacity for rational agency

---

48   Rousseau, *Social Contract*, p. 61.
49   Rousseau, *Social Contract*, p. 65.
50   LLFC 199.

and self-direction. A rational agent is master of herself and she is free to the extent that she obeys the primary maxim of pure practical reason: '*So act that you use humanity, whether in your own person or in the person of any other, always at the same time as an end, never merely as a means.*'[51] Green embraces fully this Kantian development of Rousseau's principle of moral freedom. He agrees with Kant that this formulation of the categorical imperative forms the justificatory basis of all valid moral principles: the agent acts well to the extent that her actions are motivated by respect for a universal moral law that accords respect to the capacity for rational agency.[52] Both philosophers hold the good will to be the highest expression of moral freedom: as Kant puts it, 'Only a rational being has the capacity to act *in accordance with the representation* of laws, that is, in accordance with principles, and has a *will*. Since *reason* is required for the derivation of actions from laws, the will is nothing other than practical reason'.[53]

This requirement grounds Kant's further contention that a society approaches perfection to the extent that it is structured as a 'kingdom of ends'. He refers to the latter in the following terms: gradually, he writes, 'there arises a systematic union of rational beings through common objective laws, that is, a kingdom, which can be called a kingdom of ends (admittedly only an ideal) because what these laws have as their purpose is just the relation of these beings to one another as ends and means'.[54] This purely abstract structure embodies formal respect for the moral equality of all rational beings, and generates more substantive claims which, when honoured, make that formal respect a lived practical reality. This maxim is the Kantian reformulation of Rousseau's idea of 'general will', in that it entails that a society constitutes a kingdom of ends to the extent that its members act out of a shared respect for the rationality of free agents.[55] Only by acting in accordance with such a principle can a rational agent manifest a proper practical acknowledgement of the 'dignity of a rational being', and only in this way can she express her highest nature as an autonomous agent. Indeed, when Kant details the system which he believes to be the political embodiment of

---

[51] Immanuel Kant, 'Groundwork of The Metaphysics of Morals' (1785), in his *Practical Philosophy*, trans. and ed. Mary J. Gregor (Cambridge: Cambridge University Press, 1996), p. 80 (Prussian Academy Edition 4:429); see PE 214. Frederick C. Beiser credits Rousseau with leading Kant to 'drastically redefine the role of reason and his conception of metaphysics' in the mid-1760s. Frederick C. Beiser, 'Kant's Intellectual Development: 1746–1781', in Paul Guyer, ed. *The Cambridge Companion to Kant* (Cambridge: Cambridge University Press, 1992), p. 43; see *ibid.*, pp. 43–45.

[52] PE 196.

[53] Kant, 'Groundwork', 65–66 (4:412).

[54] Kant, 'Groundwork', 83 (4:433). See 'Kant' 124.

[55] Kant, 'Groundwork', 83–86 (4:434–36).

the kingdom of ends, he refers explicitly to 'right' as the 'expression of the general will', in a manner that brings to mind Green's subsequent character-isation of Rousseau's conception of the general will as 'an impartial and disinterested will for the common good'.[56]

The fundamental point to appreciate in this section is as follows. Green endorses the central claim of the ethics of both Rousseau and Kant: namely, that a claim has authority over an individual only to the extent that it pre-supposes values that are freely endorsed by the individual against whom that claim is being made. This is because only to the extent that the individual freely endorses the claim is she morally free: only then is she subject to a law that she has set for herself. This endorsement can be both explicit and implicit. For Rousseau as a romantic, implicit free endorsement at the level of personal virtue is entailed by the demands of her 'authentic' nature; and for Kant it is entailed by the demands of the individual's rationality alone. In relation to the free society Kant and, in some moods, Rousseau conceptualise free endorsement of collective norms through the device of the social contract. Green insists on both the Kantian claim that the individual endorses those values that are entailed by her rationality, and the Rousseauian claim that the individual endorses the commitments entailed by her distinctively human nature (conceived in Green's own romantic or neo-Aristotelian terms). In this way, Green enriches Kant's rather procedural kingdom of ends by emphasising the individual's innate drive to realise not merely her nature as a rational agent, but also her nature as a being with other higher capacities, such as those of acting courageously, wisely and moderately in ways that are both complex and historically-informed. Moderating the primitivist thrust of Rousseauianism, Green holds that these capacities for virtuous action have been manifested in a plethora of mag-nificent achievements in the humanities, arts and sciences, of selfless acts and collective institutions. These achievements constitute the 'realisation of the soul's faculties in certain pursuits and achievements, and in a certain organisation of life'; they are the 'evidence of its true vocation which the human spirit has so far yielded in arts and sciences, in moral and political achievement', which point towards 'a better social order than any that now is'.[57] They are the products of individuals guided by the desire to serve the common good and enriching it as they do so (something that becomes clearer below in chapter four).

It has been established in this section and the one preceding it that Green makes the common good the focal point both of his social theory and of his

---

[56] Immanuel Kant, 'On the common saying: That may be correct in theory, but it is of no use in practice', in his *Practical Philosophy*, pp. 292–93 (Prussian Academy Edition 8:292). PPO 69.

[57] PE 254, 354; see also PE 352–53.

reinterpretation of a powerful intellectual tradition whose key figures include Aristotle, Rousseau and Kant.[58] He argues that an enriching common good encapsulates shared meanings and values which allow individuals to live together as a vibrant and yet stable community. In the enriching community of the type valued by Green, the common good is constituted by meanings and values of an historically-located free society. The institutions of such a society help to remove the most severe external impediments to individual self-realisation in a particularised cultural environment, without crushing the opportunities for the individual to lead a self-directed life. An enriching common good thereby constitutes the heart of a concrete community in which each citizen can form and act on her own judgements regarding her own true good, and yet can do so without destroying the social conditions required for that self-directed life to continue to be possible.

Moreover, this section has indicated how Green's conception of the endorsement of the common good does not carry the oppressive implications that many critics have found in it.[59] Green does not value all common goods equally, because he does not value all types of society equally. As has been shown, Green relates his 'common good' to Kant's development of Rousseau's 'moral freedom' and the 'general will' as the fundamental principles of the 'categorical imperative' and the 'kingdom of ends'. More than this, Green himself develops the Kantian position via his addition of a form of Aristotelian eudaimonism. In this way, Green's common good is not the basis of a free-standing social theory in which all common goods are equally valuable, as some critics seem to believe. Rather, it is just one element of his philosophical system, and can be properly understood only when it is read in light of the theory of human flourishing that has been set out since the beginning of MSF. Green values citizenship which serves the common good of one's society only to the extent that the society is one which facilitates the development of all its members' determinate true goods. As will become

---

[58] Hegel did much the same of course, but it is notable that Green does not refer to Hegel when analysing and developing his own formulation of this argument. Possibly, this is an example of Green following his own advice to 'sit rather looser to the "dialectical" method than Dr. [John] Caird has done' in his *Introduction to the Philosophy of Religion*, and to 'recast' Hegelian philosophy 'in a freer form, working to the same end from a beginning more likely to commend itself to the exoteric world, and by a method less liable to misapprehension' (IPR 146). Regarding Green's great many non-Hegelian influences, see MSF §2.III.

[59] Many critics seem to have revelled in the morbid gratification of bolstering their own 'scholarly' standing by having confirmed the prejudices of their post-Victorian peer-group. This enjoyment is evident particularly in the indulgent rhetorical flourishes of critics such as Michael St John Packe, Harold Prichard and Richard Crossman.

clear in chapter four, to the extent that social norms and institutions fail to facilitate individual self-realisation, every citizen has an at least *prima facie* duty to seek to reform them, something that will require them to resist established norms, possibly using violence. Green does not subordinate the individual to the collective then, in the sense that he does not deny the intrinsic worth of the individual, her interests and her conscientious judgement.

Green's conceptualisation of an enriching common good enables him to establish a number of other claims. For instance, it allows him to show that upholding this common good helps to maintain an orderly and fair reconciliation of rights and other claims within the body politic. It does this to the extent that members endorse it as a set of authoritative standards by which to plan and judge their own actions and those of their fellows. With reference to this shared scheme of meanings and values, a just reconciliation can be achieved among what would be otherwise a chaos of conventional or purely individualist institutions and rights. The former conventional meanings, values and institutions tend to be chaotic because they have arisen out of the contingency of historical events. The chaos of the latter reflects the arbitrary private interests and power that individuals tend to valorise when considering themselves, wrongly, to be atomistic agents. In this way, the common good is the structural principle of Green's eudaimonically-sensitive kingdom of ends.[60] Yet, this apparent move towards uniformity runs counter to another fundamental tendency within Green's social theory. Before considering these issues in §3.VII, it is important to consider certain remaining philosophical issues in §3.IV–V, before §3.VI considers the vital question of the demands of social justice that are generated by the inequalities of real societies.

IV

The Non-competitiveness of the Common Good

It is necessary now to consider an important objection to Green's claim that the true good is an inherently common good. A.J.M. Milne argues that Green fails to grasp the fatal implications of finitude for any ethics of self-realisation: 'Resources are limited and the opportunities for the development of gifts and capacities are finite. Not everyone who has the ability can become a

---

60 PE 326. In such cases, Green's invocation of the common good recalls Mazzini: 'where there is not a common Principle, recognised, accepted, and developed by all, there is no true Nation, no People; but only a multitude, a fortuitous agglomeration of men whom circumstances have called together, and whom circumstances may again divide.' Giuseppe Mazzini, 'The Duties of Man', in his *Life and Writings,* ed. Emilie Ashurst, 6 vols., second edition (London: Smith, Elder, 1891), vol. 4, p. 278.

first violinist in a symphony orchestra or a university teacher'.[61] This objection may rest upon a purely empirical point: as a matter of fact there are insufficient material resources for everyone to become fully self-realised, making competition for these resources inevitable. If this is the objection, then Green's theory remains intact. His point is, firstly, that in such circumstances, no one could ever be completely self-realised, although some people may be closer to being so than others. Secondly, once a minimum level of property has been secured for everyone, the existence of inequalities does not inhibit self-realisation to the extent Milne alleges. In essence, even though a certain level of material well-being and security is necessary if the individual is to have a real opportunity to realise her true good, the true good itself remains a spiritual condition rather than a material one.[62] (See chapters nine and ten below.)

Milne's claim might be slightly different. He could be arguing that some social forms are inherently competitive, and so anyone who chooses to develop herself by engaging in them must compete with other people. First violinist might be an inherently competitive social role, as is 'being the richest person in the world' or 'being the most powerful individual'. All of these roles are intelligible only on the assumption that other people exist who are, for example, the second violin or poorer or less powerful. Yet, the present

---

[61] A.J.M. Milne, 'The Common Good and Rights in T.H. Green's Ethical and Political Thought', in Andrew Vincent, ed., *The Philosophy of T.H. Green* (Aldershot: Gower, 1986), p. 69; see also *ibid.*, pp. 69–70. See also A.J.M. Milne, 'The Idealist Criticism of Utilitarian Social Philosophy', *Archives Européenes de Sociologie*, 8 (1967), 328–29; Sidgwick, *Lectures on the Ethics*, pp. 67–69, 106; Henry Sidgwick, *Outlines of the History of Ethics for English Readers*, fifth edition (London: MacMillan, 1902), p. 260; Hastings Rashdall, *The Theory of Good and Evil*, 2 vols. (London: Oxford University Press, 1924), vol. 2, pp. 98–101; Carritt, *Theory of Morals*, pp. 61–62; H.D. Lewis, 'The Individualism of T.H. Green', in his *Freedom and History* (London: George Allen and Unwin, 1962), pp. 90–104, especially pp. 98–104 *passim*; H.D. Lewis, 'T.H. Green and Rousseau', in his *Freedom*, pp. 129–30; Kemp, 'T.H. Green and The Ethics of Self-realisation', 238–39; Cacoullos, *Thomas Hill Green*, pp. 120–22, 133–44 *passim*; Craig A. Smith, 'Individual and Society in T.H. Green's Theory of Virtue', *History of Political Thought*, 2:1 (1981), 200–01; Richard Bellamy, 'T.H. Green and the Morality of Victorian Liberalism', in Richard Bellamy, ed., *Victorian Liberalism: Nineteenth century political thought and practice* (London: Routledge, 1990), pp. 141–42; Thomas Hurka, *Perfectionism* (Oxford: Oxford University Press, 1993), p. 67; but see Fairbrother, *Philosophy of Thomas Hill Green*, pp. 178, 184–86; G.F. Barbour 'Green and Sidgwick on the Community of the Good', *Philosophical Review*, 17 (1908), 149–66; Gaus, *Modern Liberal Theory*, pp. 68–74 *passim*.

[62] Vincent *et al.*, *Philosophy, Politics and Citizenship*, pp. 24–26; Peter P. Nicholson, 'A Moral View of Politics: T.H. Green and the British idealists', *Political Studies*, 31 (1987), 120–22, Nicholson, *Political Philosophy*, pp. 195–96. Bellamy denies this claim (Bellamy, 'T.H. Green and the Morality of Victorian Liberalism', 141).

existence of inherently hierarchical social roles such as these does little to undermine Green's position as a critical theory. On Green's logic, to the extent that such roles are intrinsically positional goods, they must be imperfect modes of instantiating human nature, meaning that they cannot form parts of a perfect kingdom of ends. Even here one must be careful however. In what sense is 'first violin' an inherently competitive social role? Certainly, it is definitionally the case that only one person can be the first violinist in any one orchestra at any one time, and consequently some people who aspire to the position will fail to have their hopes realised, at least for the time being. Yet, this does not mean that the holder of that role should be accorded greater status than any other member of the orchestra, any more than a professor need be lionised in an academic context. That such roles tend to be accorded higher status than many others is a contingent cultural fact. Different functions need not imply different personal worth of the individuals fulfilling those roles. Even differences of authority, such as the power to issue orders to others, need not imply higher social standing. Similarly although the first violinist will have different modes of self-realisation available to her, this is logically compatible with different but equivalent opportunities being open to everyone else. Equal status and equivalent opportunities for self-realisation would seem to be core features of a Greenian kingdom of ends, which consequently could contain first violinists and professors (although such people would have to be rather more modest than many of the current occupants of these roles!).

Milne's objection from scarcity would invalidate Green's claim that the true good is a common good only if it could be established that some aspect of the true good was inherently competitive and that this inherent competitiveness was a necessary facet of this aspect of the true good.[63] It is not enough to establish that, given the empirical conditions of the world as it is or even as it ever could be, the particular and necessary aspects of the true good could never be expressed in any mode of living which was to any degree inherently uncompetitive. This fact would only establish something upon which Green himself insists frequently: that our world and we ourselves are doomed to imperfection for all time. We are attempting to manifest human nature under the constraints of a physical world and an animal form. Yet, Milne does not even come close to attempting to establish that the very idea of the true good is necessarily competitive. In philosophical terms, even extreme inequality and scarcity are irrelevant to the logical coherence of Green's conception of the common good. Nevertheless, things are very different at the level of practice, as becomes clear in §3.VI.

---

63   Milne, 'Common Good and Rights', 70–75. See Mukhopadhyay, *Ethics of Obedience*, p. 57.

V
How Selfless Does Green Want Us to Be?

Another serious objection arises at this point. Even though they might agree that Green respects the individual and her judgement on the nature of the common good, some generally-sympathetic scholars have found other reasons to worry about this core aspect of his system. One of the most significant criticisms of this type is that Green accords intrinsic worth to only a limited range of the individual's interests, namely those that arise from her conception of herself as a citizen, daughter, wife or mother, as a member of the local council or school board. In short, some critics have argued that ultimately Green values only those of the individual's interests which arise from the common goods of the groups to which they belong. Such criticisms are addressed in this section.

Maria Dimova-Cookson bases much of her analysis of Green's theory of the common good on a distinction she draws between the individual's 'ordinary goods' and her 'moral good'. An ordinary good is an object which the individual values irrespective of her relationships with other people, such as her love of Weimar films or the music of David Bowie. The moral good, on the other hand, is 'intended by its agent as a good common between him and others'; in other words, it is the good which the individual values because she conceives its attainment to be beneficial for both herself and for others.[64] Dimova-Cookson claims that 'Green's theory of the common good is a further explanation of his views on the moral ideal', citing as examples Green's references to 'the work of keeping a family comfortably alive', 'the composition of a book on an abstruse subject' and the 'sanitation of a town'.[65] Elsewhere, Green refers to the 'better management of an estate, or the better drainage of the town where he lives, or the better education of his family, or the better administration of justice'.[66] He also refers to the individual's 'advancement of some branch of knowledge, or the improvement of public health, or the endeavour after "personal holiness"', all of which represent some form of the 'bettering of the life which is at once his and the society's'.[67] Dimova-Cookson uses her distinction between ordinary goods and moral goods 'to articulate two different conceptions of the common good' with which she argues Green operates.

In the first case, the common good is realised to the extent that every citizen helps all others to obtain their respective ordinary goods.[68] Dimova-

---

[64] Dimova-Cookson, *T.H. Green's Moral and Political Philosophy*, p. 97.
[65] PE 239, 235, quoted in Dimova-Cookson, *T.H. Green's Moral and Political Philosophy*, p. 95.
[66] PE 135.
[67] PE 239.
[68] Dimova-Cookson, *T.H. Green's Moral and Political Philosophy*, pp. 99–100.

Cookson highlights the most paradoxical implication of this conception: the individual can serve the common good only to the extent that she has transformed her highest good into a state of being in which she helps others to realise their ordinary goods, a transformation that is possible only when the individual suppresses her own efforts to secure her own ordinary goods. Dimova-Cookson objects that this conception of the common good fails Kant's universalisability test, thereby violating one of Green's most fundamental ethical principles: 'The elimination of the self-centred framework', in which agents seek to gain their ordinary goods as fully as they can, 'would simultaneously imply a destruction of the possibility of doing good to others', because it would require the 'elimination' of everyone's ordinary goods.[69] The second conception of the common good highlighted by Dimova-Cookson is realised to the extent that the agent seeks the good of the community as a whole, conceived as a kingdom of ends. Dimova-Cookson conceives of this kingdom as a set of social arrangements designed to respect each individual member 'as an end' in herself. She interprets this to mean that 'each person is [to be] valued simply on account of his human nature. This implies that everyone deserves social welfare and justice regardless of whether they act as moral agents or not'.[70] Even though it is presented in an analytic frame, Dimova-Cookson's objections have been presented elsewhere in more historical terms. Many scholars have argued that the Evangelical strand of Victorian thought undervalues the pursuit of what are, on at least one level, purely private goals.[71]

Avital Simhony has attempted to answer the philosophical objection by arguing that when invoking a distinction between 'one's concern for one's personal development and moral concern for the well-being of others' in this way, scholars 'entirely exclud[e]' the 'possibility of non-contingent connection between... personal and moral concerns'.[72] She surveys alternative approaches proposed by Joseph Raz and Lawrence Blum, both of which reject this 'dichotomous or confrontational view of morality', thereby exposing the error of believing that furthering 'one's own development and serving others are... mutually exclusive'.[73] In response to Simhony's attempted defence of Green, it is important to emphasise that Dimova-Cookson and others do not deny the possibility that some agents will sometimes realise their

---

69　Dimova-Cookson, *T.H. Green's Moral and Political Philosophy*, p. 99.

70　Dimova-Cookson, *T.H. Green's Moral and Political Philosophy*, p. 102.

71　Richter, *Politics of Conscience*, pp. 129–35; T.C. Hammond, *Perfect Freedom: An introduction to Christian ethics* (London: Inter-Varsity Fellowship, n.d.), pp. 207–08; H.D. Lewis, 'Does the Good Will Define its Own Content? — a study of T.H. Green's *Prolegomena to Ethics*', in his *Freedom*, pp. 41–47.

72　Avital Simhony, Review of Colin Tyler, *Thomas Hill Green...*, *Bradley Studies*, 5:1 (Spring 1999), 100.

73　Simhony, Review of Tyler, *Green*, p. 102; see *ibid.*, pp. 101–04.

own true good through social service. The problem that Simhony fails to resolve is that, for much of the time, Green seems to assume that individuals can find meaning and worth in their lives *only* by serving the common good, something that seems to entail that the individual's true good can be gained only vicariously. Here, Dimova-Cookson's worries reassert themselves.

One must be careful here not to assume that Green is claiming all efforts to further one's own interests through social service count as efforts to serve the common good. Simhony gestures towards many of the ways in which individuals can realise themselves through social service. In some of the examples she gives, individuals increase their own private options for intrinsically-valuable actions by maintaining a set of enriching social forms, while in other of her examples individuals genuinely find self-satisfaction directly in helping those less fortunate than themselves. Simhony seems to neglect the fact that only in performing the second type of activity does the individual attempt to serve the common good in a Greenian sense. Ultimately, the first type of activity is motivated solely by the individual's desire to further her own private interests, something that, only incidentally, requires her to take part in a collective enterprise. In the first case, the agent is motivated by her own interests alone, whereas she is motivated by the intrinsic worth of her fellows in the second. Despite what Simhony implies, acting out of enlightened self-interest is not the same as acting for the common good. It still seems that Green disregards those of the individual's interests which do not relate to serving a common good as such.

Nevertheless, some of the examples that Green gives of service to the common good appear to aim at the agent's purely personal development. He refers to the development of the individual's 'faculties which find expression not in his dealings with other men, but in the arts and sciences'.[74] These examples support a more sympathetic reading, one which emphasises the central role played in Green's theory by eudaimonia understood as 'the full exercise or realisation of the soul's faculties in accordance with its proper excellence, which was an excellence of thought, speculative and practical'.[75] Yet, these examples are atypical, and it is undeniable that usually Green is reticent about attributing intrinsic worth to the individual's pursuit of what Dimova-Cookson calls 'ordinary goods'. For example, for the most part he portrays the efforts of the self-absorbed artist or scientist as having true worth only to the extent that the results of their work help other people.[76] He argues that it is only as the artist or scientist conceives of her

---

[74] PE 370; see also Nicholson, *Political Philosophy*, p. 81; Gerald F. Gaus, 'T.H. Green, Bernard Bosanquet and the Philosophy of Coherence', in C.L. Ten, ed., *Routledge History of Philosophy, Volume VII, The Nineteenth Century* (London: Routledge, 1994), p. 417.

[75] PE 254.

[76] For example, PE 135, 148, 289–90, 370–71, 380–81.

personal development as having some wider social benefit that she can gain the highest degree of true and permanent self-satisfaction. Green considers the duty of the musician in times of social and political instability, concluding that the question which must be asked when assessing the correct course of action is 'Has [the musician] talent to serve mankind – to contribute to the perfection of the human soul – more as a musician than in any other way? Only if he has, will he be justified in making music his main pursuit'.[77]

So, does this mean that Green fails to accord proper weight to the individual's pursuit of her own ordinary goods? If he did, then Richard Bellamy would be correct to portray Green's ethics of the common good as entailing the identification of 'self-realisation with self-determination, and both with self-abnegation'.[78] In that situation, only the individual's capacities for helping others would play any determining role in Green's normative theory. Other idealists noticed this possible implication as well.[79] Indeed, if this were to be Green's position, he would not be sufficiently true to his own romantic and Kantian roots (see §2.III).[80]

A possible response emerges from the fact that, as many of Green's followers have emphasised, it is only when everyone is fully developed and all members of society are treated as moral equals and understand each other as such, that anyone can attain her true good to its fullest degree and complexity.[81] Here, it seems that Green makes little of the distinction between self-regarding and other-regarding potentials partly because of his theory of intersubjectivity: developing one's own talents necessarily entails developing the talents of every person with whom one interacts. For this reason, all members of the kingdom of ends should work to realise the full range of their own respective capacities to their highest degree, as well as to facilitate the self-realisation of all their fellows. This is a necessary consequence of the intersubjective twist that Green gives to the categorical imperative to respect

---

[77] PE 381.

[78] Richard Bellamy, *Liberalism and Modern Society: An historical argument* (Oxford: Polity, 1992), p. 92; see 'Works of Fiction' 37–38; PE 302, 376–77, 380; also Richter, *Politics of Conscience*, pp. 255–59; J.D. Mabbott, *State and the Citizen: An introduction to political philosophy*, second edition (London: Hutchinson University Library, 1967 [1948]) p. 73n1; Germino, *Machiavelli to Marx*, pp. 266–67; O'Sullivan, *Problem of Political Obligation*, pp. 160–61; Simhony, 'T.H. Green: The common good society', 234–37.

[79] Bernard Bosanquet, 'Recent Criticisms of Green's Ethics', in his *Science and Philosophy, and other essays,* ed. J.H. Muirhead and R.C. Bosanquet (London: George Allen and Unwin, 1927), pp. 174–81.

[80] See further Barbour, 'Green and Sidgwick on the Community of the Good', *passim*; Mukhopadhyay, *Ethics of Obedience*, pp. 56–57; Gaus, *Modern Liberal Theory*, p. 105.

[81] Bosanquet, 'Recent Criticisms', 174–81; also see Nettleship, 'Memoir', cxlvii–cxlix.

'humanity, whether in your own person or in the person of any other'.[82] It forms the basis of his appeal to social justice that is explored in the next section.

VI

Social Justice and the Common Good

The practical realities of life have direct implications for questions of justice (something that will become still clearer in chapters nine and ten). In this regard, Green recognises something that is neglected by many of the critics of his theory of the common good. The extreme impartiality of the categorical imperative means that where an agent already enjoys opportunities to act rationally while others do not, it becomes her duty to do what she can to liberate others from oppressive social conditions. Consequently, the categorical imperative requires the individual to delay her own efforts at self-satisfaction to the extent that is required to raise everyone to the same level. As Green puts it:

> 'It is no time to enjoy the pleasures of eye and ear, of search for knowledge, of friendly intercourse, of applauded speech or writing, while the mass of men whom we call our brethren, and whom we declare to be meant with us for eternal destinies, are left without the chance, which only the help of others can gain for them, of making themselves in act what in possibility we believe them to be.'[83]

Ideally we would live in societies of self-realising, self-reliant and virtuous individuals.[84] Yet, Green is acutely conscious of how far all past and current societies have been from achieving this ideal.[85] Green sees it as self-indulgent, immoral and ultimately self-defeating to focus upon one's personal development when millions of people live in wretched conditions. Hence, his guiding concern is to remove the miserable conditions into which many agents, not least women, find themselves condemned by vagaries of birth, gender and fortune.[86]

> 'The calls for such sacrifice arise from that enfranchisement of all men, which, though in itself but negative in its nature ['because amounting merely to the denial to any one of a right to use others as his instruments or property'], carries with it for the responsive conscience a claim on the part of all men to such positive help from all men as is needed to make their freedom real.'[87]

A well-ordered society is one in which each member does the most she can for herself while still being able to rely on assistance from others when faced

---

[82] Kant, 'Groundwork', 80 (4:429); PE 192–98.
[83] PE 270; see also PE 273–76.
[84] PE 271.
[85] DSF 6.
[86] PE 267.
[87] PE 270.

with excessively adverse circumstances. Indeed, Green dedicates several pages of the *Prolegomena* to attacking the ancient Greeks for building the magnificent achievements of a tiny minority in, say, art and philosophy on the oppression of the vast majority of their population.[88] When looking at the slaves, the 'Greek saw a supply of possibly serviceable labour, having no end or function but to be made really serviceable to the privileged few'.[89] Green insists that no matter how extraordinary the works of Socrates, Plato, Aristotle, or any other of the ancient Greeks, one should always remember that their achievements came at a huge cost: the society that fostered them was built on the brutal oppression of a vast slave population.[90] Consequently, when assessing the worth of such triumphs, one should always ask whether the achievements of any particular society are worth the costs that had to be incurred to maintain the society that made them possible.[91] For Green, it is a definitional requirement of justice that, in A.C. Bradley's words, 'no one should seek the good, either of himself or of anyone else, by means which hinder the good of others'.[92] One should always look to the common good, rather than merely sectional privileges, whether those privileges are your own or those of past masters.

In this sense, Green defends the common good on grounds of social justice. In the most 'abstract' terms, he understands 'justice' to mean respecting the fact that 'there is something due from every man to every man, simply as his due'.[93] More specifically, he argues that the individual is just when she is 'not serving a friend or kinsman or countryman in a manner prejudicial to any one else'.[94] An individual with a developed 'sense of justice' is one 'who will be just before he is generous; who will not merely postpone his own interest to his friend's, but who, before he gratifies an "altruistic" inclination, will be careful to enquire how in doing so he would affect others who are not the object of his inclination'.[95] Green states the core of his theory of justice in the following terms, a few sentences later.

> 'The essential thing is that he applies no other standard in judging of the well-being of others than in judging of his own, and that he will not promote his own well-being or that of one whom he loves or likes, from whom he has received service or expects it, at the cost of impeding in any way the well-

---

[88] PE 270–75 *passim*, especially PE 274.

[89] PE 270.

[90] PE 275.

[91] PE 273.

[92] A.C. Bradley, 'Analytical table of Contents', in PE xxvi. Bradley renders Green's second requirement of justice as being that one should not 'measure the good of different persons by different standards'. See PE 270.

[93] PE 211.

[94] PE 213.

[95] PE 212.

being of one who is nothing to him but a man, or whom he involuntarily dislikes; that he will not do this knowingly, and that he is habitually on the look-out to know whether his actions will have this effect or not.'[96]

Where an individual has developed a 'constant and uniform' concern not to act badly, even if she does not actively 'do all that [s]he ought', she has achieved the 'habit of practical justice' which Green describes as 'at least the negative principle of all virtue'.[97] The individual's purely 'negative' respect for justice might not earn 'universal or very hearty admiration' for her, given that it does not motivate her to actively promote the positive demands of justice.[98] Nevertheless, it has moral value in itself and forms a necessary element of a more full-blooded concern for justice.

Green argues that the negative principle of justice underpins conventional morality and institutions, even if frequently individuals fail to honour it in practice.[99] Even when it is instantiated in conventional morality however, the principle is too general to provide the individual with definite practical guidance. Green argues that, for the just individual, the 'condition' of 'ideal conduct' is that it is *alike* for the real good of all men concerned in or affected by it', with that 'real good of all men' being 'estimated on the same principle', and so constituting 'a like claim in all men'.[100] Even though determinate claims of justice can be made only where one has a clear conception of the nature of the 'real' or true good understood as a 'theory of well-being', the specific content of one's conception of the true good cannot be distinguished from concerns regarding justice as such, with the abstract structure of the latter being derived solely from the 'idea of human equality'.[101] This principle must be combined with a more fully developed conception of the true good if it is to provide practical guidance to the individual who wishes to perform actions that are not merely 'negatively' just (they are not actively unjust), but also 'just' in the positive sense of actively promoting the demands of fairness. Justice requires that voluntary institutions and the state actively help individuals where circumstances prevent them from helping themselves. This highly significant aspect of Green's social and political theory is dealt with at great length below (chapters seven and ten).

Concerns might arise regarding the type of impartiality required by Green's theory of justice and the common good. He argues that the demands of justice should take priority over all concerns of partiality: no one should

---

[96] PE 212.
[97] PE 212.
[98] PE 213.
[99] PE 213.
[100] PE 212, 211.
[101] PE 212.

favour anyone else due to their connections of friendship, 'family, status, or nation'.[102] Contemporary theorists have attacked such an apparently simplistic impartialist view, pointing to the many plausible examples where it would seem wrong not to favour those to whom one is especially close.[103] These cases can be either serious or trivial. For example, I take time off work to care for my own mother before I do the same for yours, or I give the last few treats to my own cat rather than to my neighbour's. These are instances where strictly impartial treatment would seem misplaced. In recognition of this fact, Green himself analyses at length the special rights and duties which exist, for example, within families or between property-owners.[104] The details of these arrangements are examined in §7.V and chapter ten. For the moment, only Green's general principles are relevant.[105] He argues that the individual 'as husband or head of a family' takes on certain rights and duties (as well as legal rights and obligations) from the fact that the family is a community with its own common good. (The same holds for all members of the family.) These rights, duties and obligations do not exist *sui generis* however. Instead, even though non-legal norms are subject to some amendment by the parties themselves, for the most part they are determined by the established social and legal norms that govern the institution of marriage in one's society. These established norms are legitimate to the extent that they are required in order to maintain a stable 'reconciliation of rights arising out of one sort of social capability with those arising out of another'.[106] Green does not appeal to a distinction between first and second-order impartiality (between impartiality in the private and public spheres respectively), as many contemporary impartialists do, because he understands that the distinction is itself socially-constructed, as are the expectations of appropriate behaviour and partiality within the respective spheres. Counterfactually, unlike many contemporary philosophers, Green does not appeal to some mythical essentially idiosyncratic 'private' sphere, populated by individuals who determine the founding norms of that part of their lives without being influenced by wider social norms.

These socially-conditioned principles of impartiality vary with the spheres (private, public, civic, economic, political and so on). They are important for Green because they form part of a freely-endorsed system of

---

[102] PE 212.

[103] Brian Barry, *Justice as Impartiality* (Oxford: Clarendon Press, 1995); Susan Mendus, *Impartiality in Moral and Political Philosophy* (Oxford: Oxford University Press, 2002); Judith Squires, 'Culture, Equality and Diversity', in Paul Kelly, ed., *Multiculturalism Reconsidered: Culture and Equality and its critics* (Cambridge: Polity, 2002), pp. 118, 121–23.

[104] PPO 211–46.

[105] PPO 141.

[106] PPO 141.

social principles which sustains a non-arbitrary and non-abusive social environment. This environment in turn facilitates individuals in their collective efforts to engage in mutually enriching and respectful forms of life. Not all principles of impartiality will serve this end equally well. For example, Green acknowledges that utilitarianism respects impartiality to some degree. Yet, he observes that it is all too easy to imagine realistic scenarios in which the concern to maximise the greatest happiness will allow 'a superior race or order' to 'plead strong justification, not indeed for causing useless pain to the inferior, but for systematically postponing the inferior's claims to happiness to its own ... or what we commonly call the oppression of the weaker by the stronger'.[107] The Kantian categorical imperative to respect rationality as an end avoids the utilitarian's problem, by asserting unequivocally the ultimate worth and equality of all persons. Yet, the categorical imperative is itself a purely formal principle. It can guide practice only to the extent that it informs the individual's reflections on the substantive demands of conventional morality.[108] Only in this way can the individual arrive at sound judgements regarding the duties arising from the particular relationships that constitute her citizenship.

VII

Personal Perspective and the Common Good

It was established in MSF §8.II that Green believes conventional morality and social forms are being disrupted continually by the emanation of aspects of human nature which up to that time have been articulated in the world only very imperfectly. Every agent both attempts to draw out the implications of her own existing beliefs and commitments, and, perhaps unconsciously, posits previously-unarticulated demands of human nature. In both ways, continually individuals tend to destabilise and enrich even the fairest societies.[109] That these tendencies emanate from individuals in unpredictable ways and without conscious design has hugely significant implications for Green's theory of the common good. To understand precisely why the implications are so significant, it is first necessary to recall a key feature of Green's philosophical system, something that formed a core subject of MSF: namely, the methodological primacy Green accords to the reciprocal processes of critical and speculative metaphysics (see also §1.II above).

A central part of Green's metaphysics is his claim that the self-realising individual uses crystallisation iteratively in her attempts to construct and reconstruct a harmonious personality of distinct elements which she can endorse freely as manifesting her own idea of her highest nature. Green con-

---

[107] PE 214.

[108] PE 215.

[109] 'Aristotle' 58; PE 301, 317–19.

ceives this constructive project as being founded upon the individual's faith that, in principle, one could find a harmony between all true meanings and values. Hence he argues that 'we only find unity in the world because we have an idea that it is there, an idea which we direct our powers to realise'.[110] He emphasises time and again, especially in the *Prolegomena*, that as the motor of personal self-realisation, this constructive process is orientated with reference to the individual's own always partially inchoate conception of an ideal fully-realised personality. This personal ideal guides the individual's efforts at self-development and social improvement.

Using such a position, Green is able to conceptualise the fundamental processes by which the individual seeks to create a truly satisfying and indeed truly free life. Crucially, he can conceptualise the idea of the individual positing an ideal of herself as a state of being to be constructed through her own actions within a social environment that facilitates such efforts. One consequence of the fluidity of this iterative process and the multifaceted personality that it tends to generate is that, to varying degrees, specific individuals will tend to conceive the linguistic and other social structures in which they are raised and live, in ways that are different to everyone else in that society. Unfortunately for Green's social theory, these differences seem to make the notion of a common good highly problematic. If everyone experiences her world differently, how can any two individuals possess anything in common? If everyone's world is a slightly different concrete expression of a shared abstract human nature, how can one endorse the same determinate common good?

To discover the answers to these questions, it will be helpful to consider an unsuccessful route for conceptualising Green's theory of the common good. Some commentators (myself included, in the first edition of this work) have drawn a distinction between 'a common good' and the 'Common Good'.[111] On this view, the 'Common Good' (capitalised) refers to that hypothetical principle of social organisation which would be shared by individuals within a perfect community (sc. one that enables its members to express the human spirit perfectly). The implication is that there is only one such ultimate ideal (the Common Good) as there is only one fully determinate human spirit. In practice, there can be, and indeed are, many 'common goods' (without capitalisation). These are particular structures of belief and values which are common to the individual subsets of humanity which

---

110 PE 149.

111 Nicholson, *Political Philosophy*, Study II; Colin Tyler, *Thomas Hill Green (1836–1882) and the Philosophical Foundations of Politics: An internal critique* (Lampeter and Lewiston, NY: Edwin Mellen, 1997), for example, pp. 96–97 and then *passim*; Matt Carter, *T.H. Green and the Development of Ethical Socialism* (Exeter and Charlottesville, VA: Imprint Academic, 2003), pp. 27–32 (Carter does not capitalise the 'perfect' Common Good).

make up different social groups. In that they logically require their holders to disagree fundamentally with members of other groups regarding the nature of the good life, common goods can only be held by imperfect beings. Of necessity, they entail disagreements where ultimately there should be concurrence. Ultimately however, disagreement is a sign of imperfection because human beings share one essence and hence one can only properly realise in one way the principles of just social and political organisation, in terms of content if not specific mode of expression. Presumably, that telos would be 'natural' in the sense Green holds certain rights to be 'natural' (§6.III). It is not that the individual is born with a determinate essence in the sense that most people are born with arms and legs, nor is it necessarily the nature the individual would have if she lived in some pre-social state of nature. Instead, it is 'natural' because it is 'the end which it is the vocation of human society to realise'.[112]

Yet, the problem with positing an even-hypothetical 'perfect' Common Good is that it seems to imply that there can be only one way to express human nature fully. This implication seems to require further that human nature is a determinate human essence. Yet, it was argued in MSF chapter four and CS §2.II that Green rejects determinate human essentialism. Human nature requires a social context if it is to gain determinate expression. If it does not have that context, then human nature must remain purely abstract. Once that social context does exist, the determinate expression of human nature must also be conditioned by the contingency embodied within and constitutive of that context.

Certainly, Green does not believe that individuals are simply passive 'subject positions', or nodes within a network of social forces. The concretisation of human nature owes more to the constructive action of crystallisation than it does to its abstract *a priori* structure. In fact, on the reading defended here and in MSF, human nature is more an initially purely abstract group of capacities to which the individual strives to give determinate expression in her character and life. In practical terms, this abstract human nature serves as a structuring principle, the gradual instantiation of which reflects three key factors: the character that the individual has built up through her prior efforts to articulate such an ideal; the sedimentation in social practices and institutions of previous efforts by members of her society to give voice to their ideals; and the contingent conditions in which the individual acts. Under such circumstances, it seems best to regard the Common Good as a heuristic fiction used by the critical citizen, an ideal projected in the hope of helping to create a better society and a better character for the individual. In short, the Common Good functions as a hypothetical and imperfectly-

---

[112] PPO 9.

specified ideal against which the common goods of actual social groups can be critically assessed.

Yet as has just been noted, Green acknowledges the individuated and perspectivist character of his theory of self-positing. Consequently, he rejects the homogenised view wherein all individuals tend to see exactly the same series of meanings and values as constituting the fundamental structure of their shared society. He accepts that the common good will be conceived differently depending on the individual's critical reflections on her prior commitments and circumstances. Moreover, as will be shown in chapter eight he founds his democratic thought not merely on his rejection of a privileged conception of the common good, but on his recognition of the inherently contested nature of the common good. As will become clear shortly however, there is a highly significant sense in which Green's acknowledgement of the inherently contested character of society's common good is perfectly compatible with his perspectivalist claim that each individual 'conceives' the other members of his society as being 'like himself, as having objects which it is their vocation to realise,… and which form part of one great social end, the same for himself as for them'.[113]

While Green is conscious of the problems that arise from focusing on the individual's personal perception of the common good, equally he believes that one should be careful not to overstate these difficulties. Firstly, it is misleading to claim, as Maria Dimova-Cookson does, that Green 'wants to assert moral attributes as facts' and 'wants to present human morality as something that is fixed and unconditional, rather than dynamic'.[114] In reality as has just been noted, Green conceives the good society as one in which individuals clash with each other (usually non-violently), regarding the precise features and implications of both the defining characteristics of the true good and the common good of the society to which they all belong.[115] These clashes will occur with varying degrees of intensity, animosity and concord, and through all types of social interaction. Some of them occur through political and economic struggles, for example through struggles to extend the franchise, or through contests between political parties, as well as through disputes between trade unions and employers (see chapters eight and ten). Others occur in more veiled form in disputes over systems of land ownership and temperance reform as well as over particular pieces of legislation, such as the Contagious Diseases Acts, the Elementary Education Act and the Factory Acts. The more extensive but less self-conscious of these disputes are implicit within the numerous and diverse interactions that individuals have with each other as well as with public and private institutions,

---

[113] PE 237.

[114] Dimova-Cookson, *T.H. Green's Moral and Political Philosophy*, pp. 91, 83.

[115] This reading is also developed in my 'Contesting the Common Good'.

on a daily basis.[116] The precise features of the true good and the common good may not be the primary focus of these interactions. The participants may not even be aware of the ramifications of their interactions for the wider consensus on the nature of these goods. Nevertheless, these are precisely the processes through which the contours of an already fairly inchoate consensus tend to be either affirmed, rejected or, more likely, gradually revised. Green holds that the more inclusive these interactions, the richer and more satisfying will participants find the shifting consensus regarding the nature of the true and common goods.

Secondly, Green sees certain forces as tending to provide centres of gravity for these disputes. For example, perceptions of the common good will tend to be most similar between people who have had similar experiences. As he puts it in his undergraduate essay on *The Duties of the University to the State*, 'Men cannot read the same books without in some measure thinking the same thoughts, nor can they fix their thoughts on the same ideals of intellectual excellence without feeling somewhat of their assimilating powers'.[117] People raised in the same cultural and social groups will tend to have similar experiences. Consequently, Green believes that, in practice, a workable consensus will tend to exist within communities. Certainly, if experiences vary too greatly within a group of people who are only nominally a community, then the common goods will not bind the citizens together with sufficient force to ensure social stability. If a society becomes too unstable, its members will be unable to act with a degree of effectiveness that is sufficient for their respective enriching self-expression and self-development. In fact, Green is emphatic that communities are worth sustaining only to the extent that individuals understand themselves to be sharing allegiances. To the extent that they do not do so, the group does not enrich its members and should be either reformed or disbanded (see chapter eight below). This is a conceptual point as well as an empirical one. There must be a relatively narrow consensus between members' judgements regarding the ultimate ends of their association if their respective conceptions of the specific norms and rules of right conduct are to ground a coherent social system. There must be a relatively significant overlap between members' conceptions of

---

[116] On the Contagious Diseases Acts of 1864, 1866 and 1868, see Peter Nicholson, 'Introduction' and Green, 'Letters to the Press: Contagious Diseases Act', 14 March 1874 (GW 5:xxvi–vii, 220–23, respectively). On land, temperance and educational reform, see LLFC, and various of Green's public documents, letters to the press, speeches and personal letters (for example, GW 5:195–486). See also Green's lectures on educational reform ('Grading', 'Elementary', 'Oxford High School'). On franchise reform, see Colin Tyler, *Idealist Political Philosophy: Pluralism and conflict in the absolute idealist tradition* (London and New York: Continuum, 2006), chapter 2.

[117] T.H. Green, 'The Duties of the University to the State' (GW 5:20).

the good life if they are to sustain one shared system of rights, duties and obligations.

John Horton has claimed that such an 'idea of the common good... is either impossible to determine or non-existent'.[118] Clearly, there is an element of truth in this objection. Yet, it is not that Green fails to recognise the divisions and conflicts in his society. Neither does he fail to appreciate that such intimacy tends to diminish as groups grow, nor that, consequently, the common good becomes less obvious and frequently less real.[119] Yet, as an analysis of what makes a society a stable and enriching community, Green's theory of the common good is not damaged by Horton's observation. In fact, quite the reverse: Green's acknowledgement of the need for a common good in the face of continual social strains forms the basis of a powerful approach to social criticism. It allows citizens to ask whether a particular society is one in which citizens are able to develop a clear and stable sense of personal identity from their interpersonal relationships. As will become evident in chapter eight, this was one reason why Green was both a committed social egalitarian and a political democrat.

In many ways, Horton's criticism serves to reinforce the profound significance of Green's localism, and the associated dangers of concentrating too heavily on the need for a single national common good. As has been shown already, Green emphasises repeatedly that, in practice, the most significant influences on the self-conceptions of most individuals are their respective participation in numerous, often parochial social groups, including families, clubs, voluntary groups and businesses. Their membership of a particular nation may have a relatively small influence. The individual's life is framed by a network of often fairly small-scale community memberships. One just has to remember the examples of the individual's 'chief interests' given in §3.V.[120] They included family life, church life and developing 'the sanitation of a town'.[121] These are all localised routine interests of concrete citizens.[122] Of necessity, they can generate rather transient communal activities. Nevertheless, they are structured by the particular common goods of the various communities, and these frequently mundane daily lives remain fundamental to the agent's self-understanding.[123] Together they constitute a large and

---

[118] Horton, *Political Obligation*, p. 74; also Sidgwick, *Lectures on the Ethics,* pp. 71–77; Arthur K. Rogers, *English and American Philosophy Since 1800: A critical survey* (New York: MacMillan, 1922), pp. 243–46; Carritt, *Theory of Morals,* pp. 64–65; Richter, *Politics of Conscience,* pp. 234–36, 259–60; Alasdair MacIntyre, *A Short History of Ethics* (London: Routledge, 1967), p. 247.

[119] Vincent *et al.*, *Philosophy, Politics and Citizenship*, p. 165.

[120] PE 228.

[121] PE 228, 232, 237.

[122] Compare PE 299.

[123] PPO 38–39.

indispensable aspect of her self-understanding and 'spiritual' life. Green gives the following example in his manuscripts.

> 'Consider life of a healthy peasant. He is interested in his parents, on whom, to begin with, he is physically dependent, and in whom, in virtue of his self-conscious nature, his interest does not cease as it seems to do with the animals when period of physical dependence is over. They become involved in the self in which he is interested, so that he cannot detach himself in thought from them, though no appetite connects him with them. Then he forms new ties – if no other, those implied in becoming a father, so that the self which he presents to himself as to be lived for in the future is conditioned by relations to children. To live for himself means to live for them.'[124]

The very ordinariness of such relationships does much to answer Horton's objection. The problem which Horton highlights is really significant only in relation to very large groups, such as a nation. It is far easier to identify a common good amongst a small group with which one's everyday life is obviously bound up. It is, in George Eliot's words, the 'incalculably diffusive' effects of these 'unhistoric acts' of people living 'hidden' lives which generate the common goods that are most significant for most individuals.[125] As will be established at length in chapter four, in this way Green's perspectivalism enriches significantly his theory of the common good rather than destroying it.

The implications of this line of argument can be brought out in the following manner. Green believes that the individual will probably be a member of many separate groups, with her identity being framed within the complex network of such interrelating and conflicting identifications.[126] The significance of the particular identifications will vary for the individual: for example, she may understand herself more in terms of membership of a group defined on the basis of gender rather than cultural membership. There is no necessary reason to prioritise the agent's identification with one group simply because it has the largest membership or the greatest power over other groups. One can think here of the case of an agent feeling her identification with and allegiance to a disempowered group more strongly than her identification with the oppressing or marginalising group or organisation. The practical spiritual life of an imperfect agent is, thus, a complex balancing of the many duties that arise from her identification with many separate groups, each of which possesses its own common good. The imper-

---

[124] 'Pleasure' 85.

[125] George Eliot, 'Middlemarch', in her *Works*, 20 vols. (New York: Jensen Society, 1910), vol. 11, p. 237. See also Bernard Bosanquet, 'Unvisited Tombs', in his *Some Suggestions in Ethics* (London: MacMillan, 1918), pp. 66–87; Bernard Bosanquet, 'On the True Conception of Another World' and 'The Kingdom of God on Earth', in his *Science and Philosophy*, pp. 320–32 and 333–51, respectively.

[126] PE 299, 309.

fections of her present consciousness and the imperfect social forms with which she identifies conflict with the agent's inherent need for coherence. These conflicts may well express themselves as impulses for what could be large-scale, even revolutionary, social, political and economic change.

VIII

Conclusion

This long chapter has analysed Green's conception and derivation of the common good. It has considered also some of the criticisms that have been levelled at it, as well as some of its previously underappreciated complexities. §II established Green's theory of the common good to be derived from the interrelation of his relational social theory and his intersubjective theory of personal spiritual development. §III developed this analysis by tracing out his incorporation of elements of the social and ethical thought of Rousseau, Kant and Aristotle. §IV rebutted the allegation that Green fails to establish the non-competitiveness of the common good, while §V asked how selfless Greenian citizens have to be. §VI highlighted the immense significance that Green's concerns for social justice have for his theory of the common good. Finally, §VII examined the relationship between his social theory and his often-overlooked perspectivalism. It is with the balancing to which this persectivalism leads that the discussion arrives at the main subject of the next chapter: Green's theory of conscientious action and social criticism.

The Social Reformer as the Self-realising Individual

I
Introduction

The preceding chapters have established that, contrary to his reputation among some critics as a crypto-authoritarian, Green sees unthinking endorsement of or mere acquiescence to social norms and legal imperatives as having no intrinsic ethical worth.[1] Quite the contrary: he is emphatic that the individual is self-realising only to the extent that she follows principles, norms and rules upon which she has reflected critically, and which she has adopted freely as her own. In the second and third chapter, these issues were examined primarily from the perspective of the origins, structure and integrity of the social context in which the individual acts. In a sense, the following chapter approaches the same issues from a different angle.[2] Specifically, this chapter explores the ways in which Green believes the individual should interact with her social context. Among other things it will be established that Green's philosophical analysis of conscience and social criticism completes the theories of morality and self-realisation that were examined in MSF, as well as the social theory analysed in chapters two and three.

Surprisingly little developed philosophical work has been done on Green's theories of conscience and social criticism. Where they have received critical attention, generally the reaction has been negative. For example, Henry Sidgwick could find no explanation of the correct method of conscientious social criticism within Green's writings, something that Sidgwick saw as a major problem with Green's social and political thought.[3] Even

---

[1] PPO 6.
[2] 'In seeking to understand its [consciousness's] reality we have to look at it from two different points of view; and the different conceptions that we form of it, as looked at from these different points, do not admit of being united, any more than do our impressions of opposite sides of the same shield' PE 68.
[3] Henry Sidgwick, *Lectures on the Ethics of T.H. Green, Mr. Herbert Spencer, and J. Martineau*, ed. E.E. Constance Jones (London: MacMillan, 1907), pp. 114–15.

though this assessment has attracted some notable supporters, the present chapter will demonstrate that Sidgwick's criticism is misplaced.[4] Green tells us enough regarding the formal conditions of social criticism and its substance to make his theory tolerably complete. That Sidgwick did not find what he wanted is probably a sign that he was trying to find more detail in Green's writings than is allowed by the subject matter.

Yet, more fundamental doubts may remain regarding Green's theory. To many twentieth-century historians and theorists, Green's focus on thick, local relationships seemed a comfortable if not complacent valorisation of the status quo, an inadequate response to the systemic power relations that subsequently became characteristic of modern civilised societies. Something like this thought might well have been in Melvin Richter's mind when he observed in 1964 that although Green's principles had been 'accepted by the fathers as bold and progressive' when Green died, just a few years later his principles 'appeared to their sons as a set of priggish *clichés*'.[5] Until recently, Green's focus on civil society might also have seemed inadequate to political philosophers, given a certain tendency on their part to obsess about the state to the exclusion of non-state power relationships at work within advanced capitalist societies. Fortunately contemporary debates have recovered some of the insights into the workings and significance of civil societies that one finds in Green.[6] In part, this is a reflection of the growing influence of Hegel's philosophy, not least as that is evident, in a highly revised form, in certain postmodernists and poststructuralists. A greater awareness of the profound significance of various forms of power within civil society has been found also in the work of multicultural theorists, theorists of the politics of recognition, identity and difference, as well as republican theorists, many of whom draw on the social theory literature which most mainstream political philosophers have wrongly tended to ignore. Nevertheless, a reconsideration of Green's own analysis of the reformist implic-

---

Jerome B. Schneewind, *Sidgwick's Ethics and Victorian Moral Philosophy* (Oxford: Clarendon Press, 1977), pp. 408–11.

Melvin Richter, *The Politics of Conscience: T.H. Green and his age* (London: Weidenfeld and Nicolson, 1964), p. 376.

I deal with these points much more fully in Colin Tyler, *Idealist Political Philosophy: Pluralism and conflict in the absolute idealist tradition* (London and New York: Continuum, 2006), chapter 5, and Colin Tyler, 'Power, alienation and performativity in capitalist societies', *European Journal of Social Theory*, 14:2 (May 2011), 161–80. Early social theorists appreciated the significance of power relationships in civil society: see, for example, Ferdinand Tönnies, 'Gemeinschaft und Gesellschaft', in his *Community and Association*, trans. Charles P. Loomis (London: Routledge and Kegan Paul, 1955), pp. 31–275, which appeared first in 1887, just five years after Green's death.

ations of the process of self-positing inherent within civil society is long overdue. That reconsideration is presented in this chapter.

The argument is structured as follows. §4.II examines Green's argument in support of his claim that social reform springs from the individual's self-alienation. §4.III introduces the main features of Green's theory of conscientious citizenship, while §4.IV examines his melding of social criticism with the individual's attempt to overcome her own moral confusions. §4.V turns to the vexed question of the role of indirect public service in Green's theory of citizenship. §4.VI suggests that conscientious citizenship is unintelligible to the extent that Green adopts a spiritual determinist theory of the will. The chapter concludes with §4.VII. Throughout his writings, Green distinguishes conscientious criticism of personal and social norms from conscientious criticism of legal imperatives (statute law, common law and so on).[7] The former are dealt with in the present chapter, with a consideration of the legal imperatives being undertaken in chapters six and seven.

II
Self-alienation as the Motor of Reform

It was established in §§2.III–IV that, in his theory of intersubjective identity formation, rather than focusing on national politics, Green places far greater significance on the individual's relationships with her family, her neighbours, her particular voluntary associations, her local council and other more immediate and personal relationships. It will be shown now that these parochial interactions are profoundly significant in numerous ways. It has also been established in §2.IV that Green conceives it as a necessary but not sufficient condition of actualising the true good of the self-realising agent that she identifies herself freely with rules of conduct which she understands as reflecting her highest nature. When an individual is living fully in accordance with her true nature — when she is fully autonomous — those meanings, values and associated activities through which she believes her true good can be gained — her 'chief interests' — form a network which interrelate to create the outer or practical life that reflects the demands of her personality.[8] The need for self-conscious action in conformity with a self-imposed law ensures that it is not sufficient for the individual's behaviour simply to accord with conventional social norms. For a conventional action to be truly valuable, the agent must perform it because she freely identifies her own true good with the norms which guide her actions.[9] Mere acquiescence does not constitute autonomous and therefore intrinsically-valuable action. The individual is truly free only to the extent that she wills subjectively a definite

---

[7] For example, PPO 4–5.

[8] PF 228.

[9] DSF 25.

end which is valuable objectively, and pursues that end in practice because she believes it to be objectively valuable. It is this contextualised ethically-guided action which constitutes the particular individual's praxis.

Green's insistence on definite agents, social contexts and circumstances has led Geoffrey Thomas to conclude that

> 'Green's morality of social roles suggests the idea of a coherent form of social organization in which each role is associated with a practice that respects the rights and serves the interests of individuals. The complete network of social roles provides the conditions in which the individual, all individuals, can achieve self-satisfaction through self-realization.'[10]

While there is much truth here, one needs to be careful about stating Green's position in the manner Thomas does. No doubt, there is a rather abstract sense in which each social role can be characterised as embodying just one practice conceived as 'a rule-governed pattern of activity'.[11] For example, 'being a parent' could be defined as 'ensuring the present and future well-being of one's child'. Yet, on another level it would be strange to characterise 'ensuring one's child's well-being' as a single practice in the way Thomas seems to do. It is difficult to think of any social role that is not a series of structured activities (rather than being simply one structured activity) upon which the agent reflects and then decides to follow in particular circum-stances. Characterising a social role as relating to merely one practice fails to capture the full complexities of most functions. Importantly in the present context, it is not an inadequacy found in Green's theory. Moreover, present-ing Green's position in the manner Thomas does, makes his position seem less nuanced and plausible than it actually is. Green himself participated in the daily grind of various civic and political campaigns, not least in relation to temperance, trade union activism, women's educational rights, university reform and as a town councillor. As many of his public speeches demon-strate, he was acutely aware of the complex strategic and tactical consider-ations of which the individual needed to take account when negotiating the vagaries of continually changing circumstances.[12]

Green conceives of true citizenship, in Gertrude Himmelfarb's words, 'as much [as] a moral as a political condition'.[13] More than this however, it is a civil condition, as Himmelfarb herself tacitly acknowledges when she claims that Green's true citizens strive continually to be 'active and useful members

---

[10] Geoffrey Thomas, *The Moral Philosophy of T.H. Green* (Oxford: Clarendon Press, 1987), p. 302.

[11] Thomas, *Moral Philosophy*, p. 283.

[12] See various of the documents which Nicholson includes in the fifth volume of Green's *Works* (GW 5 *passim*).

[13] Gertrude Himmelfarb, *Poverty and Compassion: The moral imagination of the late Victorians* (New York: Alfred A. Knopf, 1991), p. 236.

of society'.[14] As will be explored in §§7.IV, 8.IV and 10.IV, in addition to his own personal crusade for temperance, land, education and electoral reform, Green's writings include many other practical examples of how one might live up to the ideal of true citizenship.[15] For instance, he argues that in his own society fulfilling one's role in ensuring 'the welfare of a family… has probably had the largest share in filling up the idea of true and permanent good'.[16] Moreover, he cites life as part of a 'nation, of a state or a church' and, in more specific terms, helping in 'the sanitation of a town'.[17] He refers to a person's need 'to get A.B. to leave off drinking' as 'a troublesome moral duty of benevolence to his neighbour'.[18]

Ultimately, the individual can only give content to the idea of acting 'in service of the state' (understood as a 'society of societies') when she is actually faced with a concrete situation. Consequently, the 'true good presents itself to men [continually] under new forms'.[19] For example, the virtues of Green's society were different from those of the Greeks.[20] Similarly, the virtues of the twentieth-first century Europe and North America will be different from those in Green's day. All of this demonstrates that, in spite of the implications of Thomas's reading, Green's theory recognises that every social role is made up of many different practices.

Green is alive to the downside of the fact that the individual can express herself only through a diverse and shifting range of specific contextualised roles and practices. These practicalities constitute the environment in which the individual can conceive a better state of the world, one that is crystallised around an ideal of the highest good that she endorses freely, and then

---

[14] Himmelfarb, *Poverty and Compassion*, p. 236; see also PPO 121–23; Richter, *Politics of Conscience*, especially pp. 344–76 *passim*. Green, speech to the Wesleyan Boy's School, Oxford, 18 December 1874 (GW 5:254).

[15] For example, 'Hume II' 4; 'Popular Philosophy'; 'English Revolution' *passim*; 'Grading'; 'Elementary'; 'Oxford High School'; PE especially 154–382 *passim*; PPO 148–246 *passim*; LLFC; see also Nettleship, 'Memoir', *passim*; John H. Muirhead, *The Service of the State: Four lectures on the political teaching of T.H. Green* (London: John Murray, 1908), pp. 7–8, 81–113 *passim*; Richter, *Politics of Conscience*, pp. 344–76.

[16] PE 229.

[17] PE 232, 229.

[18] PPO 118. Here, Green might be thinking of his own brother, with whom he lived for a time in Oxford in an ultimately unsuccessful attempt to save him from alcoholism (Nettleship, 'Memoir', xxxvii).

[19] PE 257. When any particular state is a state 'as such', its members recognise it to be the 'society of societies, the society in which all their claims upon each other are mutually adjusted' (PPO 141).

[20] Terence H. Irwin, 'Eminent Victorians and Greek Ethics: Sidgwick, Green and Aristotle', in Bart Schultz, ed., *Essays on Henry Sidgwick* (Cambridge: Cambridge University Press, 1992), pp. 279–310.

seeks to realise through her actions (§§1.II, 2.IV, 3.VII). He is very sensitive to the structural constraints that each role and practice imposes on the agent's capacity for self-expression and, consequently, to the restrictions that it creates for their opportunities for social criticism and reform.[21] Furthermore, he emphasises that no matter how creative the individual is in reforming the boundaries of her stations in life, in practice she can never transcend completely the limitations of her initial socialisation, and so can never create a completely novel world for herself. As Richter puts it, 'individuals within a given society do not construct infinitely varied ideals'.[22] This makes the individual's situation necessarily tragic: the circumstances required for her to have any practical possibility of a degree of self-realisation, themselves prevent her from ever achieving complete self-realisation.[23]

> 'Granted the most entire devotion to the attainment of objects contributory to human perfection, the very condition of his effectually promoting that end is that the objects in which he is actually interested, and upon which he really exercises himself, should be of limited range. The idea, unexpressed and inexpressible, of some absolute and all-embracing end is, no doubt, the source of such devotion, but it can only take effect in the fulfilment of some particular function in which it finds but restricted utterance.'[24]

Indeed, at several points Green echoes F.H. Bradley, claiming that the individual's limited practical ability to transcend social forms means that 'Each has primarily to fulfil the duties of his station'.[25] It is because Green, Bradley and other British idealists claim such things that some readers have accused them of being excessively conservative, as was noted above. Nevertheless, as has been established already (MSF §6.III; CS §3.III), like Bradley Green is emphatic that to the extent the individual does not freely endorse her roles, she does not recognise herself in her actions and so is not autonomous when she fulfils their demands. To that degree, her life is cramped and she is not truly free. As Green observes, in the self-consciousness of an alienated individual, conventional roles and practices 'do not form an object which, as contemplated, he can harmonise with the other objects which he seeks to understand, nor, as a practical object, do they form one in the attainment of which he can satisfy himself'.[26]

---

21 PE 182–83.

22 Richter, *Politics of Conscience*, p. 208.

23 Tragic 'not so much' in the sense of 'the war of good against evil as the war of good against good', A.C. Bradley, 'Hegel's Theory of Tragedy', in his *Oxford Lectures on Poetry* (London: MacMillan, 1965), p. 75. See also my *Idealist Political Philosophy*, chapter 1 *passim*.

24 PE 183.

25 PE 183; see PE 313, 338.

26 DSF 24.

Unfortunately, no human being can ever attain perfection. For one thing, the animal aspects of human life make it impossible for any agent to recognise her true good in all its clarity and complexity, and to seek to realise that good in practice.[27] For another, when faced with the inevitable ambiguity, incoherence and fragmentation of both her social world and her personality (deficiencies reflective of the limitations of the conceptual resources available in herself and her world), the individual has to acknowledge that 'He is always something potentially, which he is not actually; always inadequate to himself; and as such, disturbed and miserable'.[28] Given that social structures exist only in and through the interactions of individuals, each of whom acts in light of her own personality and her own understanding of those structures, the necessary imperfection of the individual entails that no society can ever be perfect either. No agent will ever be brought up in a way which perfectly expresses a complete and coherent conception of her inherent nature and, therefore, no one will ever attain a state of perfect abiding satisfaction in the life which her social environment prompts and allows her to live. There will always be unavoidable conflicts between the numerous roles and virtues according to which she is expected, and expects herself, to live.[29] Given her need for harmony in her life, she cannot identify fully with such a fragmentary scheme and the virtues and practices to which it gives rise. Consequently, this necessarily imperfect individual constantly faces tragic choices, a fate that is reinforced by the fact that she is embedded firmly within imperfect societies.

Green highlights two key consequences of the individual's recognition of the incoherences and other inadequacies of her previously-accepted meanings and values. Firstly, the individual's spiritual growth will be hindered by her lack of a social structure in which to operate and with which she identifies.[30] Indeed, these fetters are inevitable given the importance of a sympathetic communal context which was outlined in §2.IV. The individual's attendant frustrations with the world in which she has been raised mean that 'there is apt to occur a revolt against conventional morality'.[31] Secondly and more positively, the individual may come to understand more fully 'the spirit underlying the letter of the obligations laid on him by society'.[32] This development arises from the fact that eventually the individual's acknowledgement of her own imperfections and those of her society prompts her to try to reconstitute established meanings and values in ways that will introduce a systematic order of living for

---

[27] PE 288.
[28] 'Works of Fiction' 29.
[29] PE 247.
[30] DSF 24.
[31] DSF 24.
[32] DSF 24.

individuals and communities corresponding to the ideal harmony 'of the capabilities, of the thinking and willing soul'.[33] It is at this point that the individual moves from juvenile nihilism to mature social criticism.

The individual can construct this harmony only to the extent that she crystallises her actions in relation to a definite conception of an ideal system of meanings and values, because her projection of a coherent system requires a definite point of orientation. In other words, the individual's attempts to revise and crystallise currently poorly organised meanings and values can be successful only to the extent that she presupposes a clear if internally-differentiated telos (MSF chapter 5; CS §§1.II, 2.IV). Consequently, Green claims that, in more concrete terms, the individual's sense of inner disharmony drives her to search for an object which is truly desirable: 'there arises a quest for some definite and consistent conception of the main ends of human achievement. Is there some one direction, common to all the forms of activity esteemed as virtuous, which explains and justifies that estim-ation?'[34] This is an internal quest, in the sense that it tends to lead the con-scientious citizen to a clearer understanding and resolution of incoherences within her own perspective on conventional meanings and values (§7.VII).

The orientating telos is not wholly conventional however. No matter how extreme the individual's break with convention, it remains the case that established meanings, values, norms, institutions and activities are, in part, collective manifestations of previous efforts to give concrete expression to the otherwise abstract human nature. When combined with her need for self-conscious identification with universalisable laws which should guide her conduct as a rational being, the fact that social values and institutions are (imperfect) manifestations of human nature has profoundly significant implications for the manner in which the individual can live her own free life. For one thing, it means that the individual's innate drive to add coherence to conventional norms is 'a reconciliation of reason with itself'.[35] Moreover, it means that constructing a more coherent conception of the meanings and values that can structure her society is a vital stage in the individual's personal development. It is for this reason that Green observes in his undergraduate essay on *The Force of Circumstances*, 'The very essence of a true reformer consists in his being the corrector and not the exponent of the common feeling of his day'.[36] Green concludes his analysis of David Hume's moral philosophy on this point.

> '[A]n "ideal" theory of ethics tampers with its only sure foundation when it depreciates respectability;... there is no other genuine "enthusiasm of human-

---

33   PE 251.
34   PE 249.
35   DSF 25.
36   FC 10.

ity" than one which has travelled the common highway of reason the life of the good neighbour and honest citizen — and can never forget that it is still only on a further stage of the same journey.'[37]

As was established in §§2.IV and 3.II–III, Green's analysis of this 'common highway of reason' underpins his theory of the true good: as a rational being with eudaimonic capacities, the individual should come to recognise that every person should live her life as

> '[her] articulation, and application to particulars of life, of that principle of an absolute value in the human person as such, of a like claim to consideration in all men, which is implied in the law and conventional morality of Christendom, but of which the application in law is from the nature of the case merely general and prohibitory, while its application in conventional morality is in fact partial and inconsistent.'[38]

Moreover, it has been established that such dedication to serving a true good signifies the need to work for a 'common well-being', something that Green equates with working to facilitate the self-realisation of all other members of one's community (§§3.III–IV).[39] The individual's existential disharmony is mitigated through praxis aimed at serving an inherently collective end, then: purposive action in support of the public realm (§3.II).

Whatever her context then, to truly act as a citizen, the individual's actions must have a real impact on the more enriching aspects of the daily lives of those living within one's community. With this thought in mind, on 5 December 1879, Green gave a speech at the Liberal Hall, Abingdon in which, echoing his great hero, John Bright, he distinguished between 'a false patriotism and a true'.[40]

> 'False patriot is a man who clamours for display of national strength without considering whether cause in which strength is to be displayed is just or no. Who seeks to gratify a passion for excitement by calling for wars, in which he will not shed his blood, without considering their effect on the permanent good of his nation. True patriot is man who will sacrifice [himself?]… to serve his nation not merely in war,… but by making the people more virtuous and

---

[37] 'Hume II' 64.

[38] PE 215.

[39] PE 232, 243.

[40] Green, 'National Loss and Gain under a Conservative Government', speech at the Liberal Hall, Abingdon, 5 December 1879 (GW 5:352). See Christopher Harvie, *The Lights of Liberalism: University liberals and the challenge of liberal democracy 1860–86* (London: Allen Lane, 1976), p. 113, and John Bright's speech in Birmingham, 29 October 1858 which particularly inspired Green (Nettleship, 'Memoir', xx–xxiv), printed in John Bright, *Speeches on Questions of Public Policy*, 2 vols., ed. J.E.T. Rogers (London: MacMillan, 1869), pp. 466–79, especially p. 478.

contented, and therefore greater and stronger with only true greatness and strength. Those who talk most about patriotism not best patriots.'[41]

He had made the point more succinctly in 1860: 'Let the flag of England be dragged through the dirt rather than sixpence be added to the taxes which weigh on the poor'.[42] Green acknowledges that many of his contemporaries made huge sacrifices in the name of a nation's alleged collective dignity or of serving 'some impersonal Humanity'.[43] Yet, he rejects such mythical entities, insisting instead that the true patriot is she who seeks to help her flesh-and-blood compatriots at the prosaic level of what would now be called social policy and 'low' politics (§§3.VI, 5.II). In the longer-term, the requirements of citizenship can have effective hold on the individual only to the extent that they find definite expression in purposive actions (praxis) performed in particular circumstances and through particular social norms and practices with which the concrete individual identifies.[44] (Green's rejection of extra-personal entities is analysed in §5.II.)

---

41   Green, 'National Loss and Gain' (GW 5:352). See also 'Loyalty'.

42   Nettleship, 'Memoir', xx–xxi.

43   PE 184, 181; PPO 89–90.

44   PPO 89–90. See Henry Scott Holland, *Lombard Street in Lent*, quoted in S.C. Carpenter, *Church and People 1789–1889* (London: SPCK, 1959 [1933]) pp. 483–84. Also, see John MacCunn, *Six Radical Thinkers: Bentham, J.S. Mill, Cobden, Carlyle, Mazzini, and T.H. Green* (London: Edward Arnold, 1907), pp. 213–66; G.F. Barbour, *A Philosophical Study of Christian Ethics* (Edinburgh and London: William Blackwood, 1911), pp. 125, 137, 394, 400; John S. MacKenzie, *A Manual of Ethics* (London: University Tutorial Press, 1929 [1883]), pp. 391–94. There are many differing histories here. For a fascinating account of the ethical movements which Green inspired, see Ian D. MacKillop, *The British Ethical Societies* (Cambridge: Cambridge University Press, 1986). For various other assessments of Green's influence in other areas see, for example, Nettleship, 'Memoir'; James Bryce, 'Thomas Hill Green', in his *Studies in Contemporary Biography* (New York: MacMillan, 1903), pp. 85–99; Y.L. Chin, *The Political Theory of Thomas Hill Green* (New York: W. Dray, 1920), pp. 125–45; Adam B. Ulam, *The Philosophical Foundations of English Socialism* (Cambridge, MA: Harvard University Press, 1951), pp. 62–71; Melvin Richter, 'Intellectual and Class Alienation: Oxford idealist diagnoses and prescriptions', *Archives Européenes de Sociologie*, 7 (1966), 1–26 *passim*; Craig Jenks, 'T.H. Green, the Oxford Philosophy of Duty and the English Middle Class', *British Journal of Sociology*, 28:4 (1977), 481–97; Michael Freeden, *The New Liberalism: An ideology of social reform*, reprinted with corrections (Oxford: Clarendon Press, 1978), pp. 16–19, 55–56; Peter Gordon and John White, *Philosophers as Educational Reformers: The influence of idealism on British educational thought and practice* (London: Routledge and Kegan Paul, 1979), *passim*; Fred Inglis, *Radical Earnestness: English social theory 1880–1980* (Oxford: Martin Robertson, 1982), pp. 26–28; W.H. Greenleaf, *The British Political Tradition, Volume Two: The ideological heritage* (London: Methuen, 1983), pp. 137–41; Andrew Vincent and Raymond Plant, *Philosophy, Politics and Citizenship: The life and thought of the British idealists* (Oxford: Basil Blackwell, 1984), *passim*; James T. Kloppenberg,

III
Social Criticism and Personal Conscience

It has been established thus far that Green holds the individual's most fundamental duty to be to critically assess conventional social structures and values, and then to follow the best judgement of her own conscience. Personal conscience is the internal oracle through which the agent tries to judge, revise and, hopefully, reconcile the competing conventional duties of her stations and her drive for self-cultivation. The most important question for a conscientious agent to ask of her conscience is, Green writes, 'Was I in this or that piece of conduct what I should be?'[45] To answer this question fruitfully, the agent should consider whether or not she has honoured the duties incumbent upon her given her particular social roles and attachments, an activity requiring engaged critical reflection on the various meanings and values inherent within her various social interactions. This is a practical and not a merely abstract enquiry. By asking this question of her particular determinate meanings and values and by being honest with herself in her answers, the individual is brought to a clearer understanding of her common goods and, therefore, her duty or duties.[46] In this way, her conception of the ideal form of virtue will become clearer, more concrete and more powerful in her mind and actions. Indeed, any attempt to rectify a situation which the agent believes to be evil will tend to bring her to a clearer comprehension of a truly good life.[47] Green summarises his position as follows.

> 'No individual can make a conscience for himself. He always needs a society to make it for him. A conscientious "heresy," religious or political, always represents some gradually maturing conviction as to social good, already implicitly involved in the ideas on which the accepted rules of conduct rest, though it may conflict with the formulae in which those ideas have been hitherto authoritatively expressed, and may lead to the overthrow of institutions which have previously contributed to their realisation.'[48]

The true citizen—the truly free agent—must engage in social criticism, then. Moreover, seeking the higher spirit of social conventions shows true loyalty to her fellows, even when the agent's search leads her into conflict with

---

Uncertain Victory: Social democracy and progressivism in European and American thought, 1870–1920 (New York and Oxford: Oxford University Press, 1986), pp. 30–34; Olive Anderson, 'The Feminism of T.H. Green: A late Victorian success story?', *History of Political Thought*, 12:4 (1991), 671–93; Himmelfarb, *Poverty and Compassion*, pp. 247–62 *passim*.

45 PE 307.
46 PE 197, 279, 306–07; PPO 3.
47 PE 307.
48 PE 321.

those fellows.[49] Green expresses the social critic's core question in the following words.

> 'How are the institutions of social life, and the rules of conventional morality, to be cleared of the alien growths which they owe to the constant co-operation of selfish passions with interest in common good, and which render them so imperfectly organic to the development of the human spirit? Above all, how is this or that individual — circumstanced as he is, and endowed, physically and mentally, as he is — to take part in the work?'[50]

Given his relational social theory, it should be no surprise that Green sees the question of social criticism as being intimately connected to the question of how the individual should deal with the numerous perplexities of conscience that she faces in her life. The conscientious attitude is 'no other than the [individual's] sense of personal responsibility for making the best of themselves in the family, the tribe, or the state, which must have actuated certain persons, many or few, in order to [produce] the establishment and recognition of any moral standards whatever.'[51] Social criticism and conscientious self-judgement are two modes of analysis, and their respective constitution and revision are inherently interrelated objects.

In the cases of both social and self-criticism, Green is emphatic that there can be no 'view from nowhere'; that is, no non-situated Archimedean point from which to assess the validity of given norms (or any other intellectual construction, such as a work of philosophy). The best that is available is either an internal critique or a criticism of one set of social and personal norms (work of philosophy and so on) from the perspective of another. This belief reflects the most fundamental structure of Green's analysis of the growth of knowledge (MSF chapter three; CS §1.II). Hence, in his unpublished manuscripts, he argues that 'In order to get [a] notion of distinct properties, (and so <u>conceive</u> the thing) we must <u>analyze</u> the confused image. The continued analysis gives us [a] more and more determinate conception'.[52] This applies to knowledge regarding values as much as to all other types of knowledge. Green clarifies what he sees as the appropriate procedure for social criticism and conscientious judgement in his very revealing — and still greatly underrated — 1866 article 'The Philosophy of Aristotle'.[53] There, he argues that the Socratic method proceeded by drawing out the underlying rationale of commonly-held beliefs so as to gain the truth. Then he writes, 'Incidentally as applied to morals, the method had a

---

[49] 'Loyalty' *passim.*
[50] PE 352; see PE 198.
[51] PE 309.
[52] MS11, T.H. Green Papers, Balliol College, Oxford, emphasis in original.
[53] See also PE 301.

far higher value. It was the correlative of the Socratic doctrine of innate moral ideas'. He continues with a revealing change of tense.

'[A]nd the method has a practical value, as the doctrine [contains] a practical truth. The truth of the doctrine lies in the fact that an unconscious always precedes a conscious morality; that men act on moral principles, embodied in law and custom, which have never distinctly become part of their individual consciousness. The value of the method lies in its power, as a process of self-examination, to awaken in a man the consciousness of the law on which, under higher guidance than his own, he has already been acting, and thus to transform it from an outward to an inward law, to be obeyed not on authority but in freedom, not under the limitations of local or temporary enactment, but in the open atmosphere of reason.'[54]

This method requires the individual to examine critically her own particular beliefs and values by asking herself whether or not they cohere with her other beliefs and values. Where they do not, she should reform them so that her beliefs form a more fully integrated system. Only when the system is integrated fully will the agent realise her true good and so gain an abiding satisfaction of her abiding self. The social critic should apply precisely the same process to conventional meanings and values.

It is best to reconsider this process in terms of David Ritchie's characterisation of Green's method as a form of critical and speculative metaphysics (MSF §3.II; CS §1.II). On this reading, Green holds that the coherence of analytic judgements derived via critical metaphysics can be assessed simply using the principle of non-contradiction. Yet, to assess the coherence of the synthetic propositions arrived at through speculative metaphysics, one must rely upon other criteria. The question is, which ones? There are no criteria against which to judge one's beliefs and values which can be truthfully called 'objective' in the sense of being demonstrably true in a manner which is essentially separable from the existing modes of human reasoning. As was noted in §2.IV, Green holds that 'Language presupposes thought as a capacity, but in us the capacity of thought is only actualised in language'.[55] To a large extent, language is a cultural construction. For Green, the criteria which the individual should apply when engaging in social criticism are derived from the modes of reasoning which are embodied in the particular conceptual frameworks that underpin her understanding of her world. These in turn arise out of the interaction of human nature as that is expressed in the particular individual, with the concrete social influences faced by that person. Hence, social criticism constitutes a manifestation of the interaction of reason as it is found in the human mind with reason as it is

---

[54] 'Aristotle' 58; cf. PE 301, 317–19.
[55] PE 183.

embodied in social institutions: as noted earlier, it is 'a reconciliation of reason with itself'.[56]

It is worth emphasising once again that this is not simply a process of harmonisation between the individual's determinate consciousness and social norms. As has been established (MSF chapter five; CS §2.IV), Green regards the individual's craving for the satisfaction of certain higher needs as an expression of the 'law of… [the] being' of the human spirit, which itself is 'a law of development in society'.[57] Consequently, social criticism is an effort to move towards a situation where the agent attains both her own true good and that of everyone else with whom she interacts on a daily basis. For this reason, conscientious social criticism arises from the clash of inherent eudaimonic and rational human drives with the modes provided for their expression by current social institutions and practices.[58] This tends to drive reform of presently imperfect institutions and practices so that the latter facilitate the better expression of agents' distinctively human needs. Only in this way can the individual continue, in Green's very Hegelian phrase, 'to reject what is temporary and accidental in [her cultural frameworks], while retaining what is essential',[59] activities which are necessary aspects of social criticism. Only in this way can the individual 'disentangle the operative ideas from their necessarily imperfect expression'.[60] In general terms, Green states that the conscientious agent should begin by asking herself,

> 'Does this or that law or usage, this or that course of action—directly or indirectly, positively or as preventive of the opposite—contribute to the better being of society, as measured by the more general establishment of conditions favourable to the attainment of the recognised virtues and excellences, by the more general attainment of those excellences in some degree, or by their attainment on the part of some persons in higher degree without detraction from the opportunities of others?'[61]

Yet, this guidance is rather vague. Consequently, frequently the agent will feel lost and confused. How Green believes she should proceed in such situations is the subject of the next section.

---

[56] DSF 25.

[57] PE 176; see PE 77, 149, 172, 183–85, 187, 190–91, 352–54, 363, 375–77, 382.

[58] Mander fails to mention the crucial interaction of the eudaimonic aspects of human nature with conventions (Mander, *British Idealism*, p. 201).

[59] PE 279.

[60] PE 319.

[61] PE 371, slightly misquoting himself from PE 354.

IV

Perplexities of Conscience

To understand what might be termed Green's 'contextualist' approach to social and personal reform in greater depth, consider his discussion of perplexities of conscience. What does Green believe the individual should do when apparently faced by conflicting duties? It is rarely recognised that he gives two incompatible responses to this question. Firstly and most famously, he argues that the individual's inability to discern her duty is not a mark of an ultimately confused moral situation: 'There is no such thing really as a conflict of duties. A man's duty under any particular set of circumstances is always one, though the conditions of the case may be so complicated and obscure as to make it difficult to decide what the duty really is.'[62] There is always really only one proper way to act but humans may have difficulty working out what it is. For Green when in this mood then, perplexities of conscience arise from conflicts between the commandments of the differing authorities which the agent reveres.[63] When bewildered in this way, 'However disposed to do what his conscience enjoins, the man finds it difficult to decide what its injunction is'.[64] Green reiterates that the proper way to act — and, therefore, the agent's duty — is to follow 'the course which contributes most to the perfect life'.[65] He claims that by bearing this end in mind, 'the soul… can harmonize all the authorities' which initially appear to the individual to have a claim on her.[66]

In his own context, Green sees no problem with these apparently rather formless general recommendations regarding the appropriate methods of personal ethical assessment and social criticism. Much of this lack of concern can be attributed to the contextualised nature of his approach. For example, he believes that, in his own day, the 'higher moral culture' of modern Christendom has developed to such an extent that there will always be a determinate answer to all moral perplexities.[67] This is a very controversial and, indeed, overly-optimistic assumption.[68] Even in specific circumstances, there is a long way to go from possessing an abstract maxim to discovering one's particular duty. More is needed to overcome the problem of the perplexity of conscience. Indeed, it was shown in §2.V that although Green

---

62 PE 324.

63 PE 314.

64 PE 321.

65 PE 324.

66 PE 327.

67 PE 354, 372.

68 H.D. Lewis, 'Does the Good Will Define its Own Content? — a study of T.H. Green's *Prolegomena to Ethics*', in his *Freedom and History* (London: George Allen and Unwin, 1962), pp. 30–35; H.D. Lewis, 'Individualism and Collectivism', in his *Freedom and History*, pp. 85–89.

disagrees with Berlin, holding instead that ultimately all true values are in harmony with each other, at the practical level he accepts the inevitability of conflicts of values which arise from human imperfection. He is emphatic that these clashes will be present as long as humans are imperfect, and humans will always be imperfect. Consequently, Green must accept value pluralism and genuine perplexity as endemic features of human life. Indeed, he does acknowledge this fact at other points in his writings, and the discussion must examine these passages next.[69]

In this second mood, Green accepts that there *can* be genuine perplexities of conscience. He argues that where one's conscience is unclear about whether to follow the norms of one's society or to perform some other course of action, the former should tend to carry more weight (see §4.II). In other words, if in doubt, one should operate on the assumption that the conventional morality of one's society indicates the better course to take. By satisfying the prescriptions and expectations of our social positions 'we can seldom go wrong; and when we have done this fully, there will seldom be much more that we can do'.[70] Even if the individual does decide to follow convention, she must be self-critical if she is to act as a truly free, self-realising agent. She must question her motives so as to ensure that she is acting out of a sense of duty: that is, according to the disinterested dictates of her conscience, and not out of some self-serving attempt to evade what she really believes to her most dutiful course. Green is emphatic on this point. The conscientious citizen should take care to assess the worth of her competing desires and hence the worth of her associated motives.

> '[I]t is not by the outward form… that we know what moral action is. We know it, so to speak, on the inner side. We know what it is in relation to us, the agents; what it is as our expression. Only thus indeed do we know it at all.'[71]

The agent should not attempt to provide non-normative redescriptions of her actions in order to make it appear that she has not acted wrongly.[72] The initial evidence from which she assesses her motives must not be reinterpreted in the light of the theory that subsequently is produced to explain it. In other words, the evidence should guide her theory rather than her theory altering her interpretation of the evidence. To this end, Green argues that it is imperative to utilise the concepts and viewpoint which represent 'the expression of that experience which is embodied, so to speak, in the habitual phraseology of men, in literature, and in the institutions of family and polit-

---

69   Lewis, 'Good Will', 35–36; H.D. Lewis, 'T.H. Green and Rousseau', in his *Freedom and History*, pp. 128–33 *passim*.
70   PE 313.
71   PE 93.
72   PE 93.

ical life'.[73] The value of her motives (thus interpreted) tends to be reflected in their contribution to the attainment of the 'ideals of permanent good' which are current at the time of action.[74] The 'ideas and ideals of permanent good' to which Green refers are the ones which constitute 'the standard of social expectation on the part of those whom [the agent] recognises as his equals'.[75] These standards express what is likely to be the highest stage of the concrete instantiation of her human nature that is currently present in the agent's world. The most reliable point from which to assess the agent's probable motive for any particular act is culturally-given, then.

Yet, this approach seems to present certain difficulties for Green's wider theory. Firstly, it appears to be a highly collectivist position with conservative implications. On an unsympathetic reading, the individual seems to be required to abdicate her powers of self-assessment in regard of her general principles of psychology and value.[76] Secondly, Green appears to be arguing that there is only one theory of human motivation current in society at any one time. This is highly simplistic. Of course, he may be assuming that there are a number of positions which cluster together tightly enough that the agent can treat the resulting common ground as the shared perspective on motivation. Green is vague here but the essential points to be made in his defence are as follows. Firstly, the ideal is always for the individual to judge her actions according to her own general theory of human motivation. That is, she should disregard the fact that she is trying to assess her own motivation in the present case and that, consequently, it is she herself who will suffer or enjoy moral blame or praise for the action. Now, given the formative influence of one's self-understanding on the nature of her actions, it is vital for the agent to understand how she believes herself to act in general: her interpretation of her own personal psychology. This tends to be the viewpoint from which she can most accurately understand the motives which issue in the specific actions.

The problem which most greatly concerns Green is that the agent will tend to be biased in judging her own actions. A disinterested expression of

---

73 PE 94.

74 PE 95.

75 PE 98.

76 George H. Sabine, 'The Social Origin of Absolute Idealism', *Journal of Philosophy, Psychology and Scientific Methods*, 12:7 (1915), 174–75; Arthur K. Rogers, *English and American Philosophy Since 1800: A critical survey* (New York: MacMillan 1922), pp. 246–48; Richard H.S. Crossman, *Government and the Governed: A history of political ideas and political practice* (London: Christophers, 1958 [1939]), pp. 196–97; Jenks, 'T.H. Green, the Oxford Philosophy of Duty and the English Middle Class' *passim*; Richard Bellamy, 'T.H. Green and the Morality of Victorian Liberalism', in his *Victorian Liberalism: Nineteenth century political thought and practice* (London: Routledge, 1990), pp. 147–48.

her psychological make-up must be found, if at all possible. Given the inter-subjective basis of the individual's character, Green argues that the external expression of that view of personal psychological motivation which is clos-est to her own self-understanding is most likely to be found in those inf-luences which helped to form her personality. Hence, using a phrase which Green uses in a slightly different context, the individual should assess the nature of his motives from the basis of the psychological theory current among the social group made up of 'those whom he recognises as his equals'.[77] Nevertheless and importantly, this is merely a 'rule of thumb', and the individual always has a duty to accept or reject it as her conscience dic-tates. Hence, Green avoids sanctioning collectivism and conservatism by insisting that the agent's conscience always has priority over social judge-ments.[78]

The second objection is that this approach overstates the homogeneity of social judgements of personal psychology. Looking at Green's theory as it stands, the objection fails to take account of the limited nature of the 'society' to which the conscientious agent should look for guidance. The citizen should look for her conscience reflected in the judgements of those people in whom she recognises herself. She should only be concerned with those whom she judges to be like herself; in other words, 'those whom he recog-nises as his equals'. This group is likely to be a far more restricted and, hence, more homogeneous group than the objection must assume if it is really to bite. Unfortunately, the situation is not so simple when we turn to a fragmented society (§§3.VII, 8.II–III). Most people now live in this situation. The individual will probably be a member of many different groups, each with its own particular common good and each with its own *prima facie* claims on the agent.[79] Moreover, these disparate social claims may well be augmented by 'some demand of the self-realising spirit which has not found expression in a recognised rule' (MSF §§5.III–IV; CS §4.II).[80]

The conscientious agent must balance all of these claims. Unfortunately, they need not be mutually compatible, given that we are constrained to live in an imperfect world. It will be remembered (from MSF §3.II; CS §2.V) that Green's monism can only perform its harmonising role fully within a perfect world. Such a world is just not available in any temporal existence humans can ever lead. Values are almost certain to clash irreconcilably in any world human beings can know. This is one sense in which Green believes that we are 'condemned' to have to make tragic choices. Unfortunately then, the

---

[77] PE 98.

[78] See also Paul Harris, 'Moral Progress and Politics: The theory of T.H. Green', *Polity*, 21 (1988–89), 560–62.

[79] PE 299, 309.

[80] PE 311. Mander (*British Idealism*, p. 201) seems to deny this fundamental element of Green's theory of critical citizenship.

second objection stands. The claim that intersubjectively-formed standards and theories of psychological motivation provide a standpoint from which the perplexed agent can engage in self-criticism and social criticism does indeed rest upon an over-optimistic assessment of the harmony and homogeneity of the individual's social life. The most the agent can do is to act in that way which she believes will probably bring about the greatest eudaimonic development of herself and her fellows. Green defends his position by arguing that 'However insufficient such safeguards may be, it remains the case that self-reflection is the only possible method of learning what is the inner man or mind that our action expresses; in other words, what that action really is'.[81]

Green avoids the temptation to give easy but false answers and comfort. For example, in a speech to the Cowley Road Mutual Improvement Society in 1877, Green is reported to have 'begged' the audience 'to cultivate reverence for the facts, and to think once, twice, thrice, and a great many times before they trusted their own judgement on any subject whatever'.[82] It was established in §§2.II, 3.II–IV and 3.VII that certain formal conditions must hold: for example, that the ideal is non-competitive and rests on a Kantian respect for persons. Showing respect here means fostering self-realisation: 'the end is that full self-conscious realisation of capabilities to which the means lies in the self-conscious exercise of the same capabilities — an exercise of them in imperfect realisation, but under the governing idea of the desirability of their fuller realisation'.[83] Green's justification of his Kantianism was examined in §3.III. It was established that the inherent logic of social relations implies (whether or not this is recognised) that rationality is a quality possessed by all humans as social beings. The drive for consistency in her life tends to push the individual to respect this rationality in her dealings with others. For this reason, the true good is a common good. It exists as our 'interests in the development of our faculties, and in the like development of those for whom we care'.[84] In this sense 'society is founded on the recognition by persons of each other, and their interest in each other, *as persons, i.e.* as beings who are ends to themselves'.[85] Only by respecting the capacity for agency and therefore promoting self-realisation in others can the individual gain an understanding of herself as a being who is also worthy of respect.[86]

---

[81] PE 94.
[82] T.H. Green, speech to the Cowley Road Mutual Improvement Society, 22 October 1877, reported in *Oxford Times,* 27 October 1877.
[83] PE 195.
[84] PE 234.
[85] PE 190.
[86] PE 190.

Unfortunately, as has been noted already, this injunction is still not very helpful when one comes to deciding how to act. How does it help the agent to determine what it means for her to *'be a person and respect others as persons'* in practice?[87] The necessary features of the ideal are not given very much real content by this requirement.[88] One of the main causes of this vagueness is the individuated nature of human self-expression. Even though every individual should have the opportunity to realise her personality and to help her fellows to do the same, 'it does not follow from this that all persons must be developed in the same way'.[89] The object sought as the true good 'will vary in different ages and with different persons, according to circumstances and idiosyncrasy'.[90] If different individuals perceive their respective determinate true goods in different ways, what sort of a guide can Green's call to always respect persons be?

In reality, this vagueness is not something which worries Green very greatly.[91] The abstract nature of the true good is imperfectly realised in the world. That is demonstrated by the contradictions present in our lives.[92] This fact, together with the complexity of all determinate morally-significant situations, undermines the validity of those approaches to ethical theorising which seek a set of determinate commandments. Hence, a determinate command is only properly understandable and authoritative in relation to its context.[93] To clarify this point, Green considers the case of two individuals who face precisely the same circumstances and who then have to decide whether or not to tell the truth even though they realise that evil consequences will also follow if they do so. He assumes that one lies whilst the other tells the truth and asks, 'who is better?': 'it would be impossible for the moral philosopher to say which action were the better or the worse of the two; because he would not know in regard to either that spiritual history [of the formation of their respective characters] upon which its moral value depends.'[94]

---

[87] Georg W.F. Hegel, *Elements of the Philosophy of Right*, ed. Allen W. Wood, trans. H.B. Nisbet (Cambridge: Cambridge University Press, 1991), §36.

[88] Muirhead, *Service of the State*, pp. 30–31.

[89] PE 191.

[90] PE 239.

[91] PE 337, 352, 376–82.

[92] PE 195.

[93] Green refers to Sir Henry Maine's very influential works on this subject occasionally (for example, PPO 84, 88). Indeed, Maine held a chair at Oxford (1869–78) for some of the time that Green was a lecturer at Balliol College. See the editorial note in T.H. Green, *Lectures on the Principles of Political Obligation, and other writings*, ed. P. Harris and J. Morrow (Cambridge: Cambridge University Press, 1986), p. 329n3.

[94] PE 316.

The specific form taken by the ideal is fundamentally dependent on the context of the action and the agent, and this context can only be assessed by the agent when she is either in a particular situation or looking back on one that she herself experienced.[95] Attempting to set down a 'timeless' moral system would be effectively to ignore the fundamental importance of the contextual nature of morality. Theorising about how she should act in hypothetical moral situations is useless as well. Only by following her conscience in actual situations will moral progress be achieved.[96] 'A judgement of the sort we call intuitive — a judgement which in fact represents long courses of habit and imagination founded on ideas — is all that the occasion admits of.'[97]

Horton pursues the objection of vagueness, arguing that ultimately Green's theory of the common good cannot overcome the 'fact of disagreement'.[98] Indeed, Green himself goes as far as to state that the spirit of ethical norms 'speaks with many voices according as men have ears to hear'.[99] Consequently, Horton argues Green cannot satisfactorily answer the question 'How are we to decide what is in the common good?'[100] As it stands, it appears that Horton is correct. Let us take one of the hardest possible cases: the conscientious slave-owner versus the conscientious slavery abolitionist.[101] Both believe as a matter of conscience that their particular cause is right. How should the citizen choose between the two positions? The first course of action may be to carry out an internal critique of the two positions. Which is the more coherent on its own terms? The intersubjective and Kantian arguments which were presented in §§2.IV and 3.III tend to favour the abolitionist line. Yet, the logic of Green's own position means that, at least in an imperfect world, he must accept the possibility of a pro-slavery case being put forward which, on the pro-slavery logic, is at least as coherent as his neo-Kantian line.[102] A pro-slavery activist may claim this is so with, for example, Aristotle's defence of natural slavery.[103] For Green the inability to choose on the grounds of coherence can only occur in an imperfect world. Nevertheless, we as humans are condemned to imperfection forever. For this reason, it appears that we can never be assured of the truth of even our most coherent beliefs. Furthermore, given that we do live in an imperfect world,

---

[95] PE 308.

[96] PE 196, 308, 327.

[97] PE 320.

[98] John Horton, *Political Obligation* (London: MacMillan, 1992), p. 74.

[99] PE 301.

[100] Horton, *Political Obligation*, p. 74.

[101] See also Lewis, 'T.H. Green and Rousseau', 131–33.

[102] For another interesting if not unproblematic interpretation of Green's theory of rights, see Derrick Darby, *Rights, Race, and Recognition* (Cambridge: Cambridge University Press, 2009), pp. 142–68.

[103] Aristotle, *Politics*, I.iii–vii.

the coherence test does not trump all other possible tests. Conscience and contextualised intuition remain pre-eminent. The discussion has not progressed at all then, for the slave-owner can simply respond to a more coherent anti-slavery line by stating that her conscience tells her that slavery is a morally-better state than non-slavery.

It is because of difficulties such as these that Green downplays the link between the philosopher and the practical citizen.[104] 'Moral philosophy as [Green] conceives it can take one only so far', Nicholson argues, '...it cannot lay down in advance how the ideal should be applied in specific circumstances. That is a matter of practical judgement, and is subject to pragmatic considerations.'[105] To ask the moral philosopher to provide the true good (and, hence, the common good) with content independently of the full details of a particular context, as for instance Lewis seems to want, is utopian and futile.[106] The desire for commandments, which moral philosophers themselves have encouraged, must be resisted: 'One is sometimes, indeed, tempted to think that Moral Philosophy is only needed to remedy the evils which it has itself caused.'[107]

What the moral philosopher can do, however, is to prescribe a negative condition of moral action.[108] She should try to bring the agent to consider whether or not her proposed course of action truly appears to her to be dutiful, or alternatively whether it is motivated essentially by selfish considerations. Furthermore, the philosopher should attempt to clarify the claims which the agent feels by exposing any ambiguities, incoherences and possible foundations which are present or implicit.[109] Even so, ultimately the agent herself must decide how she should act.[110] All the philosopher can do is try to help the agent to gain a clearer and more critical understanding of herself and her beliefs. This limiting of the role of philosophy to one of interpretation extends into all of its branches. For example, in a manuscript from the mid-1860s, Green writes:

> 'The metaphysician, as he is told depreciatingly but with truth, adds nothing to the sum of existing knowledge... Penetrating the intelligible world, he seeks to disentangle its elements, and to "put them together" again no longer as a material presented from without, but as the complex realisation, the organized body, of the spirit which contemplates them. (He is not a mathem-

---

[104] PE 196, 327. See W.H. Fairbrother, *The Philosophy of Thomas Hill Green* (London: Methuen, 1900), pp. 185–87; Thomas, *Moral Philosophy of T.H. Green,* pp. 370–71.

[105] Peter P Nicholson, *The Political Philosophy of the British Idealists: Selected studies* (Cambridge: Cambridge University Press, 1990), p. 79.

[106] PE 317. Lewis, 'Good Will', *passim*; Lewis, 'T.H. Green and Rousseau', 131–33.

[107] PE 311.

[108] PE 316–17.

[109] PE 322.

[110] PE 316.

atician, or chemist, a physiologist or psychologist, but he re-adjusts (or ought to readjust) the processes pursued by all in a new order of unity and necessity, as successive determinations of the Divine spirit, whose thought "he thinks after Him".)... The ridicule which the assertion of such an office excites is a witness to its difficulty and remoteness from ordinary interests.'[111]

As a philosopher—rather than as 'a man or a citizen'—the agent should not attempt to recommend better courses of action, then.[112] Indeed, as a philosopher she should not attempt to make any active contribution to the direction of the spiritual development of those around her or even try to make others want to develop themselves.[113] Such active involvement is her duty as a member of her society and not as a philosopher: her 'immediate business as a philosopher is not to strengthen or heighten this aspiration much less to bring it into existence, but to understand it'.[114] Nevertheless, the individual cannot impose this understanding upon another agent, even when she is fulfilling her role as a 'man or a citizen' or a preacher.[115] Certainly, the case she can make for acting in a certain manner in the particular circumstances might awaken her fellows' obedience to their respective consciences. Yet, such obedience arises only when the individual has a personality that is receptive to the claim. It will be receptive only once the agent's abstract human nature has been determined in a certain way over the course of the life which she has lived to that point.

Ultimately, then, the agent must rely upon her own honest, conscientious convictions. This is one reason why Green's own epitaph—which also serves as the theme of his lay sermon on *Faith*—is so appropriate.[116] It is an unavoidable conclusion of his methodology that 'we walk by faith, not by sight'. In a manner of speaking, this is the source of Horton's criticism. His attack can be rephrased as the observation that, 'Green provides little way to adjudicate between people whose faiths contradict each other'. If faith and conscience are the ultimate guides in matter of belief and value, what are the implications for 'the fact of disagreement'?[117] As has been stated already, moral conversion is the proper task of the man, citizen or preacher, rather than the moral philosopher. Poetry and polemic, as well as reasoned argument persuasively put, are all potentially legitimate methods of promoting reflection. In the end, there are few universally-applicable limits on the types of action which can be used to pursue the cause of personal development.

---

[111] 'Rudiment' 2.

[112] PE 327.

[113] PE 327.

[114] PE 327.

[115] PE 313.

[116] 'Faith' 253. Green is buried in St. Sepulchre's Cemetery, Oxford, just inside the walls when coming from the Walton Street entrance.

[117] Horton, *Political Obligation*, p. 74.

The agent should use whatever method her conscience deems most appropriate in the circumstances. This may mean war or literature, legislation or quiet personal example. (Related issues are pursued in §8.IV.)

To conclude this section, one more issue should be considered. Even though Green insists that conscientious action is the core of distinctively human agency, he is very aware that self-reflection can be harmful or self-indulgent when carried to the extreme. For example, the overly-conscientious individual may be so busy with 'a kind of devotion to great objects or to public service' that she is apt to ignore the question of whether or not there is some other course of action that would be better able to achieve the ends which she believes should be brought about.[118] Often, those individuals who act without reflecting on the abstract ideal of virtuous action can achieve a greater number of their truly valuable objects and achieve them in a better manner than those who constantly concern themselves with their motives and the philosophical (or quasi-philosophical) basis of their ethical judgements. Echoing his concerns regarding the false patriot (§4.II), Green attacks those people

> 'who pride themselves on conformity to a standard of virtue (which cannot be the highest, or they would not credit themselves with conforming to it), and who so hug their reputation with themselves for acting conscientiously that in difficult situations they will not act at all.'[119]

Certainly, being aware of one's motives to some extent is a necessary part of truly moral action.[120] The truly moral agent asks herself whether or not she did her duty to the best of her ability, paying proper regard to the 'circumstances and effects' of her action.[121] The criticism applies only in extreme cases. Recognition of the true nature of one's motives is bad only to the extent that the agent is being self-indulgent. Green's fundamental point is that the conscientious moral agent should ask herself whether or not she has done the best that she could in the past and at present. Furthermore, she should do so because she honestly wants to fulfil her duties. To my mind, Green's refusal to make the world seem an easy place for a good person to live in, is to be applauded rather than portrayed as an avoidable fault.[122]

---

[118] PE 297.

[119] PE 297.

[120] PE 298, 305, 322–25.

[121] PE 305.

[122] Compare A.D. Lindsay, 'Introduction', in T.H. Green, *Lectures on the Principles of Political Obligation* (London: Longmans, 1941), pp. xviii–xix.

V
Citizenship and the 'Cunning of Reason'

Thus far, Green's emphasis has been on direct public service. One reason for this is his belief that the good consequences of any particular action are solely the result of the good intentions of the agents involved (even where on balance the agent acts from evil motives).[123] He gives the example of the leader of a political movement who acts out of selfish motives rather than for duty's sake. He concludes that, 'The good in the effect of the movement will really correspond to the degree of good will which has been exerted in bringing it about; and the effects of any selfishness in its promoters will appear in some limitation to the good which it brings to society'.[124]

Green does not hold this position unambiguously. Disinterested citizenship is not the only progressive force which he identifies and these alternatives create inconsistencies within his writings. For example, there is an interesting and highly significant passage in his lectures on Kant's ethics which clearly shows how close his conception of public service comes at times to the thought of Kant himself, Adam Smith and John Stuart Mill. All four philosophers argue that human actions can have unintended beneficial consequences. In Smith's case, narrowly self-interested actions tend to bring economic benefits to everyone through the operation of the 'invisible hand'. For Kant, human development can arise from actions that are not morally good (see §5.II). In the case of Mill, a situation in which each individual is allowed to be an eccentric fosters the maximisation of human capacities in all their diversity throughout the society. In a similar vein, Green writes,

> 'a man may be living for objects in the effort after which he takes no positive thought for the good of others, without being therefore selfish. An artist or man of science, who "lives for his work" without troubling himself with philanthropy, is yet not living for an object merely private to himself. His special interest may be shared by no one, but the work which results from it, the machine constructed, the picture painted, the minute step forward in knowledge, that is the man's good as attained, is a good for which others are the better.'[125]

In addition to Smith, Kant and Mill, this passage has clear affinities with Hegel's 'cunning of reason'.[126] Reason is cunning for Hegel in the sense that the actions of agents have consequences which on the one hand push human life in general to develop, whilst on the other hand bring the downfall of the agents themselves: 'it sets the passions to work for itself, while that which

---

[123] PE 295; PPO 104, 106.

[124] PE 295; see also PPO 127–31.

[125] 'Kant' 123; see also PPO 163.

[126] George W.F. Hegel, *The Philosophy of History*, trans. J. Sibree (New York: Dover, 1959 [1858]), pp. 20–37; see Tyler, *Idealist Political Philosophy*, pp. 6–16.

develops its existence through such impulsion pays the penalty, and suffers loss.'[127] For example, often violence, especially in war, brings progress in unforeseen ways. Consequently and famously, Hegel characterizes 'History as the slaughter-bench at which the happiness of peoples, the wisdom of States, and the virtue of individuals have been victimized'.[128] Usually, Green is not as pessimistic as Hegel. Usually, he does not argue that, of necessity, History victimises the virtue of its agents and, to this extent, Cowling is incorrect when he argues that 'Green... has a fully Hegelian sense of the deviousness of all social action'.[129] Nevertheless, at one point in his *Lectures on the Principles of Political Obligation*, Green does claim that,

> 'It may be that, according to the divine scheme of the world, such wrong-doing [as occurs in and as the result of war] is an element in a process by which men gradually approximate more nearly to good (in the sense of a good will). We cannot think of God as a moral being without supposing this to be the case.'[130]

Green differs from Hegel in the strength of his pity for the victims of conflict. His thought seems to be that a truly good Creator must give back a net benefit to compensate for the suffering caused by war. This is one point where Green's religious faith and optimism overwhelm his good sense.

Green's two incompatible arguments concerning the status of ultimately beneficial actions do not fit together very easily.[131] In adopting the 'invisible hand' approach, he accepts that agents may unintentionally promote human well-being. Yet, with the 'good intentions' line which justifies citizenship, he argues that there must always be some motive to do good if good consequences are to follow. The latter claim excludes the former. Which line should be favoured? The second is Green's later thought and the one which best accords with the argument that he values public service understood in any very straightforward sense. Nevertheless, it is far less satisfactory than the first argument at the philosophical level, although at least one commentator has accepted the idea.[132] The claim that only good motives have good consequences is, as Bertrand Russell puts it in the marginalia of his copy of the *Prolegomena to Ethics*, simply an 'arbitrary assumption'.[133]

---

127 Hegel, *Philosophy of History*, 33.
128 Hegel, *Philosophy of History*, 21.
129 Maurice Cowling, 'The Use of Political Philosophy in Mill, Green and Bentham', *Historical Studies*, 5 (1965), 150.
130 PPO 163.
131 For example, I.M. Greengarten, *Thomas Hill Green and the Development of Liberal-Democratic Thought* (Toronto: University of Toronto Press, 1981), pp. 42–43.
132 MacKenzie, *Manual of Ethics*, p. 355n1.
133 Bertrand Russell's copy is a third edition (that is 1890) and is held in the Special Collection of the J.B. Morrell Library at the University of York. It is signed 'B Russell. Trin. Coll. Camb.. July 1893'. For other interesting views on this claim of

The other approach ('the invisible hand' argument) is more plausible when it comes to explaining some if not all social improvements. Self-centred action often promotes the common good. Certainly, the idea that actions can serve the common good unintentionally, does not fit easily with Green's endorsement of the Kantian requirement to act out of reverence for the moral law.[134] To be consistent with the remainder of his ethics, Green's conception of public service must include the requirement that the citizen is determined to action by the very idea of duty in itself. The structure of his argument logically commits him to the conclusion that the action of an artist or scientist 'who "lives for his work"'[135] cannot ultimately be of moral value in any straightforward sense. Yet, the consequences of selfish actions can still have ethical value even when the actions were not performed out of reverence for the moral law. This can be true even of selfish actions, to the extent that the latter are formulated and performed within the framework of a stable set of social norms and practices. At that point, even actions performed from an individual's evil motives carry into action the beneficial influences embodied within those norms and practices. Green captures this fascinating yet often-overlooked argument in the following example in his *Principles of Political Obligation*, which it is worth quoting at length.

> 'We look at the action e.g. of Napoleon with reference merely to the selfishness of his motives. We forget how far his motives, in respect of their concrete reality, in respect of the actual nature of the ends pursued as distinct from the particular relation in which those ends stood to his personality, were made for him by influences with which his selfishness had nothing to do. It was not his selfishness that made France a nation, or presented to him continuously an end consisting in the national aggrandisement of France, or at particular periods such ends as the expulsion of the Austrians from Italy, the establishment of a centralised political order in France on the basis of social equality, the promulgation of the civil code, the maintenance of the French system along the Rhine. His selfishness gave a particular character to his pursuit of

---

Green's, see Fairbrother, *Philosophy of Thomas Hill Green*, p. 178; Sidgwick, *Lectures on the Ethics*, p. 46; W.D. Lamont, *An Introduction to Green's Moral Philosophy* (London: George Allen and Unwin, 1934), pp. 208–11; Lewis, 'Good Will', 30–33; Lewis, 'T.H. Green and Rousseau', 120–29 *passim*; Noël O'Sullivan, *The Problem of Political Obligation* (New York: Garland, 1987), pp. 167–68. In his hurry to condemn Bosanquet for committing this error, Hobhouse implies that Green does not support this claim as well (Leonard T. Hobhouse, *The Metaphysical Theory of the State: A criticism* (London: George Allen and Unwin, 1918), pp. 17–18).

[134] Kant himself was clear that moral development can result from actions that are either morally-neutral or wrong, as his writings on history show (for example, Immanuel Kant, 'The Idea for a Universal History with a Cosmopolitan Purpose', in his *Political Writings*, second edition, ed. Hans Reiss (Cambridge: Cambridge University Press, 1991), pp. 41–53). Moreover, see O'Sullivan, *Problem of Political Obligation*, pp. 157–58.

[135] 'Kant' 123.

these ends, and (so far as it did so) did so for evil. Finally it led him into a train of action altogether mischievous. But at each stage of his career, if we would understand what his particular agency really was, we must take account of his ends in their full character, as determined by influences with which his passion for glory no doubt co-operated, but which did not originate with it or with him, and in some measure represented the struggle of mankind towards perfection.'[136]

Green's 'invisible hand' argument points out these uncomfortable facts, whereas his 'good intentions' argument does not. Nevertheless, the Napoleon case operates at a far more profound level than the 'invisible hand' argument. It shows a very significant way in which to formulate a 'cunning of reason' argument without invoking a notion of a quasi-divine agent, such as Hegel's very particular conception of 'Reason', which 'sets the passion [of man] to work for itself'.[137] Instead, Green highlights the fact that, in order to motivate a large number of individuals to agree to fight in a war (as Napoleon did) or to lead a large political party, even the most self-interested agent must appeal to popularly-recognised values, such as the rule of law (in the Napoleonic Civil Code, say). In so doing, the selfish agent spreads those values and the benefits that come with those values.

VI

Conscientious Action and Spiritual Determinism

There is a final difficulty for Green. To this point, it has been assumed that Green is adopting his self-interventionist theory of the will. Yet, it was established in MSF §5.II that at times he adopts an alternative approach: spiritual determinism. MSF argued that this second theory of the will is more in harmony with the main thrust of the rest of his philosophy than is his self-interventionism. Whether or not one agrees with this assessment, Green's spiritual determinism makes his theory of conscientious action very difficult to sustain. Henry Calderwood saw this clearly.

> 'A philosophy which accounts for all things by "the action of a free or self-conditioned and eternal mind," has by its own structure created a difficulty in the way of shaping a theory of personal obligation; for an injunction to conform to law seems as unmeaning in a nature which is the "reproduction of an eternal consciousness," as in a "being who is simply the result of natural forces".'[138]

What becomes of Green's call to consult one's conscience if he adopts the spiritual determinist line? What becomes of his call to judge one's actions by

---

[136] PPO 129; see PPO 128–30. Mander (*British Idealism*, p. 208) makes this point as well.

[137] Hegel, *Philosophy of History*, p. 33.

[138] Henry Calderwood, 'Another View of Green's Last Work', *Mind* 10 os (1885), 81.

the standards of one's social group when faced with a perplexity of con science? In short, what becomes of the injunction to become a conscientious citizen when the very structure of Green's argument precludes the agent from acting in any way except that in which she is pushed automatically by the interaction of her abstract human nature, her determinate personality and her particular circumstances? Moreover, if the agent cannot choose voluntarily to act otherwise than in fact she does, in what sense can she be held responsible for anything? The most fundamental aspect of these points were dealt with at some length in MSF chapter five. Adopting the spiritual development line, all that is lost from what is currently the favoured reading of Green's thought is the idea that conscientious action is voluntary in the sense that the agent could have acted otherwise than in fact she did. Nevertheless, this is a very big 'all', as it alters fundamentally the nature of his moral and political thought from the way he understood himself and the way in which generally he is read now.

VII

Conclusion

This chapter has covered a lot of ground. §4.II analysed the role played by alienation in Green's theory of self-reform. It argued that, taken together, the perspectivalist and constructivist features of both his social theory and his theory of intersubjective identity-formation make alienation a ubiquitous human experience. That alienation is a perennial facet of human life ensures that true citizenship is always critical, with a tendency towards dispute and even social conflict. §4.III explored in greater depth the link between personal conscience and social reform, before §4.IV turned to the perplexities of practical reason. §4.V considered the extent to which Green's theory of citizenship recalled Hegel's 'cunning of reason', while §4.VI asked what alters within Green's theory if one adopts his spiritual determinist theory of the will. The next chapter examines some further issues related to Green's theory of progress, before chapter six begins the analysis of his political and economic thought which occupies the remainder of the book.

5

Further Issues Regarding Green's Attitude to Progress

I
Introduction

The previous chapters have shown that Green bases his mature ethics and social theory on three key claims. The first is that personal worth stems from the individual's realisation of her highest capacities as a rational being with eudaimonic capacities. The second is that, as a rational being, every individual is under a categorical imperative to respect those qualities that she values in herself, even when those qualities are instantiated in others.[1] Thirdly, Green argues that, when understood correctly, the categorical imperative is inherently practical (§2.IV): it requires all rational agents to show respect in practice for rationality as an end-in-itself. For this reason, at the heart of Green's conception of the well-ordered society stands the idea of a kingdom of ends founded on the common good of humans as beings with higher capacities. He observes in his undated *Notes on Moral Philosophy* that

> 'With most men, as strangers, one can only deal on [a] footing of *right*. But in such dealing the good man respects [the] right of others not merely as [a] condition of his own right being respected, but as [an] *allos autis* [other self] — as that which he has taken into himself and loves as himself.'[2]

Green develops this thought more formally in the *Prolegomena*: 'perfect morality,' he writes, is realised as the 'ideal of a society in which every one shall treat every one else as his neighbour — in which to every rational agent the well-being or perfection of every other such agent shall be included in that perfection of himself for which he lives'.[3]

Yet, Green recognises that these epochal ideas have histories; they have emerged in civilised societies over the course of many generations. He comments on the historical character of these ideals repeatedly, not least in his analysis of modern conceptions of virtue: for example, he writes that 'the

---

[1] PE 199.
[2] 'Moral Philosophy' 2, emphasis in original, additions by Harris *et al.*
[3] PE 205.

interests of the "pure heart" have become really more determinate, its demands upon itself fuller, in the Christian society than they were to the most enlightened and conscientious [ancient] Greek'.[4] Or again: 'unless mankind has lived its last two thousand years in vain, the formal and provisional account of the good should mean more for us than it does for the [ancient] Greeks.'[5] Such passages have led many scholars to claim that Green's ethical and social thought relies on a largely unstated theory of progress.

This chapter considers the allegedly progressivist elements of Green's ethics. As might seem appropriate for a chapter on progress, §5.II introduces the analysis by considering Green's changing relationship to progressivism. The section begins by considering Green's changing relationship to Mazzinianism and Italian unification in the 1850s and 1860s. Next, it establishes that while the mature Green regards human development as being in some sense 'natural', he does not believe it to be inevitable. Nevertheless, he does see good reasons for believing that societies have progressed in the past and will continue to do so. §5.III considers Paul Harris's objection that Green's mature conception of development makes it impossible to judge whether or not humans have developed over time. §5.IV examines the problems associated with Green's spiritual determinist perspective on human development. §5.V draws the chapter to a close. In many ways, this relatively short chapter establishes little that has not been defended at much greater length and depth in MSF and the earlier chapters of the current book. Nevertheless, it earns its place here in that it counters a common misreading of Green (that he relies on an implicit progressivism), and it brings together a number of previously-established points in new and revealing ways.

II
Italy, Mazzinianism and the Progress of Humanity

Green's greatest interest in Italy stemmed from the struggles for Italian unification in the 1850s and 1860s. In this, he was not alone at Oxford. The leading Italian republican Giuseppe Mazzini enjoyed many friendships and acquaintances during the years he spent in exile in England, and many of these were found among scholars at Oxford and especially Balliol College's Old Mortality Society. He knew Goldwin Smith and Benjamin Jowett as well as James Bryce who in 1860 even tried to join Garbaldi's Thousand.[6] Mazzini

---

4   PE 253.
5   PE 252.
6   G. Howard's contemporary sketch of Mazzini talking to Jowett is reproduced in Geoffrey Faber, *Jowett: A portrait with background* (London: Faber and Faber, 1957), p. 366. Faber dates it to 1868, but Abbott and Campbell imply that Jowett first met Mazzini in 1871 (Evelyn Abbott and Lewis Campbell, *The Life and Letters of*

was a friend of the Oxford astronomer J.P. Nichol, whose son John Nichol was part of the same Balliol circle, both father and son being admirers of Mazzini, with the father being a member of Mazzini's 'Society of the Friends of Italy' and the son donating funds to Mazzini's cause.[7] Mazzini influenced those college fellows who professed to be republicans, such as A.C. Bradley, Edward Caird, A.V. Dicey, Algernon Swinburne, Arnold Toynbee and Green himself.[8] In Alberto de Sanctis's words, 'At the Old Mortality Society it was possible to breathe an air which was deeply impregnated by Mazzinian suggestions'.[9] Christopher Harvie has observed that,

> 'Mazzini's ideology was scarcely lucid or cohesive, but in two significant ways he was influential: he demanded a devotion to the ideal of democratic nationalism which was religious rather than calculating; he argued that politics was a moral rather than a functional activity. The university men, re-interpreting the evangelical tradition on similar lines, welcomed the sanction of a man honoured by a movement to which they were anyway sympathetic.'[10]

Harvie goes on to highlight the 'particular esteem in which Mazzini was held by T.H. Green and his disciples'.[11] This seems something of an over-statement given Swinburne's almost fanatical hero-worship of Mazzini.[12] Nevertheless, Harvie is correct that Green admired Mazzini greatly and that Green's disciples did much to encourage study of Mazzini. Bolton King published a biography of Mazzini in 1902,[13] while Green's student and

---

Benjamin Jowett, M.A. Master of Balliol College, Oxford, 2 vols. (London: John Murray, 1897), vol. 2, pp. 10–12).

7   E.F. Richards, ed., *Mazzini's Letters to an English Family 1861–72*, 3 vols. (London: John Lane, n.d.), vol. 1, pp. 193–94, 315; vol. 2, pp. 91–97 *passim*, 125, 143, 149; vol. 3, p. 241&n. Denis Mack Smith, *Mazzini* (New Haven and London: Yale University Press, 1994), p. 126.

8   Smith, *Mazzini*, pp. 190–91, and Christopher Harvie, *The Lights of Liberalism: University liberals and the challenge of democracy 1860–86* (London: Allen Lane, 1976), pp. 100–05. William Angus Knight, *Memoir of John Nichol, Professor of English Literature in the University of Glasgow* (Glasgow: James MacLehose, 1896), p. 140. Edmund Gosse, *The Life of Algernon Charles Swinburne* (London: MacMillan, 1917), *passim*.

9   Alberto de Sanctis, *The 'Puritan' Democracy of Thomas Hill Green, with some unpublished writings* (Exeter and Charlottesville, VA: Imprint Academic, 2005), p. 31.

10 Harvie, *Lights*, pp. 103–04.

11 Harvie, *Lights*, p. 104.

12 'On his reappearance at Balliol [after the Easter vacation of 1858], Swinburne's rites of incantation before the portraits of Mazzini and Orsini became more extravagant than ever. In these performances he was humorously supported by the sympathy of T.H. Green, but other fellow-undergraduates regarded them as silly and almost blasphemous.' Gosse, *Swinburne*, p. 55.

13 Bolton King, *Mazzini* (London: J.M. Dent, 1902).

cousin Charles Edwyn Vaughan venerated Mazzini in his *Studies in the History of Political Philosophy* (1925), in a large chapter edited posthumously by another of Green's students A.C. Bradley.[14] Another student of Green (and indeed of Edward Caird at Glasgow), John MacCunn included Mazzini as one of 'six radical thinkers' in his 1907 book of the same name.[15]

Green was particularly struck by Giuseppe Mazzini's efforts to establish a self-determining cooperative Italian republic in the 1850s and 1860s. Italy's need for a decentralised self-determining, broadly egalitarian republic weighed heavily with Green, who recorded being made 'very gloomy' by Garibaldi's agreement to the settlement of September 1860, whereby Piedmont joined with and dominated the majority of the remaining Italian regions under the constitutional monarchy of Victor Emmanuel II. Many radicals saw Garibaldi's acquiescence as a betrayal of the free Italian cause, and in a private letter of the time Green lamented the fact that,

> 'Garibaldi is evidently not strong enough to take at all a high tone, and thus I fear the Mazzinian or federal program, which I have no doubt is really the best, will have to give way, for want of public virtue, to Cavour's. I can't think that a Piedmontese king of all Italy, without federal limitations, would ever be trustworthy, or that Italy can ever be permanently safe with Rome and Venetia in the hands of foreigners.'[16]

Mazzinianism placed associations such as the family and the nation at the heart of its programme. It held that together they act as the main vehicles for the realisation in the world of Humanity's highest potentials. For Mazzini, the family and especially the nation anchor the individual's development, something that in turn enables the individual to gain her own sense of existence and existential location. Against this background, in the 1860s at least Green endorsed Mazzini's assessment of the roots of Italy's problems: currently, the Italian working classes were not sufficiently virtuous to build a republic based on cooperative principles for themselves, let alone to sustain it for any length of time.[17] It was because of that deficiency that both Green and Mazzini were resigned to the futility, for the time being at least, of Mazzinianism as a public policy. In 1858, Mazzini observed:

> 'whatever be the end and aim towards which we are created, we can only reach it through the progressive development and exercise of our intellectual faculties. Our faculties are the instruments of labour given to us by God. It is

---

[14] Charles Edwyn Vaughan, *Studies in the History of Political Philosophy before and after Rousseau*, 2 vols. (Manchester: University of Manchester Press, 1925), vol. 1, pp. ix, vi, and vol. 2, chapter VI.

[15] John MacCunn, *Six Radical Thinkers: Bentham. J.S. Mill, Cobden, Carlyle, Mazzini, T.H. Green* (London: Edward Arnold, 1907), chapter V.

[16] Green quoted in *Memoir*, p. xlii.

[17] Mack, *Mazzini*, pp. 137–42.

therefore a necessity that their development be aided and promoted, and their exercise protected and free.'[18]

One of the core contentions of the 'School of Progressive Movement' with which Mazzini identified himself was that human beings are 'creatures capable of rational, social, intellectual progress *solely through the medium of association:* a progress to which none may assign a limit'.[19] Our common nature is as beings whom God created in 'resemblance' to Himself, beings that gradually come to manifest some but never all of the potentials of Humanity through their interactions with one another. Moreover, Mazzini understood the individual to be the vehicle for 'a providential law of progress and perfectibility' of Humanity.[20] Humans are driven by an inner 'law of existence, [which] urges every living being to the fuller development of all the germs, the faculties, the forces, the *life* within it'. 'Tradition', as the repository of the proven wisdom of the past, combines with the individual's thirst to achieve 'aims impossible of realisation within the limits of earthly existence'. When not hindered by external forces and harsh socio-economic conditions, this awakens the individual's 'innate' 'tendency to association' and her related respect for the '*duty* of self-sacrifice' in the interests of a collective entity, Humanity, whose life extends across generations.

Regarding the agents of this development, Alberto de Sanctis has highlighted Mazzini's attacks on Thomas Carlyle's hero-worship: 'Mazzini accused Carlyle of being unable to recognise that Humanity played a more important role than individuals [in human development]'.[21] Mazzini saw hero-worship as being 'entirely inconsistent with democracy'.[22] Human development requires the development of peoples organised as nations that are not merely unified and strong, but also self-governing. In fact, although de Sanctis does not claim this, Mazzini pushed his position so far that, in effect if not intention, he reduced individuals to mere parts of a collective whole. Hence he claimed in *The Duties of Man* (1860) that 'humanity is one sole being, and must be governed by one sole law', and 'only by entire humanity can the design of God be fully accomplished here below'.[23] Echoing both J.G. Fichte and Carlyle, Mazzini even went so far as to characterise human development as the advance of the 'Divine Idea' or God through

---

18 Joseph Mazzini, 'The Duties of Man', in his *Life and Writings,* ed. Emilie Ashurst, 6 vols., second edition (London: Smith, Elder, 1891), vol. 4, p. 307).

19 Mazzini, 'Duties', p. 259. Joseph Mazzini, 'On the History of the French Revolution, by Thomas Carlyle' [1843], in Ashurt, ed., *Life*, vol. 4, p. 130.

20 Mazzini, 'French Revolution', p. 131.

21 De Sanctis, *Puritan*, p. 31.

22 De Sanctis, *Puritan*, p. 31; see also *ibid.*, pp. 37–38.

23 Mazzini, 'Duties', 268.

Humanity.[24] Not only did Mazzini see Humanity as gradually manifesting God, but he claimed that this means the individual is valuable because he enables Humanity to do so, and *only* to the extent that he does so. He expressed the idea forcefully in 1843.

> 'We have begun to suspect, not only that there is upon the earth something greater, more holy, more divine than the individual—namely, Humanity—the collective being always living, learning, advancing toward God, of which we are but the instruments; but that it is alone from the summit of this collective idea, from the conception of the Universal Mind, "of which," as Emerson says, "each individual man is one more incarnation," that we can derive our mission, the rule of our life, the aim of our societies.'[25]

Along similar lines, in his 1867 *Lectures on the English Revolution* Green claimed that his then-self-professed Hegelian philosophy could recover the progressive spirit that animated England briefly during the Interregnum, and present that spirit 'cleared and ripened' as a guide for political agitation.[26] In this way, the British nation, Europe and ultimately all Humanity could progress. On the face of it at least, Green's 1866 position accorded with that of Mazzini, even if Mazzini himself did not invoke Hegel. Yet, the type of philosophy that Green used to conceptualise the 'national spirit' changed significantly over the course of his life, and his mature position differs markedly from that of Mazzini in certain crucial respects. By 1881, Green had reached a critical but still respectful distance from Hegel, arguing that one should seek to achieve much the same end as Hegel but without being tied dogmatically to Hegel's dialectical method.[27] This shift in Green's position is reflected in the fact that while he seems to continue to admire Mazzini, at least from the late 1870s onwards Green is careful to reject the conception of a spirit of Humanity or the nation existing over and above the lives of individuals.

---

[24] Mazzini, 'Duties', 230, 260, 286. 'Humanity is the Word, living in God. The Spirit of God fecundates it, and manifests itself through it, in greater purity and activity from epoch to epoch, now through the instrumentality of an individual, now through that of a people.'/ 'From labour to labour, from belief to belief, Humanity gradually acquires a clearer perception of its own life, of its own mission, of its God, and of His law.' /'Humanity is the *successive* incarnation of God.' Mazzini, 'Duties', 25.

[25] Mazzini, 'On the Genius and Tendency of the Writings of Thomas Carlyle' (first published in October 1843], in Ashurst, ed., *Life*, col. 4, pp. 73–74.

[26] 'English Revolution' (GW 3:364). Green characterised his own philosophy explicitly as Hegelian in a letter to James Bryce, 23 March 1866 (GW 5:418).

[27] IPR 138–43. On Green as a reconciler of Kant and Aristotle, see David G. Ritchie, *The Principles of State Interference: Four essays on the political philosophy of Mr. Herbert Spencer, J.S. Mill, and T.H. Green*, third edition (London: Swan Sonnenschein, 1902), pp. 139–40.

The key themes of Green's mature attitude to progress should be familiar from the preceding chapters of this book. Possibly thinking of Mazzini's claim that 'Strictly speaking, you cannot… separate your life from that of humanity. You live in it, by it, and for it',[28] Green argues at length in the *Prolegomena* that 'there can be nothing in a nation however exalted its mission, or in a society however perfectly organised, which is not in the persons composing the nation or the society. Our ultimate standard of worth is an ideal of *personal* worth. All other values are relative to value for, of, or in a person'.[29] A few pages later Green develops this claim in the following way.

> '[W]hatever moral capacity must be presupposed [to exist in individuals], it is only actualised through the habits, institutions, and laws in virtue of which the individuals form a nation. But it is none the less true that the life of the nation has no real existence except as the life of the individuals composing the nation, a life determined by their intercourse with each other, and deriving its peculiar features from the conditions of that intercourse… Since it is only through its existence as our self-consciousness that we know anything of spirit at all, to hold that a spirit can exist except as a self-conscious subject is self-contradictory. A "national spirit" is not something in the air.'[30]

The national spirit still exists for the mature Green, but only in the fluid and multifaceted character that is generated by the similarly fluid and multifaceted daily interactions of all its individual members. Bearing in mind the analysis of Green's mature relational social ontology presented in chapters two and three, it is clear that his mature position differed in crucial respects from Mazzini's holistic organicism. Moreover, as W.J. Mander acknowledges, Green's position 'would seem to rule out any understanding of the Absolute or eternal consciousness as something in which finite minds are lost or absorbed'.[31]

Mazzini was not the only writer whom Green both admired greatly in some areas, but whose theory of progress he came to reject. In his 1784 article *The Idea for a Universal History with a Cosmopolitan Purpose*, Kant attempts to reinforce his ethics by appealing to certain controversial progressivist claims. Specifically, he argues that a belief in the moral freedom of the rational agent who is integrated into a kingdom of ends has become more widely and forcefully held in civilised societies. Kant sees a dual aspect to this phenomenon. On the one hand, he argues that, as an event in the phenomenal world, the progress of humanity should be understood as

---

28 Mazzini, 'Duties', 269.
29 PE 184.
30 PE 185.
31 W.J. Mander, *British Idealism: A history* (Oxford: Oxford University Press, 2011), p. 208. But see MSF chapter four.

being 'determined in accordance with natural laws'.[32] On the other, the belief that humanity is not subject to the 'rule of blind chance' is a noble myth, the widespread belief in which helps to prevent human relationships from descending into 'a hell of evils'.[33]

Green's mature attitude to this aspect of Kant's ethics extends his reaction to Mazzini. He rejects Kant's contentions, firstly, that it is meaningful to claim that humanity can progress as a corporate entity, and, secondly, that any progress that does occur should be viewed as being a consequence of the operation of 'natural laws'.[34] Nevertheless, Green points out that, as the kingdom of ends is founded upon the imperatives of reason and as reason must be present in even the most underdeveloped form of society, every social group contains the seeds of the Kantian ideal.

> 'If we are right in ascribing to Reason a function of union in the life that we know; if we are right in holding that through it we are conscious of ourselves, and of others as ourselves, — through it accordingly that we can seek to make the best of ourselves and of others with ourselves, and that in this sense Reason is the basis of society, because the source at once of the establishment of equal practical rules in a common interest, and of self-imposed subjection to those rules; then we are entitled to hold that Reason fulfilled a function intrinsically the same in the most primitive associations of man with man, between which and the actual institutions of family and commune, of state and nation, there has been any continuity of development.'[35]

As was noted at the beginning of this chapter, by the late 1870s this development has reached such a point in civilised societies that, echoing Kant once again, Green describes the belief in fundamental human equality as 'almost an axiom of popular Ethics': 'when we are free from private bias, we do not seriously dispute its validity.'[36] All sane adults in modern societies are recognised as having valid claims to possess the same basic rights.[37] For example, normally the individual's 'free enjoyment and disposal of the fruits of his labour, is guaranteed to every one, on condition of his respecting the like freedom in others'.[38]

Green's optimism regarding the degree of respect paid to this principle in his society may seem strange given his acute sensitivity to the severe problems faced in his own society, an awareness evidenced by his extensive work

---

[32]   Immanuel Kant, 'The Idea for a Universal History with a Cosmopolitan Purpose', in his *Political Writings*, ed. Hans Reiss, second edition (Cambridge: Cambridge University Press, 1991), p. 41.

[33]   Kant, 'Universal History', 48.

[34]   PE 202–05.

[35]   PE 204. Compare W.G. de Burgh, *From Morality to Religion* (London: MacDonald and Evans, 1908), p. 273.

[36]   PE 206.

[37]   PE 280.

[38]   PE 210.

to improve the lives of the disadvantaged (see, for example, §3.VI and chapter ten below).[39] Indeed, Green is clear that, no matter how strong the hold exerted by the principle as an idea, there is a long way to go until he and his fellow citizens live up to the ideal in practice. Nevertheless, still Green insists that, as an empirical fact, the claim that all humans should be accorded the same basic respect is embedded within the 'higher moral culture of Christendom', as the latter is instantiated in the 'conscience of those citizens of the modern world who are most responsive to the higher influences of their time'.[40] In the mid-Victorian age, he argues, respect for the idea if for not the practice of the fundamental moral equality of all human beings is overridden generally only in times of war. More than this, Green believes that, over time, the conscientious citizen is tending to move towards a more adequate practical recognition of the true good.[41] This process of development has entailed a gradual widening of the group of people whom the individual understands to be her fellows and hence a widening of that group 'towards whom and between whom accordingly obligations are understood to exist'.[42] Consequently, he believes that the development of a broadly-shared conception of the true good has led to the development of a broadly-shared conception of the common good as well.

Such passages have led some scholars to describe even the mature Green as presenting an evolutionary theory of ethics.[43] Yet, that characterisation is misleading. Green does not define the moral ideal as the end which necess-arily is gaining wider acceptance, as Thakurdas alleges.[44] Paul Harris and Richard Bellamy are correct to reject the claim of Lewis and others, that Green sees progress as inevitable, a claim that has led some critics to accuse him an 'incurable optimism' that reflects a cultural prejudice of his time.[45]

---

[39] Olive Anderson, 'The Feminism of T.H. Green: A late Victorian success story?', *History of Political Thought*, 12:4 (1991), 671–93; PE 263.

[40] PE 354, 207, 210.

[41] See John H. Muirhead, *The Service of the State: Four lectures on the political teaching of T.H. Green* (London: John Murray, 1908), pp. 68–74; Mark Bevir, 'Welfarism, Socialism and Religion: On T.H. Green and others', *Review of Politics*, 55 (1993), 655–57.

[42] PE 206; 206–17.

[43] Frank Thakurdas, *The English Utilitarians and the Idealists: An introductory study to the development of English political theory in the eighteenth and nineteenth centuries* (Delhi: Vishal, 1978), for example, p. 222.

[44] Compare John R. Rodman, 'Introduction', in John Rodman, ed., *The Political Theory of T.H. Green: Selected writings* (New York: Appleton-Century-Crofts, 1964), pp. 10–11.

[45] Paul Harris, 'Moral Progress and Politics: The theory of T.H. Green', *Polity*, 21 (1988–89), 559–60; Richard Bellamy, 'T.H. Green and the Morality of Victorian Liberalism', in Richard Bellamy, ed., *Victorian Liberalism: Nineteenth century political thought and practice* (London: Routledge, 1990), p. 136; H.D. Lewis, 'Does

Certainly, in a speech of 1877 Green did claim that '*society by an inevitable process* was becoming more and more democratic, and in the future he thought the question whether it should be a healthy democracy depended upon whether they could cure the people of the national habit of drunkenness'.[46] Yet, in reality this passage lends little support to those who claim that Green regarded human development as inevitable. Firstly, Green sees only 'democracy' as 'inevitable'; 'healthy democracy' is not. His point is only that more sections of the population are being enfranchised, something that, in itself, says nothing about how thoughtfully they will use the vote. Secondly, Green's claim regarding the widening of the franchise relates specifically to the direction of political change in Britain in the late-1870s, following the 1867 Reform Act.[47] It says nothing about the 'metaphysical' inevitability of that trend, nor indeed its strength.

Similarly, Green's discussion in the *Prolegomena* of the growth of the area of the common good offers no solid evidence that he holds human progress to be inevitable, and neither does his related analysis of the relative worth of Greek and modern virtues.[48] Instead, his discussion is thoroughly Aristotelian: 'if habit is strengthened by exercise', then, in fact, greater social inclusion will tend to lend greater impetus to human development.[49] Even

---

the Good Will Define its Own Content?—a study of T.H. Green's *Prolegomena to Ethics*', in his *Freedom and History* (London: George Allen and Unwin, 1962), pp. 36–41; H.D. Lewis, 'Individualism and Collectivism—a study of T.H. Green', in his *Freedom and History*, p. 84. Also, see John H. Hallowell, *Main Currents in Modern Political Thought* (New York: Holt, Reinhart and Winston, 1950), p. 282; S.I. Benn and R.S. Peters, *Social Principles and the Democratic State* (London: George Allen and Unwin, 1959), p. 60; Melvin Richter, *The Politics of Conscience: T.H. Green and his age* (London: Weidenfeld and Nicolson, 1964), pp. 114, 253, 262; Dante Germino, *Machiavelli to Marx: Modern western political thought* (Chicago and London: University of Chicago Press, 1972), p. 272; James T. Kloppenberg, *Uncertain Victory: Social democracy and progressivism in European and American thought, 1870–1920* (New York and Oxford: Oxford University Press, 1986), p. 32. 'Incurable optimism': Kenneth R. Hoover, 'Liberalism and the Idealist Philosophy of Thomas Hill Green', *Western Political Quarterly*, 26 (1973), 556, 564–65; Mark Bevir, *The Making of British Socialism* (Princeton and Oxford: Princeton University Press, 2011), pp. 224–33 *passim*.

[46] Speech to the Church of England Temperance Society, Merton College, Oxford, 30 October 1877, reported in *Oxford Chronicle*, 3rd November 1877 (GW 5:305, emphasis added).

[47] See Colin Tyler, *Idealist Political Philosophy: Pluralism and conflict in the absolute idealist tradition* (London and New York: Continuum, 2006), chapter 2. It was a political tide that led to the 1884 Representation of the People Act and eventually the widening of the franchise to women, citizens between 18 years old and 21 years old, and so on.

[48] PE 206–18 *passim*, 246–90 *passim*.

[49] PE 208.

when read in conjunction with his 1877 remarks regarding the franchise and his acknowledgement in the *Prolegomena* of the increasing egalitarianism of British society, it remains the case that constitutions are always liable to change and, where they are not treated with care, they may well degenerate.[50]

Does Green's lack of a theory of progress harm his ethics and social theory? Kenneth R. Hoover has argued that the 'assumption of automatic progress is essential to Green's idealism, but not to the defense of liberal values. The potential for progress rather than the historical reality of progress is the crucial point in the justification of liberal values'.[51] The last point may be true as long as by the 'potential for progress' is meant that liberalism must possess an attainable standard of conduct for it to be a viable moral and political theory. Yet, to the extent that Hoover's first assertion is intelligible at all, it simply does not hold water. There is no plausible reason why 'automatic progress' must be assumed if Green is to have a viable idealist philosophy. Rejecting the inevitability of, or even the mere tendency for, moral progress simply moves him closer to Aristotle and away from Hegel, in the sense that it means cultures can become better *or* worse over time rather than always tending to progress. Consequently, progress is something we must work for and not wait for (see chapters four and eight).[52] This gives another reason for characterizing Green as an 'English Aristotle' rather than an English Kant or an English Hegel.[53]

III

Spiritual Determinism and Human Development

There is another reason for Green to be sceptical about the claim that human progress is inevitable. If one adopts what is nowadays the most widely-endorsed, self-interventionist reading of Green's theory of the will, ultim-

---

[50]   Compare Aristotle, *Politics*, Books V and VI *passim*.

[51]   Hoover, 'Liberalism', 564–65.

[52]   See also the quotation from T.H. Green, public meeting of the Oxford Reform Club, 25 March 1867 (GW 5:227), which appears as one of the epigraphs at the start of the book.

[53]   John MacCunn, *Six Radical Thinkers: Bentham, J.S. Mill, Cobden, Carlyle, Mazzini, and T.H. Green* (London: Edward Arnold, 1907), p. 253; the phrase recurs in Amal Mukhopadhyay, *The Ethics of Obedience: A study of the philosophy of T.H. Green* (Calcutta: World Press Private, 1967), p. 196; see Nettleship, 'Memoir', lxx–lxxii *passim*. On Kant, Fichte and Hegel's respective theories of History, see Tyler, *Idealist Political Philosophy*, pp. 6–16. Mander's interpretation presents Green as being far more mystical (Mander, *British Idealism*, pp. 199–201). Mander's Green believes that human societies progress due to the agency of the eternal consciousness. For the root of my profound disagreement with Mander here, see MSF chapter four.

ately human progress must be the result of individual choices. Yet, there is no good reason to believe that a person who can act voluntarily will necessarily tend to choose a path of progress. Wrong actions and regression are just as likely. It was established in MSF §5.II that, at times, Green operates with a different, non-voluntaristic theory of the will. In these moods, Green rejects the idea that an agent can be drawn in one direction by 'a calm, still voice', and in another by her irrational animality. Instead, he argues that positing the existence of such a dualism fundamentally misunderstands the nature of distinctively human agency. The crucial assumption of the dualist position is that the rationally-guided will is essentially separable from the agent's desires. This assumption underlies the determinist/indeterminist debate, and Green believes that it is this point which makes the whole debate futile. Characterising the will as 'merely the strongest desire' neglects the necessity of the action of the individual's consciousness of the desires that she experiences.[54] As Green writes, it masks the 'self-distinguishing and self-realising consciousness, through which, as a transforming medium, these influences must pass before they can take effect in a moral action at all'.[55] It is in this way that the agent's will is fundamentally an expression of her consciousness as it acts automatically in the circumstances it faces, and, ultimately, it creates.[56] Bernard Bosanquet expresses this thought very clearly when he writes that 'In short, then, all logical activity is a world of content reshaping itself by its own spirit and laws in presence of new suggestions'.[57] Green's support for such a view underlies his assertion that

> '[t]he idea of the good... is an idea, if the expression may be allowed, which gradually creates its own filling... Acting in us, to begin with, as a demand which is ignorant of what will satisfy itself, it only arrives at a more definite consciousness of its own nature and tendency through reflection on its own creations—on habits and institutions and modes of life which, as a demand not reflected upon, it has brought into being.'[58]

Yet, if the individual cannot consciously choose how to act (as the spiritual determinist line entails), how does she come to express her conception of her highest nature through her will? The answer is that the agent's knowledge of the world 'activates' the desires which are inherent in her otherwise abstract human nature. Consequently, the development of an individual's consciousness is the progressive actualisation of her conception of her highest capacities. It is the progressive activating of the spiritual desires which

---

[54] PE 145.

[55] PE 145.

[56] For example, PE 303, 311; PPO 131, 165.

[57] Bernard Bosanquet, *The Principle of Individuality and Value* (London: MacMillan, 1912), p. 333.

[58] PE 241.

manifests her otherwise abstract but abiding human nature through her practice. Consider the following case. An agent tries to understand the world as it is presented to her, for example using current scientific, religious, and moral theories. This is an act of intellect. In that these theories are never completely coherent—either they never manage to fully explain the agent's observations of the world, or they fail to do so without contradicting another part of the theory—the agent feels them to be unsatisfactory. She wishes to alter the theory in order to avoid such incoherences. This wish is a non-voluntary response and it tends to be progressive (in Green's eyes at least).

Turning to the normative realm next. For Green, the fully self-realised agent would recognise herself as desiring a collection of objects which are interrelated in such a way that she conceives each particular desire to be part of a totally coherent system of desires and motives which express her high-est human capacities.[59] The agent improves to the extent that she 'unites successive wants in the idea of a general need for which provision is to be made, and holds together the successive wants and fillings as the connected but distinct incidents of an inner life'.[60] For the agent to possess a coherent view of the world then, she must recognise its inseparability from the action of her consciousness. Furthermore, she must recognise that 'we only find unity in the world because we have an idea that it is there, an idea which we direct our powers to realise'.[61]

The key point in the present context is that, for Green, individuals feel a need to understand the world as a coherent environment in which to live, and it is a central contention of the spiritual determinist line that they con-struct its coherence through a non-conscious act of will and, therefore, intell-ect. As long as the agent recognises that the objects in which habitually she seeks her self-satisfaction do not bring her lasting satisfaction, she has the possibility of regret and, hence, self-improvement. This dual process brings to her 'both the inchoate impulse to realise the conception [of being better], and the possibility of its realisation'.[62] Again, reform is not sought volun-tarily but arises out of an impulse of the individual which is an expression of her nature rather than a consequence of her voluntary choice. A belief in the tendency of humanity to progress is no more secure if one adopts the spirit-ual determinist rather than the self-interventionist line. The problem is that, in both cases, 'as one fragment of the truth is grasped, another has escaped us'.[63] Green would have no sound philosophical reason for believing that

---

59   PE 85.
60   PE 90.
61   PE 149.
62   PE 110.
63   IPR 145.

progress is inevitable. It is just as well, then, that he does not believe it to be so.

IV

How Useful is Green's Criterion of Development?

Even if Green does not believe progress to be inevitable, he does believe that it has occurred since the time of the Greeks. Paul Harris has objected to even this limited and commonly-made claim.[64] Harris asks,

> 'If the moral quality of an action depends on the conscious motive from which it was done and if we can never really know the motives of others' actions, how then can we say that one person's action is morally better or worse than another's? And if we cannot make that kind of judgement, how can we tell whether or not there has been moral progress of the large-scale kind that concerns Green?'[65]

Harris argues that the structure of Green's theory of the will precludes him from ever having a reasonable assurance of any other agent's true motives.[66] As a result, we must judge an action's worth by assessing the worth of its consequences. Yet, the worth of these consequences is determined solely by the act's tendency to promote actions which proceed from a better will. Harris's first objection reappears. He concludes that, in order to assess the worth of an agent's motives, 'It may be that we are reduced to intuition and self-reflection, but they hardly seem adequate bases for these judgements'.[67]

Yet, if Harris is arguing that one can never gain a reasonable idea of a person's motives (for example, not even in actual cases which we witness for ourselves), then his objection would be highly implausible. On the other hand, if he is arguing that the calculation is open to such a degree of error that one should not base a theory of large-scale historical progress upon it, then his attack is more telling. We cannot have the necessary intimate experience of those epochs in which we do not live our own daily lives, making it a lot harder, if not simply impossible, to assess whether or not individuals' wills coincide with the claims of their highest nature more now than they did in earlier ages. Indeed, Green himself uses this criticism against over-ambitious historians in his *Lectures on the Principles of Political Obligation*.[68] In fact, the question of the virtue of agents now relative to those of the past has

---

[64] Paul Harris, 'Moral Progress and Politics: The theory of T.H. Green', *Polity*, 21 (1988–89), 558–59; also made by Jerome B. Schneewind, *Sidgwick's Ethics and Victorian Moral Philosophy* (Oxford: Clarendon Press, 1977), p. 411.

[65] Harris, 'Moral Progress', 558.

[66] Harris, 'Moral Progress', 559.

[67] Harris, 'Moral Progress', 559.

[68] PPO 111–12.

significant implications for neither Green's wider philosophical system, nor the political theory that he builds upon it.

Yet, Harris' objection rests on a misunderstanding of Green's central point. Green himself accepts that 'according to his lights the [ancient] Greek might be as conscientious as any of us [moderns]'.[69] He argues that progress is not measured by purer or stronger moral motives, but by the general increase of the range of the agent's morally-relevant community and in the growth of a clearer conception of her duties. Green seems to hold that, as an empirical fact, the 'acceptance of humanitarian ideas' (that is, the acknowledgement of the equal moral worth of each individual, irrespective of her 'race or religion or [social] status') to be a 'natural fulfilment of a capability given in reason itself'.[70] He claims also that human nature draws the individual to realise that capability in her own personality and daily life.

Harris does acknowledge that Green believes progress occurs through the development of social institutions: that is, through the gradual extension of the area of the true and common good as well as through its better articulation in social practices and expectations. Yet, Harris objects that, on Green's own account, it is not enough for individuals to perform an action which merely coincides with the outward act required by duty. Action is worthy to the extent that it is performed consciously for the duty's sake. He concludes that 'Green's argument is plainly unsatisfactory', as what should be important is the actual and not the potential motive: the agent's actual, and not merely his potential, motive of acting for duty's sake.[71] The former may be implicit in the latter, but merely being implicit in this sense is not sufficient to make an action truly valuable. Nonetheless, Green need only assume that all other things are equal: namely, that agents alive today are just as dutiful as those who were raised in previous epochs. Granting that seemingly uncontroversial assumption, there is still moral progress if

---

69   PE 206.

70   PE 209, 207; see further PE 186–87. 'The whole moral life is, in fact, a process in which, though it be sometimes like a stream that seems to run backward, man, as an unrealised self, is constantly fusing the skirts of the alien matter that surrounds him, and fashioning the world of his desires to a universe adequate to himself. / To the individual man, no doubt, the absoluteness of his limitations never wholly vanishes. The dream that it can do so is the frenzy of philosophy' ('Aristotle' 86). Or again, '[The development of] our actual knowledge remains a piecemeal process. We spell out the relations of things one by one; we pass from condition to condition, from effect to effect; but, as one fragment of the truth is grasped, another has escaped us, and we never reach that totality of apprehension through which alone we could know the world as it is and God in it. This is the infirmity of our discursive understanding. If in one sense it reveals God, in another it hides him.' (IPR 145)

71   Harris, 'Moral Progress', 559.

societies have come to be based on a more inclusive conception of the moral community and a more refined scheme of rights, duties and obligations.

The final point to be made has been noted repeatedly both in MSF and above. Green is emphatic that none of us can ever be actually what we are potentially. We can only ever be a partial instantiation of human nature. Moreover, he accepts that the drive to improve is a tendency which 'special selfish interests can withstand'.[72] It appears that the individual's tendency to progress is a 'natural' feature of human life in a sense related to that in which certain rights are 'natural': that is, it is the individual's 'vocation' — her calling—to develop. Even so, this does not mean that development is inevitable, because the animal elements of the individual's existence in the world constantly hinder human development.[73] Indeed, it has been acknowledged already (§5.III) that in principle this hindrance can be so severe as to cause degeneration among individuals and the societies they constitute.

V

Conclusion

This short chapter has shown (in §5.II) that Green's mature theory of progress differed from the position he had held in the mid-1860s, and countered the claim that Green believed progress was inevitable. §III established that his beliefs regarding the likelihood of progress are the same whether one interprets him as holding a spiritual determinist theory of the will or a self-interventionist theory. §IV argued that Green's core criterion of development does not relate to the question of whether modern agents tend to be more motivated than ancient ones to act out of reverence for the moral law. Green assumes that there has been little or no change in that regard. Rather he considers the content of their respective conceptions of virtue and right action. As such, Green employs a perfectly serviceable core criterion of development.

Even though Green does not believe long-term progress to be inevitable, he does believe that an individual's drive to develop will tend to become stronger as she constructs increasingly concrete and coherent conceptions of her highest nature and of the attractions of attaining its enduring satisfaction. In this way, the individual's self-realisation is self-perpetuating: as she develops, her drive to seek what at least appears to be a better state becomes a more powerful 'moving influence' in her.[74] Her rejection of claims

---

72 PE 209.

73 Noël O'Sullivan, *The Problem of Political Obligation* (New York: Garland, 1987), pp. 138–39. Lancaster fails to realise that Green believes perfection must elude us (Lane W. Lancaster, *The Masters of Political Thought, Volume III, Hegel to Dewey* (London: George G. Harrap, 1959), pp. 225–26).

74 PE 180.

that duties spring from ideas of, for example, gender or social status, in favour of the idea of the obligation to all individuals as rational beings, acts as a spur to moral progress and frees the agent to realise her truly human potentials. Consequently: 'Faculties which social repression and separation prevent from development, take new life from the enlarged co-operation which the recognition of equal claims in all men brings with it'.[75] This belief has very significant civil and political implications, as will become evident in the following chapters.

---

75 PE 208. For example, see Green's speech to the Oxford Reform League, 25 March 1867, reported in *Oxford Chronicle and Berks and Bucks Gazette*, 30 March 1867 (GW 5:226–32); and his speech to the Loyal Wellington Lodge of Odd Fellows, 25 February 1868, reported in *Oxford Chronicle and Berks and Bucks Gazette*, 29 February 1868 (GW 5:232–36). This thought grounds Green's calls for the extension of the franchise.

6

Recognition, Rights, Duties and Obligations

'moral duties I always distinguish from legal obligations'[1]

I

Introduction

Green's *Lectures on the Principles of Political Obligation* has been variously received. Rex Martin describes it as 'perhaps the finest book in the philosophy of rights written to date'.[2] John Bowle argues that it offers 'the most valuable, closely reasoned, and practical case for Victorian humanism'.[3] On the other hand, Geoffrey Thomas characterises it 'as one attempt, not itself of privileged importance but rather partial and at times precarious, to draw out the political implications of an ethical theory'.[4] A.J. Ayer judged it to be a 'respectable but hardly an inspiring work'.[5] More fundamentally, Craig Smith once argued that the text is inherently confused and was probably corrupted by its original editor, R.L. Nettleship.[6] Even though Paul Harris and John Morrow established that the text has not been corrupted to any major extent, this did not alter the fact that, for many years, positive assessments of the *Principles,* of the type presented by Martin and Bowle, were in the minority.[7] Since the late-1990s however, this aspect of Green's works has

---

[1] PPO 1.

[2] Rex Martin, 'Green on Natural Rights in Hobbes, Spinoza and Locke', in Andrew Vincent, ed., *The Philosophy of T.H. Green* (Aldershot: Gower, 1986), p. 104.

[3] John Bowle, *Politics and Opinion in the Nineteenth Century: An historical introduction* (Oxford: Arden, 1954), p. 275.

[4] Geoffrey Thomas, *The Moral Philosophy of T.H. Green* (Oxford: Clarendon Press, 1987), p. 363.

[5] Alfred J. Ayer, *Metaphysics and Common Sense* (London: MacMillan, 1969), p. 240.

[6] Craig A. Smith, 'The Individual and Society in T.H. Green's Theory of Virtue', *History of Political Thought*, 2:1 (1981), 187–201.

[7] Paul Harris and John Morrow, 'Did Nettleship Corrupt Green's Lectures? A comment on Smith', *History of Political Thought*, 4:3 (1985), 643–46; see also Ben Wempe, *T.H. Green's Theory of Positive Freedom: From metaphysics to positive freedom*

received increasingly favourable notice. In addition to Martin's continued work in this area, David Boucher, Derrick Darby, Gerald Gaus, Avital Simhony and others have urged readers to return to Green's theory of rights in particular.[8]

This chapter analyses the general principles of Green's philosophy of rights. Particular attention is paid to his theory of recognition and the role which it plays in the ontology of moral rights and duties. §II examines preliminary matters, including Green's distinction between moral rights and duties on the one hand, and legal rights and obligations on the other, before turning to his critique of the natural rights tradition. §III compares Green's theory of community, rights and recognition with that of Johann G. Fichte, before §IV attempts to resolve some of the main confusions that one finds in the secondary literature on Green's theory of recognition. §V establishes that the structure of Green's theory necessarily precludes the environment, animals and the severely mentally disabled from possessing intrinsic moral rights. §VI takes seriously Green's claim that 'every theory of rights in detail' requires 'a corresponding theory of punishment in detail'.[9] §VII summarises the chapter, as a bridge to the analysis of Green's theory of the state which is developed in chapter seven.

A number of caveats are in order before beginning the reconstruction and analysis of Green's theory of rights. Firstly, this chapter and the two following it are premised almost exclusively upon the self-interventionist strands of Green's writings on the will, which he presupposes throughout his political writings. Only in §8.V is this presupposition questioned, with an analysis of the implications for Green's political philosophy of adopting the spiritual determinist theory of the will. Secondly, it will be seen in the course of this chapter that between Green's ethical and his political philosophy, 'the

---

(Exeter and Charlottesville, VA: Imprint Academic, 2004), p. 129; Peter P. Nicholson, 'A Moral View of Politics: T.H. Green and the British idealists', *Political Studies*, 35 (1987), 116–17.

8   For example, Rex Martin, 'T.H. Green on individual rights and the common good', in Avital Simhony and David Weinstein, eds., *The New Liberalism: Reconciling liberty and community* (Cambridge: Cambridge University Press, 2001), pp. 49–68; Timothy Hinton, 'The Perfectionist Liberalism of T.H. Green', *Social Theory and Practice*, 27:3 (July 2001), 473–99; David Boucher, *The Limits of Ethics in International Relations: Natural law, natural rights, and human rights in transition* (Oxford: Oxford University Press, 2009), pp. 223–44 *passim*; Gerald Gaus, 'The Rights Recognition Thesis: Defending and extending Green', in Maria Dimova-Cookson and W.J. Mander, eds., *T.H. Green: Ethics, metaphysics and political philosophy* (Oxford: Clarendon Press, 2006), pp. 209–235; Avital Simhony, 'Rights that Bind: T.H. Green on rights and community', in Dimova-Cookson *et al.*, eds., *T.H. Green*, pp. 236–61; see Derrick Darby, *Rights, Race, and Recognition* (Cambridge: Cambridge University Press, 2009), pp. 142–68.

9   PPO 177.

distinction was rather one of form and method than of matter and substance'.[10] At the same time, there is great deal of truth in Nettleship's observation that 'the lectures on *The principles of political obligation* form in some degree an illustrative commentary on the *Prolegomena to ethics*'.[11] Indeed, Green gave them as parts of a single cycle of professorial lectures. Now the discussion can begin with an examination of the formal structures of rights, duties and obligations.

II

Preliminaries: Moral Duties, Legal Obligations and the Natural Rights Tradition

Green's theory of the public and political spheres presupposes his theory of 'distinctively human action'. As was outlined in MSF chapter five, Green understands the latter to be that type of action which expresses the higher nature of man. Ultimately, this higher nature is only manifest in the world in individual personalities. Importantly, Green has established that expression of this nature and its links to the animal form of human life relies upon the existence of a sympathetic context for action. In the social sphere, such a context is framed by deep attachments to institutions such as the family, civil associations and political movements.[12] These claims have significant implications for Green's public philosophy. In particular, they are fundamental to his theory of rights, duties and obligations and to his theory of the state. It is to the first of these—the theory of rights, duties and obligations—that the discussion must turn now.

Contemporary philosophical analyses tend to focus upon the normative status and grounding of rights rather than upon the conditions of their existence. Viewed from this contemporary perspective, Green's theory of rights is bound to appear strange, if not fundamentally confused. Green holds rights as such to be social categories, and argues that rights are valid to the extent that they are underpinned by morally-valid claims. In other words, he conceives of rights as such to be 'institutions of civil life' which are created and maintained in the actual practices of the members of society, and which reflect the ways in which members 'generally' view one another.[13] Green uses the term 'rights' to refer to particular titles held by members of particular categories of agents either to act in certain ways without interference from other agents, or to secure positive behaviour from other agents or institutions. He holds that rights exist to the extent that the members of the

---

10 F.C. Conybeare, 'On Professor Green's Political Philosophy', *National Review*, 13 (1889), 773.

11 Nettleship, 'Memoir', cxlix.

12 PPO 25.

13 PPO 8, 2.

society under consideration habitually structure their patterns of action in light of the perceived authority of these titles. In this sense, rights are created, structured and sustained by their practical 'acknowledgement' by members of the relevant society, or as Green also puts, by 'social recognition' (or synonymously, social 'acknowledgement').[14] Recognition is significant for Green because he holds that rights and their associated claims on others are 'real' (or 'exist') only to the extent that they motivate the individual to act in accordance with them. Problems arise when scholars assume that rights require legal enforcement: that they motivate the individual in the correct way and to the correct degree only to the extent that an external agency (such as the agents of the legal and penal systems) enforce them over members of society.[15] In reality, there is no necessary or uniform link between a right's motivating force and legal enforcement of it. In fact, as will become clear below, Green is acutely conscious that external enforcement tends to reduce the likelihood that the most fundamental rights and duties will motivate the individual in an appropriate manner and to an appropriate degree.

Consequently, in his *Lectures on the Principles of Political Obligation*, Green draws a sharp conceptual distinction between a 'duty' and an 'obligation'.[16] The former is a moral imperative and therefore refers necessarily to the agent's motivation for action, whereas ultimately the latter relies on the fear of punishment and makes no essential reference to the quality of the agent's motivation, merely requiring the performance of certain patterns of behaviour (not killing someone, for example, or paying one's taxes).[17] Conceptually if not always in practice, the latter can be enforced through legal sanctions whereas the former cannot. One cannot have an obligation to perform one's duty because that would require the agent to force himself to

---

14 On 'acknowledgement', see for example PPO 107, 143, 201; on 'social recognition', see PPO 139, 142, 144, 145, 176, 214, 235.

15 For example, Thom Brooks, 'T.H. Green's Theory of Punishment', *History of Political Thought*, 24:4 (Winter 2003), 685–701 *passim*.

16 For interesting and concise discussions of this distinction see Conybeare, 'On Professor Green's Political Philosophy', 776–77; A.J.M. Milne, *The Social Philosophy of English Idealism* (London: Allen and Unwin, 1962), pp. 125–27; Paul Harris, 'Green's Theory of Political Obligation and Obedience', in Vincent, ed., *The Philosophy of T.H. Green*, pp. 128–29 and Wempe, *Positive Freedom,* p. 46. Green is adopting a distinction which — with various differences of terminology — is used by many other philosophers. For example, see John Locke, *A Letter Concerning Toleration*, ed. John Horton and Susan Mendus (London and New York: Routledge, 1991), pp. 18–19; Benedict de Spinoza, 'Tractatus Theologico-Politicus', in his *Political Writings*, ed. A.G. Wernham (Oxford: Clarendon, 1958), chapter XVI; Immanuel Kant, *The Metaphysics of Morals*, trans. Mary Gregor (Cambridge: Cambridge University Press, 1991), pp. 218–21.

17 PPO 10.

act from a certain motive: that is, out of a sense of duty. In reality, all that can be enforced is the performance of 'external acts'.[18] These are deeds which are carried out intentionally (the agent wills to perform them) although not necessarily for the sake of duty. Such deeds are only the performance of 'certain motions of the bodily members which produce certain effects in the material world'.[19] For this reason, the law should not be concerned to produce acts which are carried out from the agent's sense of duty.[20] The most the law can hope to achieve is the occurrence of the same behaviour that is required by duty. As Green puts it, the law 'has nothing to do with the motive of the actions or omissions, on which, however, the moral value of them depends'.[21] Legal enforcement of behaviour is necessary in certain instances because it is better that some outward acts or omissions are performed out of fear of punishment rather than not being performed at all.[22] In this way, Green maintains a distinction between moral rights and duties on the one hand, and legal rights and obligations on the other.[23]

Green justifies reciprocal rights and duties on the contention that without living under such a system, the individual would face severe hindrances to her own eudaimonic and rational development: rights and duties 'arise out of, and are necessary for the fulfilment of, a moral capacity without which a man would not be a man'.[24] Yet, they are more than merely a 'negative' condition of man's self-perfection.[25] Without a system of rights and duties which corresponds to the conception of a common good with which members identify their own true well-being, there could be no society and, as has been established in the preceding chapters, without a society there can be no determinate persons.

> '[T]hat I may have a life which I can call my own, I must not only be conscious of myself and of ends which I present to myself as mine; I must be able to reckon on a certain freedom of action and acquisition for the attainment of those ends, and this can only be secured through common recognition of this

---

18 PPO 10.
19 PPO 13.
20 PPO 137.
21 PPO 13.
22 PPO 16.
23 Green's success in this regard was missed by Harold A. Prichard, *Moral Obligation: Essays and lectures* (Oxford: Clarendon Press, 1949), *passim* and Frank Thakurdas, *The English Utilitarians and the Idealists: An introductory study of the development of English political theory in the eighteenth and nineteenth centuries* (Delhi: Vishal, 1978), p. 31.
24 PPO 30.
25 PPO 103.

freedom on the part of each other by members of a society, as being for a common good.'[26]

Defined and predictable spaces must be secured for the performance of distinctively human actions by concrete individuals, otherwise those individuals could not develop personalities with which they can freely identify and pursue their own true goods. This justification logically entails that the most basic right which an individual can possess is the right to live a positively free life (see MSF §6.III; CS §§1.IV, 2.II).[27] Indeed, this is a precondition of all other rights in the sense that all other rights are of no use without the basic right to self-determination.[28]

Green's claim that the capacity for being determined to action by one's own conception of a common good is the basis of all rights forms the foundation of his attack on the 'natural rights' tradition of Spinoza, Hobbes and Locke.[29] His attack sheds significant light on his own positive position. For the social contract theorists he analyses, certain rights are possessed by every human being irrespective of the right-holder's cultural background, and are made known to her through her exercise of her non-culturally conditioned reason.[30] Consequently, the specifics of a person's upbringing fundamentally affect neither her rational understanding of these rights nor the legitimacy of her claim to hold them. Critics such as Prichard and Lancaster have claimed that Green rejects this approach because he holds that individuals have rights and obligations only at the state's behest.[31] Yet, it should be clear, especially given Green's moral theory, that this authoritarian reading must rest upon a very twisted interpretation of Green's text.[32]

---

[26] PPO 114.

[27] PPO 148–56.

[28] PPO 155.

[29] PPO 7–31 *passim*, 32–63, 113, 178–79, 214–16; see de Spinoza, 'Tractatus Theologico-Politicus', 125–43 *passim*; Thomas Hobbes, *Leviathan*, ed. Richard Tuck (Cambridge: Cambridge University Press, 1991), pp. 91–111; John Locke, 'Second Treatise', in his *Two Treatise of Government*, ed. Peter Laslett (Cambridge: Cambridge University Press, 1988), §§4–15; see also Milne, *Social Philosophy*, pp. 127–33 *passim*; Amal K. Mukhopadhyay, *The Ethics of Obedience: A study of the philosophy of T.H. Green* (Calcutta: World Private, 1967), pp. 83–87; Ann R. Cacoullos, *Thomas Hill Green: Philosopher of rights* (New York: Twayne, 1974), pp. 14–15; I.M. Greengarten, *Thomas Hill Green and the Development of Liberal-Democratic Thought* (Toronto: University of Toronto Press, 1981), pp. 52–55, 58–60; Martin, 'Green on Natural Rights'; Wempe, *T.H. Green's Theory of Positive Freedom* pp. 132–38 *passim*; Martin, 'T.H. Green on individual rights', pp. 51–57.

[30] PPO 113.

[31] Prichard, *Moral Obligation*, pp. 57–66; Lane W. Lancaster, *The Masters of Political Thought: Volume III, Hegel to Dewey* (London: George G. Harrap, 1959), *passim*.

[32] See Cacoullos, *Thomas Hill Green*, pp. 75–76 for another attack upon Prichard's reading.

He is explicit and emphatic that he rejects the natural rights tradition because he believes the latter fails to appreciate 'the development of society and of man through society'.[33] The natural rights tradition is fundamentally flawed because it assumes the concrete expressions of the higher capacities of the individual to be ultimately separable from her society and its norms. In this manner, the tradition neglects the situated nature of every human consciousness and life, something for which Green argues strongly throughout his writings. In this sense, natural rights theorists present a theory which leaves 'out of sight the process by which men have been clothed with rights and duties'.[34] This fundamental defect has serious implications. For one thing, it tends to lead natural rights theorists to extend rights, duties and obligations which have arisen in one setting into other very different settings too quickly, and without due care that these rights and so on are justified in the new settings. Green sees the root problem with the social contract tradition as lying in its neglect of the profound roles played by intersubjective recognition in the constitution of personal identity, rights and duties.[35] That Green avoids this problem in his own theory will become clearer in the remainder of this chapter. In this regard, while many scholars have noted, in general terms, that there are similarities between Green's theory of recognition and that of Johann G. Fichte, no one has explored the precise nature of these similarities and indeed differences.[36] The next section presents such an analysis (see also MSF §§2.III–IV *passim*).

III

Green and Fichte on Community, Rights and Recognition

Edward Caird observed that: 'the philosopher Fichte is said to have made a feast to celebrate the moment in which his child first said "I"; as if then the child had distinctively compassed the act of self-consciousness, and asserted his claim to the rank of an independent spiritual subject.'[37] To understand Fichte's political thought and Green's relationship to it, it is necessary to appreciate its roots in Fichte's transcendental idealism. For Fichte, Kant fails to appreciate the full implications of Kantianism: Kant fails to recognise that

---

[33] PPO 113.

[34] PPO 113.

[35] Rex Martin constructs his whole discussion of Green's theory of recognition along these lines in his 'T.H. Green on individual rights', 51–57.

[36] Paul Harris and John Morrow, 'Introduction', to T.H. Green, *Lectures on the Principles of Political Obligation, and other writings*, ed. Paul Harris and John Morrow (Cambridge: Cambridge University Press, 1986), pp. 2, 7–8. Thom Brooks, Review of Colin Tyler, *Thomas Hill Green (1836–1882)... Bulletin of the Hegel Society of Great Britain*, nos. 51–52 (2005), 143.

[37] Edward Caird, *The Evolution of Religion*, 2 vols. (Glasgow: James MacLehose, 1899 [1893]), vol. 1, pp. 177–78.

critical philosophy demonstrates the inherently 'self-positing' nature of the individual's 'ego' or 'I'. Fichte himself starts from Kant's claim that human beings possess knowledge, not mere belief. He endorses Kant's conclusion that transcendental analysis establishes that each mind interprets and organises sense-data for itself, making each one active in constructing its experiences and hence its world. For Fichte, a crucial implication of this activity is that in examining the elements of these experienced worlds, the individual examines experiences that are underpinned by the mind's own 'intellectual intuitions'.[38] Consequently, even when the individual considers her own existence, she can only examine the mind's experiences of itself as an 'active' being.[39] Ultimately, this means that she can never know any 'substratum' that might underpin this power of acting.[40] Instead, each individual mind can conceive itself only as the particular being that has posited, through its 'intellectual intuitions', its particular concrete self and particular concrete world.[41]

Entailed in the act of self-positing is the positing of an object or another consciousness which gives meaning to one's own identity by way of contrast.[42] In this manner, the I and the non-I are mutually defining. The individual's interpretation of the structure of that concrete reciprocal relation determines the concrete identities of the participants: hence the agent is an I because of and in the ways that she understands herself to be recognised by a Thou. Her concrete self-conceptions and social worlds result from these various, concrete, multifaceted and ongoing acts of self-positing and recognition.

As was shown at length in chapter two, Green develops precisely the same argument in the *Prolegomena*. He insists on the mind's creation of its own 'worlds' 'of experience' and 'of practice' (MSF chapter three).[43] He argues that the concept of 'reality' only has meaning when understood as knowledge 'for us',[44] and denies the possibility of making meaningful statements regarding an undetermined 'Ego or self', understood as something existing in 'abstraction from the facts of our inner experience'.[45] He emphasises thought's relational structure, and the associated claim that: 'some

38 Terry Pinkard, *German Philosophy, 1760 to 1860: The legacy of idealism* (Cambridge: Cambridge University Press, 2002), pp. 109–12.

39 Johann G. Fichte, *The System of Ethics*, trans. Daniel Breazeale and Guenter Zöller (Cambridge: Cambridge University Press, 2005), pp. 7–17.

40 Johann G. Fichte, *Foundations of Natural Right*, ed. F. Neuhouser, trans. M. Baur (Cambridge: Cambridge University Press, 2000), p. 1n; Fichte, *Ethics*, pp. 34–41.

41 Fichte, *Right*, pp. 1–3.

42 Fichte, *Right*, pp. 4–6.

43 PE 10, 38–45 *passim*, 49–51, 55–56, 64, 76, 86–87, 124, 204.

44 For example, PE 9, 12–14, 19.

45 PE 100; compare PE 98–102.

practical recognition of personality by another, of an "I" by a "Thou" and a "Thou" by an "I," is necessary to any practical consciousness of it, to any such consciousness of it as can express itself in act' (§2.IV).[46] Moreover, at times Green uses Fichte's phrase, the 'Divine Idea'.[47] As has been noted, Green's equivalent goes by many names, but scholars tend to favour one of its least used names: the 'eternal consciousness' (MSF chapter 4; CS §1.III). This concept has attracted much largely undeserved criticism. Many critics have seen it as a mystical notion. Yet, Green's derivation is rather more clearly stated than is implied by such a view. He argues that the individual's presupposition that she knows things requires her to posit the existence of an ideal single, perfectly coherent if presently inchoate system of meanings and values.[48] This postulate of theoretical and practical reason is what Green means by the eternal consciousness. Consequently, he holds that the phrase 'divine idea' is meaningless when applied to an unsituated and undefined 'absolute and all-embracing end'.[49] It 'can only take effect in the fulfilment of some particular function in which it finds [concrete] but restricted utterance'.[50] Fichte agrees: the divine idea is a phantom unless it is situated in the definite practices of real individuals. Only thus can the individual develop a definite personality, because only thus can she express herself and be recognised by others as a discrete concrete person.

For both Fichte and Green the particular acts in which the person is recognised (including acts of self-recognition) are partly acts of 'attributing or conferring a normative status' of a certain sort on that person.[51] This becomes especially significant when combined with the claim that the clarity and stability of the individual's self-understanding is a function of the clarity and stability of the ways in which she perceives herself to be recognised by both herself and others. Significantly, Fichte and Green agree that the individual can live in accordance with her highest nature as a particular determinate rational agent only to the extent that she has a clear and stable sense of her own identity, and to the extent that her environment allows her to act in accordance with that particular determinate identity. It is for this reason that Green and Fichte insist on the need for rights, duties and obligations to be socially embedded. Green clarifies the nature of this embeddedness by claiming that

> 'It is not in so far as I can do this or that that I have a right to do this or that, but so far as I recognise myself and am recognised by others as able to do this

---

46 PE 190; also PE 201.
47 PE 183, 184, 190, 247.
48 PE 14, 26, 70, 132, 134,149, 195, 221.
49 PE 183.
50 PE 183.
51 Pinkard, *German*, p. 121.

or that for the sake of a common good, or so far as in the consciousness of myself and others I have a function relative to this end.'[52]

In other words, systems of rights and duties and systems of legal rights and obligations are legitimate only to the extent that they are recognised as being the systems which best serve the agent's attainment of her telos.[53] It was established in §3.III that this telos is an end which the 'rights-recognising-and-claiming agent' perceives as being common to both herself and the other members of those communities with which she identifies herself.[54] In short, to possess a conception of her telos which is sufficiently determinate to generate and justify concrete rights and duties, the individual must be socialised within the moralising institutions of a community.

Remembering Green's theory of intersubjectivity outlined in chapter two, the process of the growth in recognition of the agent's own worth presupp-oses her practical recognition of the worth of the persons with whom she forms a community.[55] Logically entailed in this act of recognition is the recognition that respecting others is a claim from duty.[56] It is in this manner that possessing rights entails that also the agent recognises her duties to others.[57] This argument completes Green's attack on the natural rights trad-ition. He argues that, in addition to its many other faults, the latter places far too much emphasis upon rights, whilst largely ignoring associated duties. Furthermore, the natural rights tradition implies that claims can be made against society. On Green's view, the fact that rights and duties exist only to the extent that they are recognised as forming part of a reciprocal social system means that the 'fact of [the agent's] not consenting [to be bound by any particular duty within this system] would be an extinction of all right on his part'.[58] For the individual to claim a right against society would require her simultaneously to deny the very basis on which she could possess any rights at all.[59]

This point must be emphasised. The legitimacy of every specific right derives from the relationships in which it stands to the specific conception of the common good which structures the society in which it obtains, and this good only exists for a person who is embedded within a culture. Claiming

---

52 PPO 38.
53 For ease of exposition, from here on the phrase 'systems of rights and duties and systems of legal rights and obligations' will be shortened in the text to 'systems of rights, duties and obligations', or, in some cases, simply 'systems of rights'.
54 PPO 25.
55 Gerald F. Gaus, *The Modern Liberal Theory of Man* (Beckenham: Croom Helm, 1983), pp. 190–91.
56 PPO 26–31.
57 PPO 21.
58 PPO 138.
59 Cacoullos, *Thomas Hill Green*, pp. 118–20.

any right implies recognition of the worth of one's fellows and hence the common good which binds one to them.[60] It is this insight which leads Green to the important conclusion that,

> 'in truth there is no such natural right to do as one likes irrespectively of society. It is on the relation to a society — to other men recognising a common good — that the individual's rights depend, as much as the gravity of a body depends on relations to other bodies. A right is a power claimed and recognised as contributory to a common good. A right against society, in distinction from a right to be treated as a member of society, is a contradiction in terms.'[61]

Rex Martin has framed Green's conception social recognition in terms of the creation of socially-endorsed or favoured modes of action or treatment.[62] Elsewhere, Martin has argued that

> 'Without [social recognition]… the rightholder would lack the proper understanding of his claim (that it was justified and that engaging the cooperation of others was justified too). Without it duties would not be in place, or could not be called on; nor would second parties conceive their conduct as normatively directed. Without it there would be no *guarantee* to an individual of what was justifiably claimed as his due and he could not count on getting what was claimed.'[63]

While there is much truth in Martin's characterisation, it does imply also that social recognition relates purely to practices and modes of action rather than to individuals. Moreover, Martin's characterisation implies that the individual is a passive inheritor of a scheme of socially-authorised modes of action rather than an active participant in their creation, maintenance and iterative revision. In reality, as it has been presented at length in the preceding chapters, for Green society is constituted solely by individuals in relation to one another, sometimes in relatively informal relationships, and sometimes in relationships that create and sustain collective institutions. Counterfactually, institutions including rights, duties and obligations exist only as parts of the practical attitudes that individuals have regarding one another and their collective lives. They do not exist in separation from those individuals. To the extent that these attitudes do not inform those interactions (either explicitly or implicitly), then they lack authority over the individual. After all, it is a cornerstone of Green's ethics that a claim has

---

[60] PPO 25.

[61] PPO 99.

[62] 'By social recognition, Green seemed to have in mind something like the following: an authoritative acknowledgment or affirmation within a society that a certain way of acting, or way of being treated, was desirable or should be permitted, together with appropriate steps taken to promote and maintain that way.' Martin, 'T.H. Green on individual rights', 51.

[63] Martin, 'Green on Natural Rights', 118–19.

authority over an individual only to the extent that it is grounded in values which the individual endorses freely (whether consciously or as a presupposition of her more determinate commitments). Only to the extent that rights and duties do so is the individual morally free (§3.III).

Possessing a sense of one's personal identity presupposes the intersubjective actualisation of one's self-consciousness, then. As Sabine puts it, 'the heightening of a sense of individuality is possible only with an increased sense of the social significance of such individuality'.[64] Indeed, it is a necessary consequence of Green's metaphysics that any particular system of moral rights has authority over the individual only to the extent that it (i) serves the common good of the society with which the individual freely identifies her highest good and personality, and (ii) is recognised by the other members of society as doing so.[65]

> 'There can be no right without a consciousness of common interest on the part of members of a society. Without this there might be certain powers on the part of individuals, but no recognition of these powers by others as powers of which they allow the exercise, nor any claim to such recognition, and without this recognition or claim to recognition there can be no right.'[66]

These aspects—the claim and the recognition—are the necessary and sufficient conditions for the existence of a moral right and duty. Once again, this argument reflects Green's idealism: as he puts it, 'There is no right but thinking makes it so—none that is not derived from some idea that men have about each other'.[67] When rights and duties are properly conceived, social recognition is founded 'on the conception of the individual as being what he really is in virtue of a function which he has to fulfil relatively to a certain end, that end being the common well-being of a society'.[68]

Their shared awareness of the need for a sympathetic environment in which rational agents can act and respect others as such leads Fichte and Green to emphasise definite and conceptually clear acts of recognition by one's state and community. For Fichte, however, public recognition is deficient to the extent that it lacks legal standing and enforcement. He holds that legal recognition of one's personality by a rational community and state has supreme importance because it is definite and stable: it tends to be promulgated publicly for the purpose of facilitating and coordinating free rational agency by citizens. Consequently, Fichte holds the ideal situation to be one

---

[64] George H. Sabine, 'The Social Origin of Absolute Idealism', *Journal of Philosophy, Psychology and Scientific Methods*, 12:7 (1915), 173.

[65] PPO 139; see also Georg W.F. Hegel, *Elements of the Philosophy of Right*, ed. Allen W. Wood, trans. H.B. Nisbet (Cambridge: Cambridge University Press, 1991), §207.

[66] PPO 31.

[67] PPO 136.

[68] PPO 38.

where individuals freely commit to become members of a legally-recognised category of persons ('particular occupation' (*Beschäftigung*), 'estate' (*Ständ*)) and to exercise the rights enjoyed by the members of that occupation as well as honouring the duties required of them.[69] (Fichte's examples include 'merchant', 'herdsman', 'fisherman', 'farmer', 'scholar', 'moral teachers of the people' or 'servants of the church', 'fine artist', 'state official', 'miners', 'hunters', 'craftsmen', 'artisans', 'factory workers' and other occupations of the 'lower estates'.)[70] At least as he was usually interpreted in Green's Britain, Fichte gives the state the role of securing strict and active membership of recognised occupations from its citizens, so as to maintain the conditions for rational agency.[71] For Fichte, the state is fully justified in compelling individuals to fulfil the role they contracted to play in society. This is Fichte's version of being 'forced to be free'.

The situation is less rigid for Green however. While appreciating the frequent need for legal recognition of particular claims, he is concerned not to restrain the existential and social processes whereby previously unarticulated spiritual needs and new conceptions of spiritually-enhancing meanings and values gain conscious expression and force for the individual, her community and her state. This concern underlies his contention that

> 'an unconscious always precedes a conscious morality:… men act on moral principles, embodied in law and custom, which have never distinctly become part of their individual consciousness… [The] process of self-examination… awaken[s] in a man the consciousness of the law on which, under higher guidance than his own, he has already been acting, and thus… transform[s] it from an outward to an inward law, to be obeyed not on authority but in freedom, not under the limitations of local or temporary enactment, but in the open atmosphere of reason.'[72]

This marks an important difference between Green and Fichte (at least as the latter was interpreted in Green's Britain). Fichte emphasises the need for the agent to be culturally-located because such location is necessary if her agency is to be manifested in ways that are definite and based on understandings that are shared with other agents. Only with such shared concrete understandings can the individual's capacity for rational agency become an object to herself and others. Being an object in this way is important for Fichte because the individual's actions and the communities that they constitute are legitimate only to the extent that they honour in practice the categorical imperative to respect rational agency as such. In other words, one can respect transcendental egos only within a kingdom of ends, and

---

[69] Fichte, *Right*, p. 170; Fichte, *Ethics*, pp. 259–62.
[70] Fichte, *Right*, pp. 170, 203, 204–05, and Fichte, *Ethics*, pp. 324–44.
[71] Fichte, *Right*, p. 187; also pp. 85–86.
[72] 'Aristotle' 58.

Fichte believes that requires one to recognise these egos as they are instantiated in determinate, culturally-conditioned forms. Green endorses all of this, yet he goes further holding that humans possess worth not simply as determinate manifestations of a transcendental rational ego. They possess worth also as beings who can realise their innate yet historically-situated eudaimonic capacities, understood as the 'spiritual principle' (or 'eternal consciousness', 'divine consciousness' or 'divine idea'). Only then does the individual become the self-conscious embodiment and appreciation of the true, right, virtuous and beautiful.[73] Again echoing Fichte, Green calls the individual's free manifestation of these qualities the 'vocation of man'.[74]

As has been noted, Green rejects the social contract idiom, even when of the ideal type adopted by Spinoza, Hobbes, Locke and Rousseau, and, by implication, Fichte and Kant.[75] He regards the contract as superfluous to the establishment of the community and the legitimacy of the state. Instead, both community and state are grounded on citizens' continuing practical if unarticulated aspiration to live together freely and fairly: the achievement of this end is their common good.[76] Fichte's position however is in line with that developed subsequently in Kant's *Metaphysics of Morals*: collective power is legitimate to the extent that it is applied in line with procedures that respect the rational agency of all those over whom it exercised.[77] On this view, considerations regarding 'non-moral' human capacities are irrelevant to the question of legitimacy. This is what Green denies: for him, in addition to needing to respect rational agency as such, the legitimacy of collective power is a function of its effects on the manifestation of the individual's eudaimonic capacities.

For Fichte, the state can legitimately enforce and maintain unaltered any determinate set of occupations where that set respects the culturally-manifested transcendental egos of its members. From Green's perspective however, the hypostatisation of occupations entailed by rigid enforcement tends to hinder the gradual articulation by and through the individual of previously merely implicit and inchoate higher capacities. It was noted earlier (§4.II) that at one apparently very Fichtean point, Green does claim: 'Each [person] has primarily to fulfil the duties of his station.'[78] Yet, this is not a reference to Fichte. It is a practical claim echoing F.H. Bradley's essay

---

73 PE 173–76.
74 PE 173.
75 PPO 32–79.
76 PPO 1–7, 80–136.
77 Kant's *Metaphysics of Morals* appeared the year after Fichte's stated his own position.
78 PE 183.

'My Station and its Duties',[79] Ultimately, both Bradley and Green insist that 'ideal morality' transcends conservatism: 'You can not confine a man to his station and its duties.'[80] The system of rights and duties tends to be in a state of constant flux (see §7.V).

Even acknowledging the shifting nature of rights and duties and despite his rejection of the 'natural rights tradition', Green does believe that there is a sense in which a certain system of rights is 'natural' to each person as a human being: 'There is a system of rights and obligations which *should be* maintained by law, whether it is so or not, and which may properly be called "*natural*",... because necessary to the end which it is the vocation of human society to realize.'[81] The hypothetical ideal society — a eudaimonic-ally-enriching kingdom of ends — would allow all of its members to be and to live as fully human beings; that is, to fully express their inherent nature by acting in a distinctively human manner. The system of rights upon which this hypothetical ideal society would be based is 'natural' in Green's eyes in the sense that it would facilitate the satisfaction of the individual's distinc-tively human needs.[82] Both the system and the needs are structured by the underlying framework of a distinctively human consciousness and cons-titute moments of the objective manifestation of the common good of a eudaimonically-enriching kingdom of ends.[83] The closer the good is to embodying such a hypothetical ideal common good, the closer the system of rights is to partaking of Green's system of natural rights.[84]

Reflecting on the recent scholarship in this area brings out a number of profoundly significant aspects of Green's theory of rights. In a particularly interesting piece, Avital Simhony takes to task those contemporary philos-ophers who see rights discourse as inherently and inextricably linked to 'competitive, selfish individualism'.[85] She rejects the claim that ascribing rights to individuals must mean that those individuals are, at root, atoms who use their rights to achieve their own primarily asocial goals. In fact, Simhony argues, the implications of ascribing rights to individuals depend on what one takes those individuals to be like: selfish or public spirited, acquisitive or generous, alienated or integrated. To the extent that the con-temporary philosopher fails to confront the intrinsically metaphysical pre-

---

[79] F.H. Bradley, *Ethical Studies*, second edition (Oxford: Clarendon Press, 1927 [1876]), Essay V.

[80] Bradley, *Ethical Studies*, p. 204.

[81] PPO 9.

[82] Adam Ulam misses this point (Adam B. Ulam, *The Philosophical Foundations of English Socialism* (Cambridge, MA: Harvard University Press, 1951), p. 36).

[83] PPO 138.

[84] On scholars' misunderstandings of the word 'partaking', see MSF §4.II.

[85] Simhony, 'Rights that Bind', 242. Simhony's chapter explores this claim and the two which follow it, at length and with great clarity.

suppositions of the conception of the person which underpin her philosophy of rights, the contemporary philosopher bases her position on her pre-philosophical prejudices. Consequently, as Simhony writes, in these cases 'the link between rights and competitive, selfish individualism' becomes 'essentially ideological'.[86]

Simhony argues that denying a necessary distance and antagonism 'between the "individual" and "society"' leads Green to adopt a 'social' not 'territorial' 'conception of rights'.[87] Systems of moral and legal rights delineate areas in which the individual's preferences should be allowed to determine her actions and ways of life, free from 'encroachments of [the] consequentialist calculations [of others], tyranny of the majority, or an over-arching community'.[88] Simhony points out that Green's alternative, the 'social' conception of rights, is akin to positions adopted by Karl Marx and Charles Taylor, among many others. On Green's view, rights exist to enable individuals to act on their judgements of how best to serve themselves and their fellow citizens. The socially-sensitive, common good-orientated Greenian citizen referred to in chapter four seeks to use her personal rights to cultivate and maintain the collective structures that facilitate the eudaimonic development of all members of her society, while honouring the categorical imperative to respect their status as rational agents.

Finally, Simhony argues that Green's social conception of rights tends to accord a greater significance to positive rights than one usually finds in the works of territorial rights philosophers.[89] On the social conception, usually it is insufficient to merely not prevent an individual from acting on her preferences; on many occasions, one is required to provide them with active assistance. One might think here of the need for social provision to the individual of an assured level of income during periods of unemployment, or a basic education and health-care that is free at the point of delivery, for anyone who is too poor or otherwise unable to provide herself with such essentials. Taken together, Simhony argues, these three parts enable Green to establish a social theory in which rights 'bind' groups together, rather than making social interactions a series of ultimately 'confrontational' encounters.

Green's social conception of rights and duties is then one part of the relational social ontology that has been analysed at length in chapters two and three of this book. No particular determinate moral right can be understood correctly except as part of a system of determinate moral rights. That is, rights derive their value from the roles they play in creating a sympathetic context for the individual's construction of what she regards as a valu-

---

[86] Simhony, 'Rights that Bind', 242.
[87] Simhony, 'Rights that Bind', 243.
[88] Simhony, 'Rights that Bind', 243.
[89] Simhony, 'Rights that Bind', 243.

able personal identity and its expression in her praxis. Obviously, this does not entail that all elements of the system stand and fall together; that rejecting one right requires one to reject all others. An element may be poorly specified or even wrongly specified without the remainder of the system being so. In fact, one of the key ways in which a social critic can identify a poorly or wrongly specified norm (including a mis-specified right) is by discerning its incongruity with other related norms (see chapter four).[90] Incoherence or gaps in the web of meanings and values by which a society is bound together (in Simhony's sense) are signs of the imperfection of that web; that is, the web's failure to live up to the ideal of being a system. It is possible that to address this problem, revisions of every element of the system are required, or even revisions to every element except the norm that originally attracted one's attention to the unsystematic nature of the web. Alternatively, the particular 'alerting' norm might be the only element that needs to be revised. Different cases require different solutions, none of which can be specified in the abstract.

Green's approach differs from those that attempt to derive rights from an allegedly natural feature or an allegedly ahistorical intuitive judgement. The fact that a person can, for example, feel pain has no intrinsic normative implications. It can become immensely significant, however, when viewed within the context of a system of meanings and values, such as our own, where pain can be avoidable or unavoidable, deserved or undeserved, and where, all other things being equal, avoidable undeserved pain is a feeling from which each person has a right to be protected.

IV

Clarifying Confusions Over Recognition

Geoffrey Thomas claims that, for Green,

'[a] right is a power which enables the agent to fulfil the requirements of a lifeplan. For moral ontology what thus grounds a right is not dependent on recognition as its necessary condition:… But in the context of a morality of social roles, only such powers as can be ascertained as necessary or appropriate to a practice have any relevance to moral or political discourse. Moral epistemology enjoys thereby a degree of separation from moral ontology.'[91]

Thomas is correct that, for Green, a right or duty is validated by its place in a system which aims at facilitating, and in part constitutes, a common good.

---

[90] Michael Walzer, *Interpretation and Social Criticism* (Cambridge, MA: Harvard University Press, 1985), chapter 2.

[91] Thomas, *Moral Philosophy of T.H. Green,* p. 355. This line is essentially the one which Hobhouse states Green does not, but should, pursue (Leonard T. Hobhouse, *The Metaphysical Theory of the State: A criticism* (London: George Allen and Unwin, 1918), pp. 119–20).

Yet, contrary to Thomas' interpretation, Green holds recognition to be a necessary aspect of the ontology as well as the epistemology of rights. In other words, to the extent that a claim is not recognised by the group whose common good it serves and partially constitutes, it does not exist as a right. As Copleston observes, the 'point is that "right" is, so to speak, a social term'.[92] It is a social entity as well for Green. Hence, the quotation from Green given by Thomas in support of his reading—that is, '"A right is a power"'[93]—must be completed with what Green writes immediately afterwards: 'A right is a power of which the exercise by the individual or by some body of men is recognised by a society either as itself directly essential to a common good or as conferred by an authority of which the maintenance is recognised as so essential.'[94] In a similar vein, Ann Cacoullos misstates Green's position when she argues that,

> 'The factor of social recognition which, according to Green, renders a power of action into a right of action is not a mental attitude, such as an opinion or intellectual realization. To recognise a power or a claim is *to act* or behave in ways appropriate to the contents of the demand.'[95]

In expressing the idea thus, Cacoullos is in danger of overstating the distance between thought and action in Green's philosophy. She should make it clearer that the character of an action is internally related to the motives of the agent performing it, and so necessarily depends upon the significance which that action has for that agent. Cacoullos's interpretation borders upon behavouralism, making it wholly inappropriate as a reading of Green.[96]

The claim that social recognition forms a necessary aspect of the ontology of a right has occasioned much confusion and criticism in other parts of the literature as well.[97] For instance, Plamenatz interprets the importance which Green places upon recognition as implying that 'men… ought not to have [rights] unless their governors or the majority of their fellow men are of the

---

[92] Frederick Copleston, *A History of Philosophy: Volume VIII, Bentham to Russell* (London: Burns and Oates, 1966), p. 175n2.

[93] Thomas, *Moral Philosophy of T.H. Green*, p. 353.

[94] PPO 103.

[95] Cacoullos, *Thomas Hill Green*, p. 95.

[96] Even though there is insufficient space to deal with this point in depth, it should be noted that Cacoullos's analysis is generally perceptive but ultimately contains many flaws (Cacoullos, *Thomas Hill Green*, pp. 86–106 *passim*). For the most part, these flaws stem from a failure to appreciate the exact nature of Green's epistemology and his conception of the Common Good and the interrelationships between the two.

[97] For example, H.D. Lewis, 'Individualism and Collectivism—a study of T.H. Green', in his *Freedom and History* (London: George Allen and Unwin, 1962), pp. 79–89 *passim*; Noël O'Sullivan, *The Problem of Political Obligation* (New York: Garland, 1987), pp. 182–88 *passim*.

opinion that they should have them'.[98] He comes to this interpretation in spite of all the passages in Green's writings which explicitly contradict the claim. Plamenatz even quotes one such passage without grasping the clear tension with his reading. Green writes: 'If the common interest requires it [i.e. a particular law], no right can be alleged against it. Neither can its enactment by popular vote enhance, nor the absence of such vote diminish, its right to be obeyed.'[99] At first sight, the second sentence here seems to imply that the legitimacy of rights does not stem from the people. It is a short step to Plamenatz's assertion that Greenian rights exist primarily at the behest of the sovereign. Yet, in context and as the first sentence quoted establishes, it is clear that Green is not objecting to the idea that people themselves determine rights in some fundamental sense. Green is rejecting the view that rights spring from the arbitrary wills of individuals in the manner alleged by social contract theorists such as Hobbes, Spinoza and, on Green's reading, in one mood Rousseau. Rights are justified by the higher and permanent needs of determinate agents. They are legitimated solely upon this basis. In fact, for Green rights are powers secured to individuals by the concrete recognition (no matter how inchoate) of the needs for certain relations to obtain between specific determinate individuals in order that they may act in a distinctively human manner. Hence, in reality none of the passages quoted by Plamenatz establish that Green believes that the legitimacy of rights and duties is based upon the subjective wills of either the majority or the government.[100] Instead, they show that rights and duties are based upon the judgements of concrete individuals regarding their own respective determinate true goods.

In another passage, Plamenatz makes clear that even if his first objection fails, he regards Green's position on the existence of natural rights as absurd.[101] He argues that,

> 'if these powers ought to be recognized [as Green argues] it follows also that they ought to be possessed, for it is only because they ought to be possessed that they ought to be recognized. Moreover, if they ought to be possessed, it is clear that the possession of them would be either itself good or else a means to the good. In either case, their want of recognition, making it impossible for their potential possessors to exercise them, diminishes or, at least, prevents the increase of what is good. It is clear, then, that this want of recognition is productive of evil, or else a hindrance to the good, in spite of the fact that no one is wronged, since no one is deprived of his rights. This paradoxical conclusion, at which we must necessarily arrive, if we start with the supposition

---

[98] John Plamenatz, *Consent, Freedom, and Political Obligation* (London: Oxford University Press, 1938), p. 90; see also H.D. Lewis, 'T.H. Green and Rousseau', in his *Freedom and History*, especially pp. 121–25.

[99] PPO 99.

[100] Plamenatz, *Consent*, pp. 90–91.

[101] Plamenatz, *Consent*, pp. 94–97.

that there exist powers which should be rights and yet are not, appears to be false.'[102]

Plamenatz fails to appreciate the link Green posits between philosophy and practice (MSF §2.II). Understanding this link is a crucial step in gaining a proper understanding of why recognition is entailed by the ontology of rights. Certainly, Green does argue that specific rights ought to be accorded to all humans when those individuals are fully developed. This is his conception of teleologically natural rights. However, the legitimacy of this 'ought' depends upon the practical context. More particularly, it depends upon the nature of the determinate entities between whom obtain the relationships implied by the possession of particular rights. Quite simply, different partially determinate individuals have different requirements in their search for self-realisation. The concrete rights which should be granted to determinate individuals depends upon their specific present imperfections; in short, different systems of rights, duties and obligations suit different determinate individuals. Moreover, it can be seen that only if his supporting argument goes through is Plamenatz justified in arguing that suffering 'evil' or being hindered in one's pursuit of the good is the only situation in which an agent can be 'wronged'. Implicitly, Green rejects this assertion and rightly so. There are many ways in which one can suffer evil without necessarily having one's rights violated.

Ultimately, even Plamenatz himself recognises that his criticism is based upon a merely terminological difference. In his next paragraph he accuses Green of 'a misuse of ordinary language'.[103] He makes this accusation even though Green wrote sixty years before Plamenatz made his criticism. Once again, Plamenatz's method pushes him to rip the text from its context. It must be asked to what extent it is realistic to assume that the 'ordinary language' of British philosophers in the late-1870s and early-1880s was comparable to the 'ordinary language' of analytic philosophers just before the Second World War. Indeed, one must question the extent to which it is ever useful to think in terms of 'ordinary language' at all in philosophical discourse in the specific and largely uncritical manner that one finds in Plamenatz and many others.[104] In Andrew Vincent's words, 'much of the time ordinary language reflects confused and half-baked theories and consequently needs to be critically understood'.[105]

---

[102] Plamenatz, *Consent*, pp. 95–96.

[103] Plamenatz, *Consent*, p. 96.

[104] Cacoullos poses this question very effectively (Cacoullos, *Thomas Hill Green*, pp. 147–48).

[105] Andrew Vincent, 'The State and Social Purpose in Idealist Political Philosophy', *History of European Ideas*, 8:3 (1987), 341.

That an individual has no moral rights or duties against society does not mean that she cannot criticise the existing system of rights and duties under which she lives, as Plamenatz and others have also alleged.[106] It is shown at length in chapters four and eight that Green is at pains to argue that no existing system is perfect and that, if she is able, the individual has a duty to remove any defects which she believes are present in her world.[107] The standard of perfection which ideally should guide the individual in constructing and implementing plans for social reform is her conscientious assessment of the tendency of the systems of rights to further the attainment of human perfection conceived as the habitual tendency to act in a distinctively human fashion.[108] As has been insisted, the determinate nature of such perfection is inextricably linked to the understanding of the world of meanings, values and possible praxis which the particular individual has gained from her society (see chapter two). Consequently, every individual has a duty to seek recognition for systems of moral and legal rights which are based upon what she believes to be a more coherent conception of the common good.[109]

In a sense, therefore, any revision of existing norms must be a modification of conventional morality and existing law. This line of reasoning leads Green to argue that where moral and legal rights which are at present granted to and placed upon the individual by her society are based upon contradictions and incoherences within the society's attempt to attain its common good, the individual should seek to be given modified and more coherent rights, duties and obligations which society does not yet recognise. The mere fact that the agent does not like a particular claim or obligation is not sufficient justification for not complying with it.[110] The individual must conscientiously believe that the claim is detrimental to the improvement of members of her society and ultimately of all human beings.

Green's position presupposes his argument from intersubjectivity (§2.IV). As he puts it: 'rights have no being except in a society of men recognising each other as *isoi kai homoioi* [equals]. They are constituted by that mutual recognition.'[111] This means that systems of moral and legal rights can possess different strengths of claims on the individuals living under them. The more fully the system approaches the 'natural' system, the stronger its claim and, therefore, the less leeway the person can have for conscientious objection

---

[106] For example, Prichard, *Moral Obligation*, pp. 57–66; Lancaster, *Masters of Political Thought, Volume III, passim*.

[107] PPO 9.

[108] PPO 20.

[109] PPO 100, 119.

[110] PPO 99.

[111] PPO 139; see also PPO 148.

(§§4.II–IV, 8.IV). Consequently, the force of the agent's moral duty, political obligation and, therefore, the legitimacy of the constitution vary as well.[112]

It is important to remember that, by definition, a moral agent understands herself as a being who is capable of sharing an absolutely desirable end with fellow moral agents. To favour her own attainment of the end which they all share as moral beings at the expense of a similar attainment by her fellows would represent a contradiction in the person's act of willing.[113]

> '[E]very moral person, is capable of [and ought to possess] rights; i.e. of bearing his part in a society in which the free exercise of his powers is secured to each member through the recognition by each of the others as entitled to the same freedom with himself.'[114]

It is from this basis that Green attacks the denial of moral (and legal) rights to slaves. Prichard ignores this argument in his highly influential polemic against Green, and this has caused many misunderstandings of Green's position.[115] Green is emphatic that 'Slavery… implies the establishment of some regular system of rights in the slave-owning society. The slave, especially the domestic slave, has the signs and effects of this system all about him' (but see §4.IV).[116] The slave is at least partially aware of her own power as a social, creative and self-realisable being, and of the social system in which she lives and which grants moral and legal rights to non-slaves on the basis of their (the non-slaves') capacities for self-realisation.[117] The moral and legal standing as well as the actual daily treatment of the slave by other slaves and non-slaves implies social recognition of her capacity for rational agency, thereby implying the existence of moral rights for her. The slave cannot help but feel a contradiction in her life (no matter how inchoate that feeling actually is). For this reason, any society which upholds the institution of slavery 'is violating a right, founded on that common human consciousness which is evinced both [1] by the language which the slave speaks and [2] by actual social relations subsisting between him and others'.[118] Firstly, the ability to communicate through language is evidence of self-conscious-

---

[112] PPO 132. This point will be returned to when Green's theory of resistance is examined in §8.IV below.

[113] PPO 138.

[114] PPO 25.

[115] Prichard, *Moral Obligation*, pp. 58–59; supported by Melvin Richter, *The Politics of Conscience: T.H. Green and his age* (London: Weidenfeld and Nicolson, 1964), pp. 244–45, 263–65; A. John Simmons, *Moral Principles and Political Obligation* (Princeton: Princeton University Press, 1979), pp. 38–39. The issue is discussed more broadly, and well, in Boucher, *Limits of Ethics*, pp. 239–40.

[116] PPO 114.

[117] PPO 140.

[118] PPO 140. Nettleship, 'Memoir', xliii–xiv.

ness because, as Green puts it, 'Language presupposes thought as a capacity, but in us the capacity of thought is only actualised in language'.[119] This point was made in MSF §2.II and CS §§1.II and 2.IV. Secondly, only agents are capable of taking part in social relationships.[120] These considerations should form the foundational moral considerations for all actual human social relationships, and lay the basis of a Greenian kingdom of ends (§3.III).

Furthermore, Green argues that the capacity to live as a member of a community entails the individual's claim to be respected by every other moral agent: 'Membership of any community is so far in principle membership of all communities as to constitute a right to be treated as a freeman by all other men, to be exempt from subjection to force except for prevention of force.'[121] It may appear strange for Green to take this line given his insistence upon the role of practical recognition in the ontology of rights.[122] Why should the individual's membership of culture A create rights against and duties towards members of culture B? To answer this question, one must firstly properly understand Green's claim that rights and duties can be implicit.[123] The key idea here is that there can be 'implicit' recognition that someone is a person (conceived as a being capable of moral action). Consider the apparently Hegelian underpinnings to Green's attitude towards slavery.[124] The slave feels alienated because she is aware of her capacity to act in a purposive manner. Yet, she has this capacity respected fully neither by others nor by herself. Yet, the master acts in a self-contradictory manner when she uses the slave as a purposive tool. Indeed, the very phrase 'purposive tool' is oxymoronic when used in this sense. Firstly, the master gives the slave orders and, therefore, must at the very least implicitly and inchoately recognise the slave as a purposive being: that is, as a being with the capacity to act in a distinctively human manner. Secondly, the master treats the slave as a tool and hence an object. This treatment entails an implicit denial of her capacity for agency. The master's action embodies two mutually incompatible visions of the slave, then. In one, the slave has the capacity to be an autonomous agent and, in the other, she is merely a tool. Both master and slave possess an at least partially inchoate recognition of the contradiction which this situation embodies. It is on the basis of the former claim that the slave has an implicit right to be accorded equal respect by everyone, including the master.

---

[119] PE 183.

[120] PE 182–83; PPO 25–31.

[121] PPO 140.

[122] Milne missed this aspect of Green's argument (Milne, *Social Philosophy*, pp. 129–30).

[123] PPO 104, 139–47 *passim*.

[124] PE 206–09, 245, 266–74 *passim*, 284, 330; DSF 6; PPO 104, 114, 117–18, 132, 140–147, 152, 154, 159, 240–41.

The force of Green's position on this issue has not always been fully appreciated even by his more sympathetic commentators. For instance, Peter Nicholson has argued that for Green, a 'man may have a "valid" claim to a "real" right, but if it is not recognised *as a legal right* then it is not a "full" or "actual" or "explicit" right but merely "implicit"'.[125] In fact, Green does not hold an implicit right to exist only where (i) a person is accorded a moral right by the self-conscious recognition given to her by the other members of her society, and (ii) this claim does not receive legal recognition as well. The slave, for instance, has an implicit moral right which arises from her awareness that the very logic of her actions and social relationships entails that she is a purposive being. As a purposive being, she is capable of pursuing a common good. In other words, it is not merely that the master must be conscious that the slave can pursue a common good and is, therefore, a distinctively human being, as Nicholson implies. The master may recognise this purposive capacity and still fail to fully recognise the moral implications of that capacity. Yet, the fact that the master does, in some sense, recognise that the capacity for purposive agency is the mark of a distinctively human agent in other contexts, means that already the slave has an implicit moral claim to equal treatment by the master.[126] It is in this way that membership of any one society gives the agent an implicit moral claim to equal treatment by all other individuals.[127] Moreover, any person who is capable of self-conscious social interaction and who is at least implicitly recognized as such, has a *prima facie* moral right to equal treatment.

V

The Environment, Animals, the Disabled and the Unborn

From this examination of the philosophical foundations of Green's theory of rights and duties, it should be clear that certain sorts of entity can never possess rights or duties, due to the very logic of Green's position. This section will examine the most obvious and important of these frequently controversial exclusions: the natural environment, animals, the irredeemably severely mentally disabled and the irredeemably severely insane. They are all excluded because they are inherently incapable of self-realisation: that is, of making themselves truly free.

---

[125] Peter P. Nicholson, *The Political Philosophy of the British Idealists: Selected studies* (Cambridge: Cambridge University Press, 1990), p. 85, emphasis added.

[126] Certainly, the importance of this point of difference between myself and Peter Nicholson should not be over-emphasised as he insists upon the significance of 'implicit social recognition' (Nicholson, *Political Philosophy*, p. 89) in other areas of Green's theory of rights (Nicholson, *Political Philosophy*, pp. 87–89). Cacoullos misses Green's argument on implicit recognition and, therefore, implicit rights (Cacoullos, *Thomas Hill Green*, especially pp. 86–106 *passim*).

[127] PPO 151.

The environment is not a purposive agent (unless one believes in some form of mysticism) and so cannot possess any rights or duties.[128] Certainly, people may have a right and even a duty to protect their natural environment. Yet, the validity of such a right or duty can only be derived from the need for such an environment to exist as a precondition of the self-realisation of persons and, for Green at least, this means individuals only. No matter how important it is to people, Nature as such cannot possess rights or duties.[129] A less extreme conclusion holds in the case of animals. Green makes two claims in this regard, although these claims merge into one another. Firstly, he argues that animals do not possess the capacity for self-consciousness and so cannot be moral entities.[130] Elsewhere, he makes the weaker claim that animals cannot possess rights or duties in human societies because humans are precluded from communicating with them and, therefore, we cannot recognise them as being capable of pursuing a common good in the morally relevant sense. Importantly, in part this means that we have no reason to think of them as purposive agents.[131] Green claims that even if they are capable of moral action, they cannot form part of our ethical community and we cannot form part of theirs, even when they learn to react habitually, say, to the ringing of a dinner bell.[132] In both cases, animals fail to meet the interrelated conditions which any rights-holder must fulfil. An animal is akin to 'a thing'.[133] For example, in the course of his discussion of punishment, Green argues that,

> 'The whipping of an ill-behaved dog is preventive, but not preventive in the sense in which the punishment of crime is so because (1) the dog's ill-conduct is not an intentional violation of a right or neglect of a known obligation, the dog having no conception of rights or obligations, and (2) for the same reason the whipping does not lead to an association of terror in the minds of other dogs with the violation of rights and neglect of obligations.'[134]

---

[128] PPO 208.

[129] John Rodman, 'What is Living and What is Dead in the Political Philosophy of T.H. Green', *Western Political Quarterly*, 26:3 (1973), 573–86 *passim*. It is interesting to note that this judgement is reflected in Green's own aesthetic appreciation of the environment. Nettleship writes, 'Nature appealed to his imagination ... as the sympathetic background to human life and the kindred revelation of a divine intelligence' (Nettleship, 'Memoir', xviii).

[130] 'Popular Philosophy' 112.

[131] PPO 139, 208; Lewis, 'Individualism and Collectivism', 86n2; Rodman, 'What is Living', 581.

[132] PE 123. Green's denial of the ability to engage in social relationships with animals is controversial for many humans. After all, it is not unusual to feel far greater understanding and concern for one's cat or dog than one does for most human beings.

[133] PPO 156, 158.

[134] PPO 187; also see PPO 200.

Green's position in relation to animals is less plausible than it is in relation to the environment. Rodman points out Green fails to mention the animal protection legislation which was passed at the same time as the other measures referred to in his *Lecture on Liberal Legislation and Freedom of Contract*.[135] This omission seems indicative of the fact that Green is simply 'not interested' in animal rights.[136] MacKenzie and especially Rodman are less sceptical than Green about ascribing some capacity for purposive agency to animals.[137] Both recognise, as Green did himself, that, on the logic of his theory, if a certain species of animal could be shown to have the capacity for purposive action, then its members should be granted at least some moral rights and duties, and even some legal rights and obligations.[138]

Even though Green denies that they have any such capacities, it would be wrong to conclude that his theory provides no justification whatsoever for seeking to minimise the suffering of animals.[139] He is explicit that, even for human beings, it is better to have more pleasure in one's life if one's self-development is not harmed by so doing: 'it is not desires for pleasures that are in themselves morally evil, but the occupation of the will by them — the direction of a man's self to this or that pleasure as his good — to the exclusion of those higher interests which cannot possess the man along with them.'[140] In itself, the 'renunciation of pleasure' has no 'moral value'.[141] He claims that beyond a rather small number of ascetics, very few philosophers have held pleasure to be worthless, and the vast majority of those who have appeared to do so have been writing carelessly. In other words, Green holds pleasure to be dangerous only to the extent that it distracts or otherwise hinders a being from realising its higher capacities, and he denies that animals have higher capacities. The implication is that one should not ignore the suffering of animals so long as addressing that suffering would not impede the self-realisation of human beings. In effect, Green adheres to a Millian scale of value: there are higher capacities (higher pleasures, for Mill of course) and lower pleasures, and realising the former has an absolute priority over the latter, yet where the former are not at stake, a life is better where it contains

---

135 Rodman, 'What is Living', 582.
136 Green quoted by Graham Wallas; repeated in Peter Clarke, *Liberals and Social Democrats* (Cambridge: Cambridge University Press, 1978), p. 14, and the editorial note in T.H. Green, *Lectures on the Principles of Political Obligation, and other writings*, p. 336n1.
137 John S. MacKenzie, *A Manual of Ethics* (London: University Tutorial Press, 1929 [1883]), pp. 212n2, 394–96; Rodman, 'What is Living', 582–83.
138 PPO 213.
139 PPO 176. On this general issue, see also W.J. Mander, *British Idealism: A history* (Oxford: Oxford University Press, 2011), pp. 236–37.
140 PE 262.
141 PE 262.

more pleasure.[142] Animals remain objects of moral concern even though they lack rights. They should be allowed to live the life that is best for them, so long as that does not hinder humans realising themselves. For example, depending on your view of the modern beauty industry, one might conclude that on Green's theory it is acceptable to test medicines on animals where no alternative testing is available, while it is not acceptable to test cosmetics.[143]

The most objectionable implication of Green's theory of rights arises with his treatment of the irredeemably and severely insane, and the irredeemably and severely mentally disabled. For Green, they are in precisely the same situation as animals because they are inherently incapable of purposive action.[144] As in the case of animals and the environment, this incapacity is significant because it entails that members of these groups are incapable of possessing rights, duties and obligations. It is perfectly understandable that some commentators balk at this sort of suggestion regarding the moral status of the insane and the mentally disabled.[145] Indeed, Green himself was uneasy about excluding them from the sphere of moral consideration. For instance, he writes,

> 'We treat life as sacred even in the human embryo, and even in hopeless idiots and lunatics recognise a right to live—a recognition which can only be rationally explained on either or both of two grounds: (1) that we do not consider either their lives or the society which a man may freely serve to be limited to this earth, and thus ascribe to them a right to live on the strength of a social capacity which under other conditions may become what it is not here; or (2) that the distinction between curable and incurable, between complete and incomplete, social incapacity is so indefinite that we cannot in any case safely assume it to be such as to extinguish the right to live. Or [(3)] perhaps it may be argued that even in cases where the incapacity is ascertainably incurable, the patient has still a social function (as undoubtedly those who are incurably ill in other ways have)—a passive function as the object of affectionate ministrations arising out of family instincts and memories—and that the right to have life protected corresponds to this passive social function.'[146]

Unfortunately, Green is grasping at straws to a very large extent. Reason (1) is invalidated if one rejects Green's claim that there is an afterlife where

---

[142] See the second chapter of John Stuart Mill's *Utilitarianism*.

[143] It is interesting here to compare Green's fellow British idealist on the moral status of animals: David George Ritchie, *Natural Rights: A criticism of political and ethical conceptions*, second edition (London: George Allen, 1903), pp. 107–11, and his 'The Rights of Animals', *International Journal of Ethics*, vol. 10 (1899/1900), 387–89.

[144] PPO 199, 206, 208, 246.

[145] For example, S.I. Benn and R.S. Peters, *Social Principles and the Democratic State* (London: George Allen and Unwin, 1959), p. 98; Brian Barry, *Political Argument* (London: Routledge and Kegan Paul, 1965), p. 311; Rodman, 'What is Living', 581–82; O'Sullivan, *Problem of Political Obligation*, pp. 184–85.

[146] PPO 154.

'aborted fetuses, idiots and lunatics' will become purposive agents.[147] Simil-arly, the third (or 'passive social function') argument fails to establish that 'the patients' — as opposed to those who care about them — have rights. This is precisely because, adopting Green's words, the patients 'are not affected by the conception of the good to which they contribute'.[148] If there really could be a passive social function which confers rights and duties, then there would be no reason why rights and duties would not be possessed by much-loved teddy bears. Green recognises this fact as his phrase 'perhaps it may be argued' indicates.[149] In fact, reason (2) (that it is too dangerous to preclude the severely insane and mentally disabled from having rights) is the most forceful explanation which Green could present on the basis of his general theory. Even so, this is a purely pragmatic justification and as such will be insecure under certain empirical conditions.

All four of these instances highlight the limitations of a moral theory which is based upon self-realisation. Ultimately the problem is that, for an entity to be able to realise itself, it must have some capacities to realise. Quite simply, some groups which many people regard as possessing at least some inherent claims to moral consideration do not possess these capacities. This is a serious problem for Green and, although this has not always been recog-nised in the literature, it is ultimately unsolvable within the fundamental structure of his argument.[150] He is simply not able to argue consistently, for example, that cruelty to animals or the severely disabled is intrinsically wrong so long as he bases his theory solely upon the ultimate value of distinctively human action. (Hence the significance of his remarks regarding animal sentience.)

Green argues legal rights and obligations are meaningless unless indiv-iduals believe that they will be enforced, and that consequently 'every theory of rights in detail' requires 'a corresponding theory of punishment in detail'.[151] For this reason, the next section examines his own theory of

---

[147] Rodman, 'What is Living', 581–82.

[148] PPO 208.

[149] See Nicholson, *Political Philosophy*, p. 87.

[150] Cacoullos, *Thomas Hill Green*, pp. 73–74.

[151] PPO 177. Alan Norrie presents an extended attack upon Green's theory of punishment which fails because it is premised upon the crude antithesis between the individual and society, something which §2.IV established Green had transcended (Alan W.Norrie, *Law, Ideology and Punishment: Retrieval and critique of the liberal idea of criminal justice* (London: Kluwer, 1991), pp. 90–104). See also Lewis, 'Individualism of T.H. Green', 90–92 *passim*; Milne, *Social Philosophy*, pp. 148–55. For an analysis of a related theory of punishment, see my '"This Danger-ous Drug of Violence": Making sense of Bernard Bosanquet's theory of punish-ment', *Collingwood and British Idealism Studies*, 7 (2000), 116–40.

punishment. As such it forms a bridge to the analysis of his theory of sovereignty and the state in the next chapter.

VI

Green's Theory of Punishment

Green's conception of punishment accords with what H.L.A. Hart later termed the 'standard' definition of punishment.

> '(i) It must involve pain or other consequences normally considered unpleasant.
> '(ii) It must be for an offence against legal rules.
> '(iii) It must be of an actual or supposed offender for his offence.
> '(iv) It must be intentionally administered by human beings other than the offender.
> '(v) It must be imposed and administered by an authority constituted by a legal system against which the offence is committed.'[152]

Hart argues that coherent theories of punishment have other necessary elements. The first, the General Justifying Aim (GJA) of punishment, refers to the goal that is sought through the application of punishment, such as retribution, deterrence, reform, annulment and the expression or communication of fundamental values. The second, the 'Distribution' of punishment, has two facets: 'liability' relating to the types of person to whom punishment may be applied legitimately, and 'amount' referring to quantity of punishment inflicted.[153]

In terms of the GJA, Green holds that where crimes are committed, the state should inflict such punishments as are most likely in the particular circumstances to 'prevent such action as interferes with the possibility of free action contributory to social good', with 'free action' being conceived as action that is 'determined by the idea of a common good'.[154] For the reasons given in §6.II, Green insists that it is not the state's business to punish immorality as such: no one can be forced to act from a morally-good motive.[155] Instead, Green argues that 'every action should be so enjoined [by law] of which the performance is found to produce conditions favourable to action proceeding from that disposition [that is, from a good will], and of which the legal injunction does not interfere with such action'.[156] In this way, punishment can help to sustain the conditions under which the individual

---

[152] H.L.A. Hart, 'Prolegomenon to the Principles of Punishment', in his *Punishment and Responsibility: Essays in the philosophy of law* (Oxford: Clarendon Press, 1968), pp. 4–5.

[153] Hart, 'Prolegomenon', 8–13.

[154] PPO 176.

[155] PPO 16, 196–97, 204, 206.

[156] PPO 16.

can realise her culturally conditioned eudaimonic and rational capacities.[157] Nevertheless, the law still does not exist to enforce morality; indeed, the individual's moral character remains beyond the reach of law because her motivation remains beyond the reach of the law. Punishment exists to sustain a system of legal rights and obligations that creates the social conditions in which individuals tend to be most free to form conscientious judgements and to put those judgements into practice. Consequently, it is deeply misleading to claim that for Kant and Green 'it is certainly possible — indeed, necessary — to legislate our physical affairs [that is, our system of penal laws] so as to incorporate moral law as best as we can'.[158] It is not that 'the unity of moral and positive law is an ideal that may never come about'.[159] Rather, it is not ideal at all, because it simply impossible for it to 'come about', not because they are 'too vague' as Brooks implies, but because of necessity morality concerns the agent's (internal) motives whereas penal law can only affect her (external) behaviour.

Green argues that 'punishment according to its true nature is retributive', 'preventive' and 'reformatory'.[160] It is preventive and reformatory in that it should seek to deter future violations by the offender and those who might otherwise have violated the system of legal rights and obligations which enables individuals to live self-determining and self-realising free lives.[161] Yet, Green also holds that for punishment to achieve its GJA it must also be retributive, because, as will be explained now, only when punishment includes a retributive element can it annul the agent's crime. Retributive punishment is punishment meted out to the agent because she deserves it as a recalcitrant member of her community. Crucially for Green, in that the criminal's sense of personal identity presupposes the meanings and values that she has violated, she recognises that she deserves to be punished: 'He sees that the punishment is his own act returning on himself, in the sense that it is the necessary outcome of his act in a society governed by the conception of rights — a conception which he appreciates and to which he does involuntary reverence.'[162] Under these conditions, retributive punishment

---

157 Brooks ignores the eudaimonic aspects of Green's true good and hence of the common good and punishment (Brooks, 'T.H. Green's Theory of Punishment', for example, 693).

158 Brooks, 'T.H. Green's Theory of Punishment', 700.

159 Brooks, 'T.H. Green's Theory of Punishment', 700.

160 PPO 178.

161 PPO 186.

162 PPO 186. Immediately prior to this passage, Green writes: 'When the specified conditions of just punishment are fulfilled, the person punished himself recognises it as just, as his due or desert, and it is so recognised by the onlooker who thinks himself into the situation. The criminal, being susceptible to the idea of

tends to remind the agent of the commitments and contexts that her person-ality presupposes. In other words, punishment of this type reminds the criminal of the values that she endorses as a member of her society.

It is vital to understand this point because it is the linchpin of Green's characterisation of punishment as annulment.[163] As was established in detail in chapters two, three and four, Green believes that an agent has a determin-ate personality only to the extent that she conceives of herself through her active membership of a living community founded upon common goods and shared values. When she violates those common goods and shared values, she undermines her own personality as well as weakening the social fabric which that personality presupposes as a context for the agent's self-understanding and her capacity to perform distinctively human actions. It is in this sense that retributive punishment annuls the agent's crime: it reaffirms the nature and authority of those meanings and values which help to constitute the criminal's personality, thereby helping to repair her self-understanding, reaffirming to her the worth of her own most fundamental values, and thereby enabling her to live a self-directed, free and distinctively human life once again. To the extent that it does these things, punishment annuls the crime and 'maintain[s]... the rights of the criminal himself'.[164] In sum, punishment has a GJA that includes elements of retribution and reform. These are valuable both intrinsically, and because together they annul the crime and respect the criminal's standing as both an agent and a free citizen.[165]

The link made in Green's theory of annulment between the offender's existential self-mutilation and her social membership also underpins his position regarding what Hart calls the 'distribution' of punishment. Firstly, Green holds that a person should be liable for punishment if she has violated intentionally a publicly-promulgated legal right or neglected an obligation that serves the common good of the society in which the violated right or obligation obtains.[166] This position accords with Hart's claim that just punishment is always of 'an offender for an offence'.[167] This is the most straightforward sense in which acts of legitimate punishment are retributive without being vengeful, retribution being possible only in relation to viol-ation of legal rights and obligations that serve the common good, while

---

public good, and through it of rights, though this idea has not been strong enough to regulate his actions, sees in the punishment its natural expression.'
[163] Brooks ignores the annulling aspects of Green's theory of punishment (Brooks, 'T.H. Green's Theory of Punishment'), as does Mander (Mander, *British Idealism*, pp. 238–39).
[164] PPO 204.
[165] On punishment's reformatory function, see PPO 204.
[166] PPO 185, 177.
[167] Hart, 'Prolegomenon', 11.

vengeance can obtain only in relation to private injuries.[168] Secondly Green holds that the 'kind and amount' of punishment 'must depend on the relative importance of the right [violated by offender] and of the extent to which its general exercise is threatened'.[169] Notice that not only does Green not accord equal significance to all legal rights and obligations, but he insists that even properly-constituted and authorised legal rights and obligations derive their value from the service they render to the realisation of the community's determinate common good. This has highly significant implications for the seriousness of particular acts of violation and punishment.

> 'A punishment is unjust... [to the extent that it] is one that is not required for the maintenance of rights, or (which comes to the same thing) if the ostensible rights for the maintenance of which the punishment is required are not real rights—not liberties of action or acquisition which there is any real public interest in maintaining.'[170]

In other words, Green denies that punishment is always legitimate even against a citizen who deliberately violates a publicly-promulgated legal right or fails to honour a publicly-promulgated obligation. He believes that to argue otherwise would be 'to put the cart before the horse for, as we have seen, rights are relative to morality, not morality to rights (the ground on which certain liberties of action and acquisition should be guaranteed as rights being that they are conditions of the moral perfection of society)'.[171]

Other considerations are also relevant when determining the appropriate amount of punishment. One should not seek to make punishment proportionate to the 'moral depravity' of the crime. Neither moral depravity nor the seriousness of punishment can be measured in any meaningful way, let alone compared with one another.[172] This makes it impossible to make punishment proportionate to the crime. Yet, Green goes further by arguing that 'neither the state nor its agent, the judge,' should attempt to inflict the same amount of pain on different individuals who have committed crimes of the same seriousness (however seriousness is measured). The same punishment (the same fine, or same jail term in the same jail, for example) will cause different people different amounts of suffering. Consequently, inflicting the same pain on different people would require different punishments, something that would mean in effect 'an end to all general rules of punishment'.[173] Instead, the state should use punishment solely to fulfil its primary role as the direct sustainer of the society's system of legal rights and

---

168 PPO 178–83.
169 PPO 177.
170 PPO 186.
171 PPO 186.
172 PPO 190.
173 PPO 192.

obligations, and thereby to act as the indirect sustainer of the more fundamental (sc. inherently-valuable) system of moral rights and duties. Green
argues that punishment is valuable to the extent that it 'associate[s] terror
with the contemplation of the crime in the mind of others who might be
tempted to commit it'.[174] In reality then, particular acts of punishment
should seek to deter prospective criminals from committing crimes in addition to deterring the perpetrator from reoffending.

Obviously, many considerations are relevant here. Importantly, unlike
where proportionality is sought, it tends to be easier to use punishment as
an effective deterrent, because it is easier to predict the effect of particular
punishments on the 'public mind' even though it remains a vague and
inexact process.[175] Indeed, in certain cases, Green is willing to envisage
different punishments for crimes that are 'equivalent, both in respect of the
rights which... [the crime] violates and of the terror needed to prevent the
recurrence of like offences'.[176] On these grounds, he argues that it is appropriate merely to imprison a 'fraudulent banker' while sentencing a burglar to
hard labour, even though fraud and burglary are equivalent crimes.

> 'The infliction of hard labour is in everyone's apprehension so different to the
> banker from what it is to the burglar, that its infliction is not needed in order
> to equalise the terror which the popular imagination associates with the
> punishment in the two cases.'[177]

Nevertheless, Green is very careful to insist that this does not mean that the
poor should always be punished more harshly than the rich. He highlights
the case of the individual who steals food because she is on the verge of
starvation. A policy of punishing such thefts harshly in order to deter a
crime committed under these extreme conditions 'would be a one-sided
application of the principle [of punishment]. It is not the business of the state
to protect one order of rights specially', namely that of private property
ownership, 'but all rights equally' including the right to have a reasonable
chance of living a free life.[178]

> 'In any tolerably organised society the condition of a man, ordinarily honest
> and industrious, who is driven to theft by hunger, will be so abnormal that
> very little terror needs to be associated with the crime as so committed in
> order to maintain the sanctity of property in the general imagination.'[179]

---

[174] PPO 193.

[175] 'The effect of the spectacle of punishment on the onlooker is independent of any
minute inquiry into the degree to which it affects the particular criminal.' PPO
193.

[176] PPO 193.

[177] PPO 193.

[178] PPO 194.

[179] PPO 194.

In fact, rather than punishing theft by imprisoning or executing its starving citizens, the state should address the root causes of the latters' extreme poverty.

Taken together, these considerations underline the fact that Green holds determining the appropriate amount of punishment in any particular case to be primarily a practical matter rather than a philosophical one.[180] In addition to the examples given above, Green considers the cases of a negligent engine-driver, a drunken murderer, a lunatic who breaks a law, a drunken mother who smothers her child in her sleep, and a man who is murdered in a fit of rage having been found to have 'tampered with the fidelity of his neighbour's wife'.[181] The same practical considerations obtain for setting appropriate boundaries between criminal offences and civil offences, many particular examples of which Green considers: 'in order to [secure] the general protection of rights, with some [offences] it is necessary to associate a certain terror, with others it is not.'[182] Moreover, these practical considerations lead Green to be cautious regarding the appropriateness of capital punishment and permanent imprisonment. Either of these punishments would be justified only if the crime required the most extreme terror to be associated with a particular crime, or if the criminal was incapable of reform.[183] Green doubts that one can even know with any confidence whether these conditions obtain. The implication of all this is significant. Contrary to what Thom Brooks for one argued, given that in every case decisions regarding guilt and the appropriate amount of punishment are intrinsically contextualised, little can be gleaned from the fact that in certain practical cases Green might have agreed or disagreed with certain other philosophers, such as John Stuart Mill, regarding the appropriate way to punish certain crimes (see also MSF §7.III).[184]

VII

Summary and Conclusion

This chapter began in §II by establishing that Green's analysis employs a distinction between moral claims on the one hand and rights, duties and obligations on the other, such that all rights, duties and obligations are derived from moral claims but not all moral claims are rights, duties and

---

180 PPO 177.

181 PPO 199, 202, 194.

182 PPO 200; for Green's consideration of different types of offence, see PPO 200–02.

183 PPO 205–06.

184 Thom Brooks, 'Was Green a Utilitarian in Practice?', *Collingwood and British Idealism Studies*, 14:1 (2008), 5–15. See also Thom Brooks, 'Hegel and the Unified Theory of Punishment', in Thom Brooks, ed., *Hegel's Philosophy of Right* (Oxford: Wiley-Blackwell, 2012), pp. 103–23 (especially pp. 117–18).

obligations. It was established that he held the existence of rights, duties and obligations to be an ontological more than a normative matter. Next, he distinguishes moral rights and duties from legal rights and obligations. Moral rights and duties help to constitute both the environment in which the agent acts and, to the extent that she internalises them, to constitute some of the contours of her personality. Legal rights and obligations share certain characteristics with moral rights and duties. Yet, they tend to exist for the agent at a greater remove from her conception of her personality. They are more clearly and stably defined than are moral rights and duties, they are articulated by a legal institution authorised constitutionally by a political institution (such as a legislature or executive), and, unlike moral rights, legal rights can be enforced as much by fear of punishment as by the agent's own sense of the rightness of obedience to them. Moral rights and duties exist to secure or constrain certain patterns of self-directed action from rational eudaimonic agents, whereas legal rights and obligations exist to secure or constrain certain patterns of behaviour from members of society.

It was established that individual determinate specifications of rights, duties and obligations are justified for Green to the extent that they form parts of systems of claims and prohibitions which sustain forms of interaction which the adherents' respective conceptions of their true goods give them reason to value or see as authoritative. To the extent that moral and legal systems are this type, each of the participants is subject to a rule which she has set for herself, and so is 'morally free', in Rousseauian and Kantian terms. In addition to both moral rights and duties and legal rights and obligations, the individual implicitly acknowledges various semi-formalised claims and counter-claims. These reflect ideas regarding the nature of both the true good and the common good that have not gained a clear and explicit voice within the individual, and do not receive explicit social acknowledgement. These implicit rights and duties reflect emerging ideas about what makes life worthwhile as well as currently inchoate entailments of other, socially-recognised claims.

§III built on this analysis by establishing that Green's theory of self-positing differs in significant respects from the much better known theory developed by Fichte, not least because Green seeks to accommodate the individual's attempts to instantiate her non-rational, eudaimonic capacities. Hence, while Fichte calls for individuals to be held rigidly to the obligations of the social roles that they contracted to occupy on becoming a full citizen, Green is concerned to allow individuals to change and develop their respective social roles in response to their continually changing self-understandings.[185] §IV explored Green's conception of recognition in greater depth, defending it against the most significant criticisms found in the secondary

---

[185] Fichte, *Right*, pp. 170, 203v05, and his *Ethics*, pp. 324–44.

literature. §V showed that the structure of Green's theory necessarily precludes the environment, animals and the severely mentally disabled from possessing intrinsic moral rights. §VI analysed Green's theory of punishment, which he sees as a necessary conclusion to his theory of rights. Having now examined Green's theory of rights, duties and obligations in some detail in itself, it must be placed within in its fully political context of the state and the power-laden economic sphere, something that is achieved in the next three chapters.

7

Sovereignty and the Greenian State

*'The real function of government… [is] to maintain conditions of life in which moral-
ity shall be possible,… [with] morality consisting in the disinterested performance of
self-imposed duties'[1]*

*'The state in its judicial function… looks not to virtue and vice but to rights and
wrongs.'[2]*

I

Introduction

Once a community has developed beyond a certain size, enforcement of the
system of legal rights and corresponding obligations which help to sustain
its system of moral rights and duties becomes a necessary aspect of its
ordered scheme of social living.[3] Political life is possible, therefore, only once
the individual is capable of feeling attachments to a large and relatively
impersonal group. The institutions in which such a citizen has been raised
will be the latest stage in a lengthy historical process. Initially the family was
the largest community with which an agent could feel her rational and
eudaimonic well-being to be bound up. Then it was the tribe, and only after
that could the state become a feasible organ for structuring group activities
in the manner that the family and the tribe had done. (The ideal but ultimately unattainable moral community would be the whole human race.)[4]
Indeed, once this stage has been reached, the existence of the state becomes a
necessary condition for the individual's realisation of her conception of her
own true good. At that point, as Paul Harris puts it, 'their rights must be

---

[1] PPO 18.
[2] PPO 204.
[3] PPO 134, 152–53, 178–80.
[4] PPO 206–17.

secured by a body capable of reconciling all claims to rights within society'.[5] The state is able to do this to the extent that it orients and orders legal rights and obligations with reference to the common good of the community.

Nevertheless, one must be careful here. Many scholars place too much importance on the legal enforcement of rights in Green's thought, arguing that all forms of rights are deficient to some degree, until they are recognised in law. As was made clear in §6.III, Green draws a very significant distinction between legal rights and obligations on the one hand, and logically and normatively prior moral rights and duties on the other. Moral rights and legal rights are fundamentally different types of entities, even if the latter should enforce behaviour which accords with or supports the background conditions for the effective functioning of the former.[6] Moral rights and duties can be honoured only when the agent appreciates their intrinsic categorical character and acts in accordance with them because of that appreciation. She can fulfil her legal rights and obligations simply by performing certain outward behaviour. Her motives for behaving as she does are irrelevant in this case. In this sense, the enforcement of legal rights and obligations forms a feature of the institutional environment in which the agent can chose to act in a manner that is either right or wrong, whereas honouring moral rights and duties expresses the agent's inherent virtues.[7]

This chapter is structured as follows. §II introduces Green's theory of the state, sovereignty and political obligation. §III examines Green's criteria for determining the legitimate area of state action and his application of those criteria to modern societies. §IV examines Green's application of his principles of state intervention to some key practical cases. §V compares Green's educational theory with that of Giuseppe Mazzini. §VI considers the problems of practical reason that are faced by Green's political theory, before §VII summarises the argument developed in course of this chapter. Chapter eight turns to Green's defence of democratic social and political institutions, in addition to analysing his interrelated theories of political change and civil disobedience.

II

Green's Theory of the State, Sovereignty and Political Obligation

Famously, Green remarks that 'We only count Russia a state by a sort of courtesy on the supposition that the power of the Czar, though subject to no constitutional control, is so far exercised in accordance with a recognised

---

5 Paul Harris, 'Moral Progress and Politics: The theory of T.H. Green', *Polity*, 21 (1988–89), 542.

6 In what follows the phrase 'moral rights' refers to moral rights and duties, while the phrase 'legal rights' refers to legal rights and obligations.

7 PPO 204.

tradition of what the public good requires as to be on the whole a sustainer of rights'.[8] R.G. Collingwood endorses Harold Laski's attack on what he sees as Green's confusion of moral judgement with careful definition: 'Was it not Green's business as a political scientist', Collingwood asks, 'to analyse facts without indulging in condemnation?'[9] In short, Collingwood characterises this dispute as being between an insistence on conceptual precision on the one hand, and Green's moralism on the other.

The broadly Hegelian conception of the modern state with which Green operates has been attacked in this manner frequently.[10] Part of the reason for the current undeservedly low reputation of Green's theory of the state is that it was misunderstood very significantly by the immediately subsequent generations of scholars and is largely ignored now. Even contemporary British idealist scholars have tended to focus much more closely on Green's conception of the common good and his theory of rights, often effectively treating the state as a mysterious 'black box' whose internal workings are rarely analysed. Yet, Green's analysis of sovereignty and the state anticipated the conceptions of states and 'quasi-states' that have been popularised in the writings of contemporary international relations theorists such as Hedley Bull, Adam Watson, Robert Jackson and others.[11] This coincidence of view has rarely if ever been noted previously. Jackson analyses states and quasi-states using a conceptual distinction between 'negative sovereignty' and 'positive sovereignty'. Negative sovereignty is the 'formal-legal condition' of 'freedom from outside interference'.[12] Positive sovereignty includes negative sovereignty, but extends it so as to become 'a substantive rather than a [merely] formal condition': 'A positively sovereign government is one which not only enjoys rights of non-intervention and other international immunities but also possesses the wherewithal to provide political goods for

---

8   PPO 132.
9   Robin G. Collingwood, 'The Three Laws of Politics', in his *Essays on Political Philosophy*, ed. D. Boucher (Oxford: Clarendon, 1989), p. 214. In this connection, also see Jim Connelly, *Metaphysics, Method and Politics: The political philosophy of R.G. Collingwood* (Exeter and Charlottesville, VA: Imprint Academic, 2003), pp. 253–61. Georg W.F. Hegel, *Elements of the Philosophy of Right*, ed. Allen W. Wood, trans. H.B. Nisbet (Cambridge: Cambridge University Press, 1991), especially §257–320.
10 Most famously in relation to the British idealists specifically, by Leonard T. Hobhouse, *The Metaphysical Theory of the State: A criticism* (London: George Allen and Unwin, 1918). For a modern defence of Hegel's conception of the state, see Robert R. Williams, *Hegel's Ethics of Recognition* (Berkeley and Los Angeles: University of California Press, 1997), chapter 13.
11 See Hedley Bull and Adam Watson, *The Expansion of International Society* (Oxford: Oxford University Press, 1984), p. 430.
12 Robert Jackson, *Quasi-states: Sovereignty, international relations and the Third World* (Cambridge: Cambridge University Press, 1990), p. 27.

its citizens.'[13] Viewing the world through this lens, Jackson observes that many contemporary 'ex-colonial states' have been recognised as states by the international society, 'hav[ing] been internationally enfranchised and possess[ing] the same external rights and responsibilities as all other sovereign states: juridical statehood'.[14] Nevertheless, many of these states fall short of the ideal of statehood as the latter is set out in international law: 'Their governments are often deficient in the political will, institutional authority, and organized power to protect human rights or provide socio-economic welfare.'[15] These are 'quasi-states', and are often run in the interests of a local elite rather than 'the citizenry at large'.[16] This conception of full sovereignty and statehood highlights three conditions: effective agency, recognition by others, and service of the well-being of one's citizens. It is a conception that forms the theoretical backbone for many leading contemporary approaches to the study of international relations including the English School and Constructivism.[17] As will become clear by the end of this section, in crucial respects it coincides with Green's conceptions of sovereignty and the state.

This section will explore Green's conceptions of these two related ideas. It will establish that he adopts Hegel's usage of the 'state', and in so doing conceives of it in a manner that is far closer to the ancient Greek understanding of the *polis* than to the standard English conception of the 'political' state.[18] For Hegel, as Green observes, the state is 'a society governed by laws and institutions and established customs which secure the common good of the members of the society — enable them to make the best of themselves — and are recognised as doing so'.[19] It will be established, firstly, that Green understands the sovereign as that person or entity which determines the actions of the administrative, judicial and military arms of the state.[20] The power to determine these actions is *de facto* sovereignty, while the authority

---

13   Jackson, *Quasi-states*, p. 29.

14   Jackson, *Quasi-states*, p. 21.

15   Jackson, *Quasi-states*, p. 21.

16   Jackson, *Quasi-states*, p. 21.

17   See many of the contributions in Thomas J. Biersteker and Cynthia Weber, eds., *State Sovereignty as Social Construct* (Cambridge: Cambridge University Press, 1996), as well as Colin Tyler, '"History's Actors"?: Insights into the "war on terror" from international relations theory', in Maurice Mullard and Bankole A. Cole, eds., *Globalisation, Citizenship and the War on Terror* (Cheltenham: Edward Elgar, 2007), pp. 32–54.

18   DSF 4–6; PPO 132–35, 141–42. Ruskin conceives of the state in this way without being an Hegelian: for example, John Ruskin, *Unto This Last: Four essays on the first principles of political economy* (London: George Allen, 1900 [1862]), §§17, 34, 37.

19   DSF 4.

20   PPO 132–36.

to do so through law-making is *de jure* sovereignty.[21] In line with a long tradition which still thrives today, Green holds an entity to be truly sovereign only to the extent that it combines *de facto* and *de jure* sovereignty. Precisely where sovereignty resides in any concrete instance is an inherently context-ualised and practical matter.

The analysis begins now with Green's theory of sovereignty, and hence political obligation. Green presents his theory as reconciling the theories of John Austin and Jean-Jacques Rousseau.[22] He begins by arguing that a core facet of being the sovereign is that one is habitually treated as the sovereign (sc. the authoritative person or body wielding supreme coercive power in the territory governed). He is influenced by Austin here.[23] If the sovereign fails to receive such habitual obedience, it lacks the capacity to act and, hence, cannot be the supreme sovereign power in a territory.[24] Critics have attacked Green for allegedly claiming that this proposition is able, on its own, to ground sovereignty.[25] In fact, Green himself sees that the Austinian condition of habitual obedience is not sufficient to do so.[26] He argues that 'So long as [Austin's] view is retained, no satisfactory answer can be given to the question by what right the sovereign compels the obedience of individuals'.[27] Austin sanctions the commands of a sovereign even when subjects obey them simply out of fear. Yet, for Green fear cannot be the foundation of a free personal life, and hence it cannot ground a just political order. As he observes: 'To represent [fear] as the basis of civil subjection is to confound the citizen with the slave.'[28] Social relationships derive their imperative character from the citizen's careful judgement that engaging in them tends to facilitate the performance of distinctively human actions.[29] Consequently, Green holds that it must be illegitimate for the individual to subordinate her own self-determination to the authority of another person or group for any

---

21 PPO 95–99.

22 PPO 84; John Austin, 'The Province of Jurisprudence Determined', in his *The Province of Jurisprudence Determined and the Uses of the Study of Jurisprudence* (London: Weidenfeld and Nicolson, 1954), Lecture VI *passim*; Jean-Jacques Rousseau, *The Social Contract*, trans. Maurice Cranston (London: Penguin, 1968), especially pp. 69–78.

23 Austin, 'Province', Lecture VI, especially 197–9.

24 PPO 113.

25 For example, Harold A. Prichard, *Moral Obligation: Essays and lectures* (Oxford: Clarendon Press, 1949), pp. 61–66.

26 PPO 84.

27 PPO 137.

28 PPO 119.

29 PPO 84; F.C. Conybeare, 'On Professor Green's Political Philosophy', *National Review*, 13 (1889), 776; Vrajendra R. Mehta, 'T.H. Green and the Problem of Political Obligation', *Indian Political Science Review*, 7 (1973), 115–24.

reason other than to actualise such a mode of living. This is Green's most fundamental objection to Austin's theory.

To avoid this problem, Green turns to the Rousseauian conception of the 'general will'.[30] As was established in §3.III, Green conceives of the general will as the will to serve the common good. He refers to it as 'that impalpable congeries of the hopes and fears of a people bound together by common interests and sympathy'.[31] To the extent that citizens do not recognise such a shared goal as the basis of their association, their society is merely a collection of individuals rather than an enriching and stable community. Consequently, the sovereign is authoritative only to the extent that citizens habitually believe it to be so, based upon their conscientious assessment of the political requirements of the common good. Habitual obedience is a necessary but not a sufficient condition of full sovereignty. Such habitual obedience must be motivated by the honest belief that generally the state which the sovereign claims to represent and serve tends to enable its citizens to actualise the common good of the community with which they identify themselves freely.[32]

When functioning properly as the head of an enriching state, the sovereign facilitates forms of living which were previously inconceivable, and in so doing the state and its sovereign enable the agent to live previously unattainable forms of distinctively human life. To understand why this is the case, it is necessary to delve more deeply into Green's conception of the state. The true nature of Green's conception of the state has been missed by at least one important recent commentator.[33] Geoffrey Thomas implies that Green conceives of the state in the classical liberal sense, where it is seen simply as a formalised and constitutionally-ordered set of institutions through which political control is exercised over citizens. In fact as was noted above, Green defines the state in an expanded manner: it is 'a body of persons, recognised by each other as having rights, and possessing certain institutions for the maintenance of those rights'.[34] Green is aware that

---

30 PPO 84; also see Lane W. Lancaster, *The Masters of Political Thought: Volume III, Hegel to Dewey* (London: George G. Harrap, 1959), pp. 208–10; Amal K. Mukhopadhyay, *The Ethics of Obedience: A study of the philosophy of T.H. Green* (Calcutta: World Press Private, 1967), pp. 90–93.

31 PPO 86.

32 Monro misses this point (D.H. Monro, 'Green, Rousseau, and the Culture Pattern', *Philosophy*, 26:9 (1951) 350–55). In many ways, Monro's own 'reformulation' of Green is identical with the latter's actual theory (Monro, 'Green, Rousseau, and the Culture Pattern', 353).

33 Geoffrey Thomas, *The Moral Philosophy of T.H. Green* (Oxford: Clarendon Press, 1987), pp. 333–41 *passim*.

34 PPO 132. This became the standard usage among the British idealists: for example, 'I use the term "State" in the full sense of what it means as a living whole, not the mere legal and political fabric, but the complex of lives and

his usage is alien to the British tradition of classical liberalism, yet he defends his alternative on the ground that it captures an institution that is central to the modern world.

> 'A word is needed to express that form of society, both according to the idea of it which has been operative in the minds of the members of the societies which have undergone the change described [i.e. from tribal to political], an idea only gradually taking shape as the change proceeded, and according to the more explicit and distinct idea of it which we form in reflecting on the process.'[35]

Of those commentators who have appreciated Green's real position, not everyone has welcomed his expansion of the term beyond its classical liberal usage.[36] Richter argues that Green's emphasis upon full realisation and, hence, practice in the Hegelian conception of the true state, together with the imperfection of any world in which humans can live, leads to 'a systematic ambiguity about all Idealist uses of the concept of the state which Green did not escape'.[37] Yet, Richter's objection is somewhat misplaced. For Hegel, 'the well-ordered state' perfectly expresses the true will of its members. Consequently, in following its norms, each member becomes morally free. Green supports Hegel up to a point.[38] He argues that Hegel is correct to emphasise the distinctively human need for a cultural framework in which to live, and that Hegel is correct also to conceive of the ideal state as a moralising system which therefore tends to assist its members to obtain their true good. Nevertheless, Green argues that he is more concerned than Hegel by the imperfection of 'empirical' states, and by the consequence that the latters' customs and institutions cause a great deal of suffering.[39] Green argues that what Hegel writes regarding the state implies that most empirical states are fairly faithful embodiments of the ideal.[40] Even though Green endorses Hegel's

---

activities, considered as the body of which that is the framework. "Society" I take to mean the same body as the State, but *minus* the attribute of exercising what is in the last resort absolute physical compulsion.' Bernard Bosanquet, *The Principle of Individuality and Value* (London: MacMillan, 1912), p. 311n1.

[35] PPO 133.

[36] For example, Melvin Richter, *The Politics of Conscience: T.H. Green and his age* (London: Weidenfeld and Nicolson, 1964), pp. 248–50; George H. Sabine, *A History of Political Theory*, rev. T.J. Thorson (Hinsdale: Dryden, 1973), pp. 666–67.

[37] Richter, *Politics of Conscience*, p. 250.

[38] DSF 5–6.

[39] The term 'empirical' is used here because Hegel calls an entity 'actual' or 'real' to the extent that it embodies its ideal. This is precisely the point at issue here in relation to empirical states.

[40] 'Legislative interference'; Hobhouse, *Metaphysical Theory*, pp. 24, 118–19 ; see also Richard Bellamy, 'A Green Revolution? Idealism, liberalism and the welfare state', *Bulletin of the Hegel Society of Great Britain*, 10 (1984), 35–36; Andrew Vincent and Raymond Plant, *Philosophy, Politics and Citizenship: The life and thought of the*

conception of the ideal state, he holds that Hegel is too optimistic regarding the worth of empirical states.

> 'To an Athenian slave, who might be used to gratify a master's lust, it would have been a mockery to speak of the state as a realisation of freedom; and perhaps it would not be much less so to speak of it as such to an untaught and under-fed denizen of a London yard with gin-shops on the right hand and on the left.'[41]

What is important in the present context is that Green believes that Hegel's way of writing about contemporary statehood underemphasises significantly the suffering caused by empirical states.

By contrast, Green himself is careful to treat the notion of the 'state' as what Max Weber would later call an 'ideal type'.[42] He argues that any observable political organisation is truly a state (and the sovereign is truly a sovereign) 'only [to the extent that it] exists as sustaining, securing, and completing' rights which arise out of social relations and the common good which binds those relations and rights together.[43] In other words, Green's notion of the state refers to the ideal form which society should take to maintain a 'settled, impartial, [and] general' system of legal rights and obligations.[44] Certainly, there are 'so-called states' which are merely 'an aggregation of individuals or communities under one ruling power' but it is clear that these are not included in Green's conception of 'a true state'.[45] Hence, there is no real bite to Richter's objection because Green's is an evaluative category against which 'so-called states' can be judged. This contrast brings out Green's anticipation of contemporary notions of the state and quasi-state in Constructivist and English School international relations (IR) scholarship which was noted above.

This coincidence of view between Green and certain IR scholars becomes even clearer as one delves more deeply into Green's writings on the ideal interrelation of the four elements covered thus far in this section

---

British idealists (Oxford: Basil Blackwell, 1984), p. 12; James T. Kloppenberg, *Uncertain Victory: social democracy and progressivism in European and American thought, 1870–1920* (New York and Oxford: Oxford University Press, 1986), pp. 395–96.

41   DSF 6. For a different assessment, see Peter Nicholson, 'T.H. Green's Doubts about Hegel's Political Philosophy', *Bulletin of the Hegel Society of Great Britain*, 31 (1995), 61–72.

42   Max Weber, *The Methodology of the Social Sciences*, ed. and trans. Edward A. Shils and Henry A. Finch (New York: Simon and Schuster, The Free Press, 1949 [1904]), pp. 88–99.

43   PPO 134. Chin misses this point (Y.L. Chin, *The Political Theory of Thomas Hill Green* (New York: W. Dray, 1920), pp. 158–59).

44   PPO 182.

45   PPO 161

(sovereignty, the sovereign, the state and the citizen). He argues that obedience to the sovereign 'is virtually conditional upon' the members of the community believing that the sovereign embodies their general will.[46]

> '[T]he ultimate power of exacting habitual obedience from the people… [is based upon] a common desire for certain ends—specially the *"pax vitaeque securitas"* ["peace and security of life"]—to which the observance of law or established usage contributes, and in most cases implies no conscious reference on the part of those whom it influences to any supreme coercive power at all.'[47]

For Green, society is prior to the state in at least two significant senses. Firstly, temporally: early societies (families and tribes) had no formalised political structures, whereas modern ones tend to have them. Secondly, conceptually: the definition of 'a state' entails the concept of 'a society'. The state is 'for its members the society of societies—the society in which all their claims upon each other are mutually adjusted'.[48] This latter conceptual relationship is fundamental because it is only through the coordination of the different spheres of the individual's activities with the spheres of her fellows that the individual can realise her capacity to lead a self-directed enriching 'distinctively human' life.[49]

> 'The state is for [its members]… the complex of those social relations out of which rights arise, so far as those rights have come to be regulated and harmonised according to a general law, which is recognised by a certain multitude of persons, and which there is sufficient power to secure against violation from without and from within. The other forms of community which precede and are independent of the formation of the state do not continue to exist outside it, nor yet are they superseded by it. They are carried on into it. They become its organic members, supporting its life and in turn maintained by it in a new harmony with each other.'[50]

A crucial point here is that a state is an internally-complex relational entity and, as such, each part can function as it should only to the extent that every other part does so as well. In fact, it is so complex that often it is not always clear or agreed which part of the state constitutes the sovereign: is it the monarch, the legislature, the executive, the people or something else?[51] Consequently, the proper functioning can be attained only through cooperative action aimed at the eudaimonic and rational development of every member of society. The members of the different 'sub-state' associations should

---

[46] PPO 84.
[47] PPO 84.
[48] PPO 141.
[49] See also Nalini Pant, *Theory of Rights: Green, Bosanquet, Spencer and Laski* (Varanasi: Vishwavidyalaya Prakashan, 1977), pp. 36–38.
[50] PPO 141.
[51] PPO 160.

recognise, therefore, that they share certain concerns—possess a common good—with those individuals who are not members of their particular association but who are members of their state (see chapter three for the analysis of this claim).

It is vital to bear this point in mind so as to head-off objections such as the one made by Bhikhu Parekh that 'Although Green saw the great value of the citizen's sense of political obligation, he did not explore its nature and basis, integrate it into his formulation and analysis of the problem of political obligation, and ask how citizens can cultivate and express a "higher feeling of political duty"'.[52] In reality, Green did all of these things at very great length. Ironically, the form of political obligation for which Parekh argues (one founded on the active fostering of a vibrant community of truly equal citizens) is precisely what motivates Green's moral, political and religious thought (see chapters eight and ten below).[53]

Green is clear that, for the most part 'so-called' states (like early societies) were not formed originally to serve the common good.[54] Yet, his fundamental point is that empirical states attain their ideal type to the extent that there is a sense of community amongst the governed and to the extent that the governed are correct in judging the state and its sovereign to be serving the best interests of the community.[55] One consequence of this need for popular, conscientious, intelligent and habitual trust in the system is that the sovereign will always be limited in its ability to act, by the political influence of these social 'ties derived from a common dwelling-place with its associations, from common memories, traditions and customs, and from the common ways of feeling and thinking which a common language and still more a common literature embodies'.[56] Pragmatically, when the sovereign is not perceived as contributing to the common good of society, or acts contrary to its customs, its position is precarious and its actions will tend to be ineffectual. In the present context, this indicates that merely acquiescing to a person or body as the sovereign is not enough to sustain the political union in practice, nor does it make that union authoritative. To the extent that passive obedience constitutes the total extent of the individual's attachment to the state, its sovereign and its laws,

---

[52] Bhikhu Parekh, 'A Misconceived Discourse on Political Obligation', *Political Studies*, 41 (1993), 248, quoting PPO 122.

[53] On the problems with Parekh's own attempts to theorise this form of political society, see Colin Tyler, 'Strangers and Compatriots: The political theory of cultural diversity', in John Rex and Gurharpal Singh, eds., *Governance in Multicultural Societies* (Aldershot: Ashgate, 2004), pp. 19–35.

[54] PPO 125.

[55] A.J.M. Milne, *The Social Philosophy of English Idealism* (London: Allen and Unwin, 1962), pp. 133–36.

[56] PPO 123.

'the result is still only the loyal subject as distinct from the intelligent patriot, i.e. as distinct from the man who so appreciates the good which in common with others he derives from the state — from the nation organised in the form of a self-governing community to which he belongs — as to have a passion for serving it — whether in the way of defending it from external attack or developing it from within.'[57]

The citizen acts as an intelligent patriot to the extent that she obeys the state and its sovereign because she judges such obedience to best foster both a stable and enriching community and the variegated concrete and distinctive humanity of its individual citizens. A community is strong and enriching to the extent that every citizen contributes actively to a collective life which best serves and embodies her common good.[58] Only to this extent will she be able to act from the pure motive of performing duty for its own sake. Only in this way can she come to act habitually in a distinctively human manner and so to gain an abiding satisfaction of her abiding self (see MSF chapter five).

Echoing Kant's essay 'Perpetual Peace', Green argues that well-ordered states (that is, states as such) are inherently peaceful, and will not come into conflict with one another.[59] Certain other types of empirical state do tend to provoke jingoism domestically, and thereby tend to be able to get their members to fight in aggressive wars. This is particularly true of states ruled by elites or where an ecclesiastical power (such as the papacy) disputes the authority of the (temporal) state.[60] Similarly, conflicts tend to arise where there is an oppressed domestic minority, such as happened with the Irish in Britain.[61] Consequently, well-ordered, broadly egalitarian and tolerant states may have to go to war in order to protect themselves against states that are not well-ordered. The relatively well-ordered state is justified in conscripting its citizens to the extent that is required to protect its character as a eudaimonically-enriching kingdom of ends, but even then the deaths caused

---

[57] PPO 122.

[58] PPO 122.

[59] PPO 166, 169. Immanuel Kant, 'Perpetual Peace: A philosophical sketch', in his *Political Writings*, second edition, ed. Hans Reiss, trans. H.B. Nisbet (Cambridge: Cambridge University Press, 1991), pp. 93–130. See also Immanuel Kant, 'The Idea for a Universal History with a Cosmopolitan Purpose', in his *Political Writings*, ed. Hans Reiss, second edition (Cambridge: Cambridge University Press, 1991), pp. 41–53, and §5.II above. Here, Green differed from Hegel: see my *Idealist Political Philosophy: Pluralism and conflict in the absolute idealist tradition* (London and New York: Continuum, 2006), pp. 6–16. A useful sketch of the historical background to Green's writings on war can be found in Alberto de Sanctis, *The 'Puritan' Democracy of Thomas Hill Green, with some unpublished writings* (Exeter and Charlottesville, VA: Imprint Academic, 2005), pp. 115–21.

[60] PPO 167.

[61] PPO 168.

by the conflict remain wrongs for which all states bear responsibility to the extent that they are badly-ordered. Nevertheless, Green goes so far as to contemplate that there might arise in the future a stable 'international court with authority resting on the consent of independent [well-ordered] states'.[62]

Given that empirical states and sovereigns fulfil their primary functions to varying degrees, in practice there can be different degrees of sovereignty and, therefore, different degrees of political obligation.[63] Green insists that the extent of sovereignty and political obligation can be assessed properly only in particular cases and only by applying two criteria. 'The political society is more complete as the freedom guaranteed is more complete both in respect [1] of the [number of] persons enjoying it and [2] of the range of possible action and acquisition over which it extends.'[64] The first criterion — the number of people ruled — springs from Green's belief that the extent of our recognised community varies and yet ultimately we are all part of one common human society.[65] In practice Green sees the second criterion — the area of political activity — as being more fundamental. He gives the example of a nomad horde which may be 'as numerous as a Greek state', but which secures very few legal rights and obligations for its members.[66] The limited scope of the rights and obligations granted in this case weakens the nomad horde's claim to possess political authority. Similarly, British colonial rule over India derives whatever authority it might have only from the fact that it is exercised in line with the general will of the Indians themselves, and to the extent that it does so in a manner that is consistent with the rule of law.[67]

---

[62] PPO 175. See also Peter P. Nicholson, 'Philosophical idealism and International Politics: A reply to Dr Savigear', *British Journal of International Studies*, 2 (1976), 76–83.

[63] Lancaster misses this point (Lane W. Lancaster, *The Masters of Political Thought: Volume III, Hegel to Dewey* (London: George G. Harrap, 1959), pp. 223–25).

[64] PPO 91.

[65] PE 206–17.

[66] PPO 91.

[67] 'The British power in India exercises a middle function between that of the Roman Empire and that of the mere tax-collecting and recruit-raising empire with which the Roman Empire has just been contrasted. It presents itself to the subject people in the first place as a tax-collector. It leaves the customary law of the people mostly untouched. But if only to a very small extent a law-making power, it is emphatically a law-maintaining one. It regulates the whole judicial administration of the country, but applies its power generally only to enforce the customary law which it finds in existence. For this reason an "habitual obedience" may fairly be said to be rendered by the Indian people to the English government, in a sense in which it could not be said to be rendered to a merely tax-collecting military power; but the habitual obedience is so rendered only because the English government presents itself to the people, not merely as a tax-collector, but as the maintainer of a customary law, which, on the whole, is the expression of the "general will"' (PPO 90).

Borderline cases exist where a tolerable degree of political authority is 'almost' attained. Green focuses on one very significant instance from his own time, which was noted at the beginning of this section.

> 'We only count Russia a state by a sort of courtesy on the supposition that the power of the Czar, though subject to no constitutional control, is so far exercised in accordance with a recognised tradition of what the public good requires as to be on the whole a sustainer of rights.'[68]

In addition to highlighting the link between the authority of the empirical state and its sovereign on the one hand, and their combined service to the common good on the other, the Russian case highlights the fact that the degree of political authority is dependent upon the means by which its position is maintained and its will is enforced.[69] For example, to the extent that the sovereign's position relies on force or its threatened use, the sovereign's rule is illegitimate. The need for the use of force domestically is an indication either that the sovereign no longer embodies the general will effectively, or that the people do not identify themselves with the understanding of the common good which the sovereign seeks to make effective.[70] In either case, there is a *prime facie* case for the empirical state or its sovereign to be either reformed or replaced. In terms of the contemporary debates regarding statehood with which this section began, under these conditions what looks like a state at first glance, on closer inspection turns out to be a 'quasi-state' or 'failed state'. Even if it has 'been internationally enfranchised and possesses the same external rights and responsibilities as all other sovereign states: juridical statehood', its government is 'deficient in the political will, institutional authority, and organized power to protect human rights or provide socio-economic welfare'.[71]

As noted earlier, Green's conceptions of the ideal state and its sovereign are his attempts to articulate the core features of the modern state. His object of analysis is an 'ideal type' of the modern state in the sense popularised by Max Weber.[72] Empirical states live up to this ideal to the extent that they possess what Jackson calls 'positive sovereignty': 'A positively sovereign government is one which not only enjoys rights of non-intervention and other international immunities but also possesses the wherewithal [and 'political will'] to provide political goods for its citizens.'[73] Green uses his conceptions of the state, sovereignty and the sovereign not merely for inter-

---

[68] PPO 132.

[69] PPO 132.

[70] PPO 93.

[71] Jackson, *Quasi-states*, p. 21. This assumes that we understand 'human rights' as socially-particularised Greenian 'natural rights' (see §6.III).

[72] Weber, *Methodology*, pp. 88–99.

[73] Jackson, *Quasi-states*, p. 29.

pretative purposes, but for evaluative ones as well. In this way, he is closer to Jackson and contemporary international relational theorists of his ilk, than he is to Weber. Green's conceptions of the ideal state and sovereign serve as conceptual and critical standards by which citizens and functionaries of empirical states can judge their own actions, as well as the actions of their own and other states.[74]

III

The Appropriate Areas for State Action

The next aspect of Green's conception of the modern state to be considered here is his claim that the government of such a state should restrict its area of activity in certain ways.[75] The fundamental considerations for the sovereign when deciding which particular areas to 'enter' — practically, which particular laws to make and enforce — are that (i) the legally-enforced system of rights and obligations should be framed in accordance with the need for individual self-development, and that (ii) it is impossible to force individuals to develop themselves. Even though the role of the state is defined in relation to morality, it is very misleading to characterise the 'aim and whole rationale of state [as being]… to make us *good*'.[76] As D.G. Ritchie puts it, the 'direct legal enforcement of morality cannot be considered expedient or inexpedient: it is *impossible*. The morality of an act depends on the state of the will of the agent, and therefore the act done under compulsion ceases to have the character of a moral act'.[77] Nevertheless, Green is a pragmatist in that he recognises the need for certain acts to be performed even when the agent's motives are not the highest ones she could have. In these cases, the state should operate on the understanding that

---

[74] In that their conception of the state has a normative dimension as well as conceptual one, Green and Jackson's respective analyses of statehood and sovereignty differ from Bernard Bosanquet's characterisation of Hegel's position: 'The object of political philosophy is to understand what a State is, and it is not necessary for this purpose that the State which is analysed should be "ideal," but only that it should be a State; just as the nature of life is represented pretty nearly as well by one living man as by another.' Bernard Bosanquet, *The Philosophical Theory of the State*, fourth edition (London: MacMillan, 1923), p. 232.

[75] See especially PPO 207–10; also John H. Muirhead, *The Service of the State: Four lectures on the political teaching of T.H. Green* (London: John Murray, 1908), pp. 87–91; Ben Wempe, *T.H. Green's Theory of Positive Freedom: From metaphysics to positive freedom* (Exeter and Charlottesville, VA: Imprint Academic, 2004), pp. 113–16.

[76] W.J. Mander, *British Idealism: A history* (Oxford: Oxford University Press, 2011), p. 230. Mander does acknowledge immediately thereafter that the state cannot 'make' the individual moral directly.

[77] David G. Ritchie, *The Principles of State Interference: Four essays on the political philosophy of Mr. Herbert Spencer, J.S. Mill, and T.H. Green*, third edition (London: Swan Sonnenschein, 1902 [1891]), p. 14; see also Ritchie, *Principles*, pp. 147–51.

'[t]hose acts should be matter of legal injunction or prohibition of which the performance or omission, irrespectively of the motive from which it proceeds, is so necessary to the existence of a society in which the moral end stated can be realised[,] that it is better for them to be done or omitted from that unworthy motive which consists in fear or hope of legal consequences than not to be done at all.'[78]

In this way, obligations are 'at once distinguished from the sphere of moral duty, and relative to it'.[79] For example, recalcitrant parents should be forced by the threat of legal sanctions to provide for the upbringing and education of their children, even if subsequently they comply only due to the fear of legal punishment.[80] Similarly, Green gives grudging support to the second Poor Law, which he sees as a necessary expedient until a widespread, self-asserting and responsible trade union movement exists in Britain (see chapter ten below). In these and all other cases, politics should be shaped by morality.

This recalls the earlier analysis of Green's theory of punishment (§6.VI). The law can attempt to produce the required behaviour using at least one of two methods. Either it can use '(1) threats of pain, and offers of reward', or '(2) the employment of physical force'.[81] Exactly which of these methods will best achieve the state's goals is dependent upon the intrinsically contingent practical circumstances of the concrete situation. In considering which method to adopt, the just legislator should bear in mind at least two general points.[82] Firstly, it is best that no action which is motivated by a sense of duty is changed into an action which is motivated by a fear of legal punishment. Secondly, those actions which tend to promote a net increase in the performance of dutiful actions should be encouraged through law. Certain laws can be passed which will not affect the motive of the particular agent.[83] Nevertheless, it may well prove necessary to prevent some dutiful actions as an unavoidable side-effect of an arrangement which on balance encourages the performance of dutiful actions. Indeed, it is difficult to envisage any state action which will not be likely to prevent some other particular dutiful action from being performed. No law should be made which, given the circumstances, is likely to produce a net impediment to the citizens' eudaimonic and rational self-development.

---

[78] PPO 15.

[79] PPO 10.

[80] Peter P. Nicholson, *The Political Philosophy of the British Idealists: Selected studies* (Cambridge: Cambridge University Press, 1990), pp. 165–71.

[81] PPO 14.

[82] PPO 16.

[83] PPO 209; LLFC 203. Mabbott misses this important point (J.D. Mabbott, *State and the Citizen: An introduction to political philosophy,* second edition (London: Hutchinson University Library, 1967 [1948]), pp. 61–69 *passim*).

Whilst these conditions do not highlight any positive requirements of law beyond the most abstract, Green argues that they do rule out certain forms of legislation. As he puts it, 'the enforcement of the outward act, of which the moral character depends on a certain motive and disposition, may often contribute to render that motive and disposition impossible'.[84] He considers three concrete instances of illegitimate restrictions which the state has imposed upon its citizens. Firstly, there are 'legal requirements of religious observance and profession of belief'.[85] In all probability, he is alluding to the former requirement to sign the Thirty Nine Articles of the Church of England in order to gain certain university appointments. He objects that such laws tend to debase religious practices, and, hence, to hinder the believer's spiritual development.[86] Secondly, certain laws tend to hinder the development of the individual's 'self-reliance': that is 'the formation of a manly conscience and sense of moral dignity'.[87] Thirdly, there are laws which close certain avenues via which the individual could pursue her self-improvement. One example here is the second Poor Law (as noted above), which, in Green's eyes and in the eyes of the Royal Commission that investigated it,[88] diminished the individual's 'moral opportunity' to care for her relatives and friends.[89] (Green's alternative to the Poor Laws is considered in chapter ten below.)

What links these instances is Green's belief that the state can most effectively enable its citizens to promote their own true development by removing the hindrances to their own realisation of their own respective determinate manifestations of the distinctively human capacities (see further MSF chapter five). In modern societies, state interference in these three areas will tend to impair the citizen's ability to make the best of herself and to help others to make the best of themselves. This does not mean that the state should restrict itself to the role of a 'nightwatchman'.[90] As Henry Sturt puts it, Green's 'main thesis is simply the truth (which needed enforcement more at that time than now) that the state is not only a liberty-and-property defence association, but a moral institution in the highest sense of the

---

84 PPO 10.
85 PPO 17.
86 See also John Locke, *A Letter Concerning Toleration*, ed. John Horton and Susan Mendus (London and New York: Routledge, 1991), pp. 17–20.
87 PPO 17.
88 See Richter, *Politics of Conscience*, p. 330. Lewis finds this particular judgement hard to comprehend (H.D. Lewis, 'Individualism and Collectivism — a study of T.H. Green', in his *Freedom and History* (London: George Allen and Unwin, 1962), pp. 69–70).
89 PPO 17.
90 'Legislative interference' 308.

term'.[91] Indeed, Green's emphasis on the moral imperative for state action under certain circumstances is a 'logical conclusion of... [his] philosophical position',[92] and at least one scholar has referred to it as Green's most valuable contribution to the development of political theory.[93] The fundamental point is conveyed by Bernard Bosanquet's contention that 'The State is in its right when it forcibly hinders a hindrance to the best life or common good. In hindering such hindrances it will indeed do positive acts'.[94]

This aspect of Green's theory can be clarified by distinguishing between those forms of state action which tend to enable members of society to develop as rational eudaimonic agents (which will be called 'state intervention' here) and those forms of state action which tend to have the opposite effect (which will be termed 'state interference'). Using this distinction, one can summarise Green's position as being that whilst state intervention is legitimate, state interference is not. In other words, state action in itself is not illegitimate, only that state interference which hinders and may even prevent individuals from being able to develop their own highest capacities, their own distinctively human natures.[95] Grounding this conclusion is Green's contention that 'society should secure to the individual every power, that is necessary for realising this capacity' of conceiving of and actualising her own true good.[96] Ultimately, the Greenian state is simply society's political instrument for carrying out certain aspects of this task.[97]

IV

The Practical Determination of State Intervention

Richter admits to being confused by Green's attempt to combine radicalism and liberalism in relation to war, private property, self-help and charity, education and temperance reform.[98] He concludes that Green holds confused positions in all these areas, and that this reflects another more pro-

---

[91] Henry Sturt, *Idoli Theatri: A criticism of Oxford thought and practice from the standpoint of personal idealism* (London: MacMillan, 1906), p. 222. On the same point, see Vincent *et al.*, *Philosophy, Politics and Citizenship*, p. 34; Thomas, *Moral Philosophy of T.H. Green*, pp. 333–63 *passim*; Andrew Vincent, 'The State and Social Purpose in Idealist Political Philosophy', *History of European Ideas*, 8:3 (1987), 333–35.

[92] Adam B. Ulam, *The Philosophical Foundations of English Socialism* (Cambridge, MA: Harvard University Press, 1951), p. 38.

[93] W.H. Greenleaf, *The British Political Tradition, Volume Two: The ideological heritage* (London: Methuen, 1983), pp. 124–37 *passim*.

[94] Bosanquet, *Philosophical Theory*, p. 178.

[95] PPO 18.

[96] PPO 29.

[97] DSF 5–6; Mukhopadhyay, *Ethics of Obedience*, pp. 119–26.

[98] Richter, *Politics of Conscience*, pp. 270, 293, 369–70. Noël O'Sullivan, *The Problem of Political Obligation* (New York: Garland, 1987), pp. 181–82 makes the same claim.

found confusion regarding the spheres of action in which the individual, civil society and the state respectively should hold sway.[99] In reality, Richter fails to appreciate the extent of Green's sensitivity to the imperfections of the world.[100] Green insists that agents can act in a distinctively human manner only once they have attained a certain minimum level of personal development. Where social influences fail to foster this minimum achievement, the state should intervene to do so. Hence, in relation to his own age and despite the possibility of 'over-legislation', Green argues that, as an empirical fact, his society is such that the individual agent has her opportunities to act well reduced by 'advancing civilisation' to such a degree that it is better to expand state intervention than it is to leave citizens at the mercy of their fellows.[101] Certainly, at present some laws do tend to 'interfere with the spontaneous action of those interests [in the service of a common good], and consequently checks the growth of the capacity which is the condition of the beneficial exercise of rights'.[102] It is for this reason that the state should restrict its actions to the careful 'removal of obstacles'.[103] Nevertheless, frequently such intervention must be undertaken.[104] Charles Sherover brings out the wider implications of Green's position.

> 'The responsibility of the positive state is… [to] undertake those activities which are deemed necessary for the general welfare and which it alone can perform. Just which of these activities require state sponsorship is, of course, the center of political debate in any modern society committed to this kind of responsibility.'[105]

At the level of practice, one especially important area for state intervention is the legal requirement for parents to ensure that their children are educated

---

[99] Richter, *Politics of Conscience*, p. 270.

[100] Sabine, *History of Political Theory*, pp. 655–59; Richard Bellamy, 'T.H. Green and the Morality of Victorian Liberalism', in Richard Bellamy, ed., *Victorian Liberalism: Nineteenth Century Political Thought and Practice* (London: Routledge, 1990), pp. 141–44; Nicholson, *Political Philosophy*, pp. 157–97 *passim*.

[101] PPO 18.

[102] PPO 209.

[103] PPO 209.

[104] Excellent histories of Green's influence in the area of state legislation include Rodman, 'Introduction', pp. 1–16; Vincent *et al.*, *Philosophy, Politics and Citizenship*, *passim*. The best examination of the internal structure of Green's philosophical position is Nicholson, *Political Philosophy*, pp. 132–97.

[105] Charles M. Sherover, ed., *The Development of the Democratic Idea: Readings from Pericles to the present* (New York: Merntor, 1974 [1968]), p. 308. Elsewhere, Sherover writes, '[t]o tell an illiterate person that he is allowed to read is rather an empty liberty; to teach him how to read is to provide a positive freedom or opportunity enabling him to do so' (Charles M. Sherover, *Time, Freedom, and the Common Good: An essay in public philosophy* (Albany, NY: State University of New York Press, 1989), p. 117).

to at least a certain level and in a certain way. Education in a precondition of the self-realisation of a child's capacity for moral agency. Similarly, it is possible for certain contracts to be made between people, and certain economic rights can be accorded, which tend to stunt the eudaimonic and rational growth of at least one of the parties.[106] These contracts and rights include the renting of bad housing, work contracts which impose conditions leading to the physical and mental injury of the worker, and certain land rights. (These issues are dealt with at great length in §7.V and chapter ten, respectively.) Passing more extensive temperance legislation works in tandem with restraints upon oppressive work contracts, land reform and all other legitimate instances of state intervention in the lives of citizens, all of which constitute necessary functions of the British state of Green's age.[107] The core point is that Green's primary political commitment is to foster the individual's capacity to perform their own distinctively human actions. This is 'intelligent' action: action which the individual undertakes with full knowledge of her goals and the best means for achieving the full realisation and exercise of all of her distinctively human capacities. Human imperfection means that this telos can never be attained perfectly. Yet, Green sees state intervention as a key device for creating the conditions under which the ideal can at least be moved towards. This liberal socialist approach is analysed in greater depth in chapters nine and ten, during the discussion of Green's qualified defences of the right to private property and of capitalism. There is no contradiction or ambivalence in Green's philosophical thought on this point then, although things will always be less clear at the level of practice.

Before moving on, it will be illuminating to give one further example of a key are of state action: legislation regarding education. To bring out some other interesting dimensions, the following section will also compare Green's position to that of one of his great heroes: Giuseppe Mazzini.

V

Green, Mazzini and Educational Reform

Green's intellectual relationship to Mazzini was introduced in §5.II. There, it was shown that while Mazzini sees progress as something that can be achieved only by Humanity conceived as a corporate entity, Green insists that it can be achieved only by individuals. It will be shown now that this difference of social ontology helps to explain a profound difference between Green's attitude to the education of citizens and that of Giuseppe Mazzini.[108]

---

[106] PPO 210.
[107] PPO 211.
[108] See Nettleship, 'Memoir', xlv–lviii; Peter Gordon and John White, *Philosophers as Educational Reformers: The influence of idealism on British educational thought and*

Where Mazzini's progressivist form of holism leads him to advocate the use of education to instil the most 'advanced' principles into the population, Green's relational social theory leads him to resist any attempt to train the working classes in how and what to think. For Mazzini, 'Education teaches in what social weal consists'.[109]

> 'The nation is bound to transmit its programme to every citizen. Every citizen should receive in the national schools a moral education, a *course of nationality* – comprising a summary view of the progress of humanity and of the history of his own country; a popular exposition of the principles directing the legislation of that country, and that elementary instruction about which we are all agreed. Every citizen should be taught in these schools the lesson of equality and love.'[110]

Mazzini insists that once this 'National Programme' has been 'transmitted' to the citizen, he should be allowed not merely to express his own views freely, but trained to do so. Yet, Mazzini is emphatic regarding how the individual should decide on the truth of their views. Relying solely on one's own conscience leads to the 'anarchy' that afflicts and divides Protestants, whereas blind acceptance of generalised beliefs of Humanity would be a form of 'tyranny'.[111] One could only be absolutely assured of one's beliefs where personal conscience and Humanity agree.[112] Yet, where these two guides differ, it is clear to which Mazzini accords the highest authority: 'God, the *Father and Educator of Humanity*, reveals His Law to Humanity through time and space... *I believe in Humanity*, sole interpreter of the law of God on earth.'[113]

Green too holds that, in a healthy society, the 'collective wisdom of the ages', in Edmund Burke's phrase, is embodied within the 'complex organisation of life, with laws and institutions, with relationships, courtesies, and charities, with arts and graces', and it is 'through... [participating in these that] the perfection [of man] is to be attained'.[114] In a lecture to the Birmingham Teachers Association that was published in 1877, Green advocates a system of compulsory education which is to be provided at the expense of the community if parents cannot afford it. Again like Mazzini, Green wishes to use the educational system to undermine the inequalities of society, with

---

     practice (London: Routledge and Kegan Paul, 1979); Richter, *Politics of Conscience*, pp. 350–62; Nicholson, *Political Philosophy*, pp. 165–77.

[109] Giuseppe Mazzini, 'The Duties of Man', in his *The Life and Writings*, ed. Emilie Ashurst, 6 vols., second edition (London: Smith, Elder, 1891), vol. 4, p. 320.

[110] Mazzini, 'Duties', 325.

[111] Mazzini, 'Duties', 248, 250.

[112] Mazzini, 'Duties', 257–58.

[113] Mazzini, 'Duties', 257, 258.

[114] DSF 23.

schools mixing children from all classes.[115] Moreover, he wishes to use it to encourage children to choose their own paths in life rather than merely following blindly the careers of their fathers.[116] Through greater use of endowments and other changes Green hopes that T.H. Huxley's 'ladder of learning' can be created in Britain.

Alongside these similarities, Green's educational theory differs from Mazzini's in important respects. Rather than aiming as Mazzini does to use the educational system to build a sense of shared nationality, Green aspires to create a system of liberal education at the end of which children will be able to pursue any career for which they have both the innate capacity and desire. In 1882 Green described an educational ladder with three rungs: the child leaving school at thirteen years old should be 'expert in arithmetic, and thoroughly able to read and write his own language'; those who left at sixteen would also study 'mathematics, with Latin or some modern language'; and those who stayed until eighteen would add Greek and an applied natural science.[117] Brighter children should then be enabled to attend university.

While Green's religious beliefs inform his attitude to 'great books' and by extension to the education required to make those books intelligible, his aspirations are far more practical and certainly less nationalistic than those of Mazzini.[118] Nevertheless, both Green's experiences as a Schools Inquiry

---

[115] 'Oxford High School' (GW 3:462).

[116] 'Grading' (GW 3:389-90). See also Green's various detailed contributions to the reports of the Schools Inquiry Commission, Taunton Commission: 'Special Report on Birmingham Free School, and General Report on the Counties of Stafford and Warwick', in Schools Inquiry Commission, vol. viii: *General Reports by Assistant Commissioners: Midland Counties and Northumberland* (London: HMSO, 1868), pp. 91–253; 'County of Buckingham' and 'County of Northampton', in Schools Inquiry Commission, vol. xii: *Special Reports of Assistant Commissioners, and Digests of Information Received: South Midlands Division* (London: HMSO, 1868), pp. 175–93, 313–79; 'County of Stafford' and 'County of Warwick', in Schools Inquiry Commission, vol. xv: *Special Reports of Assistant Commissioners, and Digests of Information Received: West Midlands Division* (London: HMSO, 1869), pp. 365–485, 669–752; and 'County of Leicester', in Schools Inquiry Commission, vol. xvi: *Special Reports of Assistant Commissioners, and Digests of Information Received: North Midlands Division* (London: HMSO, 1868), pp. 17–90 (see Nicholson, *Political Philosophy*, p. 315).

[117] 'Oxford High School' (GW 3:461).

[118] 'In great books and great examples, in the gathering fulness of spiritual utterance which we trace through the history of literature, in the self-denying love which we have known from the cradle, in the moralising influences of civil life, in the closer fellowship of the Christian society, in the sacramental ordinances which represent that fellowship, in common worship, in the message of the preachers through which, amid diversity of stammering tongues, one spirit still speaks — here God's sunshine is shed abroad without us' (WG 248).

Assistant Commissioner in the mid-1860s and his subsequent university career showed him the difficulties in realising these hopes in practice. Reform is hindered by middle-class parents' conventional aspirations for their children, as well as by more technical issues relating to the organisation of the school system.[119] Not only this but he wishes to see an extensive reform of the English university system. Green put it in the following way during a speech that he gave under the auspices of the Oxford Reform League, predominantly to working men, during the agitation that led to the passing of the 1867 Reform Act.

> 'As for the educated class—it is hard to know what that means. Every one who wears a good coat, or reads the *Times* or the *Saturday Review*, believes himself to belong to the educated class. (Laughter.)... But the present system of higher education in England is a protected and exclusive system. It is so in consequence of the artificial system of expense which is kept up at the Universities, and of the endowments—the unequal distribution of endowments—of the established Church. Thus those who share in the higher education, while they gain enough learning by it, gain a great deal of the spirit of protection and exclusion which it fosters. Well, then, we must make up our minds to the opposition of the capitalists and the educated classes.'[120]

Green argues that the radical reform of all levels of education is a precondition of the creation of what has been called here a eudaimonically-enriching kingdom of ends. Only with parliamentary reform would Britain get educational reform, because only then would one end 'government by oligarchy of wealth, fenced round and protected by a system of law, which makes many poor to make a few rich, and which, as a matter of history, has done its best to keep the mass of the people abject and ignorant, in order to secure the supremacy of a class. (Cheers)'.[121] It was for this reason that Green himself helped create and for some time ran cheap accommodation to house poorer Balliol students, as well as campaigning (successfully) for the admission of women to degree-bearing courses at the University of Oxford. At his death, he was also in the process of helping to reorganise secondary schools in Birmingham and to improve the pay of assistant masters there, something which earned him significant thanks in the local educational establishment.[122]

In a sense, both Mazzini and Green want to use education as a method of social engineering.[123] Yet, whereas Mazzini's approach is explicitly directed towards nationalistic purposes, Green seeks to restructure educational pro-

---

119 'Grading' (GW 3:387).
120 T.H. Green, report of his speech, 'The Reform Bill', to the Oxford Reform League, Oxford Town Hall, 25 March 1867 (GW 5:228).
121 Green, 'Reform Bill' (GW 5: 228–29).
122 Nettleship, 'Memoir', lv.
123 'Grading' (GW 3:387–90) and 'Oxford High School' (GW 3:475–76).

vision in order to enable all children to find and live lives that suit them personally. In other words, Mazzini's theory recalls, say, Fichte's use of education to build patriotism in his *Addresses to the German Nation* (1808), whereas Green's does not (see §6.III).[124] Similarly, Green's position differs from the one Plato defends in *The Republic* in that Plato wants people to find the role that suits them best from among all the roles required for the *polis* to function as a unity.[125] Plato's roles are constructed to serve social necessity and in that sense they are determined prior to the needs of the individual. Green's occupations on the other hand change over time partly in response to the gradual development of the range of human activities that are socially-recognised as tending to liberate the individual's potentials. In short, Plato's roles derive ultimately from a hierarchical form of holistic organicism, whereas Green uses a relational social theory to justify an egalitarian community of self-directing citizens. The educational system associated with this community should be similarly egalitarian. His goal is a situation in which,

> 'each citizen will have open to him at least the precious companionship of the best books in his own language, and the knowledge necessary to make him really independent; when all who have a special taste for learning will have open to them what has hitherto been unpleasantly called the "education of gentlemen." I confess to hoping for a time when that phrase will have lost its meaning, because the sort of education which alone makes the gentleman in any true sense will be within the reach of all. As it was the aspiration of Moses that all the Lord's people should be prophets, so with all seriousness and reverence we may hope and pray for a condition of English society in which all honest citizens will recognise themselves and be recognised by each other as gentlemen.'[126]

It should be clear by now that Mazzini and Green share a world-view that seeks to combine a profound concern for the poor, with a belief in the existence of national identities and an appreciation of the practical need for organisation and leadership in social reform. Both appeal to considerations of the common good to resolve these problems. Yet, this section has indicated that, whereas Mazzini believes that education should be used to make citizens loyal to the common good and hence to the nation, Green holds that the state should act so as to ensure that education enables the individual to develop her own personality as a free and equal citizen with rational and eudaimonic potentials.

---

[124] Johann G. Fichte, *Reden an die deutsche Nation* [*Addresses to the German Nation*], see the second address for a sketch of Fichte's basic position. This is only to note the coincidence of views, not to claim any direct influence of Fichte on Mazzini.

[125] Plato, *The Republic*, 367e–376c.

[126] 'Oxford High School' 475–76.

V

Practical Reason and the Limits of Political Philosophy

Despite what was established in the preceding two sections, it might be concluded that, even if Green is unconcerned by the practical vagueness of his position on state action, its open-endedness throws great doubt on the liberal credentials of his wider political theory.[127] Yet, as has been shown in chapter four, Green insists that the more determinate conceptions of the requirements of personal virtue can only spring from reflections on the specific demands of one's conscience.[128] As a result, his theory cannot justify repression of one's conscience.[129] This means that at most levels the popular allegation that potentially Green's theory justifies despotism fails due to its misunderstanding of the workings of the individual's best life and self-development.[130] Nevertheless, things are not so straightforward in certain cases, as Green does advocate the suppression of certain types of desire in the interests of fostering the agent's true freedom. It is this contention which allegedly creates the problem for the liberal elements of his political theory.

The implications of the objection come out most starkly in relation to Green's work for temperance reform. Green argues that circumspect state action in these and similar areas is often legitimate because a 'right' to harm oneself to the extent of destroying the possibility of pursuing a common good is self-contradictory.[131] This line of thought also underlies his vehement reaction against the ease with which alcohol was available in his time. Famously, he argues that,

> 'Drunkenness in the head of a family means, as a rule, the impoverishment and degradation of all members of the family; and the presence of a drink-shop at the corner of a street means, as a rule, the drunkenness of a certain number of heads of families in that street. Remove the drink-shops, and as the experience of many happy communities sufficiently shows, you almost, perhaps in time altogether, remove the drunkenness.'[132]

---

127 See Richter, *Politics of Conscience*, pp. 286–87; Michael J. Phillips, 'Thomas Hill Green, Positive Freedom and the United States Supreme Court', *Emory Law Journal*, 25 (1976), 77–78; Wempe, *T.H. Green's Theory of Positive Freedom*, especially pp. 127–28.

128 PE 308.

129 PPO 176–206 *passim*.

130 Isaiah Berlin, 'Introduction', in his *Four Essays on Liberty* (Oxford: Oxford University Press, 1969), p. xlix$n$1.

131 Possibly for the same reason, Green describes suicide as 'ludicrously wrong' (LMPP 159–60). He adds shortly afterwards: 'Suicide and murder are unsound, and come under physical laws; men may lose their free will by physical causes' (p. 162). Nevertheless, he writes nothing regarding the legitimacy or otherwise of the state making attempted suicide a criminal offence.

132 LLFC 210.

Green goes so far as to argue that without such restrictions upon the sale of alcohol, all other measures aimed at improving human lives will be largely ineffectual. Without the stricter control of alcohol sales, the frequently self-reliant individual is merely a potentially good person who fails to realise her own higher potentials.[133] Many commentators regard Green's position here as merely a rather quaint expression of an exaggerated Evangelical preoccupation with the evils of drink.[134] Yet, these critical reactions to Green demonstrate a certain ignorance of or insensitivity to the degree and consequences of drunkenness within mid- and late-Victorian Britain. There was extensive alcoholism, particularly among the working classes.[135] The seriousness of the problem was most apparent among children. The equivalent situation in today's terms is living in a society where harmful drugs are widely available and used, and where crime and destitution reflect that fact even among children. One needs only to think of sections of most large European and American cities at the moment to recognise how serious such a situation is. This is directly equivalent to the situation Green is addressing.

With this point in mind, one can consider the following familiar scenario. The drug addict wishes to give up heroin. Doing so would allow her to develop her skills and talents as a moral being and, on Green's terms, to become more fully human. Should the addict be forced to give up heroin by another individual or an organisation such as the state? On one view, it seems that Green would say that she should. The addict's desire to overcome heroin is her 'higher', more real, desire. Indeed, even if the agent never expresses any wish to quit her habit, Green seems committed to arguing that she should be coerced to do so. She should be 'forced to be free'.[136] For Green the drug addict who says that she does not wish to give up drugs is having her conscience overpowered by her animal imperfections (see MSF chapters five and six). In short, the real problem arises where one is uncertain whether or not the agent is following her conscience. In the case of alcoholics and other drug addicts, Green is clear that they are not.[137] Nevertheless, as has been

---

[133] PPO 21–22.

[134] For example, Kenneth R. Hoover, 'Liberalism and the Idealist Philosophy of Thomas Hill Green', *Western Political Quarterly*, 13 (1973), 560; Bellamy, 'T.H. Green and the Morality of Victorian Liberalism', 142–44 *passim*.

[135] See Peter P. Nicholson, 'T.H. Green and State Action: Liquor legislation', *History of Political Thought*, 6 (1987), 517–50, and Brian Harrison, *Drink and the Victorians: The temperance question in England 1815–1872* (London: Faber and Faber, 1971).

[136] Rousseau, *Social Contract*, p. 64.

[137] For example, on alcohol see LLFC 199, 209–12; see also Nettleship, 'Memoir', cxv–cxviii; Richter, *Politics of Conscience*, pp. 362–70; Gerald F. Gaus, *The Modern Liberal Theory of Man* (Beckenham: Croom Helm, 1983), pp. 178–82; Nicholson, 'T.H. Green and State Action'; Nicholson, *Political Philosophy*, pp. 177–88 *passim*. On education, see especially 'Grading'; 'Elementary'; 'Oxford High School'; Gordon

noted in §7.IV, there will be some cases where the state cannot avoid supp- ressing conscientious actions. This is because some restriction of personal subjective freedom seems to follow almost inevitably and frequently from the fact that one body of law applies equally to all citizens. Often, the law attempts to facilitate and protect intrinsically non-coercive social relation- ships. Moreover the law applies generally, but always to cases that are, in some ways, unique. This leads to both the granting and the denial of legal options that are inappropriate in some particular concrete cases.

Consider Green's analysis of family rights. He begins by rejecting poly- gamy as being incompatible with the quality and degree of concrete inter- personal intimacy that is required to foster and sustain distinctive elements of a personality which family life makes possible. These elements help to form a life in which the individual conceives 'of his own good' as including 'a conception of the well-being of others, connected with him by sexual relations or by relations which arise out of these. He must conceive of the well-being of these others as a permanent [spiritual] object bound up with his own'.[138] Only when such a permanent relation is central to the husband's sense of self will the wants of the wife tend to be 'permanently provided for' and will the children enjoy 'a recognised claim for shelter and sustenance'.[139] Only when such a bond exists between family members will there tend to be what Green calls, quoting the *Digest* from the *Code of Justinian*, 'sharing an entire life' or an 'indivisible common life'.[140] Only then can family life fulfil its social function of 'domestic training' or 'moral education', by which Green seems to mean the development of the individual's capacity for self- less love and caring for others.[141] He claims that it is possible for marriage to fulfil this social function only where it is based on monogamous families. Moreover, even if each adult family member has different (gender- determined) roles and associated rights, duties and obligations, an enriching family is possible only to the extent that every adult member is respected as an equal irrespective of their gender. He argues that, in order to foster the requisite familial bond, the state should encourage weddings to be cond- ucted 'in the presence of religious congregations and with religious rites'.[142] At the same time, he does not believe that the state should make these

---

et al., *Philosophers as Educational Reformers*; Nicholson, *Political Philosophy*, pp. 168– 71, 315.

[138] PPO 236.

[139] PPO 235.

[140] PPO 240. The translations are by Paul Harris and John Morrow in their edition of Green's *Political Obligation*, the original Latin phrases being '*consortium omnis vitae*' and '*individua vitae consuetudo*', respectively.

[141] PPO 240, 242.

[142] PPO 245.

religious elements compulsory, and hence he holds that civil marriages should be recognised in law.

Even though Green never questions the husband's legal standing as head of the household, he is very concerned to ensure that the utmost possible is done to ensure that women are not disempowered by marriage and that children are protected. In this regard, he is concerned especially with the legal right for divorce. He argues that where the recognised grounds for divorce obtain, it should be made 'cheap and easy' for the wronged party to gain a divorce irrespective of their gender.[143] That said, his position does have elements which might seem unduly restrictive to modern eyes. For example, he holds that divorce should be possible only on grounds of adultery, as adultery tends to destroy the intimate ties that form the heart of a healthy marriage. He argues that the option of a divorce being granted simply 'at the pleasure of one of the parties' infringes the right of the other party.[144] It does this by tending to discourage both parties from committing fully to a properly shared life, and it prevents the woman who does so commit herself from ever finding another husband or committing herself so completely again. Similarly, Green does not wish divorce to be obtainable on grounds of insanity (the lunatic might recover), cruelty or incompatibility (both which he believes would tend to encourage unhappy spouses to act in those ways towards one another).[145] To protect the rights of the ex-wives and children, the state should force recalcitrant ex-husbands to provide the requisite financial support following divorce.

Green's discussion of family rights, especially his defence of the rights to marry, to have children and to divorce, is instructive in the context of the present discussion regarding the unavoidable injustices of the law. Throughout his analysis, Green seems torn in several directions. On the one hand, he is conscious of the distinctive characteristic of family rights: they are rights that particular individuals exercise over other particular individuals for the performance of and abstention from certain behaviour.[146] Importantly, this right is not held against any other individual, such as a stranger or even a friend. As such, family rights regulate the details of the free lives of individuals in ways that, for example, the right to own private property does not.[147] Significantly, family rights are inherently reciprocal: the husband's rights over his wife create like rights of the wife over the husband. On the other hand, family rights exist to facilitate socially-valuable forms of life that rely not on claims and counter-claims, but rather on mutual love and self-

---

[143] PPO 243.
[144] PPO 242.
[145] PPO 246.
[146] PPO 233.
[147] PPO 235–37.

lessness between individuals: in this way they create a unique 'indivisible common life'.[148] Constantly, however, family rights as legal entities risk formalising and hence destroying the intimacy they exist to serve.

Moreover, Green is conscious that each family develops in its own way, and that consequently their own subtle dynamics seem to be constantly constrained and distorted by laws which have to treat particular instances as representatives of generalised social categories. The attendant complexities are evident in his continual recourse to the tendencies of the law, rather than those consequences that are inevitable in practice, let alone its allegedly necessary consequences. Unfortunately, the law's likely effect on one family may well not be found in another. As a result, the same law will have different impacts on different families. For some it will be beneficial on balance, whereas for others it will do more harm than good. It is difficult to reach a solid practical judgement under these conditions. For example, Green attempts to establish that divorce should be obtainable due to adultery, but not on grounds of insanity, cruelty or incompatibility. Yet, it is not clear why the arguments in support of adultery do not apply to the other grounds. One could only arrive at decisions that best serve Green's ultimate telos (individual self-realisation) by considering cases in their own irreducible complexities. In short, the central problem is the one noted above: law applies generally, but always to cases that are, in some ways, unique, something that leads to both the granting and the denial of legal options that are inappropriate to some particular concrete cases. Case-by-case tailoring would destroy the notion of a single set of laws which binds together everyone subject to it within the same state. It would undermine the notion of a kingdom of ends in which all individuals are treated as free and equal citizens.

Consequently, unless one can identify universally-valid empirical arguments that could protect individuals absolutely, there will always be a danger that some people's welfare will be sacrificed to increase the welfare of others, even if 'welfare' is understood in terms of the protection of individual rights (see MSF chapter eight).[149] Yet, it is extremely difficult to imagine concrete, realistic and yet universally-valid empirical arguments of this type.

The awkwardness of Green's discussion of family rights reflects a more general problem facing applied political philosophy. As Ben Wempe has written: 'Green is prepared to leave things to their own course, it would

---

[148] PPO 238, 240.

[149] PE 273; LLFC 199; Thomas, *Moral Philosophy*, pp. 359–60. David Cummiskey, *Kantian Consequentialism* (New York and Oxford: Oxford University Press, 1996); David Weinstein, 'Between Kantianism and Consequentialism in T.H. Green's Moral Philosophy', *Political Studies*, 41:4 (1993), 618–635.

seem, as long as this produces the right result; if not, he seems to be saying, the use of force is appropriate in all those cases in which this result is nevertheless needed'.[150] At its most damaging, however, Wempe's criticism seems to be merely an acknowledgement of the salience of pragmatic considerations in every instance of the exercise of practical reason. It is a problem for any applied philosophy which ascribes any significance to the consequences of one's principles, rather than being a problem which confronts Green alone.

VII

Conclusion

This chapter has covered some important ground. It was established in §7.II that, as for Greenian political action more generally, the primary function of the Greenian state is to maintain a social environment in which each individual can live a self-determined, multifaceted, enriching and free life. For the state, this means maintaining the legal rights and obligations that correspond to the common good of the governed society, with the latter being understood as an ordered community of self-directing yet socially-responsible citizens. The state is sovereign to the extent that (i) it fulfils this function, and (ii) its rule is judged to be authoritative by those whom it governs. The extent and nature of legitimate state action was analysed in §7.III, before §7.IV examined the processes whereby a determination can be made of the practical extent of state intervention. §V compared Green's theory of education with that of Mazzini, whereas doubts regarding the liberal aspects of his political theory were addressed in §7.VI.

There are a number of points to draw out of this chapter. As has been explored in the earlier chapters of this book, Green holds that individual human beings are ultimately the only agents in the world. Their drives for self-realisation and inner peace can be satisfied only to the extent that the individual lives a coherent life, a life which is a self-conscious practical instantiation of her human nature. For this reason, the perfected human life would be founded on a practical recognition of the duty to respect persons. Only to the extent that particular individuals endorse in practice the cultural groups and institutions who exercise coercive power over them as being objective manifestations of their own highest nature as agents, do these groups and institutions possess true spiritual worth. Similarly, Green argues that the state is constituted by certain types of interrelations between individual human beings.

As has been established in §§7.II–III, social norms have value only to the extent that the individual identifies with them freely and conscientiously as

---

[150] Wempe, *Positive Freedom*, p. 114.

a citizen, rather than out of either selfishness or fear. As Green writes in his manuscripts, 'Slave, as a slave, can't be moral'.[151] The agent's '"will is autonomous," [when it] conforms to the law which the will itself constitutes'.[152] A command lacks intrinsic normative weight to the extent that it is obeyed out of fear rather than because the person obeying it judges it to bind her categorically.[153]

> 'The law, merely as law or as an external command, is a source of bondage in a double sense. [1] Presenting to man a command which yet it does not give him power to obey, it destroys the freedom of the life in which he does what he likes without recognising any reason why he should not….; it thus puts him in bondage to *fear*, and [2] at the same time, exciting a wish for obedience to itself which other desires (*phronema sarkos* [desires of the flesh]) prevent from being accomplished, it makes the man feel the bondage of the *flesh*.'[154]

In the first instance, the agent does not identify with 'the law' in such a way that she can conceive of it as a true claim of duty, and so she does not revere it for its own sake. In the second instance, she is led to feel her own imperfection more clearly, thereby heightening her feeling of self-alienation. The imposition of such rules onto the individual's life constitutes a powerful source of inner disharmony for her. This fact is crucial for present purposes because the rules governing an individual's life only have value to the extent that they facilitate her efforts at self-realisation. The development of the individual equates with the increasing harmonisation of her inner life. Consequently, any attempted authoritarianism would be necessarily both illegitimate and ineffective.[155] The specific path of the individual's development depends on the particular manifestation of her highest capacities. The increased self-harmonisation which this process of manifestation entails can be achieved only by allowing the contradictions within the agent's character to work themselves out gradually and for themselves. Consequently, this working out of the contradictions within the agent's inner life can only be successful to the extent that the underlying principle of the agent's consciousness as expressed in her conscience is allowed a truly free reign in the world of practice.

The details of the future steps in this path must remain unknowable until the individual has actually progressed along them. There is no way in which an external authority, including the state, can claim better knowledge than she has regarding the details of her future progress. In this way, 'social guidance' of the individual to a truly 'free' life is an impossibility as it involves a

---

151 MS15, T.H. Green Papers, Balliol College, University of Oxford.
152 DSF 22.
153 PE 325.
154 DSF 2.
155 PPO 100.

self-contradiction. All that can happen is that the individual is forced to perform outward acts whilst still feeling inner disharmony: 'all that a purely
external authority can impose is a command enforced by fear.'[156] This type of
agency is not what Green means by 'true freedom' (see MSF chapter six).
Indeed, he states explicitly that 'of course there can be no [true] freedom
among men who act not willingly but under compulsion'.[157] Green rejects
the claim that the individual is bound to the rules of 'her' society whether or
not she identifies with them. His theory is incompatible with the dualistic
position ascribed to him by Isaiah Berlin.[158] Indeed, Ian Bradley has gone as
far as to argue that 'Green had invoked the idea of the common good of
society not as a rationale for collectivism, but a spur to a more strenuous
individualism'.[159] Bradley's interpretation may rely on a rather strange use
of the term 'individualism', but his underlying point is valid.[160]

Having explored the most basic structures of the Greenian state and its
sovereign in this chapter, the next chapter considers to the role of the citizen
within that state. In particular, it examines Green's democratic thought, his
theory of dissent, the implications for his theory of the contemporary fact of
cultural diversity, and the individual's duty to engage in civil disobedience,
rebellion and even revolution under certain circumstances.

---

[156] PE 325; see also PPO 10–19 *passim*.

[157] LLFC 199.

[158] Ann R. Cacoullos, *Thomas Hill Green: Philosopher of rights* (New York: Twayne,
1974), pp. 112–22 *passim*.

[159] Ian Bradley, *The Optimists: Themes and personalities in Victorian Liberalism* (London:
Faber and Faber, 1980), p. 220.

[160] Vincent *et al.*, *Philosophy, Politics and Citizenship*, p. 27; Kloppenberg, *Uncertain
Victory*, pp. 186–87, 189.

8

Democracy and the Conscientious Rebel

I
Introduction

It will be remembered from the opening of this book that L.T. Hobhouse identifies 'two conditions' which must be fulfilled if a political theory is to constitute a form of liberal socialism. Firstly, it must be 'democratic', in the sense that it must 'emerge from the efforts of society as a whole to secure a fuller measure of justice, and a better organization of mutual aid. It must engage the efforts and respond to the genuine desires not of a handful of superior beings, but of great masses of men'. Secondly, it must 'give the average man free play in the personal life for which he really cares. It must be founded on liberty, and must make not for the suppression but for the development of personality'.[1] In line with this conception, the preceding two chapters of this book have explored the institutional facets of Green's political theory. In addition to examining Green's theory of moral rights and duties, chapter six analysed his theory of legal rights and obligations together with its associated theory of punishment, while chapter seven examined his theory of the state, sovereignty and the sovereign. Appropriate institutional structures are necessary aspects of any eudaimonically-enriching kingdom of ends beyond the smallest and most simple.[2] Nevertheless, Green recognises that institutions derive their value from the roles they play in facilitating the active life of individual citizens. No matter how elegant its institutional structures, the life and value of community originates solely in the conscientious actions of its individual members. In the same way, even a well-governed society is lifeless to the extent that it rules over passive subjects.

It should not be surprising that Green insists on the need for a vital citizen body, given what was established in MSF and what has been argued

---

1   Leonard T. Hobhouse, *Liberalism* (London: Williams and Norgate, n.d. [1911]), pp. 172–73.
2   PPO 119.

above. Chapters two and three of the present book established that Green's social theory understands communities as the relationships that individuals sustain with one another. The different perspectives that individuals hold on shared meanings and values ensures that the common good is open to constant debate and revision. In fact, it has been shown that Green sees gradual change as the normal state of both a healthy individual and a healthy community. The practices employed and given public voice through institutions facilitate this change by providing relatively stable points with reference to which individuals can understand and interact with one another. Shared institutions provide shared points of orientation between individual citizens, even when those citizens hold very different attitudes to one another. For example, the fact all parties agree that, constitutionally, sovereignty in the UK resides with the Crown in Parliament enables a dialogue to take place between those who wish to maintain the status quo, those who wish to abolish the monarchy, those who wish to radically reform Parliament, and even those who wish to dissolve the UK into England, Ireland, Scotland and Wales. Similarly, existing laws on marriage provide common terms of reference for both sides in the debates regarding the appropriateness or otherwise of the legal rights of long-term gay and lesbian partnerships. In the terminology employed earlier (for example, MSF §3.II; CS §1.II), institutions are indispensable features of the shared landscapes through which individuals can crystallise their respective self-conceptions and their respective interpretations and evaluations of the various communities they help to constitute with others.

This chapter analyses the positions Green defends regarding the ways in which individuals should interact with each other as citizens. The discussion is structured as follows. §II examines Green's democratic theory, focusing on his attitude to local participation and the extension of the franchise. §III argues that it is possible to reconcile Green's theory of the ideal state with the contemporary fact of cultural diversity. §IV analyses his theory of civil disobedience and political change. §V considers briefly the effects on the analysis presented in this chapter when one adopts Green's spiritual determinist theory of the will rather than his self-interventionist theory. §VI summarises the argument of this chapter and the conclusions that it reaches.

II

Democratic Participation

Green was well-known in Oxford for his radicalism and in particular for his enthusiasm for the democratisation of British society and politics. He insisted that political decisions should be made by those responsible people who are likely to be affected by their outcomes.[3] He insisted that the franchise should be extended to every section of society that has shown its members would generally wield political power intelligently and conscientiously.[4] To this end, he spoke on many public platforms in favour of what became the 1867 Reform Act. He argued that the vote should be extended to every adult male resident of an urban borough in the UK. He argued against the retention of any property qualification for the vote and rejected Tory calls to manipulate reforms so as to ensure continuing political dominance by the aristocracy and middle classes. He held that in these ways, the 1867 Reform Act could help to break the hold that landed power had over the House of Commons, even if it could not affect directly their dominance in the House of Lords. Yet, ultimately his most important reasons for seeking the extension of the franchise were not pragmatic, but instead arose naturally out of his wider social theory. He made this clear on many occasions, including in a speech that he gave on 25 February 1868, to celebrate the passing of the 1867 legislation.

> 'We said, and we were much derided for saying so, that citizenship only makes the moral man; that citizenship only gives that self-respect, which is the true basis of respect of others, and without which there is no lasting social order or real morality. If we were asked what result we looked for from the enfranchisement of the people, we said, that is not the present question; untie the man's legs, and then it will be time to speculate how he will walk.'[5]

Green did not wish to see the franchise extended because he believed that the poor would then vote for a particular body of legislation that Green himself supported. Neither was it a purely pragmatic move by Green the Advanced Liberal, to undermine the electoral base of his Conservative enemies.[6]

---

3   For a different angle (the metaphysical basis of Green's theory of citizenship), see David Boucher and Andrew Vincent, *British Idealism and Political Theory* (Edinburgh: Edinburgh University Press, 2000), chapter 1. For more historical detail, see Alberto de Sanctis, *The 'Puritan' Democracy of Thomas Hill Green, with some unpublished writings* (Exeter and Charlottesville, VA: Imprint Academic, 2005), chapter three, and especially Denys P. Leighton, *The Greenian Moment: T.H. Green, religion and political argument in Victorian Britain* (Exeter and Charlottesville, VA: Imprint Academic, 2004), chapters four and five. Conybeare resists Green's move (F.C. Conybeare, 'On Professor Green's Political Philosophy', *National Review*, 13 (1889), 771–87 *passim*).

4   For the details of Green's developing position on franchise reform in Britain, see my *Idealist Political Philosophy*, chapter 2. References to the incidents and claims made in the next paragraphs can be found there as well.

5   Green's speech to the Loyal Wellington Lodge of Odd Fellows, 25 February 1868, (GW 5:234), also quoted in Nettleship, 'Memoir', cxii.

6   In fact, the workers elected the Conservatives in 1874, much to many Liberals' huge disappointment, Green's included (see my *Idealist Political Philosophy*, pp. 80–84).

Instead, he supported the extension of the franchise because he believed it would move society closer to becoming a kingdom of ends, it would recognise the moral and intellectual qualities of the newly-enfranchised citizens, and it would force existing voters and politicians to exercise their political judgement and power in a more responsible manner.[7] The whole society would benefit as a result; as he writes in the *Prolegomena*: 'Faculties which social repression and separation prevent from development, take new life from the enlarged co-operation which the recognition of equal claims in all men brings with it' (see §5.V).[8] He develops the political implications of this position explicitly in *The Principles of Political Obligation*.

> 'That active interest in the service of the state, which makes patriotism in the better sense, can hardly arise while the individual's relation to the state is that of a passive recipient of protection in the exercise of his rights of person and property... If he is to have a higher feeling of political duty, he must take part in the work of the state. He must have a share, direct or indirect, by himself acting as a member or by voting for the members of supreme or provincial assemblies, in making and maintaining the laws which he obeys. Only thus will he learn to regard the work of the state as a whole, and to transfer to the whole the interest which otherwise his particular experience would lead him to feel only in that part of its work that goes to the maintenance of his own and his neighbour's rights.'[9]

Moreover, only when political inclusion is combined with an active and deep identification with one's political community, one's 'fatherland', would the individual live up to the true ideal of citizenship.

Nevertheless, in the debates leading up to the passing of the second Reform Act, Green does not push this line on active citizenship to its apparently logical conclusion by seeking the immediate extension of the franchise to the whole adult population. There is no call, for example, to enfranchise women and the rural poor. Support for only piecemeal extension of voting rights had been Green's position for many years. For instance, at an Oxford Union debate on 15 May 1858, he and John Nichol proposed the motion: 'That it is the undoubted right of every Englishman to possess the suffrage, and that, as the time has not yet arrived to carry this principle into effect without serious danger, every means should be taken, by liberal development of education, to bring it about'.[10] Even though full enfranchisement was the ultimate goal, Green held that it would be unwise to widen the vote

---

[7] See Green's speech to the Oxford Reform League, 25 March 1867 (GW 5:266-32).

[8] PE 208.

[9] PPO 122.

[10] *Debates of the Oxford Union*, Oxford, 1895 quoted in Christopher Harvie, *The Lights of Liberalism: University liberals and challenge of liberal democracy* (London: Allen Lane, 1976), p. 118. Also see Melvin Richter, *The Politics of Conscience: T.H. Green and his age* (London: Weidenfeld and Nicolson, 1964), pp. 328-29.

to the whole adult population before they were ready for such responsibility. A key part of the problem was that one could only enfranchise
individuals as members of social groups, rather than assessing the personal
qualities of each separate individual. Groups could prove themselves to be
made up of generally responsible citizens of course. For example, a sufficient
proportion of the British aristocracy and middle classes were content to
enfranchise urban workers through the Second Reform Act, in no small part
due to the virtue shown by Lancashire workers when, from 1861 to 1863, the
latter were willing to suffer significant hardships rather than handle cotton
harvested by American slaves. It could work the other way of course. For
example, Green withdrew his support for the enfranchisement of agricultural workers in national elections, following the return of a Conservative
government by newly-enfranchised workers in 1874. He believed that agricultural workers had also acted irresponsibly by 'suddenly striking in the
midst of harvest in hay-time, with the very object of causing the farmer
loss'.[11] In other words, Green came to believe that the agricultural poor were
not yet ready to vote responsibly in national elections.

For these reasons, Green called for the creation of a decentralised democracy, governed at the national level by a Parliament containing a House of
Lords which had been reformed in such a way as to make it a truly represen-
tative institution and not merely a force for vested class interests.[12] With
these conditions in mind, Green argues the following in the *Principles of
Political Obligation*.

> 'The size of modern states renders necessary the substitution of a rep-
> resentative system for one in which the citizens shared directly in legislation,
> and this so far tends to weaken the active interest of the citizens in the
> commonwealth, though the evil may be partly counteracted by giving
> increased importance to municipal or communal administration.'[13]

---

[11] Charles Alan Fyffe, Recollection regarding Green, in Colin Tyler, ed., 'Recoll-
      ections Regarding Thomas Hill Green', *Collingwood and British Idealism Studies*,
      14:2 (2008), 70. See further Colin Tyler, *Idealist Political Philosophy: Pluralism and
      conflict in the absolute idealist tradition* (London and New York: Continuum, 2006),
      pp. 80–84.

[12] Richter, *Politics of Conscience*, pp. 343–44, especially p. 344n.

[13] PPO 119. Inevitably, human imperfection tends to create serious tensions
      between the need for personal contact in the creation of a real feeling of duty and
      the internationalism inherent in the fundamental human need to respect all
      persons, irrespective of their race, gender and so on (A.J.M. Milne, *The Social
      Philosophy of English Idealism* (London: Allen Lane, 1962), pp. 147–48; J.D. Mabbott,
      The State and the Citizen: An introduction to political philosophy (London: Hutchinson
      University Library, 1967 [1948]), pp. 83–84. PPO 175; see Peter P. Nicholson, *The
      Political Philosophy of the British Idealists: Selected studies* (Cambridge: Cambridge
      University Press, 1990), pp. 77–78. For discussions of Green's theory of inter-

The final sub-clause is significant. Green believes neither that all politics should be national, nor that the agricultural poor should be denied all opportunities to participate politically. Indeed, he was a firm advocate of their participation at the local and municipal levels even when he had come to the view that they were not ready for national franchise.[14] Among many other things, participation is a form of education. More than this, however, social, economic and political participation helps to develop the individual's innate capacities to assert her judgement in an intelligent and yet forceful way. Obviously, this is the Greenian civic ideal which has been analysed and defended at great length in chapters two, three and four of the present book. Despite its continuing and very significant appeal to many of us, some scholars have argued that Green's decentralised participatory ideal is no longer practicable.

> 'The social and political changes wrought by the industrial revolutions and the creation of a mass electorate rendered this idealized conception of notable politics [i.e. one based upon disinterested and well-informed decision-making by a political elite for the common good] an anachronism. *The radical belief that it could simply be extended through increased popular participation to include the entire citizen body has proved an illusion.*'[15]

Even were this to be the case, it lends little support to the claim that the value of the ideal depends so completely on its practicability. In fact, Green's ideal of a participatory eudaimonically-enriching kingdom of ends retains significant appeal across the political spectra in Europe and North America. Green's political theory continues to offer a valuable normative standard against which to judge those political forms which do exist in practice.

When it is read in light of the remainder of his social theory, this section has indicated that Green provides a powerful philosophical justification for decentralised participatory democracy. Concrete moral and civil rights and duties can spring only from concrete social relationships. Popular local government (sc. 'local and customary administration') tends to be better at maintaining that concreteness.[16] Green argues that decentralisation tends to encourage the intimacy of rights-holder and duty-ower which is necessary for a common good to command and receive citizens' concrete habitual obedience. Green does concede that whether or not in practice 'that "civil sense", that appreciation of common good, on the part of the subjects, which is as necessary to free or political society as the direction of law to the main-

---

national relations, see §7.II above. For Green on democracy, see also Tyler, *Idealist Political Philosophy*, chapter 2.

[14] See Olive Anderson, 'The Feminism of T.H. Green: A late Victorian success story?', *History of Political Thought*, 12:4 (1991), 671–93.

[15] Richard Bellamy, *Liberalism and Modern Society: An historical argument* (Oxford: Polity, 1992), p. 4, emphasis added.

[16] PPO 93. LLFC 202; Richter, *Politics of Conscience*, pp. 348–49, 366–68.

tenance of common good, can be kept alive without the active participation of the people in legislative function, is a question of circumstances which perhaps does not admit of unqualified answer'.[17] Nevertheless, as is clear from what has been established in this section as well as many of the earlier chapters of this book, Green is emphatic that the more developed a community, the closer the practical link between a free society on the one hand and active, responsible and inclusive citizenship on the other.

III

Cultural Diversity and the Greenian State

§3.VII highlighted the increased cultural heterogeneity which marks modern societies. The ensuing apparent fragmentation of determinate higher interests within these societies seems to pose serious problems for Green's theory of political obligation and his associated call for greater public service for the common good. Can modern culturally-diverse societies ever approach Green's ideal participatory state, or must they remain archetypal 'so-called states', in the sense of being 'an aggregation of individuals or communities under one ruling power'?[18] (See §7.II.) It seems clear that Green himself would have thought culturally-diverse communities could not combine to form stable and enriching Greenian states. In this regard, it is worth quoting §123 of the *Principles of Political Obligation* in full.

> 'Even then... [the individual's] patriotism will hardly be the passion which it needs to be, unless his judgment of what he owes to the state is quickened by a feeling of which the "patria," the fatherland, the seat of one's home, is the natural object; and of this feeling the state becomes the object only so far as it is an organisation of a people to whom the individual feels himself bound by ties analogous to those which bind him to his family, ties derived from a common dwelling-place with its associations, from common memories, traditions and customs, and from the common ways of feeling and thinking which a common language and still more a common literature embodies. Such an organisation of an homogeneous people the modern state in most cases is (the two Austrian states being the most conspicuous exceptions), and such the Roman state emphatically was not.'[19]

It would be easy to conclude from this passage that Green's political theory cannot accommodate much cultural heterogeneity, and certainly not the degree of diversity that has become characteristic of many contemporary societies.[20] In short, it might be alleged that Green's theory presupposes the existence of a nation and that, necessarily, this implies the presence of a

---

17 PPO 119.
18 PPO 161.
19 PPO 123.
20 Japan and the Scandinavian countries are rare current examples of wealthy countries with low levels of cultural diversity.

culturally-homogeneous community of a type which culturally-pluralistic societies cannot accommodate.[21]

It will be suggested in this section and the one which follows it that the simple fact that many different cultural groups coexist under the rule of one government does not entail that the people can be at best merely a 'so-called state'. In other words, it will be argued that Green's theory does not entail a degree of cultural homogeneity which is and must remain absent in most modern societies. One can begin to see that a Greenian common good can exist without extreme homogeneity if one turns to Bhikhu Parekh's conception of minority groups within a culturally-diverse society.[22]

> '[T]here are territorially dispersed but culturally distinct groups who wish to preserve their ways of life… These groups wish to participate as equal citizens in the collective life of the community, but they also wish to preserve their way of life and demand recognition of their cultural identities.'[23]

This type of culturally-diverse society possesses a Greenian common good to the extent that each of its members conceives of their cultural groups as being intrinsically part of the wider society, the political manifestation of which forms the state. Under these conditions, 'Neither [particular interests nor "the sense of common interest"] would be what it is without the other, but in the state neither retains any separate reality'.[24] Precisely how, indeed whether or not, this cultural perception can be achieved depends upon the whole context of the concrete citizen's life. It is a matter of practice far more

---

[21] PPO 182; see Richard Bellamy, 'T.H. Green and the Morality of Victorian Liberalism', in Richard Bellamy, ed., *Victorian Liberalism: Nineteenth century political thought and practice* (London: Routledge, 1990), p. 148.

[22] The only article which I have found which purports to focus directly upon Green's thought in regard to multiculturalism is Paul Rich, 'T.H. Green, Lord Scarman and the Issue of Ethnic Minority Rights in English Liberal Thought', *Ethnic and Racial Studies*, 10:2 (1987), 149–68. Unfortunately, in the end it does not deal with these issues in significant depth. For my own considerations of Parekh's theory of cultural pluralism, see Colin Tyler, 'The Implications of Parekh's Cultural Pluralism', *Politics*, 16:3 (September 1996), 151–57; 'Cultural Pluralism: A response to Seglow's reply', *Politics*, 18:2 (May 1998), 107–10; 'Strangers and Compatriots: The politics of cultural diversity', in J Rex and G Singh (eds.), *Governance in Multicultural Societies* (Aldershot: Ashgate, 2004), pp. 19–35; and *Idealist Political Philosophy: Pluralism and conflict in the absolute idealist tradition* (London and New York: Continuum, 2006), chapter 5 *passim*. For my own position on these issues, see my 'Power, alienation and performativity in capitalist societies', *European Journal of Social Theory* 14:2 (May 2011), 161–80.

[23] Bhikhu Parekh, 'Cultural Diversity and Liberal Democracy', in David Beetham, ed., *Defining and Measuring Democracy* (London: Sage, 1994), pp. 200, 201.

[24] 'Kant' 62; see also I.M. Greengarten, *Thomas Hill Green and the Development of Liberal-Democratic Thought* (Toronto: University of Toronto Press, 1981), pp. 51–52.

than theory.[25] Nevertheless, Green's philosophical position does give grounds for optimism. He is emphatic that 'A state presupposes other forms of community, with the rights that arise out of them, and only exists as sustaining, securing, and completing them'.[26] Shortly after this passage, he characterises the state as 'a society of societies — the society in which all their claims upon each other are mutually adjusted'.[27] Or again, the state lives up to its 'idea' to the extent that it is 'the reconciler and sustainer of the rights that arise out of the social relations of men'.[28] Crucially, in every case the state should attempt to reconcile the rights that arise from social relationships; it should seek neither to disregard or suppress them, nor to culturally assimilate the populations that are constituted by those social relationships. Green acknowledges explicitly that the imperfections of his present society will tend to be overcome as new rights, duties and obligations begin to arise out of 'the claim for recognition on the part of families and tribes living on the same territory with those which in community form the state but [which are] living at first in some relation of subjection to them'.[29] This passage describes perfectly the situation of many contemporary disadvantaged cultural groups.

Secondly, it is important to remember that there were diverse groups within Victorian British society.[30] Green does tend to refer to the primary example of families as sub-state societies, but he also mentions 'oppressed populations', 'alien' religious denominations such as the Roman Catholics in predominantly Protestant countries, and slave societies that grow up under the noses of the slave-owners.[31] The most significant politically-marginalised group in Green's Britain were the Catholics. They formed a community which attracted much popular suspicion amongst the Protestant majority. Green himself has no great love of the Catholic religion.[32] Importantly, how-

---

[25] In Green's terms, this is one manifestation of the fact, indicated in chapter four, that philosophy cannot provide all of the answers. Only the most abstract considerations can be set out in advance of actual situations.

[26] PPO 134.

[27] PPO 141.

[28] PPO 142.

[29] PPO 135. See also W.J. Mander, *British Idealism: A history* (Oxford: Oxford University Press, 2011), pp. 230–31, and Ann R. Cacoullos, *Thomas Hill Green: Philosopher of rights* (New York: Twayne, 1974), pp. 98–99.

[30] 'Legislative Interference' *passim*.

[31] PPO 167–68, 140–41, 152.

[32] Primarily, Green objects to Roman Catholicism's tendency to discourage the individual from seeking practical moral guidance from her own conscience. He objects that Catholicism encourages its adherents to look to 'an ecclesiastical power external to the state under which they live, [something that means they] are necessarily in certain relations alien to that state' (PPO 167). A group which is

ever, Green does not argue that Catholics are incapable of being active British patriots. In fact, the only significant political problem caused by the presence of Catholics in British society is their allegiance to the Pope as a political power, broadly conceived. A Catholic can be as much of a citizen as a Protestant can, so long as she pays the same habitual obedience to the state as does the Protestant. In precisely the same manner, there is no problem in accommodating, for instance, a modern British Muslim who owes her primary constitutional allegiance to the British state (understood as a 'society of societies').[33] The British Muslim is perfectly capable of perceiving the other members of the British state as her fellows: that is, of sharing a common good with them and contributing actively to British life. She can be a member of a particular sub-culture and yet still understand herself as primarily British, and structure her actions to serve the common good of inherently British communities and ultimately of Green's expanded conception of the British state (see §7.II).[34] The crucial point is that, to use Parekh's words, such persons can 'seek the cultural space to lead and transmit their ways of life and an opportunity to make their contributions to the collective life'.[35] They are true 'patriots' in Green's sense of the term: that is, they seek to foster a vibrant society which in turn fosters the good life for all members of society by contributing to the free play of their higher capacities in a situation of what remains, in a very important sense, cultural diversity.

There are good reasons to be optimistic about the possibility of maintaining such a Greenian multi-ethnic society. Firstly, all of the participants manifest the same abstract human nature, under animal limitations.[36] As Green writes in his manuscripts, 'The constructive action of reason upon sense in moral life of mankind is a gradual process. A formal unity pervades it,... [even though] its results (a) [in] different ages and nations (b) in different individuals of same age and nation, vary greatly'.[37] The second reason for optimism is that in this context, we are by definition dealing with people who *want* to make valuable contributions to the collective life. Hence,

---

'alien' in this sense cannot ally itself completely with the dominant society and so cannot partake fully of that society's common good.

[33] PPO 22–24, 51–59, 91, 93, 98, 113, 119, 141. This reconciliation will be less likely in an empirical state that is more racially-divided, such as the United States of America, but see Derrick Darby, *Rights, Race, and Recognition* (Cambridge: Cambridge University Press, 2009), pp. 142–68.

[34] I use the example of the British state here for ease of exposition. The European Union may also serve as a good example eventually.

[35] Parekh, 'Cultural Diversity and Liberal Democracy', p. 200.

[36] 'Moral Philosophy' *passim*.

[37] 'Sittlichkeit', 14–15. Muirhead argues in a slightly different context that 'while the forms of civilisation with which we are dealing are manifold, it is the same human will that is working in all' (John H. Muirhead, *The Service of the State: Four lectures on the political teaching of T.H. Green* (London: John Murray, 1908), p. 110).

already they value and respect the other forms of life of the other groups which together constitute the state. Such a desire is a necessary feature of the Parekhian conception of cultural pluralism. Other types of cultural group may well seek formal political independence and, in those cases, one must be far more sceptical about the prospects of ever discovering or producing a common good for the society as a whole. Nevertheless, it is definitional of the cultural groups under consideration here that they wish to form a culturally pluralistic society.

The third reason for optimism is that, by definition, the Greenian state acts impartially in the sense that it finds 'its primary function... [in] maintaining law equally in the interest of all,... [not] in the interest of [particular] classes'.[38] For it to serve the interests of merely one sectional association, such as the interests of one dominant cultural group, at the expense of the common good would be for it to undermine its own authority. Ann Cacoullos sums up Green's fundamental presupposition very well when she observes that, 'rights, for Green, reflect not a homogeneous society but one where there is mutual respect among persons'.[39] As the previous chapter established, the primary function of the Greenian sovereign is the promotion of the common good via the impartial maintenance of that system of legal rights and obligations on which the political existence of the population is grounded, with this political existence being the reconciliation of the sub-state social relationships that continue to coexist between the various social groups. After all, as has just been noted, the Greenian state is a 'political society' in the sense of being a 'societies of societies'.[40]

> 'It is not... supreme coercive power, simply as such, but supreme coercive power exercised in a certain way and for certain ends, that makes a state; viz. exercised according to law, written or customary, and for the maintenance of rights... The office of the sovereign, as an institution of such a society [whose members recognise each other as possessing rights], is to protect those rights from invasion, either from without, from foreign nations, or from within, from members of society who cease to behave as such.'[41]

Empirical states live up to their ideal to the extent that they uphold the common good in a disinterested manner so that every member of society gains equally from her activity within the political union. This means that the sovereign should do its best to provide everyone with the spaces which personally they need to develop their particular talents and capacities.[42] This is a precondition of its authority. Yet, it has been established already that diff-

---

[38] PPO 121.
[39] Cacoullos, *Thomas Hill Green*, p. 99.
[40] PPO 22–24, 51–59, 91, 93, 98, 113, 119, 141.
[41] PPO 132.
[42] PPO 166.

erent individuals identify with the community through their performances of different roles within that community (§§2.IV, 3.VII). This means that there can be variations in authority between different members of society. Indeed, probably there always will be such differences in our inherently imperfect world. Consequently, although everyone should be treated equally, there should be different treatment for different individuals at the level of practice. Again, Green's theory coincides with many of the recent debates concerning cultural pluralism.[43] The most important point to keep in mind at present is that what Green excludes from his model is different treatment on the grounds of factors which are irrelevant to the individual's highest attachment to her society. What he can accommodate are culturally-sensitive political structures.

To reiterate the fundamental point then and to conclude this section, by definition in Parekhian societies there is a sufficiently strong perception of commonality to ensure that each individual cares for and respects all other members of the state.[44] There does not need to be a complete identity of interests for such sense of a common good to exist.[45] What is required for the state to fulfil its 'true end... as the sustainer and harmoniser of social relations' is a 'collective life' which every citizen values and towards which she wishes to contribute actively.[46] For such a life to be possible, at the very least, all claims within the state must be successfully adjusted in the sense of being harmonised in ways that help sustain a reasonably stable and enriching social, political and economic collective life.[47] Yet, while this harmony is necessary for the existence of a vibrant community, it is not a sufficient condition. In fact, when one turns to Green's theories of political change and dissent, there seem to be very good reasons for thinking that something very like a Greenian multicultural community could survive even greater social tensions and conflicts.[48] Hopefully, this will become clear in the next section.

IV

Political Change, Rebellion and Dissent

It has been established that Green conceives human progress as being manifested in the development of social and political institutions and practices. Social change was analysed in chapter four, and political change will be

---

[43] See Tyler, 'Strangers and Compatriots'.

[44] PPO 122–23.

[45] Andrew Vincent and Raymond Plant, *Philosophy, Politics and Citizenship: The life and thought of the British idealists* (Oxford: Basil Blackwell, 1984), p. 29.

[46] PPO 143.

[47] Again, what classes as 'reasonably stable and enriching' is a practical, rather than a theoretical, question.

[48] I develop what is in effect a Greenian model of cultural accommodation in Tyler, 'Performativity, alienation and power in capitalist societies'.

analysed now. It is important to examine the abstract nature of this developmental process in greater detail as it informs Green's theory of civil disobedience and highlights the inherently conflictual nature of 'politics', broadly
conceived. Moreover, it helps to reinforce the defence of a Greenian culturally-diverse state which was presented in the previous section. It will
become clear that although it is true, in Mander's words, that for Green,
citizens have a 'duty to *serve* [the state] not simply a duty to *obey* [it]', Green
also insists that at times serving the state at its best requires the individual to
disobey the commands that in fact it issues.[49] At times, in other words, a
citizen shows greatest loyalty to the state by defying its orders.

Green welcomes the fact that new rights, duties and obligations arise as
societies mature. Such changes can have a number of causes. Yet, they all
occur 'upon new conditions arising, or upon elements of social good being
taken account of which had been overlooked before, or upon persons being
taken into the reckoning as capable of participating in the social well-being
who had previously been treated merely as means to its attainment'.[50] Elsewhere, Green is more specific, and highlights five possible sources of such
new rights, duties and obligations.[51] The first of these sources has been mentioned already in relation to cultural pluralism (see §8.III). It is 'the claim for
recognition on the part of families and tribes living on the same territory
with those which in community form the state but living at first in some
relation of subjection to them'.[52] This claim arises out of a growing recognition of the possession and normative significance of some common characteristic which is deemed to be relevant when ascribing rights to particular
individuals.

The second source of new rights and obligations is the growing recognition of the validity of claiming respect for members of 'external communities ("external" territorially)'.[53] This recognition can arise through either
conquest or 'voluntary combination (as with the Swiss cantons and the
United States of America)'.[54] In both cases, the combined communities are
ruled by the same state and share the same system of legal rights and obligations. A contemporary example of this movement would be the growing
power and authority of the European Union. Thirdly, new rights arise out of
the increased complexity of interactions which the existence of a state makes
possible. Green argues that such new rights arise 'especially in regard to
property'.[55] One could think of new restrictions on the freedom of contracts

---

[49] Mander , *British Idealism*, p. 233. Mander recognises this fact (*ibid.*, p. 235).
[50] PPO 142.
[51] PPO 135.
[52] PPO 135.
[53] PPO 135.
[54] PPO 135; PE 216.
[55] PPO 135.

in the labour market.[56] This category will be returned to in chapter ten. Fourthly, new rights and obligations arise out of the need for effective administration within the state.[57] For instance, UK Parliamentary Select Committees now possess the right to call witnesses where previously they did not.[58] Lastly, changes in the 'situations of life' which the state facilitates 'make new modes of protecting the people a matter virtually of right'.[59] Urbanisation is the example of such a 'situation of life', given by Green himself. In each of these five ways, the creation of the state 'leads to a development and moralisation of man beyond the stage which they must have reached before it could be possible'.[60] No matter which of these five causes is the source of political change in any particular instance, the developmental process results from the revision of existing public norms in accordance with their own inherent higher logics and in response to new circumstances (§§4.II–III).

There is something paradoxical about extending Green's argument regarding the gradual perfecting of the system of reciprocal rights and claims to the political realm in the manner Green himself does. This oddity is frequently missed. It has been shown in §§3.II–III that, although ultimately unattainable, the ideal state would serve the ideal common good: that is, the common good of a concrete ideal eudaimonically-enriching kingdom of ends. As such, its function would be to protect and enforce those rights and obligations which arise out of the associated ideal relationships.[61] For this reason, citizens of an ideal state would always honour fully those rights and obligations which that particular manifestation of political society pre-scribes. Rights and obligations only exist, in the sense of being under-standable by the conscientious agent and habitually guiding her conduct, to the extent that she has realised her rational and eudaimonic capacities. An ideal system of natural rights and obligations would constitute a 'fence' around perfect individuals, protecting them from interference from other perfect individuals (see §6.III). Yet, if individuals were ever to be developed fully, then no one would need to be protected by legally-enforced claims (by obligations). Certainly, moral rights and duties would remain as guides to action, but perfect agents would respect them fully simply out of a sense of duty. Legal rights and obligations, on the other hand, would be unnecessary if the individual were ever to realise the end which it is her vocation to real-ise. Hence, there are no truly natural rights which need to be enforced through the legal system. At one point in his *Lectures on the Principles of*

---

[56] LLFC 194–99.

[57] PPO 135.

[58] See also Nicholson, *Political Philosophy*, p. 94.

[59] PPO 135.

[60] PPO 135.

[61] PPO 140.

Political Obligation, Green does seem to recognise this implication, but he does not emphasise it, nor does he trace out its further implications, nor does he hold to it in the remainder of his writings.[62]

Unfortunately, no individual, no society, no system of rights and obligations and no state, can ever be completely perfect. This fact is pivotal within Green's thought, as has been shown in numerous ways throughout this book. Missing this argument has led at least two influential commentators to interpret Green as arguing that conventional rights, duties and obligations gain their legitimacy from the command of the political sovereign.[63] If these critics were to be correct, then Green would be defending the worst form of conservatism. In fact, as has been established in chapter 4 Green's thought can have very radical ethical, social and political implications.[64] Quite simply, he is emphatic that the imperfection of every empirical state means that 'we cannot apply this rule [of perfect obedience] in practice'.[65]

In March 1860 Green read an essay on 'National Life' to Oxford's Old Mortality Society. A.V. Dicey, another of the society's members, observed many years later, 'One sentence sticks in my recollection: "Let the flag of England be dragged through the dirt rather than sixpence be added to the taxes which weigh on the poor"'.[66] As Dicey recalled, 'At a time when we were thinking of what one may call romantic politics he kept constantly pointing out to us the evil of pauperism. I suppose that both his sympathies & his power of imagination led him to realize much more clearly than most of us the actual sufferings of the poor'.[67] Most strikingly, as an undergraduate Green's concern for the poor turned him against the 'volunteer rifle corps' that were formed in England following the Chartist uprisings of 1848, and especially after 1852. Even though they took on the character of recreational clubs during the 1860s, initially the corps were organised on a county basis, and became especially prominent from 1859 amid growing fears of possible attacks by the French forces of Louis Napoleon, following an attempt on the latter's life (wrongly) believed to have been perpetrated

---

62 PPO 189; see Crane Brinton, *English Political Thought in the Nineteenth Century* (New York: Harper and Brothers, 1962), pp. 216–17.

63 Harold A. Prichard, *Moral Obligation: Essays and lectures* (Oxford: Clarendon Press, 1949), pp. 57–66; H.D. Lewis, 'T.H. Green and Rousseau', in his *Freedom and History* (London: George Allen and Unwin, 1962), pp. 105–33; also see Lane W. Lancaster, *The Masters of Political Thought: Volume Three, Hegel to Dewey* (London: George G. Harrap, 1959), pp. 224, 228–34.

64 'Loyalty' *passim*.

65 PPO 143.

66 Nettleship, 'Memoir', xx–xxi.

67 Albert V. Dicey, 'Recollection', in Tyler, ed.,'Recollections Regarding Thomas Hill Green', 22–23.

by Mazzinians.[68] Some corps were happy to exceed their ostensibly defensive remit. For example, although some members of the South Devon Volunteer Rifle Corp may have joined out of patriotism or even simply for their own entertainment, one of its leading members boasted in a letter to *The Times* of September 1857 that the corps themselves were used as a threat to keep to poor in line during the economic depression.[69] Around this time, Green railed against the formation of volunteer corps in a letter to his family.

> 'Fools talk at Oxford of its being desirable, in order that the gentry may keep down the chartists in the possible contingency of a rising. I should like to learn the use of the arm that I might be able to desert to the people, if it came to such a pass. After all we do not know what may arise from the hunger produced by a European war.'[70]

While it is unclear how serious the undergraduate Green was about joining the poor in a possible third English civil war, this remark does at least give a very strong indication of the depths of his radical sympathies as an undergraduate. Moreover while Green's feelings moderated in later years, he retained an intense identification with the poor until his death in 1882. Indeed, as was established earlier (§§4.II–III), even in later life Green insisted that the citizen should break or seek to change certain conventional norms of her community if social development is to occur.

> 'The general principle that the citizen must never act otherwise than as a citizen does not carry with it an obligation under all conditions to conform to the law of his state, since those laws may be inconsistent with the true end of the state as the sustainer and harmoniser of social relations.'[71]

For this reason, as Green himself recognises, he is required to produce a viable doctrine of civil disobedience, rebellion and dissent. He argues that

---

68   See for example 'The Probability of Attack and Means of Defence', *The Examiner*, as reprinted in *The Times*, 26 January 1852, p. 8. Denis Mack Smith, *Mazzini* (New Haven, CT, and London: Yale University Press, 1994), pp. 121–22.

69   'As a county magistrate, I can also testify to the value of our corps in domestic disturbances. Before its formation, during a bread riot we had to send to Exeter for military in aid of the special constables. On a similar occasion, recently, it was quite sufficient to announce that the Rifles would assemble at the Town-hall on the night on which disturbance was threatened to swear in some members, and all was perfectly tranquil.' The author of the letter recorded proudly that the 'complement for Torquay was promptly raised and officered by gentlemen resident in the town, the privates and non-commissioned officers being principally young tradesmen, clerks, and some of all classes who wished to support the system [of "volunteer corps"], or who enjoyed the skirmishing and target practice.' 'A Member of the Committee', 'Letter to the Editor: Volunteer Rifle Corps', *The Times*, 26 September 1857, p. 6.

70   Nettleship, 'Memoir', xxiv.

71   PPO 143. Milne, *Social Philosophy*, pp. 136–44.

the citizen has a duty to rebel against, and if necessary overthrow, the political organs of the state under certain circumstances irrespectively of whether there is a law 'acknowledged or half-acknowledged, written or customary' to do so.[72] Hence, even though the individual can be forced to submit to the laws of her state, she has a duty to obey the state only as far as she believes that, in her specific circumstances, doing so is the best method of furthering the distinctively human development of that portion of mankind with which she identifies her true good.[73] She must always act with 'reference to the needs or good of society'.[74] When the individual believes that the sovereign is hindering human development, she has a positive duty to engage in civil disobedience.[75] Ultimately, the individual should decide for herself whether or not it does so in any particular instance (§§4.III–IV).[76] If the agent does decide that the sovereign should be resisted, she should think carefully about the best method to adopt. Green argues that in a relatively democratic system such as Britain's, the best method will probably be through the established constitutional procedures.[77] In this case, the dissenter should obey the law as it stands presently, whilst still working to get it changed. If the citizen of a broadly democratic system does not obey the law which she is seeking to change, then unnecessary harm is likely to be done to her fellow citizens' chances of living in accordance with the common good. In fact, although some commentators have argued that Green understates the existence and seriousness of social strife arising out of debates surrounding the legitimacy of certain rights, duties and obligations, he is fully alive to these difficulties.[78] Apart from the passages in his published writings where he mentions such conflicts,[79] he demonstrates his appreciation of their moral implications in many of his speeches. Constantly, he makes his fiercest attacks against those

---

72   PPO 107.

73   See Paul Harris, 'Green's Theory of Political Obligation and Obedience', in Andrew Vincent, ed., *The Philosophy of T.H. Green* (Aldershot: Gower, 1986), pp. 127–42; Geoffrey Thomas, *The Moral Philosophy of T.H. Green* (Oxford: Clarendon Press, 1987), pp. 356–59.

74   PPO 143.

75   Lancaster misses this vital point: Lane W. Lancaster, *The Masters of Political Thought: Volume Three, Hegel to Dewey* (London: George G. Harrap, 1959), pp. 224–25, 228–34 *passim*.

76   PPO 100.

77   PPO 100.

78   For example, Adam B. Ulam, *The Philosophical Foundations of English Socialism* (Cambridge: Harvard University Press, 1951), p. 37; Lancaster, *Masters of Political Thought*, p. 219.

79   For example, LLFC.

individuals and groups who resist or push for reforms on the basis of their own vested interests.[80]

Obviously, socio-economic and political difficulties do arise where previously-favoured citizens lose some of their previous advantages. Nevertheless, Green insists that the fact that the 'old' rights are 'violated' is not a legitimate reason for refusing to fulfil one's new obligations and the new laws. The authority of the previous system of rights and obligations was derived from its contribution to the common good. With the development of the conception of the common good or a development of a better awareness of how to foster a better common good most effectively, the authority of the old system declines. If legal enforcement of a particular system of rights and obligations is justified because it is required to ensure the well-being of the whole community now, then morally it is irrelevant that, previously, citizens had rights which a revised system does not honour. Social development 'suggests the necessity of some further regulation of the individual's liberty to do as he pleases'.[81] In short, where changes occur in the 'social judgement' regarding the best system for securing attainment of the common good (because the common good itself changes), this transfers authority to the new system.[82]

Some scholars have claimed that Green's position accords the individual's personal judgement very little weight relative to the collective will of the groups that dominate her society.[83] Indeed, Richter claims that Green's criterion for state action 'was moralistic, involving the determination by upper-class persons of those moral traits to be encouraged; it excluded from consideration the economic arrangements of the society, as well as the

---

[80] This is one recurring theme of the speeches which Nicholson has collated. For instance, it forms the main subject of Green's addresses to the Oxford Reform League, 25 March 1867 (GW 5:226–32); The Special Conference on the Government's Intoxicating Liquor Bill, 6 May 1874 (GW 5:243–44); National Agricultural Labourers' Union, 9 December 1874 (GW 5:246–50); Oxford West Ward Liberal Association, 20 September 1876 (GW 5:263–69); Abingdon Liberal Association, 5 December 1879 (GW 5:247–55); National Church Reform Union at Merton College, 7 December 1881 (GW 5:376–86); and the last speech he was ever scheduled to make, to the Oxford Liberal Associations, 15 March 1882, the manuscript of which (entitled *Liberalism in Birmingham*) survives in Balliol College library (GW 5:401–04). There are many other examples which could be given as well.

[81] PPO 142.

[82] PPO 142.

[83] Prichard, *Moral Obligation*, pp. 57–66; S.I. Benn and R.S. Peters, *Social Principles and the Democratic State* (London: George Allen and Unwin, 1959), pp. 97, 326; Lewis, 'T.H. Green and Rousseau', *passim*; Peter Robbins, *The British Hegelians 1875–1925* (New York: Garland, 1982), pp. 67–69; Noël O'Sullivan, *The Problem of Political Obligation* (New York: Garland, 1987), pp. 182–88 *passim*.

possibility that the interests and tastes of middle-class reformers might not be those of the working classes'.[84] This is an extraordinary allegation to make. Firstly, nowhere does Green exclude the economic sphere from criticism (see chapter ten below). Secondly, it is unclear whether Richter's elite is the upper or the middle classes. Thirdly and most importantly in the present instance, Green makes no claim regarding the special authority of the conscientious judgement of this elite. Strangely, Richter ignores Green's calls for the extension of the franchise and the subsequent development of new rights.

Green himself asks, 'Is... the general judgement as to the requirements of social well-being so absolutely authoritative that no individual right can exist against it?'[85] He argues that it is not. For a right to be fully legitimate, it must be 'acknowledged' or 'recognised' as being necessary for the common good of society.[86] A claimable right is a right whose 'exercise should be contributory to some social good which the public conscience is capable of appreciating—*not necessarily one which in the existing prevalence of private interests can obtain due acknowledgment*, but still one of which men in their actions and language show themselves to be aware'.[87] This point was made in chapter six, when Green's conception of implicit recognition was introduced. I will not repeat the argument here, beyond reiterating that the individual conscientious agent must decide for herself precisely what and how to resist.

Undisputed legal rights should be respected by the competing parties when claimed by both the members of their own group and the members of the groups with whom they disagree on other matters. Yet, even allowing for this common obligation, Green highlights four other cases in which the nature of the individual's constitutional duty is especially unclear.[88] Firstly, problems arise to the extent that sovereignty is disputed. In these cases, the authority of the nominal sovereign's commands is disputed by a significant proportion of the citizenry even though another significant portion accept it.[89] Examples in Green's time were found in Ireland and America. He argues that in such cases, no truly legal right or obligation exists on either side.[90] This position is perfectly in line with his earlier justification of rights and obligations. Every structured social system is based upon the citizens' mutual recognition of the system's contribution to the attainment of a

---

84   Richter, *Politics of Conscience*, p. 296.
85   PPO 143.
86   PPO 143.
87   PPO 143, emphasis added.
88   'Constitutional duties' seems a more appropriate expression than 'constitutional obligations', as legal obligations arise from constitutional arrangements, and so are both ontologically and normatively prior to them.
89   PPO 101.
90   PPO 103.

commonly-recognised shared good. Where no such good exists, there can be neither a common path nor a mutually-accepted political process for deciding the correct path. Consequently, there can be no full right as such. This lack of full legal right fundamentally undermines the legitimacy of any claim to sovereignty in the disputed area. The non-existence of a legitimate and legally-enforceable right does not mean that the individual cannot reach a conscientious judgement regarding which side in the dispute is 'better' and which is 'worse'.[91] Such a judgement is possible and should be based upon her careful assessment of the relative consequences of victory for each particular side. In short, the side whose victory would promote most effectively the social preconditions of individual self-development is the better one. Green uses the example of the American civil war and favours the abolitionists over the supporters of slavery. As well as being intrinsically valuable, their victory most effectively promoted a more developed recognition of human dignity (see §§3.III, 5.IV).[92]

The second type of difficulty which a political reformer can face when trying to gauge the nature and extent of her constitutional duty arises when 'the government is so conducted that there are no legal means of obtaining the repeal of a law'.[93] Green highlights three conditions which should be borne in mind when trying to decide whether or not dissent is justified in such a situation.[94] Firstly, is it possible to resist the sovereign on the particular matter without subverting the whole political system? If it is not, then resistance will tend to be wrong. Secondly, if the political system is going to be subverted by resistance, is the character of the body politic such that the act of subversion will lead to anarchy? If it is, then again resistance tends to be wrong. Thirdly (and this is also Green's third type of general difficulty facing the political reformer), has the system been so corrupted by private interests that there is no longer a common good supporting the sovereign and the 'so-called' state which it serves?[95] If it has been so corrupted, then revolution is justified. The fourth type of difficulty with gauging one's political duty arises when a particular political measure can be resisted without seriously risking the destruction of the 'social order and the fabric of settled rights'.[96] Once again, resistance is justified only to the extent that the individual acts on the conscientious belief that it will further the eudaimonic and

---

[91] PPO 104.
[92] PPO 104.
[93] PPO 101.
[94] PPO 109.
[95] PPO 101.
[96] PPO 101.

rational development of mankind more effectively than any other available course of action.[97]

From what has been established so far, it can be seen that commentators such as I.M. Greengarten are mistaken when they argue that 'No attempt is made [by Green] to come to terms with the moral dilemma confronting the conscientious citizen when a system of law and government obstructs, rather than assists, the attainment of the common good'.[98] Similarly, they are misguided to assert that 'One cannot escape the conclusion that when the chips are down, timidity and bourgeois punctiliousness prevail over the person and social justice in Green's liberalism'.[99] Certainly, there is a mood in which Green does argue that, as a matter of prudence, it is usually better to presume that one is wrong to believe that there is a duty to resist in a particular case unless it is 'the attitude of the mass of the people' as well as one's own.[100] It is prudent not simply because one has a greater chance of success if resistance is supported by the majority of the population, but mainly because one's judgement is less likely to be in error.[101] Yet, even here Green recognises that 'On the other hand, it is under the worst governments that the public spirit is most crushed' (see §5.II regarding the Italian civil war).[102] In these cases, the minority *should* revolt without obvious popular support if they believe the situation demands it.

Green is well aware that often this advice will not be very helpful in practice (§4.IV): 'Simply I should answer, [the individual should follow] the general rule of looking to the moral good of mankind.'[103] He acknowledges that even when the conscientious citizen is armed with knowledge of such principles, she faces a very difficult task. An error of judgement is less likely if one attempts to make one's judgement with the smallest self-regard that one can. Nevertheless, ultimately Green is realistic about the situation: 'there

---

97 Lindsay sums up this whole approach very well when he argues that, for Green, 'Our appeal is to be from the State as it is to the State as it reasonably might be, considering what its citizens are' (A.D. Lindsay, 'Introduction', in T.H. Green, *Lectures on the Principles of Political Obligation* (London: Longmans, 1941), p. xvii).

98 Greengarten, *Thomas Hill Green,* p. 67. For an excellent attack on Greengarten's interpretation of Green's theory of civil disobedience, see John Morrow, 'Review article: Ancestors, Legacies and Traditions: British idealism in the history of political thought', *History of Political Thought*, 6 (1985), 497–99.

99 Dante Germino, *Machiavelli to Marx: Modern western political thought* (Chicago and London: University of Chicago Press, 1972), p. 271.

100 PPO 109.

101 Again, to some commentators, this claim has unacceptably conservative overtones: for example, Wilfred Harrison, *Conflict and Compromise: The history of British political thought* (New York: Free, 1965), p. 240; Germino, *Machiavelli to Marx*, pp. 263, 266–67, 270–71; Greengarten, *Thomas Hill Green*, pp. 66–70.

102 PPO 108.

103 PPO 106.

are times of political difficulty in which the line of conduct adopted may have the most important effect, but in which it is very hard to know what is the proper line to take.'[104] The seriousness of this 'admission' has been over-emphasised by some commentators.[105] Quite simply, Green recognises that the nature of the subject-matter entails that theoretical maxims can provide little practical guidance. The most the philosopher can do is to encourage citizens to follow their respective consciences. Indeed, it is important to remember that the logic of Green's position ultimately makes the individual conscience the basic moral and political 'unit'.[106] The fundamental point in this part of his analysis is that where the individual considers the situation to be uncertain, conscientious action is vital: simple prudence is not suffic-ient. Green accepts even that consciously applying these criteria in practice would probably prevent many revolutions which otherwise would be of net social benefit. For this reason, he argues that the criteria outlined in this sec-tion will be of service probably only to the subsequent analyst of the revol-ution.

> 'No doubt revolutionists do and must to a great extent "go it blind"… [T]he estimate of… [whether or not] an act should or should not have been done, is not one which we could expect the [revolutionary] agent himself to have made. The effort to make it would have paralysed his power of action.'[107]

It is not very important to the conscientious agent that identifying the best action is often very difficult on the basis of these principles, then. Principles are at best guides for conscience, and ultimately it is careful conscientious judgement in concrete situations, rather than pondering over the dictates of a philosopher, which should guide the true political reformer.[108] Germino is clearly mistaken when he claims that Green's thought exhibits an 'insensit-ivity to the importance of spontaneity'.[109]

V

Spiritual Determinism

The discussion of Green's political philosophy in this chapter and the pre-ceding ones has assumed that he is adopting his self-interventionist theory of the will (see MSF §5.II). All that remains in this chapter is to draw out the implications of adopting the alternative spiritual determinist line instead.

---

[104] PPO 106.

[105] For example, Richter, *Politics of Conscience*, pp. 265–66.

[106] PPO 108.

[107] PPO 110.

[108] Norman Wintrop, 'Liberal-Democratic Theory: The New Liberalism', in Norman Wintrop, ed., *Liberal Democratic Theory and its Critics* (London: Croom Helm, 1983), p. 99.

[109] Germino, *Machiavelli to Marx*, p. 263.

The implications are certainly important. It will be remembered from §6.II that moral and legal rights exist to secure spaces for moral action: they allow the individual to act on her choices without undue hindrance from other agents. That is the problematic point when one adopts the deterministic position. The latter entails the rejection of the idea that an individual can ever make a real choice (sc. can choose to act otherwise than in fact she did). This conclusion appears to deprive rights of their rationale.

Fortunately for Green, the situation is not as bleak as this analysis makes it appear. On the determinist reading, rights, duties and obligations constitute important aspects of the individual's conceptual landscape. Consequently, they form important aspects of the circumstances with which her consciousness and conscience react. Reflecting what was established in §4.VI, political change and civil disobedience should now be characterised as 'automatic' manifestations of 'the primary demands of human consciousness'.[110] The attempt to modify rights and so on is the communication of human reason with itself. This is because rights are objective if imperfect manifestations of prior determinations of the human nature in precisely the same manner as all other social institutions (§2.IV). Viewing Green's political theory in this way might require us making radical changes to our understanding of Green's political philosophy, but at least the resulting system is internally consistent.

VI

Conclusion

This chapter has analysed Green's theory of participatory democracy and his theories of civil dissent. §8.II used Green's attitude to franchise reform in the run-up to the passing of the 1867 Second Reform Act to explore the link he posits between political participation and responsible citizenship. §8.III argued that Green's theory of government and politics can accommodate a significant degree of cultural diversity. This is an important point, given the attention paid in §3.VII to the social fragmentation which is characteristic of the modern age. §8.IV examined the interrelationships that exist between Green's neglected theories of political change and dissent. §8.V demonstrated that Green's political thought remains coherent even if one assumes his spiritual determinist theory of the will rather than his self-interventionism. The following chapters consider Green's application of his liberal socialist principles to modern capitalism.

---

[110] PPO 137.

9

The Principles of Green's Political Economy

I

Introduction

While Green is now widely recognised as a significant political thinker, his writings on political economy have a more ambiguous standing. As becomes clear in this chapter and the one that follows it, scholars disagree about the cogency and continuing relevance of this aspect of his thought, as well as about its long-term historical influence on such major innovations as the British welfare state. The impact of anyone's work can never be measured with any degree of precision of course, whether one wishes to deny the influence of Green's political economy or to acknowledge it. Nevertheless, there is much to be said for Alon Kadish's contention that Green's thought fostered a profound shift of perspective in the orthodox political economy at Oxford and, through its influential alumni, in many other areas of the public life of Britain and the world.[1] It is hard to deny the influence of his political economy thought on his immediate circle. Green's thought encouraged friends such as John Addington Symonds to become socialists (MSF chapter 2). Most notably, it also set Sidney Ball, David Ritchie and Arnold Toynbee on the roads to social reform and socialism, and through them he exerted an important influence on the wider public debate on these issues in Britain for many years following his death. Not least in importance here is Green's well-documented influence on the University Extension Movement.[2] Nevertheless, Kadish might well be correct that 'few of those who followed the

---

[1] 'Hence one might consider the rejection of J.S. Mill's economics as a response to a general trend prevalent at Oxford at the time to replace Mill's philosophy by Green's Idealism, transformed into an internal issue and strengthened by the criticism of Mill by Toynbee, Rogers, and Jevons. It is doubtful whether any of the views on internal issues were a purely spontaneous reaction by a purely intellectual process of theoretical analysis and study.' Alon Kadish, *The Oxford Economists in the Late Nineteenth Century* (Oxford: Clarendon Press, 1982), p. 287.

[2] See, for example, Alon Kadish, *Apostle Arnold: The life and death of Arnold Toynbee, 1852–83* (Notre Dame: Duke University Press, 1987).

example of T.H. Green were much concerned with the finer points of his philosophy… Their main concern was with its applications'.[3]

Even though the 'finer points' of Green's thought may have escaped the group who were taught by Ritchie, Ball and their ilk, what did matter intensely was the general tenor of Green's political economy, a tenor captured well by the words Sir Henry Jones uses to describe the approach of Green's great friend and intellectual compatriot, Edward Caird.

> 'It verily was a "new and sympathetic economy" which Caird desired and at bottom sought for through all of his social efforts in this field [of factory reform and the extension of women's employment rights] — an "economy" which should no longer be a theory that, in its evaluation of human wants and human efforts to supply them, *left out the human qualities.'*[4]

The same concern to humanise economics is reflected in the emphasis Green placed on the fact that no one can be secure in the development of their higher faculties if they are on the verge of starvation or at risk of becoming so: 'Until life has been so organised as to afford some regular relief from the pressure of animal wants, an interest in what Aristotle calls ["living well" or "well-being"], as distinct from [merely "living"], cannot emerge.'[5] Consequently, not only should the economic system provide each individual with opportunities to acquire 'property in the immediate necessaries of life' through her own labour, but it should also provide the individual with opportunities to work to acquire 'such property as will at least enable him to develop a sense of responsibility' and to pursue plans that she believes will realise her higher good.[6] Green emphasises various ways in which economic activity plays a central role in the individual's self-expression and, therefore,

---

3   Kadish, *Oxford Economists*, pp. 16, 38; see also Kadish, *Oxford Economists*, pp. 24, 26, 42, 77, 161, 198, 280.

4   Sir Henry Jones and John H. Muirhead, *The Life and Philosophy of Edward Caird, LL.D., D.C.L.* (Glasgow: MacLehose, Jackson, 1921), p. 119. For Caird's political economy, see his 'Lectures on Moral Philosophy: Social Ethics', in Colin Tyler, ed., *Unpublished Manuscripts in British Idealism: Political philosophy, theology and social thought*, 2 vols. (Exeter and Charlottesville, VA: Imprint Academic, 2008), vol. 2, pp. 64–78, and his 'Lecture on Political Economy', in Tyler, ed., *Unpublished Manuscripts*, vol. 2, pp. 153–63. See also Caird's pamphlets on political economy which are printed in the eleventh volume of Edward Caird, *Collected Works*, ed. Colin Tyler, 12 vols. (Bristol: Thoemmes, 1998). Caird lectured on political economy for many years during his time as Professor of Moral Philosophy at the University of Glasgow (1866–93). See also, Colin Tyler, *Idealist Political Philosophy: Conflict and pluralism in the absolute idealist tradition* (London: Continuum, 2006), chapter 3, and Colin Tyler, 'The Liberal Hegelianism of Edward Caird: Or, how to transcend the social economics of Kant and the romantics', *International Journal of Social Economics*, 37:11 (November 2010), 852–66.

5   PE 240.

6   PPO 221.

in her self-realisation. Consequently, it is vital to examine his writings on economics in order to complete this critical reconstruction of his liberal socialism.

Green's political economy presupposes his social and political theory, especially his general theory of rights. These have been explored in depth already in this book, and the current chapter presupposes that earlier analysis. This chapter examines the most fundamental principles of his political economy. §II examines Green's understanding of the key theoretical relationships between private property rights, his rejection of utility-maximisation as the basis for such rights, and self-realisation. §III establishes that many attacks launched against Green stem from critics' failure to distinguish sufficiently clearly between the roles played respectively by free exchange, free trade and capitalism in Green's thought. §IV explores some further complexities and problems with the principles of his political economy. §V reviews the chapter's main conclusions. From this analysis of Green's theory of the economic structure of the ideal type of a eudaimonically-enriching kingdom of ends, the subsequent chapter turns to the practical requirements for state intervention and civic action to counter the abuses of power perpetrated by the rich in the most advanced capitalist economies. Green's shift from abstract to applied political economy reflects a widespread assumption of British political economists at this time that the free market should be treated as the best possible economic system unless practical difficulties indicated the need for targeted state intervention.[7] As becomes clear in chapter ten, Green was more willing than many to accept that, in practice, capitalism had become a deeply flawed expression of the ideal type of a truly free market.

II

Property, Utility and Self-realisation

Green's analyses of the moral status of the right to private property and of capitalism assume that the 'supply of the means of living has been sufficiently secured to allow room for a consideration of the ends of living'.[8] The requisite level is determined by the needs for '[i] means of subsistence,' and '[ii] material to work upon'.[9] Once this minimum has been achieved, the individual's security in her holdings of private property is important because

'A necessary condition at once of the growth of a free morality, i.e. a certain behaviour of men determined by an understanding of moral relations and by

---

[7] Derek Fraser, *The Evolution of the Welfare State*, fourth edition (Houndsmills: Palgrave MacMillan, 2009), pp. 146–47.

[8] PE 241.

[9] 'Pol. Econ.' 1, additions by Harris *et al.*

the value which they set on them as understood, and of the conception of those relations as relations between all men, is that free play should be given to every man's powers of appropriation. Moral freedom is not the same thing as a control over the outward circumstances and appliances of life. It is the end to which such control is a generally necessary means and which gives it its value.'[10]

Green begins his analysis of the principles of political economy with a consideration of two then-fashionable but competing theories of the right to private property. The first claims that private property rights originate in first occupancy.[11] Green objects that this approach fails to establish why a person should have a *right* to the things that she is the first person to 'occupy'. Essentially the same objection holds for the second approach, which is the historical method as it was popularised by Sir Henry Maine.[12] Green argues that

'such an investigation [into the historical origins of the right to private property], however valuable in itself, leaves untouched the questions, (1) what it is in the nature of men that makes it possible for them, and moves them, to appropriate; (2) why it is that they conceive of themselves and each other as having a right in their appropriations; (3) on what ground is this conception treated as of moral authority — as one that should be acted on.'[13]

These questions frame Green's own related analyses of the right to private property and of capitalism.[14] Regarding the first question, he argues that persons appropriate things as part of their efforts to achieve self-expression and hence self-realisation.[15] '(1) Appropriation is an expression of will; of the individual's effort to give reality to a conception of his own good; of his consciousness of a possible self-satisfaction as an object to be attained.'[16] It should not be surprising that this is Green's position given the profound significance he places on his theory of the will in his wider philosophical sys-

---

10   PPO 219.
11   PPO 213. Harris and Morrow cite Hume's *Treatise* as an influence here: David Hume, *A Treatise of Human Nature*, ed. L.A. Selby-Bigge, second edition, rev. P.H. Nidditch (Oxford: Clarendon, 1978), pp. 505–07; editorial note in T.H. Green, *Lectures on the Principles of Political Obligation, and other writings*, ed. Paul Harris and John Morrow (Cambridge: Cambridge University Press, 1986), p. 338, §N, n.2.
12   PPO 211–13; Sir Henry Maine, *Ancient Law: Its connections with the early history of society and its relation to modern ideas*, with introduction and notes by Sir Frederick Pollock (London: John Murray, 1920 [1861]), chapter VIII.
13   PPO 212.
14   Ernest Barker, *Political Thought in England from Herbert Spencer to the Present Day* (London: Williams and Norgate, 1915), pp. 53–58.
15   Peter P. Nicholson, *The Political Philosophy of the British Idealists: Selected studies* (Cambridge: Cambridge University Press, 1990), pp. 95–99.
16   PPO 213.

tem, particularly his core notion of distinctively human action.[17] It will be remembered from MSF chapter five that Green believes every individual feels driven to express and, hence, develop her highest nature through purposive actions. Frequently, this expression requires the use of 'things' (conceived as non-purposive objects). Such objects form the means through which the individual can put into practice a plan which she believes serves her highest nature. The security which arises with the right to hold an object as her own (that is, to have the right to determine its use) expresses the permanence of the owner's highest capacities, and so serves to legitimate her claim to be respected as a purposive agent, both to herself and to other persons.[18] In line with Green's broader theory of rights, he holds an agent's right to private property presupposes recognition by society that appropriation by individuals should be guaranteed and should be redeemable only on the individual's wish.[19]

Becoming more distinctively human and, hence, more truly free does not mean satisfying fleeting desires, as these are, in Green's eyes, a reflection of the individual's animality.[20] When 'raw materials' are used in a distinctively human fashion, 'These things, so taken and fashioned, cease to be external as they were before. They become a sort of extension of the man's organs — the constant apparatus through which he gives reality to his ideas and wishes'.[21] These 'ideas and wishes' are expressed through the agent's will, with that

---

[17] PPO 217. John H. Muirhead, *The Service of the State: Four lectures on the political teaching of T.H. Green* (London: John Murray, 1908), pp. 74–78; John Morrow, 'Property and Personal Development: An interpretation of T.H. Green's political philosophy', *Politics: Journal of the Australasian Political Science Association,* 18 (1981), 88; James T. Kloppenberg, *Uncertain Victory: Social democratic and progressivism in European and American thought, 1870–1290* (New York and Oxford: Oxford University Press, 1986), pp. 179–82.

[18] Rodman asserts that Green's emphasis on 'permanence' in his theory of property is a reaction to the decline of religious faith in this society and to an increased scepticism about the possibility of an eternal afterlife (John R. Rodman, 'What is Living and What is Dead in the Political Philosophy of T.H. Green', *Western Political Quarterly,* 26:3 (1973), 579–80). This is an interesting, if unevidenced, claim.

[19] PPO 214; Muirhead, *Service of the State,* pp. 78–80.

[20] Geoffrey Thomas, *The Moral Philosophy of T.H. Green* (Oxford: Clarendon Press, 1987), pp. 342–49; Nicholson, *Political Philosophy,* pp. 99–115 *passim.* Morrow gives the best treatment of this subject in the previous literature (Morrow, 'Property and Personal Development'). There is insufficient space here to assess Lewis's claim that, in regard to property at least, *'in all essentials the position of Green is the same as that of Locke.'* (H.D. Lewis, 'Individualism and Collectivism — a study of T.H. Green', in his *Freedom and History* (London: George Allen and Unwin, 1962), p. 72.) For the relationship between Green and Locke's theory of property, see Morrow, 'Property and Personal Development', 88–89.

[21] PPO 214.

'will' equating to 'a constant principle, operative in all men qualified for any form of society, however frequently overborne by passing impulses, in vir-tue of which each seeks to give reality to the conception of a well-being which he necessarily regards as common to himself with others' (see MSF, chapters five and six).[22] Each individual should be secured the right to hold property privately so that she may use it in a manner which expresses her conscientious assessment of her highest and permanent interests.

Emphasising the role played by the concept of 'permanence' within Green's position on property has other important implications. For example, the Canadian Marxist C.B. MacPherson distinguishes between two asser-tions which have been made to justify liberal democracy and capitalism. 'The first claim is that the liberal-democratic society… maximises individual satisfactions or utilities… [and] does so equitably: that it maximises the satisfactions to which, on some concept of equity, each individual is entitled.'[23] The other claim is that this type of socio-economic system 'max-imizes men's human powers, that is, their potential for using and devel-oping their uniquely human capacities'.[24] MacPherson observes that, to many scholars, Green, J.S. Mill 'and the whole subsequent liberal-democratic tradition' produces 'an uneasy compromise between the two views of man's essence, and, correspondingly, an unsure mixture of the two maximizing claims made for the liberal-democratic society'.[25]

Even though MacPherson is explicit that he does not defend this claim himself, Philip Hansen does so in a highly perceptive and, in many ways, very persuasive attack on Green's theory of property.[26] Despite its strengths, ultimately Hansen's argument fails. He writes,

'Green remarks that "the transition from mere want to consciousness of a wanted object, implies the presence of the want to a subject which disting-uishes itself from it and is constant throughout successive stages of the want." [PE 85] As Green does not specify the wants he has in mind (other than that they must be transformed into objects of desire suitable for the attainment of the moral ideal), nor dispute the sorts of "mere" wants that Utilitarianism

---

22 PPO 217.
23 C.B. MacPherson, *Democratic Theory: Essays in retrieval* (Oxford: Clarendon, 1973), p. 4.
24 MacPherson, *Democratic Theory*, p. 4.
25 MacPherson, *Democratic Theory*, p. 5. See also MacPherson, *Democratic Theory*, for example, pp. 10, 32, 50; C.B. MacPherson, *Political Theory of Possessive Individual-ism: Hobbes to Locke* (Oxford: Oxford University Press, 1962), pp. 2–3; I.M. Greengarten, *Thomas Hill Green and the Development of Liberal-Democratic Thought* (Toronto: University of Toronto Press, 1981), pp. 100–09 *passim*; Andrew Vincent and Raymond Plant, *Philosophy, Politics and Citizenship: The life and thought of the British idealists* (Oxford: Basil Blackwell, 1984), p. 33.
26 MacPherson, *Democratic Theory*, p. 11n4.

posited, we may assume that Green's treatment of wants is an important basis for his moralization of the market.'[27]

Hansen is arguing, then, that Green endorses what MacPherson calls the 'utility-maximising' model of the human spirit. Yet, Hansen (and, given the nature of their respective criticisms, probably MacPherson and Greengarten as well) fails to recognise just how restricted the range of what may be termed developmentally valuable wants really is in Green's theory. Green does not attach primary value to the alleged maximisation of utility-satisfaction produced by capitalism. He does not conflate 'man-as-utility-maximiser' with 'man-as-potential-realiser'.[28] In fact, explicitly he recognises the differences and rejects the former while fervently championing the latter.[29] Green's primary reason for doing so stems from the role played by the concept of distinctively human action in his justification of private property. As was noted at the very beginning of this chapter, Green seeks to humanise political economy, and so to reclaim it from the far more utilitarian classical tradition. Richard Bellamy observes, 'Green contended that in an ideal free market [the right to private] property would be treated as an aspect of the common good and the possibilities for possession as part of one's self-realisation would become open to all'.[30] As Ernest Barker put it: 'It is only by the free action of individual wills that the social good is attained'.[31] In other words, for Green the individual needs private property in order to express her highest capabilities, and formally at least, free exchange is the best system to facilitate this expression by individuals.

This section has established that Green bases his political economy on the need to foster the social and economic conditions that enable the individual to realise her distinctively human capacities. Just as significantly, it has established that he grounds his position on considerations of self-realisation rather than utility-maximisation. In this way, his political economy accords with his wider philosophical system. The next section turns to what is in many ways the keystone of Green's political economy: his defence of free exchange between property-owning citizens. It might seem strange for Green to champion a property system that is based on individual ownership and exchange, given that his theory of citizenship has at its heart the needs

---

27 Phillip Hansen, 'T.H. Green and the Moralization of the Market', *Canadian Journal of Political and Social Theory*, 1:1 (1977), 98.

28 See also John Morrow, 'Review article: Ancestors, Legacies and Traditions: British idealism in the history of political thought', *History of Political Thought*, 6 (1985), 499–504.

29 Implicitly, Morrow questions whether or not Green does this (Morrow, 'Ancestors, Legacies and Traditions', 501).

30 Richard Bellamy, *Liberalism and Modern Society: An historical argument* (Oxford: Polity, 1992), pp. 42–43.

31 Barker, *Political Thought*, p. 55.

of the common good. This paradox is particularly acute for those who see capitalism as being based on the maximisation of utility rather than self-realisation. These issues are addressed also in the next section.

III

Free Exchange, Free Trade and Capitalism

MacPherson criticises Green for allegedly conflating capitalism with the truly free market and allegedly holding that, thus understood, capitalism always tends to maximise the development of the agent's 'uniquely human capacities'.[32] In the course of his response to this claim, Peter Nicholson argues that, for Green,

> 'the right to [private] property, like every right, is not absolute but historically relative. Green is led to a qualified defence of capitalism, but only of capitalism in and for the circumstances of his own time. There is no conceptual tie between Green's moral and political theory and capitalism or any other specific form of economy… [His attachment to capitalism] clearly remains open to revision in the light of economic, technological and social change and of new moral ideas.'[33]

Green does indeed emphasise the importance of historical change in moral ideals. Yet, it must not be forgotten that his is a teleological theory. The individual's telos is to freely actualise her own distinctively human nature by expressing her will in the 'world of practice' (MSF chapters five and six). True freedom necessarily requires that the individual follows her conscience, and does so for the sake of duty itself (MSF §6.III). The agent requires secure and known opportunities if she is to act on these conscientious judgements. For this reason, she should be accorded the right to decide how to use the materials which she believes are required for the successful implementation of the courses of action that she endorses. Green concludes from this fact that the right to own private property occupies a special place within the system of natural rights and duties (where 'natural' is used in Green's teleological sense (§6.III)). Certainly, Nicholson is correct that, for Green, until the individual's society has developed certain characteristics, the normative status of the right to private property depends above all upon the role which the right plays in the imperfect lives of imperfect individuals. Despite this qualification, however, Green is emphatic also that, given the individual's highest nature as a self-determining being, the right to private property is more 'natural' in his very Aristotelian sense of 'natural' than, for instance, a system of communal property rights. Consequently, there is a sense in which Green *does* believe that the system of private property rights is 'absolute' and not merely 'historically relative'.

---

[32] MacPherson, *Democratic Theory*, p. 4.
[33] Nicholson, *Political Philosophy*, p. 114.

Green argues that property rights have been accorded throughout history which imperfectly reflect the most coherent relationship between possession and the individual's will.[34] For example, two types of imperfect property rights are manifested in the kinship system. As the clan rather than the clan member owns certain property especially land, the individual is hindered in her efforts to implement her plans.[35] Secondly, the community is restricted to clan members rather than encompassing all possible agents. Yet, such a situation cannot bring abiding satisfaction to a human being as it represents a limitation on the possibilities for the development of the individual's higher capacities through a more complex and nuanced series of social relationships (§5.V). As Green observes: 'Faculties which social repression and separation prevent from development, take new life from the enlarged co-operation which the recognition of equal claims in all men brings with it.'[36]

Notice that as Green's ideal is a kingdom of ends, he is emphatic that any society such as the ancient polis of Plato and Aristotle which fails to recognise 'the proper and equal sacredness of all women, as self-determining and self-respecting persons' is necessarily imperfect.[37] His theory is essentially gender-blind.[38] Respecting persons requires, firstly, that all members of society are accorded the same rights 'without distinction of sex'. This is 'negative equality before the law'.[39] Secondly, it requires that women be accorded 'positive equality of conditions and a more real possibility for women to make their own career in life'.[40] In other words, whether male or female, married or single, the social structure should accord everyone significant opportunities to express their own conception of their highest natures. Consequently, every person should be accorded the same general rights in regard of property, irrespective of gender.

---

[34] PPO 217.

[35] PPO 220.

[36] PE 208. For example, see Green's speech to the Oxford Reform Club, 25 March 1867 (GW 5:226–32), and to the Loyal Wellington Lodge of Odd Fellows, 25 February 1868 (GW 5.232–36). This thought grounds Green's calls for a (limited) extension of the franchise (Tyler, *Idealist Political Philosophy*, chapter 2).

[37] PE 267.

[38] See Olive Anderson, 'The Feminism of T.H. Green: A late Victorian success story?', *History of Political Thought*, 12:4 (1991), 671–93, and Denys P. Leighton, *The Greenian Moment: T.H. Green, religion and political argument in Victorian Britain* (Exeter and Charlottesville, VA: Imprint Academic, 2004), especially pp. 302–09. For a more general analysis of British idealist defences of women's rights, see David Boucher, *The Limits of Ethics in International Relations: Natural law, natural rights, and human rights in transition* (Oxford: Oxford University Press, 2009), pp. 337–42.

[39] PE 267.

[40] PE 267.

What light does this analysis shed on the MacPherson/Nicholson debate concerning the nature of Green's attachment to capitalism? To a large extent, it depends upon how 'capitalism' is defined. Green does not tell us very clearly what he understands by the term. He appears to see free exchange between agents as a necessary feature of ideal modes of economic inter-action, with 'free' entailing that the agent's choices regarding which parts of her private property to exchange, and at what rates, are not determined by the will of the other parties to the exchange except as an unplanned consequence of the interaction of supply and demand. If private property rights are special in the way which I have argued they are for Green, then the same logic of justification applies to free exchange between individuals. Yet, this logic does not apply to a more sophisticated, non-Greenian conception of 'capitalism'.[41] In other words, Green favours free exchange over those economic systems which, in theory at least, do not make the individual the controller of her own economic choices. Consequently, Green's attachment is to the ideal type of free market, and is justified by his conception of free agency in the sense that he sees this type of market as tending to best facilitate the economic activities of perfectly conscientious citizens.[42] Free exchange attracts Green because he believes it has the potential to make the individual the primary economic decision-making unit in the same manner that his metaphysics of action established the individual to be the primary decision-making unit in the world of practice more generally (MSF chapter four). It is in this sense that he has a special attachment to free exchange, in the same way that he has a special attachment to the right to private property. He is emphatic that 'All restrictions on freedom of wholesome trade are really based on special class interests, and must disappear with the realisation of that idea of individual right, founded on the capacity of every man for free contribution to social good, which is the true idea of the state'.[43] Such class interests restrict individual agency and so are marks of an imperfect culture.

Green applies precisely the same logic to international trade, thereby arriving at a position closely akin to those endorsed by liberals such as John Stuart Mill (even if republicans such as Giuseppe Mazzini were more scep-

---

[41] Usually, the latter is taken to mean something along the lines of, 'An economic arrangement, defined by the predominant existence of capital and wage labour, the former consisting of accumulations in the hands of private (i.e. non-government) owners, including corporations and joint stock companies, the latter consisting in the activities of labourers, who exchange their labour hours (or, according to Marxian theory, their labour power) for wages, paid from the stock of capital' (Roger Scruton, *The Palgrave MacMillan Dictionary of Political Thought*, third edition (Houndsmill: Palgrave MacMillan, 2007), p. 78).

[42] Morrow, 'Property and Personal Development', 88. See §7.III on Green's use of ideal types in other contexts.

[43] PPO 174.

tical).[44] He is emphatic in his rejection of protectionist policies and colonial-ism, on the grounds that among other things, both impede the significant benefits that international free trade can bring (see §7.II). He accepts that, even though political economists have proven international trade tends to increase the wealth of all participants, international conflict still tends to erupt from 'national jealousies in regard to colonial extensions, hostile tariffs and the effort of each nation to exclude others from its markets'.[45] Often, 'commercial jealousy' encourages the 'people of one nation' to attack their economically-successful neighbours, something that was absent from Mill's analysis in his *Principles of Political Economy*.[46] Nevertheless, Green is unwav-ering in his belief that 'freer and more full' international trade tends to encourage the 'sense of common interests between [peoples], which [other-wise] war would infringe'.[47] When combined with the individual's innate desire to form enriching communities and whether intended by capitalists or not, truly free trade tends to promote the non-economic well-being of indiv-iduals and nations.[48] Hence, free international trade tends to promote the 'idea of justice, as a relation which *should* subsist between all mankind as well as between members of the same state', and eventually the idea of the rights of foreigners as human beings can 'come to act on men's minds as independently of all calculation of their several interests as does the idea which regulates the conduct of the good citizen'.[49]

Not all of Green's interpreters have been satisfied with his theory. Andrew Vincent and Raymond Plant conclude their assessment of Green's justification of the right to private property by claiming that he 'wished to justify a system of responsible enterprise, ultimately a form of humanized capitalism'.[50] Yet, they seem to include Green in their claim that

---

44 John Stuart Mill, *Collected Works, Volume III – The Principles of Political Economy with Some of Their Applications to Social Philosophy (Books III–V and Appendices)*, ed. John M. Robson, Introduction by V.W. Bladen (Toronto: University of Toronto Press, London: Routledge and Kegan Paul, 1965), Book 3, Chapter 17, §5, pp. 581–82. Giuseppe Mazzini, 'The Duties of Man', in his *Life and Writings*, 6 vols., ed. Emilie Ashurst (London: Elder, Smith, 1896), vol. 4, pp. 339–41.

45 PPO 162. In this regard, it is interesting to read the following of his under-graduate essays: 'Can Interference with Foreign Nations in any Case by Justif-ied?', 'British Rule and Policy in India' and 'Conservatism' (GW 5:15–19, 22–24, 28–30).

46 PPO 162. Mill, *Principles*, Book 3, Chapter 17, §5.

47 PPO 174. Again, Green's undergraduate essays are of interest here, particularly 'The Effect of Commerce of the Mind of a Nation' (GW 5:3–5).

48 PE 281.

49 PPO 174.

50 Vincent *et al.*, *Philosophy, Politics and Citizenship*, p. 31; also Vincent *et al.*, *Philo-sophy, Politics and Citizenship*, pp. 30–34, 85–86, 119; Andrew Vincent, 'The State and Social Purpose in Idealist Political Philosophy', *History of European Ideas*, 8:3

'The Idealists overall had an ambiguous view of property, competition and capitalism. It was as if they wanted to achieve a unity of the competitive instinct with the moral and rational good, within a moralized form of competition, yet all the time realizing that the two were exclusive, and providing no detailed account of an institutional resolution of the conflict.'[51]

Green is clear that there are real and serious questions to be answered when assessing any claim to allow, for example, the unimpeded accumulation of wealth by individuals or the existence of inequalities of wealth.[52] Green is required to make a difficult decision, for as Andrew Reeve has noted, he must choose 'between equal but limited powers [of alienation and bequest of property], and extended powers with unequal results. Green seems to have favoured the latter, but J.S. Mill and Rawls give more weight to the distributional problem'.[53] Yet, it is worth quoting Green's formulation of the general problem in full.

'Now clearly, if an inequality of fortunes, of the kind which naturally arises from the admission of these two forms of freedom [that is, freedom to trade and to bequeath], necessarily results in the existence of a proletariate, practically excluded from such ownership as is needed to moralise a man, there would be a contradiction between our theory of the right of [private] property and the actual consequence of admitting the right according to the theory; for the theory logically necessitates freedom both in trading and in the disposition of his property by the owner, so long as he does not interfere with the like freedom on the part of others; and in other ways as well its realisation implies inequality.'[54]

Green insists that if inequalities of wealth entail the existence of absolute poverty, then there is a fundamental problem for his justification of private property rights. Consequently, it is vital for his justification of capitalism that any harmful practices or institutions which currently attend capitalism are attached only contingently to the right to private property and the system of market exchange. At root, Green's problem is to find some system whereby resources will be distributed in a manner that is sensitive to the plans of conscientious agents. The complication is that differences in the talents of determinate individuals mean that the latter require different

---

(1987), 345–46; Melvin Richter, *The Politics of Conscience: T.H. Green and his age* (London: Weidenfeld and Nicolson, 1964), p. 290; Gerald Gaus, *The Modern Liberal Theory of Man* (Beckenham: Croom Helm, 1983), pp. 241–43 *passim*.

51 Vincent *et al.*, *Philosophy, Politics and Citizenship*, p. 32. A similar objection to Vincent and Plant's position is made by Nicholson (Peter P. Nicholson, 'A Moral View of Politics: T.H. Green and the British idealists', *Political Studies*, 35 (1987), 120–22). See Crane Brinton, *English Political Thought in the Nineteenth Century* (New York: Harper and Brothers, 1962), pp. 218–24.

52 PPO 222.

53 Andrew Reeve, *Property* (London: MacMillan, 1986), p. 162.

54 PPO 222.

materials through which to actualise their respective conceptions of their highest natures and those of their fellow citizens.[55] The artist requires one set of materials and the scholar requires another. Green considers two methods by which this distribution could occur. The first relies on the distribution of resources to individuals 'by society'.[56] He objects that this method 'would imply a complete regulation of [the individual's] life [by society]'.[57] The alternative is to trust individuals to obtain the resources they need for themselves through capitalism. He argues that, although market transactions can be used to exploit the poor, it is not inevitable that such transactions will be anything except the facilitators of a truly just distribution of resources.[58] There might be ways of constructing a legal and institutional architecture that will promote the latter end. Nevertheless, Green is far from complacent regarding the practical difficulties of doing so, as becomes clear when one examines his treatment of the rights of bequest and inheritance, and his position on land reform. Before turning to those vital issues in the next chapter, it is necessary to consider a number of other criticisms that have been levelled at the assumptions and principles of Green's political economy.

IV

Some Other Possible Criticisms of the
Principles of Green's Political Economy

First, David Crossley has objected to Green's claim that a system of truly free exchange need not be a zero-sum economic game.[59] Green argues that in fact there is good reason to believe in the existence of a tendency of the stock of capital to increase steadily and, hence, for wealth to increase. As Elizabeth and Richard Jay note, 'he shares with most progressives after Mill a belief that the economic problem of wealth-creation has been superseded by the political problem of its distribution'.[60] Some scholars have seen this as a very complicated and unusual point.[61] Yet, in reality Green is assuming that the economy will continue to grow in the future as it has in the past. He is optimistic that the process of free trade, when combined with a free labour market, will lead to a reduction in the proportion of the population who cannot meet their basic needs as self-realising human beings.[62]

---

[55] PPO 223.

[56] PPO 223

[57] PPO 223.

[58] PPO 224.

[59] PPO 226; 'Pol. Econ.' 1. David Crossley, 'T.H. Green on Property and Moral Responsibility', *Logical Analysis and History of Philosophy*, 6 (2003), 209–10.

[60] Elizabeth Jay and Richard Jay, eds., *Critics of Capitalism: Victorian reactions to 'political economy'* (Cambridge: Cambridge University Press, 1992), p. 179.

[61] Crossley, 'T.H. Green on Property', 209–10.

[62] 'Pol. Econ.' 1, 4, 6.

Moreover, Crossley has claimed that Green fails to discuss the idle poor.[63] In reality, Green does discuss them, arguing that their lack of effort is due primarily to the culture of dependence and servility in which they have been raised. Green does not view their lack of effort as a necessary condition for or effect of the capitalist system. In other words, the 'impoverished and reckless proletariate', labouring so inefficiently throughout Europe, is not a necessary accompaniment of the working of the capitalist system.[64] The culture that they have internalised retains the marks of the violence and domination which characterised the transition from feudalism to the modern capitalist epoch. As Green puts it, 'The original landowners were conquerors', and 'Landless countrymen, whose ancestors were serfs, are the parents of the proletariate of great towns'.[65] Certainly, Green's analysis of the causes of poverty have led Marxist scholars such as Greengarten to argue that Green held the 'problem of the proletariat' to be 'a problem, not of economics, but of consciousness'.[66] Yet, this characterisation neglects the crucial fact that, even though initially Green emphasises individual consciousness, he is emphatic that consciousness is determined by the interaction of consciousness and circumstances (MSF §§3.II-III). This is one of the main reasons why he emphasises the importance of the material conditions in which the spiritual person lives. Greengarten oversimplifies greatly and consequently misrepresents Green's position in crucial respects.

Next, James W. Harris has objected that Green develops his theory in a manner that is profoundly metaphysical, bordering on the mystical. He starts by quoting one of the passages from Green's *Principles of Political Obligation* that has just been quoted here.

> '[Appropriation] implies the conception of himself on the part of the appropriator as a permanent subject for whose use, as instruments of satisfaction and expression, he takes and fashions certain external things—certain things external to his bodily members. These things, so taken and fashioned, cease to be external as they were before. They become a sort of extension of the man's organs—the constant apparatus through which he gives reality to his idea and wishes.'[67]

Harris finds some highly counterintuitive implications of such a 'fanciful' theory, not least that 'it appears incompatible with freedom to transmit

---

[63] Crossley, 'T.H. Green on Property', 205.

[64] PPO 227, 228.

[65] PPO 228, 229.

[66] Greengarten, *Thomas Hill Green*, p. 81, see also pp. 81–85 *passim*. Ulam presents this criticism as well, although in milder terms (Adam B. Ulam, *The Philosophical Foundations of English Socialism* (Cambridge, MA: Harvard University Press, 1951), p. 30).

[67] PPO 214, quoted in J.W. Harris, *Property and Justice* (Oxford: Oxford University Press, 2002), p. 221.

[one's property to another]'.[68] Harris claims that for Green these objects 'are part of me' and so I can allow others to use them 'just as only I can authorize anyone to make use of my body'.[69] From this Harris objects: 'But it would surely be paradoxical if, because these things are part of me, I assert that they would also be part of him to whom I sell them or give them away'.[70] The implication seems to be that, once appropriated, the object is forever an essential part of the appropriator as a paw is to a cat. In other words, Harris seems to interpret Green as claiming that appropriation (almost literally?) joins the individual's body to the appropriate object, thereby making the object (almost literally?) part of her in the way that her organs and appendages are.

Harris's reading of Green is bizarre. He places almost the whole weight of his extremely hostile interpretation on the passage quoted above, a passage that he rips from its context. Moreover, he ignores the compatibility of that passage with Green's repeated assertions that appropriating an object accords the appropriator the right to use to the object to express her will in the world of practice.[71] A more accurate and more coherent reading of the passage just quoted establishes that appropriated objects become precisely what Green says they are: simply, they are the 'constant instruments of [the appropriator's] satisfaction and expression' of her will; they are the 'apparatus through which he gives reality to his idea and wishes'. There is nothing particularly metaphysical about this claim, and certainly there is nothing mystical. Green's claim is quite unremarkable and he never implies otherwise. Appropriation creates a right to use the object, and does so in such manner as accords with the 'permanence' of the appropriator's distinctively human nature.

Obviously, some aspects of Green's political economy are harder to defend. For example, at one point in the *Principles of Political Obligation*, Green argues that one should protect the right to private property those who use their property in a manner that is 'demoralising to themselves *and others*'.[72] Immediately afterwards, he states that interventions in the individual's private property rights are justified only where she uses those rights to prevent others from gaining private property for themselves. 'Demoralising' refers to something other than this, then. This makes the phrase 'and others' problematic, given Green's wider theory. It is not clear why a rights-holder should not have her private property rights abrogated to the extent that her

[68] Harris, *Property and Justice*, pp. 302, 221.
[69] Harris, *Property and Justice*, pp. 221, 222.
[70] Harris, *Property and Justice*, p. 222.
[71] Eventually, Harris does acknowledge that Green makes this 'second' argument, but never does he recognise the coherence of Green's argument as a whole (Harris, *Property and Justice*, pp. 302–03).
[72] PPO 221, emphasis added.

use of them harms the development of other persons. Indeed, as chapter ten will show at length, Green appeals to precisely this consideration in his just-ification of intervention with freedom of contract and other economic rights. It is a key part of his wider liberal socialism. As Monro notes, in relation to other difficult situations such as the clash between the parents' alleged rights over their children, and the child's right to be educated, Green is emphatic that rights derive their legitimacy from their contribution to the develop-ment of the individual's distinctively human potentials, and that the former is invalidated to the extent that the use of parental power tends to harm the well-being of the child.[73] Certainly, the justification of non-interference in the private property rights of the owner who produces detrimental effects upon her own moral development is more secure than the parental rights. This is because there is far stronger social recognition that the agent should be accorded a significant and inviolable sphere of freedom from interference in relation to her use of objects, than there is in relation to her rights over per-sons. A sphere of private control of objects is necessary to provide the opp-ortunity for conscientious action. Yet, the property-owner whose use of her property harms the capacities of others to make the best of themselves infringes the latters' true freedom, and as such it would seem that, on Green's fundamental principles, the right should be subject to limitation. Rights are valid only to the extent that they tend to facilitate the realisation of the individual's conception of her permanent and highest nature. In the present case, Green seems to lose sight of that requirement temporarily.

There are other controversial elements to Green's political economy. For example, one might well question his belief that were capitalism to live up to its ideal in practice then it would tend to distribute wealth to all sectors of the society in the manner that would best serve the realisation of the com-mon good. Moreover, one might be sceptical regarding Green's claim that *'in the general sense...* [the] interests of capital and labour are identical'.[74] Never-theless, one should still entertain the possibility that, as a matter of fact, the continued existence of capitalism does not presuppose forms of action which are inherently competitive and exploitative.[75] In all probability Green's

---

73 D.H. Monro, 'Green, Rousseau, and the Culture Pattern', *Philosophy*, 26:99 (1951), 353–57 *passim*.

74 'Pol. Econ.' 6, addition by Harris and Morrow. See Hansen, 'T.H. Green and the Moralization of the Market', 109–13; Greengarten, *Thomas Hill Green*, pp. 100–09 *passim*, 124–27, 131–41 *passim*; Thomas Hurka, *Perfectionism* (Oxford: Oxford University Press, 1993), pp. 183–85.

75 See Ulam, *Philosophical Foundations*, pp. 66–67; Hansen, 'T.H. Green and the Moralization of the Market' *passim*; C.B. MacPherson, 'The Economic Penetration of Political Theory: Some hypotheses', in his *The Rise and Fall of Economic Justice* (Oxford: Oxford University Press, 1978), pp. 113–15 *passim*; Nicholson, 'A Moral View of Politics', 120–22 *passim*.

optimism regarding capitalism's potential benefits for all reflects the influences of Hegel, Mazzini, the non-Marxist strands of classical political economy and the Manchester School.[76] Yet, his key claim remains that capitalism offers the hope and not the current reality of great net benefits. It offers hope because at its best, it is a system of free exchange between individuals, and as an ideal type, free exchange enables the conscientious citizen to act in the manner which she believes will best serve the common good of her society. At the same time, Green is well aware of the distance between the ideal and the daily realities of European capitalism. It is for this reason that he places such great significance on land reform and the need to remove the impediments which landlords place on production of and free trade in agricultural goods. This is one of the main issues addressed in the next chapter.

V

Conclusion

This chapter has analysed the most fundamental principles of Green's political economy. Green is concerned to create and protect opportunities for individuals to treat each other morally through their economic interactions. In other words, he seeks to develop a political economy that accords with his wider social and political theory, and thereby with his philosophical system as a whole. Hence and as was noted in §9.I, the principles of Green's economic thought are influenced profoundly by his desire to humanise the political economy of the classical economic tradition of Adam Smith, David Ricardo and to some degree John Stuart Mill. To this end, §II established that contrary to the allegation of some Marxists, Green rejects utility-maximisation as the basis for private property rights, appealing instead to the intrinsic and profound importance of personal self-realisation. In this way, his political economy is the natural continuation of his wider philosophical system. §III showed that one can never properly understand Green's position on the economy unless one distinguishes clearly between free exchange, free trade and capitalism. §IV explored other complexities and problems that scholars have found with the principles of Green's political economy.

Thus far however, the discussion has focused on economic relationships that would be found within his ideal type of a eudaimonically-enriching

---

[76] Georg W.F. Hegel, *Elements of the Philosophy of Right*, ed. Allen W. Wood, trans. H.B. Nisbet (Cambridge: Cambridge University Press, 1991), §§41–47; Mazzini, 'Duties', 346–47. Harris and Morrow cite J.S. Mill's *Principles of Political Economy* as the main influence here (editorial note in T.H. Green, *Lectures*, p. 339n11) as does Nicholson, 'A Moral View of Politics', 118. In particular, they highlight Books II and IV, chapter xi. (Probably, they mean Book V, chapter xi as there is no Book IV, chapter xi.)

kingdom of ends. In this way, it accords with a widespread assumption of political economists in Green's day, which Derek Fraser captures nicely: '*Laissez-faire* was... a widely held, deeply felt aspiration that ought, in the best of all possible worlds, to be the ideal. The onus of proof, so to speak, was on the prosecution, those who challenged the ideal and claimed it to be inappropriate.'[77] Green is acutely aware that the economic world is far from perfect. Consequently, he cannot rest content with a merely abstract economic analysis. With this thought in mind, the next chapter turns to the final stage of his liberal socialism: his analysis of the practical shortcomings of capitalism and the associated needs for state intervention, welfarism, cooperatives and the trade union movement.

---

[77] Fraser, *Evolution*, p. 146.

10

Capitalism, Cooperatives, Trade Unions and the Welfare State

I

Introduction

Green was born the son of the rector to the Yorkshire hamlet of Birkin on 7 April 1836. He lived there until he left for Rugby School in 1850. In this way, he spent the Hungry Forties among destitute northern peasants. No doubt this was one of the key formative experiences which gave him the great concern for the poor that later struck so many people so forcefully at Oxford, whether in the university or the wider town (see MSF §1.II). This concern was just as strong in the late 1870s and early 1880s, during what was yet another serious economic depression. Green was far from alone in this. Detailed studies and popular works had established that extreme destitution was not a recent or merely temporary phenomenon: increasingly, Victorians were coming to realise that British poverty was widespread and entrenched.[1] The economic downturn of the 1870s severely tested the widely-held faith in limitless growth and that faith was 'shattered' two or three years

---

[1] Some of the most significant studies and popular works included Thomas Carlyle, *Past and Present* (London: Chapman and Hall, 1843) and Henry Mayhew, *London Labour and the London Poor*, 4 vols. (London: privately printed, 1851–61), as well as Friedrich Engels, *The Condition of the Working Class in England*, trans. F. Kelley Wischnewetzky (London: Swan Sonnenschein, 1892 [1845]) although the latter was less widely read that the first two works. While other works were available by Edward Denison, James Greenwood, John Hollingshead, James Yeames and others, some of the most significant studies were yet to be published, most notably Charles Booth, *The Life and Labour of the People in London* (1889; 17 volumes published by 1903) and B.S. Rowntree, *Poverty: A study of town life* (1901). The extreme poverty of London's East End was exposed in during the reporting of the Jack the Ripper murders in 1888, not least through Henry Massingham's articles in *The Star* newspaper.

after Green's death in 1882 when the depression intensified still further.[2] There was a widespread and growing recognition, in Lady Bell's words, of 'how terribly near the margin of disaster the man, even the thrifty man, walks... The spectre of illness and disability is always confronting the working man'.[3] She might well have added to illness and disability the perennial danger of unemployment even for the otherwise industrious.

As was noted at the end of the previous chapter then, free exchange might have been an abstract ideal for Green as it was for many others in the 1870s, but the realities of the time were very far from ideal. It will be established in this chapter that long before the rise of British socialism in the years immediately following his death in 1882, Green recognised that pauperism and poverty could not be solved by merely leaving capitalism to run its course. As he put it in his 1867 'Lectures on Moral and Political Philosophy', advocates of laissez faire pretended that their approach was 'not theoretical but practical; but it really is most ideal': 'The theory will want six or seven generations to work itself out. This is surely most theoretical.'[4]

The previous chapter explored the fundamental principles that underpin Green's political economy. As such, it was concerned predominantly with his conception of the economic relationships that would obtain within the ideal type of a eudaimonically-enriching kingdom of ends. The present chapter turns to the imperfect world of practice, analysing in particular Green's liberal socialist position on state intervention in the economy, his grudging acceptance of the current necessity of state-based income redistribution and his concomitant hopes for the continued growth of conscientious cooperatives and trade unions. Specifically, §II indicates Green's significance in relation to the New Liberalism which emerged in the years following his death, before sketching his position on the individual's right of bequest and inheritance. §III argues for the continuing relevance of his wider practical political economy, by showing that the concerns which motivated Green's fervent advocacy of land reform anticipated in revealing and unexpected ways the principles that underpin J.K. Galbraith's subsequent analysis of the technostructure. §IV draws out the practical implications of Green's political economy, by comparing it with the radical republicanism of Giuseppe Mazzini. Particular attention is paid to Green's acknowledgement of the current necessity of the Poor Law, and his great hope that welfarism would be rendered obsolete by the growth of robust and responsible British trade

---

2   Derek Fraser, *The Evolution of the British Welfare State*, fourth edition (Houndsmill: Palgrave MacMillan, 2009), p. 160.

3   Quoted in Fraser, *Evolution*, p. 165.

4   LMPP 152–53. There is a very clear and accurate statement of this move in John Morrow, 'Private Property, Liberal Subjects and the State', in David Weinstein and Avital Simhony, eds., *The New Liberalism: Reconciling liberty and community* (Cambridge: Cambridge University Press, 2001), pp. 96–101.

unions and a healthy cooperative movement §V draws together many of the proceeding lines of argument to establish finally that Green's practical political economy is indeed a form of liberal socialism. The contours of his position are highlighted via a series of comparisons with the variety of nearly-contemporaneous socialist theories of Friedrich Engels, L.T. Hobhouse, Robert Owen, Karl Marx, William Morris, David Ritchie, R.H. Tawney and Arnold Toynbee. §VI draws together the leading strands of the analysis presented in this chapter.

II
Green, the New Liberalism and the Right of Bequest

Green is widely recognised as a key figure in the epochal shift in British politics and social policy from the old liberalism to the dawn of the New Liberalism (see also §10.V below). One can begin to understand why he is so significant when one considers his 1881 *Lecture on Liberal Legislation and Freedom of Contract*. He begins this very famous address to working-men by pointing out an apparent problem with the liberal credentials of recent Liberal-supported Acts of Parliament. Specifically, he mentions the Ground Game Act, the Employers' Liability Act, the Factory Acts and the Education Acts of 1876 and 1880.[5] These and other pieces of legislation were supported by the Liberal Party even though they were laws which regulated contracts between sane adults. How could one justify the shift from what would now be termed 'the freeing up of markets' which occurred in the previous generation of Liberal politics, to the regulation of markets in Green's own generation, given that the principle of maximising individual freedom was used to justify both types of legislation?[6]

Green's answer is implicit within the theory outlined above. Firstly, from a certain perspective, all legitimate reform is essentially the same.[7] It always aims at moving the reformer's imperfect society towards being a more concrete and eudaimonically-enriching kingdom of ends. As was established in §§3.II–III, promoting the common good of such a society is synonymous with facilitating the true freedom of the individual (sc. acting in a distinctively human manner).[8] Freedom from interference by unjust laws and practices, rather than intervention by a benevolent state, is a key phase in the development of a just society. This corresponded to the initial period of

---

[5] LLFC 194–99.
[6] This paradox is not of solely historical interest. Wempe, for one, sees the shift as a philosophical problem for modern interventionist liberals as well (Ben Wempe, *T.H. Green's Theory of Positive Freedom: From metaphysics to positive freedom* (Exeter and Charlottesville, VA: Imprint Academic, 2004), pp. 196–201 *passim*).
[7] LLFC 195–96.
[8] LLFC 199–200.

Liberal activity, the age of John Bright, Richard Cobden and the Manchester School. Yet, the next stage in social development was the construction of just but interventionist laws and practices. That was the period which Green held Britain was entering in his day. Increasingly, Liberals were coming to recognise that,

> 'freedom of contract, freedom in all the forms of doing what one will with one's own, is valuable only as a means to an end. That end is what I call free-dom in the positive sense: in other words, the liberation of the powers of all men equally for contributions to a common good. No one has a right to do what he will with his own in such a way as to contravene this end.'[9]

In this way, any contract that is 'an instrument of disguised oppression' must be invalid for Green.[10] Such a device merely perpetuates the situation in which the 'labourer stumbled through a helpless, hopeless life to a pau-per's grave'.[11] Such contracts include voluntary slavery and all other arr-angements which on balance commodify any of the participants, even where all of the parties *in a sense* give their consent: 'No contract is valid in which human persons, willingly or unwillingly, are dealt with as commodities, because such contracts of necessity defeat the end for which alone society enforces contracts at all.'[12] One cannot possess a right to consent to this sort of arrangement because the validity of all rights and duties derives from the service which on the whole they render to the true well-being of all its mem-bers.

Green is far from complacent regarding the practical difficulties of con-structing a legal and institutional architecture that will promote a truly just distribution of resources among citizens. His acknowledgement of the imm-ense attendant difficulties underpins his treatment of the reform of British (and, by implication, European) capitalism addressed in this chapter. This section introduces the type of reasoning Green employs in this regard by considering a more limited example of its use: his analysis of the inter-connected rights of bequest and inheritance. Then, the analysis will consider the far more complex matter of Green's position on land reform, and from there the discussion moves to the still more ambitious question of the archi-tecture of his practical political economy more generally.

Green starts his analysis of the disposal of the individual's private prop-erty after her death from the proposition that everyone should be free to bequeath her wealth 'as he likes among his children (or, if he has none,

---

9   LLFC 200.
10 LLFC 209.
11 Green's speech to the National Agricultural Labourers' Union, Oxford, 9 Decem-ber 1874 (GW 5:250).
12 LLFC 201; see also PPO 159.

among others)'.[13] Andrew Reeve has objected that it is unclear whether Green takes the 'primary right' to be that of bequest or of inheritance.[14] Green claims the right of bequest gains its authority from the role which it plays in allowing the individual to plan for the future given that such plans should take account of those for whom the individual cares and who will survive her.[15] Furthermore, the *prima facie* claim that children have upon their parents for an at least minimal level of care and consideration seems to imply that they have a right to inherit. Yet, the right to bequeath remains primary for Green in that he believes it tends to better facilitate the performance of distinctively human actions than does the essentially passive right to inherit. The most significant practical difficulties for Green are that both the right to bequeath and the right to inherit can easily lead to, firstly, inequalities of wealth and hence of opportunities for self-realisation; and, secondly, to the creation of a group of people who have done nothing to earn their wealth and advantages. Green believes there is nothing necessarily wrong with either of these situations. For example, the undeservedly wealthy can make useful contributions to the common good whether voluntarily or under compulsion, for instance through taxation. Primarily, the problem is that an unchecked right to inherit can and frequently does perpetuate inequalities that are so vast and entrenched that they effectively deny the poor a reasonable chance to escape their poverty. It is important to notice, however, that Green does not object to inequality *per se*, merely to such inequalities as effectively deny the poor opportunities to gain a level of private property that is sufficient for them to be able to put their will into practice. In other words, he objects to domination rather than to relative inequality.[16] There might be other reasons for regulating the extent of inequalities of wealth (such as to maintain an effective sense of common duties to a shared community), but they do not arise from the iniquity of inequality *per se* (see §3.VI).

Green concedes that difficulties do arise in practice, and that these need correction. When addressing these difficulties, he focuses upon those measures which affect the right of bequest rather than inheritance because he believes that the former are more likely to prolong and propagate harmful

---

13 PPO 224. Reeve misses this last clause when he argues that Green neglects the childless (Andrew Reeve, *Property* (London: MacMillan, 1986), p. 160).

14 Reeve, *Property*, p. 160.

15 PPO 224.

16 Mander alleges that Green seeks an equal distribution of property (W.J. Mander, *British Idealism: A history* (Oxford: Oxford University Press, 2011), p. 237). Yet, this seems to miss the more fundamental point outlined here. That Green did not seek to equalise property as a good in itself is recognised by Alberto de Sanctis, *The 'Puritan' Democracy of Thomas Hill Green, with some unpublished writings* (Exeter and Charlottesville, VA: Imprint Academic, 2005), p. 157.

concentrations of wealth. Nevertheless, he rejects any practice that will tend to reduce citizens' opportunities to distribute their wealth through bequest on any basis which furthers their own respective conceptions of the common good. In short, he denies the legitimacy of any practice which prescribes a particular distribution of property. Under this heading, Green includes any law or custom of primogeniture, as well as any obligation for the bequeather to distribute her property equally amongst her children.[17] Precisely which laws are required depends largely on the particular circumstances obtaining at the time.

In a similar vein to this nuanced discussion of the rights to bequeath and to inherit, Green attacks peerages for requiring a great deal of personal wealth, and rejects 'the power of settlement [of landed estates] allowed by English law'.[18] In fact, Green traces many of capitalism's current deficiencies, including the problem of endemic grinding poverty for some, to the fact that in modern Europe the right to private property has been arranged in such a manner that now many people 'have not the chance of providing means for a free moral life, of developing and giving reality or expression to a good will, an interest in social well-being'.[19] Instead, they are condemned to labour for the subsistence of themselves and those people for whom they care. In effect, possessing a legal right to hold property privately is meaningless for these people: in this sense, 'property is theft'.[20] Against this background, it is instructive to consider Green's position on what he sees as the most fundamental economic issue of his time: land reform.

III

Land and the Technostructure

Green's engagement with the realities of his time has led some scholars to conclude that his economic thought is now outdated. Indeed, for Ulam Green was outdated even in the 1880s: 'It is characteristic that [Green] probes most deeply into the question of *property in land* and touches but

---

17   PPO 224–25; LLFC 205–06.
18   PPO 225.
19   PPO 220, 210.
20   PPO 220, 221, 226. Here, Green recalls Giuseppe Mazzini, 'The Duties of Man', in his *Life and Writings*, ed. Emilie Ashurst, 6 vols., second edition (London: Smith, Elder, 1891), vol. 4, p. 348, and Pierre-Joseph Proudhon, *What is Property? An inquiry into the principle of right and of government,* trans. Benjamin R. Tucker (New York: Dover, 1970 [first French edition 1840]), chapter one. It seems very likely that Green got the point from Mazzini (for the textual evidence, see §10.V below). Moreover, all of the Proudhonian elements in Green's economic writings can be found in Mazzini's chapter on the economic question in *The Duties of Man*.

incidentally upon industrial problems of the age.'[21] Other readers have claimed that Green was more forward-looking than this but in the wrong way. Hence, Greengarten argues that Green's calls for the careful regulation of land holdings by the state 'are clearly designed to hasten the development of capitalist methods of production in the cultivation and general use of the land'.[22] More significantly still, even if one does not see Green as being behind his own times, the land reforms which he saw as central factors in social and economic development are claimed to be marginal issues in the advanced corporate capitalist world of the twenty-first century.

Yet, the situation is nowhere near as straightforward as the critics assume. Green conceives the key economic problem of his time to be that the system of land tenure is based on legal rights that are unjustifiable, in that they work against the common good.[23] Land, like labour, is a special commodity: 'It is from the land, or through the land, that the raw material of all wealth is obtained. It is only upon the land that we can live; only across the land that we can move from place to place.'[24] Landlords have been granted rights which are harmful to the well-being of the society as a whole. They have been given many opportunities for selfishness and control of other persons and, frequently, these opportunities have been seized. For example, the landlord has been allowed

> '[to use] his land [so] as to make it unserviceable to the wants of men (e.g. by turning fertile land into a forest), and [to take] liberties with it incompatible with the conditions of general freedom and health; e.g. by clearing out a village and leaving the people to pick up house-room as they can elsewhere — a practice common under the old poor-law, when the distinction between closed and open villages grew up — or, on the other hand, by building houses in unhealthy places or of unhealthy structure, by stopping up means of communication, or forbidding the erection of dissenting chapels.'[25]

Moreover, the practice of tenant-farming had diminished seriously peasants' incentives to improve the land they worked, especially where, as in Ireland, farmers had very little power relative to the landlords.[26] Clearly, as Green's friend George C. Brodrick established in his important 1881 book *English*

---

21   Adam B. Ulam, *The Philosophical Foundations of English Socialism* (Cambridge, MA: Harvard University Press, 1951), p. 39.

22   I.M. Greengarten, *Thomas Hill Green and the Development of Liberal-Democratic Thought* (Toronto: University of Toronto Press, 1981), p. 86.

23   PPO 194, 204–09, 229.

24   LLFC 205.

25   PPO 229. A 'closed village' was a village encompassed on a single landed estate, where the landowner controlled almost all aspects of life: who could live in the village, what shops could trade, what goods could be bought and sold and so on.

26   See M. Longfield, 'The Tenure of Land in Ireland', in J.W. Probyn, ed., *Systems of Land Tenure in Various Countries* (London: Cassell, Petter, Galpin, 1876), pp. 1–92.

Land and English Landlords, this practice caused great social harm.[27] Good land went uncultivated and good farmers starved as a result. Only through reform of the system of land tenure could self-realisation become a viable goal for the peasantry, as indeed only through reform of the terms and conditions of industrial employment could it become a reality for the proletariat.[28] Crucially, in the countryside the 'poverty and recklessness' of the lower classes 'can be cured only by such legislation as will give the agricultural labourer some real interest in the soil'.[29]

Richard Bellamy has argued that, no matter how laudable Green's goal and analysis may have been in the 1870s and 1880s, subsequent structural changes mean that Green's political economy has dangerous implications in contemporary circumstances.

> 'Within the pluralistic and complex mass societies of today, dominated as they are by imposing structures of corporate and bureaucratic powers and an intricate international market, the Victorian moral code of self-improvement has become little more than a useful fiction for justifying forms of oppression and privilege akin to those liberals originally sought to remove.'[30]

It will be shown now that far from rendering his political economy obsolete, in reality Green's reasons for placing land at the centre of his plans for the reform of mid-Victorian capitalism highlight the significance of other sectors in advanced early twenty-first-century economies. As we have seen, Green holds that the state should regulate the system of land tenure very carefully due to land's scarcity and due to the various significant effects that the system has on the lives of all citizens. Agriculture was the most important economic sector in Green's day in the same way that nowadays the global economy is based on finance, information and natural resources such as oil. In other words, it is vital to appreciate that Green's primary goal is to structure the most fundamental sectors of the economy in the manner that is most likely to serve the common good given the prevailing economic structure and circumstances. He held that in his day one should reform the system of

---

27 George C. Brodrick, *English Land and English Landlords: An Enquiry into the Origin and Characters of the English Land System, with Proposals for its Reform* (London: Cassell, Petter, Galpin, 1881). See also Brodrick, 'The Law and Custom of Primogeniture' and C. Wren Hoskins 'The Land Laws of England', in Probyn, ed., *Systems of Land Tenure*, pp. 93–168, 169–212, respectively. See Green's speech to the Agricultural Labourers' Union, 23 October 1872, reported in the *Oxford Chronicle and Berks and Bucks Gazette*, 26 October 1872 (GW 5:238–41). LLFC 205–09.

28 LLFC 200–04.

29 Green's speech to the Wellington Lodge of Odd Fellows, 25 February 1868 (GW 5:234, 235), also quoted in Nettleship, 'Memoir', cxii.

30 Richard Bellamy, 'Introduction', in Richard Bellamy, ed., *Victorian Liberalism: Nineteenth century political thought and practice* (London: Routledge, 1990), p. 12.

private property rights in land so as to promote this end.[31] In short, although Green emphasised strongly the extension of private ownership of land to the peasantry, he did so primarily upon empirical grounds. Consequently, changed economic realities require changed policy responses. Green himself recognises that the principles of his political economics yield different results in different times.

One can begin to see this more clearly by reflecting on the fact that Green's discussion of land reform is a clear application of his fundamental principle that the individual's right to private property should be abrogated only to the extent that 'possession of property by one man interferes with the possession of property by another; when one set of men are secured in the power of getting and keeping the means of realising their will, in such a way that others are practically denied the power'.[32] The mere fact that a person wastes her opportunity to use her property well is not a sufficient ground for interfering with her right to own private property.

Green's endorsement of free exchange between individuals and the ideal type of the free market (that is, a network of perfectly free exchanges between responsible conscientious individuals) (§9.III) when combined with his condemnation of economic oppression, brings to mind J.K. Galbraith's hopes in the twentieth century that the market system can function as a corrective to the abuses perpetrated by the technostructure. Galbraith characterises the former (the market system) as the interaction of a plurality of relatively small producers in which the same people who own the business control it on a daily basis, with no single firm or cartel being able to determine prices.[33] While the guiding motivation for such firms remains the profit motive and economic activity is based on competition between self-interested firms, the system itself is relatively stable and its outcomes are relatively fair. Galbraith contrasts this collection of small producers with the 'technostructure' or 'planning system'. This is founded upon expert technical knowledge that is collectivised and bureaucratised in large complex businesses.[34] Eventually the concentration of technical knowledge leads to the rise of corporate capitalism, wherein ownership is divorced from control, and, while the profit-motive remains important in the technostructure, nonprofit factors such as market-share acquire a special significance. For Galbraith, the technostructure and the market system co-exist, although increasingly the technostructure is coming to dominate the market system and eventually the state. Galbraith concludes that a free society is possible

---

[31] Hence he endorses the established legal right of the British state to compulsorily purchase of land under certain circumstances, in 1881 (LLFC 205).

[32] PPO 221.

[33] John K. Galbraith, *Economics and the Public Purpose* (Boston: Houghton Mifflin, 1973), pp. 48–53.

[34] Galbraith, *Economics and the Public Purpose*, p. 88.

only to the extent that the technostructure has been dismantled and the market system has been freed. Once that has been achieved, the state will be able to foster the proper functioning of a society in which the well-being of its citizens is the guiding ideal of collective life.[35] In this way, Galbraith seeks to create a 'good society' in which 'citizens... have personal liberty: basic well-being, racial and ethnic equality, the opportunities for a rewarding life'.[36]

Certainly, there are important differences between Green and Galbraith. Galbraith is far more willing to believe that purely self-interested actions will bring net social benefits (although see also §4.V). As has been shown (§9.III), for Green free exchange is a precondition of virtuous action wherein the individual deliberately orients her economic activities to serve the common good. Nevertheless, there are significant affinities between Galbraith's position and that of Green. Galbraith echoes Green's claim that the ideal free market is a precondition of a free and enabling society, and only to the extent that it exists will one be able to counter the oppression perpetrated by economically-powerful minorities. Like Galbraith, Green does not give 'a thoroughgoing justification of the capitalist market economy', as Greengarten claims Green does.[37] In fact both Green and Galbraith are emphatic that, as the culture of modern capitalist societies is imperfect, the outcomes of capitalist economic systems will be similarly imperfect. The existence of concentrations of economic power creates great social evils, which in turn create the need for positive state intervention in the workings of capitalism.[38] Just as Galbraith calls for the emancipation of the society and the state from the power of the technostructure, Green advocates robust government intervention to address the abusive power of landlords. Similarly and as will become clear shortly, the concerns driving Galbraith's response to the technostructure are closely akin to those which lead Green to advocate the creation of workers cooperatives (§10.V). Indeed, Green argues that it is not merely the right of the state and trade unions to counter abuse of power by landlords, it is their positive duty.[39] In this way, Green writing in the late-1870s and early-1880s anticipated Galbraith's observation from the mid-1990s that 'trade union power' should be protected in and by 'the good society', 'for worker organization remains a major civilising factor in mod-

---

[35] See, for example, Galbraith, *Economics and the Public Purpose*, chapter 24.

[36] John K. Galbraith, *The Good Society: The humane agenda* (London: Sinclair-Stevenson, 1996), p. 4.

[37] Greengarten, *Thomas Hill Green*, p. 87.

[38] PPO 230–31.

[39] For instance, see his speech to the Agricultural Labourers' Union, 23 October 1872 (GW 5:238–41). For more on Green's attitude to trade unions see Melvin Richter, *The Politics of Conscience: T.H. Green and his age* (London: Weidenfeld and Nicolson, 1964), pp. 329–30.

ern economic life'.[40] In short, both Green and Galbraith see careful but often forceful mass action against concentrations of economic power as being integral to the proper functioning of the sorts of market economy that must exist if the individual is to be able to realise herself in a complex modern society (§10.V).

This chapter has established so far that, for all of the significance Green places on free exchange, he recognises it is almost inevitable that capitalism will oppress the poor in various ways in practice. Certainly, it is possible to imagine a relatively unfettered market between imperfect citizens in which the state does not interfere. Yet, this would be very different from the free market that would exist between citizens who have attained their telos. The free markets that currently exist in the world are marked by harmful power asymmetries and hence exploitation, both of which are incompatible with the existence of a range of significant opportunities for free action, something Green believes to be required for the promotion of the common good of a eudaimonically-enriching kingdom of ends.

Green is deeply concerned by the profound changes that are happening to the European economies in the 1870s and 1880s.[41] He is emphatic throughout his writings and speeches that, as practised, capitalism fails consistently to secure the physical and mental health as well as eudaimonic and rational development of the poor. His concerns are reflected in the fact that, politically, he identifies strongly and publicly with the radical, 'Advanced' or 'Constructive' wing of the Liberal Party.[42] Such links have been explored at length by several recent scholars.[43] Famously, he insists on the need for progressive legislation in areas such as health and education to ensure the 'young citizens' grow 'up in such health and with so much knowledge as is necessary for their real freedom'.[44] Indeed for this reason, Paul Harris and John Morrow claim that Green would have been strongly supportive of the

---

[40] Galbraith, *Good Society*, p. 66.

[41] For Green's discussion of certain economic theories, see LLFC, 'Pol. Econ.' and PPO 211–32. In addition, Green shows clear debts to Hegel's justification of the right to private property as the means through which individual wills manifest themselves, see LMPP 175–76, 180.

[42] Peter P. Nicholson, *The Political Philosophy of the British Idealists: Selected studies* (Cambridge: Cambridge University Press, 1990), pp. 162–65.

[43] Matt Carter, *T.H. Green and the Development of Ethical Socialism* (Exeter and Charlottesville, VA: Imprint Academic, 2003); Denys P. Leighton, *The Greenian Moment: T.H. Green, religion and political argument in Victorian Britain* (Exeter and Charlottesville, VA: Imprint Academic, 2004) and Colin Tyler, *Idealist Political Philosophy: Pluralism and conflict in the absolute idealist tradition* (London and New York: Continuum, 2006), chapter 3.

[44] LLFC 203.

British welfare state.[45] Michael Freeden has denied that, as a matter of fact, Green's writings had any significant influence in this regard.[46] Yet, it seems difficult to deny that Green did provide intellectual justifications for at least two of the three pillars of the welfare state: namely, on the one hand the legal protection of the well-being of the members of particular social groups in the face of endemic economic exploitation and oppression, and, on the other hand, state provision of certain basic levels of education and health care.[47] This point comes through clearly in his manuscripts: '[A g]reat obs-

---

[45] Editorial note in T.H. Green, *Lectures on the Principles of Political Obligation, and other writings*, ed. Paul Harris and John Morrow (Cambridge: Cambridge University Press, 1986), p. 346n26. See further John H. Hallowell, *Main Currents in Modern Political Thought* (New York: Holt, Rinehart and Winston, 1950), p. 286; Lane W. Lancaster, *The Masters of Political Thought: Volume Three, Hegel to Dewey* (London: George G. Harrap, 1959), p. 228; Harry Holloway, 'Mill and Green on the Modern Welfare State', *Western Political Quarterly*, 13 (1960), 389–405 *passim*; David Thomson, 'Conclusion: The Idea of Equality', in David Thomson, ed., *Political Ideas* (Harmondsworth: Penguin, 1969), pp. 196–200; Vincent J. Knapp, 'T.H. Green on the Exorability of Property', *Agora*, 1 (1969), 57; M.M. Sankhdher, 'T.H. Green: The forerunner of the welfare state', *Indian Journal of Political Science*, 30 (1969), 148–64; M.M. Sankhdher, 'T.H. Green's Concept of the Welfare State', *Journal of Political Studies*, 3 (1970), 1–21; Dante Germino, *Machiavelli to Marx: Modern western political thought* (Chicago and London: University of Chicago Press, 1972), pp. 262–65 *passim*; Frank Thakurdas, *The English Utilitarians and the Idealists: An introductory study to the development of English political thought in the eighteenth and nineteenth centuries* (Delhi: Vishal, 1978), pp. 200, 302–08; Gerald Gaus, *The Modern Liberal Theory of Man* (Beckenham: Croom Helm, 1983), pp. 255–57; Andrew Vincent and Raymond Plant, *Philosophy, Politics and Citizenship: The life and thought of the British idealists* (Oxford: Basil Blackwell, 1984), pp. 181–82; James T. Kloppenberg, *Uncertain Victory: Social democracy and progressivism in European and American thought, 1870–1920* (New York and Oxford: Oxford University Press, 1986), for example, pp. 147, 280; Thomas Hurka, *Perfectionism* (Oxford: Oxford University Press, 1993), pp. 147–48. Muirhead appears to have missed this point in his discussion of Green's attitude to a possible policy of ensuring full employment through state action (John H. Muirhead, *The Service of the State: Four lectures on the political teaching of T.H. Green* (London: John Murray, 1908), pp. 99–100). Clarke disagrees with those commentators who claim that Green was 'an architect of the welfare state' (Peter Clarke, *Liberals and Social Democrats* (Cambridge: Cambridge University Press, 1978), p. 15).

[46] Michael Freeden, *The New Liberalism: An ideology of social reform,* reprinted with corrections (Oxford: Clarendon Press, 1986 [1978]), pp. 17–18. For a different view, see Yuichi Shionoya, 'The Oxford Approach to the Philosophical Foundations of the Welfare State', in Roger E. Backhouse and Tamotsu Nishizawa, eds., *No Wealth But Life: Welfare economics and the welfare state, 1880–1945* (Cambridge: Cambridge University Press, 2010), pp. 91–113.

[47] The 'Welfare State… is a system of social organisation which restricts free market operations in three principal ways: by the designation of certain groups, such as children or factory workers, whose rights are guaranteed and whose welfare is

tacle to such free development is disease & as [the] conditions of disease — specially in connection with [the] mode of work & housing — come to be better understood, [the] office of the state, under [the] limitations aforesaid, seems almost indefinitely to extend.'[48] Yet, one should be circumspect here. Green is arguing for an increase in state expenditure on health and education, but this was from a very low level. The Victorian state spent nothing like the amount modern European governments spend in these areas.

Support for Paul Harris and John Morrow's claim that Green's writings influenced the development of the third pillar, state-led targeted income redistribution, can be found in Green's belief that 'Left to itself, or to the operation of a casual benevolence, a degraded population perpetuates and increases itself'.[49] It remains an open question, however, whether an ordered and principled system of welfare supports is possible only when it is controlled by the state. Richter has established that Green believes that it is not.[50] By the same token, there is nothing to say that the state should never undertake this task, given changed circumstances or changed interpretations of existing circumstances.

Ultimately, as in all cases of practical action, Green holds that the best course depends upon the specific empirical circumstances. It is a matter of practical judgement. As was established in §7.III, Green argues that laws are required which will give real power to virtuous citizens in their pursuit of their respective conceptions of the common good of an enabling society (§3.VII). By freeing the agent from the need to occupy most of her time with the process of securing the most basic material conditions of a truly free life for herself and her family, the just state enables the agent and those people for whom she cares to develop their higher faculties more effectively.[51] Green's concerns in all these areas indicate that his attitude to capitalism is far less glib than some scholars allege, and his solutions are far more practical and nuanced.

It is important to remember that Green holds the right to private property rights to be valuable to the extent that it enables individuals to exercise

---

protected by the community; by the delivery of services such as medical care or education, so that no citizen shall be deprived of access to them; and by transfer payments which maintain income in times of exceptional need, such as parenthood, or of interruption of earnings caused by such things as sickness and unemployment.' Fraser, *Evolution*, p. 1.

[48] T.H. Green, 'Notes on Lectures on Kant's Moral Philosophy' (MS10a, T.H. Green Papers, Balliol College, Oxford), p. 28, quoted in Ben Wempe, *Beyond Equality: A study of T.H. Green's theory of positive freedom* (Leiden: Eburon, 1986), p. 202.

[49] LLFC 203.

[50] PE 305; Richter, *Politics of Conscience*, pp. 336–43 *passim*; Nicholson, *Political Philosophy*, pp. 166–68 *passim*.

[51] LLFC 199–203.

the right to live a 'free life', understood as 'the right to use the life according to the motions of… [the individual's] own will'.[52] The preconditions of a free life cannot be specified in abstraction from a concrete situation. They have to be linked to the 'social function[s]' to which the individual belongs ('artist and man of letters… tiller of land and the smith'): 'those functions are various and the means required for their fulfilment are various.'[53] Consequently, in practice legitimate property-holdings will be distributed unequally (§9.III). The question becomes how to decide who receives what. Green considers two options.

> 'Either… the various apparatus needed for various functions must be provided for individuals by society, which would imply a complete regulation of life incompatible with that highest object of human attainment, a free morality; or we must trust for its provision to individual effort, which will imply inequality between the property of different persons.'[54]

Ultimately, Green adopts a composite position: the state should provide means of support for those who, though of respectable character, fall on hard times. Wealth will be distributed unequally, and everyone should work for their own living except where circumstances prevent them from doing so; yet, there should be no right to support where one's poverty results from one's laziness. For Green, the most effective safeguards against poverty are personal virtue, an assertive conscientious character and education. To the extent that these are deficient, the individual is little better than a slave.[55]

This situation can be improved still further when workers and peasants band together to form savings societies. Such collective action creates opportunities for the 'better sort of labourers' to become capitalists themselves 'to the extent often of owning their houses and a good deal of furniture, of having an interest in stores, and of belonging to benefit-societies through which they make provision for the future'.[56] The poor need proper 'education and self-discipline' and an effective will to make more of themselves.[57] He insists that ultimately it is an irreducibly practical question what precise method is best able to foster personal development, and that the answer depends significantly on the empirical circumstances in which it is asked. Nevertheless, his emphasis on personal character and the self-directed life, like the unpredictability of personal eudaimonic development, makes him deeply sceptical regarding centralised socialism of the type associated in his day

---

52   PPO 151.
53   PPO 223.
54   PPO 223.
55   PPO 229; Mazzini, 'Duties', 343.
56   PPO 227.
57   PPO 227.

whether, fairly or not, with Fichte (see MSF §1.II; CS §6.III).[58] Hence, it is no surprise that Green shows a very strong preference for cooperative movements over centralised socialism when discussing the economic reforms in Germany in the early 1860s: 'the artisans (who are strong at Berlin, though I fear not elsewhere) seem to be free from the worse forms of socialism, and under the guidance of Schulaze-Delitsch to be developing schemes of cooperation and self-help.'[59] These reservations regarding the appropriateness of state action to solve economic problems (rather than merely to ameliorate them temporarily) becomes even clearer when one compares Green's position to that of Mazzini.

Various similarities between Green's theory of rights and that of Mazzini have been drawn out earlier in this book (§5.V). It is revealing to extend this analysis by comparing their respective derivations of the right to private property and the state's role in enforcing it. Many scholars have criticised Green's economic theory on the grounds that it is unrealistic and that it shows limited knowledge of the more specialist sources of his time.[60] Yet,

---

[58] The lack of an extended discussion of Fichte's political thought by Green makes it unclear whether he made this link between Fichte and centralised socialism. For a contemporary 'non-centralist' reading of Fichte, see Nedim Nomer, 'Fichte and the Idea of Liberal Socialism', *Journal of Political Philosophy*, 13:1 (2005), 139–59, and Nedim Nomer, 'Fichte and the relationship between self-positing and rights', *Journal of History of Philosophy*, 48:4 (2010), 469–90.

[59] Nettleship, 'Memoir', xlii.

[60] For instance, Ernest Barker, *Political Thought in England from Herbert Spencer to the Present Day* (London: Williams and Norgate, 1915), pp. 57–58; Y.L. Chin, *The Political Theory of Thomas Hill Green* (New York: W. Dray 1920), pp. 160–61; Ulam, *Philosophical Foundations*, pp. 66–67; H.D. Lewis, 'Individualism and Collectivism — a study of T.H. Green', in his *Freedom and History* (London: George Allen and Unwin, 1962) pp. 70–79; H.D. Lewis, 'Individualism of T.H. Green', in his *Freedom and History*, pp. 100–04; A.J.M. Milne, *The Social Philosophy of English Idealism* (London: Allen and Unwin, 1962), pp. 157–59; Amal K. Mukhopadhyay, *The Ethics of Obedience: A study of the philosophy of T.H. Green* (Calcutta: World Press Private, 1967), pp. 149–54; Vrajendra R. Mehta, 'T.H. Green and the Revision of English Liberal Theory', *Indian Journal of Political Science*, 35 (1974), 42–49 *passim*; Phillip Hansen, 'T.H. Green and the Moralization of the Market', *Canadian Journal of Political and Social Theory*, 1:1 (1977), 91–117; Andrew Lawless, 'T.H. Green and the British Liberal Tradition', *Canadian Journal of Political and Social Theory*, 2:2 (1978), 142–55; Phillip Hansen, 'T.H. Green and the Limits of Liberalism: A response to Professor Lawless', *Canadian Journal of Political and Social Theory*, 2:2 (1978), 156–58; Thakurdas, *English Utilitarians and the Idealists*, pp. 202–03; Ken Coates, *Work-ins, Sit-ins and Industrial Democracy* (Nottingham: Spokesman, 1981), p. 156; Vincent *et al.*, *Philosophy, Politics and Citizenship*, pp. 174–78 *passim*; Wempe, *Beyond Equality*, pp. 196–201; Peter P. Nicholson, 'A Moral View of Politics: T.H. Green and the British idealists', *Political Studies*, 35 (1987), 118; Richard Bellamy, 'T.H. Green and the Morality of Victorian Liberalism', in Bellamy, ed., *Victorian Liberalism*, pp. 144–47.

frequently this ignorance has been overstated. In addition to drawing on Hegel's *Philosophy of Right*, Green's analysis of property rights in *Principles of Political Obligation* is indebted heavily to Mazzini's radical political economy. These similarities will be explored now. It will be established that even Green's divergences from Mazzinianism reinforce his great contemporary relevance.

IV

Green and Mazzini on Welfarism and Trade Unions

Throughout his life, Mazzini called on working-class Italians to seize the opportunity to develop their virtue and quality of life, in the face of the 'moral evil[s]' around them. In *The Duties of Man* (1860), he reminded poor Italians that 'there is progress in the class to which you belong; a progress historical and continuous, and which has overcome greater difficulties'.[61] He continued:

> 'You were first *slaves*, then *serfs*. Now you are *hirelings*. You have emancipated yourselves from slavery and then from serfdom. Why should you not emancipate yourselves from the yoke of *hire*, and become free producers, and masters of the totality of production which you create?'[62]

In a striking echo of this passage, Green writes in *The Principles of Political Obligation* that: 'Landless countrymen, whose ancestors were serfs, are the parents of the proletariate of great towns.'[63] For Green the acquiescence to poverty by Britain's industrial classes is simply a continuation of the old serf mentality, although with a changed appearance reflecting the gradual shift away from agriculture to 'mining' and 'manufacture'. Green finds the cause of this acquiescence in the structures of relief upon which the poor of his day have to rely.

> '[M]en whose life has been one of virtually forced labour, relieved by church-charities or the poor law (which in part took the place of these charities)… were thus in no condition to contract freely for the sale of their labour, and had nothing of that sense of family responsibility which might have made them insist on having the chance of saving.'[64]

Early in *The Principles of Political Obligation*, Green had identified the Poor Law as one of the 'legal institutions which take away the occasion for the exercise of certain moral virtues', in that it removes the 'occasion for the exercise of parental forethought, filial reverence, and neighbourly kind-

---

61   Mazzini, 'Duties', 343.
62   Mazzini, 'Duties', 343.
63   PPO 229.
64   PPO 229.

ness'.[65] It will become clear below that Green is particularly concerned that, whether intended by its supporters or not, in this way the Poor Law tends to reinforce the servile mentality that prevents the proletariat and the peasantry from asserting themselves collectively against capitalists and large landowners. In this way, he holds that, irrespective of the motives of its creators and administrators, poor relief serves to control the poor as much as to benefit them.[66] This is not to say that Green believes the Poor Law should be abolished immediately. He is adamant that changing any law because one sees it as a device of 'paternal government' risks exposing those currently benefitting from it to influences and powers that would prevent them from ever being able to exercise and develop their moral virtues.[67] On a closely related point, Crossley claims that Green fails to discuss the deserving poor; indeed, he berates Green for not doing so.[68] In reality, Green argues that as laws in place across Europe in the 1870s and 1880s regarding land ownership, game laws and employment rights give huge power to a small proportion of the population, the Poor Law remains necessary to protect the deserving British working class from further deprivation.[69] Until the harmful laws are changed, adapting his words from a speech of 1872, the deserving poor will continue to 'have that given to them as charity that they ought to demand as a right'.[70]

Once again like Mazzini, Green is emphatic that state socialism and minimal government alike run great risks of reducing the individual's chances of leading a self-directed, virtuous life.[71] As Mazzini puts it, an overactive socialist state denies the 'essential elements of human life — such as Religion, Association, Liberty' and private property.[72] Green holds that, in the circum-

---

[65] PPO 17.

[66] The 'conspiratorial' model of welfare history sees this as a deliberate mode of social control. See Fraser, *Evolution*, pp. 7–9, and Kathleen C. Martin, *Hard and Unreal Advice: Mothers, science and Victorian poverty experts* (Houndsmill: Palgrave MacMillan, 2007).

[67] LMPP 152–53.

[68] 'Green really needs to sort this out in greater detail and to face the question of whether poor relief is an entitlement or to be viewed as state largesse, in the same league as private charity.' David Crossley, 'T.H. Green on Property and Moral Responsibility', *Logical Analysis and History of Philosophy*, 6 (2003), 206n33.

[69] LLFC *passim*. Green, speech to the Agricultural Labourers Union, 23 October 1874 (GW 5:240).

[70] Green, speech to the Agricultural Labourers Union, 23 October 1874 (GW 5:240).

[71] John Stuart Mill adopted the same position in his *Principles of Political Economy* (which we know Green read) and his *Auguste Comte and Positivism* (which he seems likely to have read), but the textual evidence (some of which is cited in the course of this chapter) implies that Green got the ideas from Mazzini rather than Mill.

[72] Mazzini, 'Duties', 346; for Mazzini's attack on 'socialism', see *ibid.*, 344–65.

stances faced by the European working classes of his day, schemes such as the Poor Law remain a necessary evil until such time as self-assertive and responsible workers and peasants join together in cooperative businesses, as German workers had done in the early 1860s.[73] It is also for this reason that, like Mazzini, Green calls for workers to set up cooperatives to buy goods more cheaply by purchasing them in bulk, as well as to escape oppressive employment by setting up cooperatively owned and run firms.[74] He places great significance on these forms of economic cooperatives because they enable workers not only to assert themselves, but also to counter exploitative capitalist-run businesses. They help otherwise vulnerable and oppressed individuals to assert themselves as self-realising beings, against the benefic-iaries of the current hierarchical social and economic structures. In this way, producer and purchasing cooperatives form key parts of the institutional framework of a contemporary Greenian kingdom of ends; they help to embed the common good of a society of free and equal citizens by tending to level current power asymmetries. In fact, Green's faith in the effectively unlimited potential for economic growth leads him to believe that well-run cooperatives will allow the poor to escape poverty even if no restraints are placed on the accumulation of wealth by the rich.[75] Green's support for the burgeoning British cooperative and trade union movements recalled a wide-spread disaffection that even potential beneficiaries of poor relief felt from the system. As one historian has observed recently: 'after 1870 the poor relief system was confining, demeaning and, above all, prohibitive. It deterred those most in need [from applying for relief].'[76]

Green's support for collective self-assertion by the poor was not a merely intellectual fancy.[77] On 26 March 1863, he attended a meeting in London

---

[73] Nettleship, 'Memoir', xlii.

[74] PPO 227.

[75] Crossley sees Green's acceptance of unlimited accumulation as creating a signif-icant ambiguity in Green's theory of property (Crossley, 'T.H. Green on Prop-erty', 211–17). On my reading, it does not so long as one accepts Green's claims regarding economic growth and so on. It is unclear why Crossley attaches such importance to Green's use of the phrase 'mere property', given that Green uses the phrase only once and even then in a rather unremarkable way: '...such property as will at least enable [the person who works for a living] to develop a sense of responsibility, as distinct from mere property in the immediate necessaries of life' (PPO 221) (see Crossley, 'T.H. Green on Property', *passim*).

[76] E.T. Hurren, *Protesting against Pauperism: Politics and poor relief in late Victorian England, 1870–1900* (London: Royal Historical Society, 2007), p. 27, as quoted in Fraser, *Evolution*, p. 173.

[77] On the British cooperative and trade union movements, see George Jacob Holyoake, *The Cooperative Movement To-day* (London: Methuen, 1891), and Alastair J. Reid, *United We Stand: A History of Britain's Trade Unions* (Harmonds-worth: Penguin, 2005).

which the trade unions had called in support of the North in the American civil war, an event chaired by John Bright.[78] Green attended at least one meeting in March 1872 in support of Oxford building workers who were striking for the introduction of a 58-hour week, and on 22 January 1877 he spoke at a public meeting of Oxford shop workers as part of the Early Closing Movement.[79] A year later, he was on the platform again, this time at a public meeting held at Oxford Town Hall by the Amalgamated Society of Railway Servants in support of the movement to prevent railway accidents, and to obtain compensation for railway servants for injuries received during their employment.[80]

Moreover, on 23 October 1872, Green seconded the proposed creation of an Oxfordshire branch of the Agricultural Labourers Union, describing himself as a 'sympathising outsider'.[81] *Jackson's Oxford Journal* reported that 'Speaking of the law of supply and demand, he said that the farmer could not and would not give more than he could afford, and the way to find out what he could afford was by common action, and [with] the Union at their back'.[82] Both the labourer and the farmer were at the mercy of the landowner, and the farmer could have his land taken off him with little warning, meaning that he would rarely invest in improvements.[83] Green's second speech to the Agricultural Labourers Union, given on 9 December 1874, made clear what he saw as the most significant functions of an agricultural trade union. [84] The first was to help labourers find work at other farms with

---

[78]   Charlotte Byron Green's notes for Richard Lewis Nettleship, I. Biography, §d, T.H. Green Papers, Balliol College, Oxford. The meeting is reported in *The Times*, 27 March 1863, p. 12e–f although Green is not mentioned. I am very grateful to Peter Nicholson for this and the other material from C.B. Green's notes, as well as for the associated newspaper references given in this paragraph of the text.

[79]   'In 1872 in a short absence of mine he mentions a builder's strike in which he took great interest—attending a public meeting', C.B. Green's notes for Nettleship. Charlotte might be referring to the meeting chaired by J.E.T. Rogers, who also helped the National Agricultural Labourers' Union (see next note). This meeting was reported in *Oxford Chronicle*, 9 March 1872, as well as 16 and 23 March, although without mentioning Green. It was also reported briefly in *Jackson's Oxford Journal*. Green's speech to 'The Early Closing Movement', Oxford Town Hall, 22 January 1877, was reported in *Oxford Chronicle*, 27 January 1877, p. 6 (GW 5:406).

[80]   See the reports in *Oxford Chronicle*, 12 January 1878, pp. 8b–d, and *Jackson's Oxford Chronicle*, 12 January 1878.

[81]   'National Agricultural Labourers' Union: Inauguration of a District for Oxfordshire', *Birmingham Daily Post*, 25 October 1872. T.H. Green, speech to the Agricultural Labourers Union (hereafter, ALU), 23 October 1872 (GW 5:238).

[82]   'National Agricultural Labourers' Union: Inauguration of a District for Oxfordshire', *Jackson's Oxford Journal*, 26 October 1872.

[83]   Speech to the ALU, 23 October 1872 (GW 5:239–40).

[84]   Speech to the ALU, 9 December 1874 (GW 5:246–50).

better working conditions or in times of unemployment. The second was to set up a strike fund, providing labourers with an income during a dispute. The third function was to provide information relating to events and conditions for workers in other parts of the countryside. Fourthly, the Union should help to support labourers where their usual employer did not offer them enough work or pay to support themselves and their family. Fifthly, the Union should 'obtain land for the labourers to occupy, not a little bit by the favour of the Clergyman or the squire, but a good substantial piece of land, from one to five acres, on which the prudent labourer might work in slack times, and in which he might invest his savings'.[85]

Certainly, even the best British trade unions were not perfect. As was noted in §8.II, Green came to worry about the virtue of workers and peasants following the victory of the Conservative Party in the 1874 General Election. As a result, after that time he began to work for temperance reform and interventionist legislation to protect workers.[86] It is partly due to this concern to raise the character of the poor through activism and even legislation that many of his friends refer to him as a socialist (MSF §1.II). Nevertheless, Green is committed to the view that in supporting and in some instances orchestrating trade disputes, the well-directed union serves rather than hinders the common good. In this way, the union serves the long-term interests of the farmers, landowners and employers as much as those of the workers and peasants. On the more general level, Green understands the common good of one's community to be an intrinsically-contested idea, that is given content and sustained by disputes regarding the fundamental nature of one's community (§3.VII).[87] Conflict between associations is a necessary part of even the most egalitarian and enabling community.

Finally, it is worth noting also that Green's active endorsement of conflict between associations seems to indicate a divergence between his position and that of Mazzini. It is important to bear in mind at this point that Mazzini was a polemicist and an ideologue, who wrote what Green's pupil Arnold Toynbee described in 1881 as 'a great book, *The Duties of Man*, which is the most simple and passionate statement published in this century of man's duties to God and his fellows'.[88] Green on the other hand was a philosopher with a very active social conscience. No matter how profound Green's agree-

---

[85]   T.H. Green, speech to the Agricultural Labourers Union, 9 December 1874 (GW 5:248).

[86]   LLFC *passim*; Tyler, *Idealist Political Philosophy*, pp. 80–91.

[87]   See Colin Tyler, 'Contesting the Common Good: T.H. Green and contemporary republicanism', in Maria Dimova-Cookson and W.J. Mander, eds., *T.H. Green: Ethics, metaphysics and political philosophy* (Oxford: Clarendon Press, 2006), pp. 262–91.

[88]   Arnold Toynbee, 'Industry and Democracy', in his *Industrial Revolution* (Newton Abbot: David and Charles Reprints, 1969 [1884]), p. 200.

ment with Mazzini's world-view, the demands of Green's profession required him to attempt to cast his position in a systematic and clear form. Doing so led Green to diverge from Mazzini at certain key points, not least over the latter's claim that the development of Humanity meant something more than the development of individual persons (§5.II). Moreover, where Mazzini viewed the state with deep suspicion favouring its replacement with a series of citizen-led associations, Green was far more willing to concede the need for state intervention in even the most utopian of realisable worlds.

This section has drawn out a number of revealing similarities and differences between Green's political economy and that of Mazzini. Both emphasise the centrality of individual effort to maintain the good society, and both recognise that, under harsh conditions, both the community and the state have a positive duty to protect individuals from needless suffering. Mazzini and Green argue that if social and economic structures are to be fair and free, then the individual should be accorded far greater opportunities to change her type of work. Both men are firm advocates of active and responsible trade unions, yet both realise that the workers are currently too servile for it to be safe to dismantle welfare schemes such as the Poor Law. Finally, where Mazzini wishes to replace the state completely with a network of associations, Green retains a strong sense of the continuing practical necessity for an enabling state to act as a sympathetic and 'powerful friend' to the vulnerable and the weak.[89]

Before concluding this analysis, it is worth locating Green's radical political economy in the landscape of some of the leading socialist theoreticians of his time. First, it is necessary to say something regarding the relationship of Green's political economy to the socialist tradition more generally.

V

Green's Political Economy and the British Socialist Tradition

a. Green and the Meaning of 'Socialism'

James Kloppenberg has observed that Green 'self-consciously and painstakingly drew connections between knowledge, responsibility, and reform, and [his] political writings represent an important, intermediate step in the convergence of socialism and liberalism towards social democracy and progressivism'.[90] This is not simply an historical matter. Green's liberal socialism remains valuable today as a source of principles with which to implement a

---

[89] LLFC 203.
[90] Kloppenberg, *Uncertain Victory*, p. 147; also George H. Sabine, *A History of Political Theory*, rev. T.L. Thorson (Hinsdale: Dryden, 1973), pp. 667–68; Mehta, 'T.H. Green and the Revision of English Liberal Theory', 48–49; Reeve, *Property*, pp. 93–94, 184–85.

radical critique of capitalism. It was noted in §10.IV that Green is explicit that, in the area of health care at least, the functional area of legitimate state action should widen over time as the conception of the true end of the state comes into contact with a better understanding of the sources of human progress and misery. In the present context, the crucial point is that, as was noted earlier, these changes are the results of differences over questions of empirical fact. They are not indicative of any inconsistency within Green's philosophical system.[91] Peter Nicholson hits the nail on the head: 'In the far from perfect societies that we know, there is a constant process, requiring much attention and effort, of deciding what are the minimum resources needed for the moral life, and checking whether or not everyone has access to them. This is the sphere of politics.'[92]

Nicholson's observation goes some way to explaining why scholars disagree so markedly regarding Green's relationship to socialism. For example, Vincent Knapp has claimed that 'Green's doctrine of the exorability of [private] property did run counter to accepted laissez-faire dogmas, but it was in no way socialistic'.[93] The analysis presented above shows that Knapp is oversimplifying hideously. Certainly, Green's theory is not materialistic and he balks at extensive state action because of his fear that it will impede self-reliance unduly. Nevertheless, he is clear also that the state should intervene in all of the areas where doing so was likely to lead to a net reduction in the hindrances to the eudaimonic development of individuals.[94] Certainly, if 'socialism' is taken to entail the rejection of all forms of private property (as it is by Knapp, Coker and Milne), then obviously Green is not and never could be a socialist. Yet, theirs is a very strange conception of 'socialism', and one that would exclude Ritchie, Toynbee, Hobhouse and Green, and every other member of the social democratic tradition and many more extreme ideologies.

Indeed, Green himself did not adopt the restricted conception of 'socialism' that one finds in Knapp and his ilk. In his fragment on political economy (which was published after Knapp, Coker and Milne had made their claims), Green defines '*practical* socialism' as '[the] doctrine (a) that wages should be regulated otherwise than by competition ([that is]: competition of

---

[91] Sabine, *History of Political Theory*, p. 664; Ann R. Cacoullos, *Thomas Hill Green: Philosopher of rights* (New York: Twayne, 1974), pp. 19–20.

[92] Nicholson, *Political Philosophy*, p. 196.

[93] Knapp, 'T.H. Green on the Exorability of Property', 63. For the same claim, see Francis Coker, *Recent Political Thought* (New York: Appleton-Century-Crofts, 1934), p. 426 and Milne, *Social Philosophy of English Idealism*, p. 156. Sankhdher argues that Green is not a Fabian socialist, although ultimately the exact structure of this claim remains unclear (Sankhdher, 'T.H. Green: The forerunner of the welfare state', *Indian Journal of Political Science*, 30 (1969), 148–64).

[94] LLFC 200–04.

labourers for employment and of masters to get work done most cheaply and quickly), and (b) that accumulation of capital should be limited'.[95] There is no mention here of a definitional aversion to all forms of private property. In fact, many socialists attack private property rights and market competition only when they become oppressive. Frequently, this entails the rejection of the right to private property in the means of production and the retention of private property in other possessions.[96] Green's theory is open-ended on this matter for the reasons which have been explained already. In principle, the perfect society requires a system of private property rights in all things. Yet, the imperfect societies in which humans are condemned to live, frequently cannot afford an unfettered system of private property rights and holdings. The moral costs are just too great. Consequently, the state usually has a duty to intervene in certain areas.

For these reasons, Green has been linked to socialism and to the social democratic tradition in particular (MSF chapter 1). Not least among those who made this link were his close friends such as John Addington Symonds.[97] As this book and MSF have sought to establish, Green's thought does much to reconcile liberalism with socialism: for example, he holds freedom from external interference to be valuable because it enables the individual to make informed choices to act well, and it is only by making such choices that she can be truly free (MSF chapter 6). This combines with his emphasis on the importance of individuals bearing the burdens of citizenship and, indeed, on their deciding to order all of their public actions towards the promotion of the common good of their fellows (see chapter 3 above). Given this link, it is instructive to compare his form of 'liberal' or 'democratic' socialism with those of other socialists of Green's time. By its nature, what follows must have the character of a series of suggestions for further research rather than a set of exhaustive comparisons.

b. Robert Owen (1771–1858)

Writing in 1813, Robert Owen complained that the economic systems of Europe were based on exclusion and oppression, with the privileged ruling over 'millions [who] have been immolated, or consigned to poverty and

---

[95] 'Pol. Econ.' 6, emphasis in original, additions by Harris and Morrow.

[96] For example, Karl Marx and Friedrich Engels, 'The Manifesto of the Communist Party', in their *Selected Works*, 2 vols. (Moscow: Foreign Languages Publishing House, 1962), vol. 1, pp. 52–54.

[97] See, for example, the letter from John Addington Symonds to Albert O. Rutson, 3 October 1885, in John Addington Symonds, *Letters*, eds., Herbert M. Schueller and Robert L. Peters (Detroit: Wayne State University Press, 1968–69), vol. 3, pp. 84–85; letter from Symonds to Charlotte Byron Green, 3 November 1886, in Symonds, *Letters*, vol. 3, p. 176; Symonds to Edward Carpenter, 21 January 1893, in Symonds, *Letters*, vol. 3, p. 808.

bereft of friends'.[98] Like Green and his ilk, Owen railed against the appalling effects of manifest inequality on both the individual and society.

> 'For it is now obvious that such a system must be destructive of the happiness of the excluded, by their seeing others enjoy what they are not permitted to possess; and also that it tends, by creating opposition from the justly injured feelings of the excluded, in proportion to the extent of the exclusion, to diminish the happiness even of the privileged: the former therefore can have no rational motive for its continuance.'[99]

Yet, Owen called for no redistribution of wealth and he advocated the retention of the established national church, although with the abolition of tests of belief for members. He sought the imposition of duties and taxes to inhibit the consumption of alcohol; no national lottery; direct taxation was to be levied according to 'ability-to-pay'; and the poor were to be educated to save and invest (a policy which Owen, if not Green, would promote by decreasing the level of poor-relief). The primary duty of the State was to set up and administer a national system of education, and to fund public works so as to ameliorate unemployment.

Even though Green shares many of these concerns and echoed several of Owen's policy prescriptions, no doubt he baulks at some key aspects of Owen's socialism. First, Owen is a utilitarian, with Jeremy Bentham even investing in his utopian community of New Lanark.[100] Second, Owen is much more sanguine than Green regarding the need to engage in social engineering. Certainly, Green would have sympathy with Owen's goal of creating the social conditions in which individuals will tend to pursue the common good. Like Owen, Green insists that lessons without pupils' criticism are, in Owen's words, 'most unjustifiable and irrational, and must prove useless or injurious to the mental faculties' (see also §7.V).[101] Yet, Owen understands human nature to be perfectly malleable, even going so far as to claim 'that greatest of all errors, [is] the notion that individuals form their own characters'.[102] Compared to Green, Owen sees education has having a far more directive function, with children being consciously moulded to recognise that their own welfare can only be realised through that of the

---

98 Robert Owen, *A New View of Society, and other writings* (London: J.M. Dent, 1927), p. 18.

99 Owen, *New View*, p. 19.

100 Owen, *New View*, pp. 17, 63.

101 Owen, *New View*, p. 24.

102 Owen, *New View*, p. 65. In short, Green would see Owen's fundamental principle as an anathema: 'Any general character, from the best to the worst, from the most ignorant to the most enlightened, may be given to any community, even to the world at large, by the application of proper means; which means are to a great extent at the command and under the control of those who have influence in the affairs of man.' Owen, *New View*, p. 16.

community. (Here, Owen's view coincides with that of Mazzini (§7.V).) Owen is confident that gradual, deliberate socialist reforms would benefit everyone, removing all poverty and crime, and hence all need for punishment.[103] Green, on the other hand, argues that individuals can realise their respective particular concrete instantiations of distinctively human capacities only as a result of their own inner tendencies, in a manner much more closely associated with J.S. Mill, William Wordsworth and others with romantic sympathies (MSF §2.III). Hence, Owen's rationalism causes him to see education and social pressure as the keys to social transformation, through the planned, centralised engineering of 'any language, sentiments, belief, or any bodily habits and manner, not contrary to human nature'.[104] Green emphasises the free development of the individual learner, and in that sense as well as many others, his socialism is far more liberal than that of Owen, without being any less concerned to address the causes and consequences of pauperism and poverty.

c. Karl Marx (1818–83) and Friedrich Engels (1820–95)

Green's relationship to Karl Marx and Friedrich Engels is revealing, especially when one focuses on the early writings of Marx and Engels as will be done here.[105] Reflecting their common debts to Aristotle and Hegel, all three value the determinate manifestation of higher human capacities, rather than social utility maximisation, and all three argue that this manifestation can be achieved best through the individual's efforts to create her own world through her own practice (§9.II). All three reject the utopianism one finds in socialists such as Robert Owen.[106] Green, Marx and Engels hold that the individual becomes a concrete person as a result of her interactions with other persons through shared social forms, as famously Marx puts it, '*man* is no abstract being squatting outside of the world. Man is *the world of man*, state, society'.[107] It is easy to overstate the differences between the idealist

---

[103] Owen, *New View*, p. 63.

[104] Owen, *New View*, p. 16.

[105] For a classic related analysis, see Herbert Marcuse, *Reason and Revolution: Hegel and the rise of social theory*, second edition (London: Routledge and Kegan Paul 1963 [1954]), pp. 389–98.

[106] 'Such fantastic pictures of future society, painted at a time when the proletariat is still in a very undeveloped state and has but a fantastic conception of its own position correspond with the first instinctive yearnings of that class for a general reconstruction of society.' Marx *et al.*, 'Manifesto of the Communist Party', p. 62.

[107] Karl Marx, 'A Contribution to the *Critique of Hegel's Philosophy of Right*. Introduction' [1843–44], in his *Early Writings*, trans. Rodney Livingston and Gregory Benton (Harmondsworth: Penguin, 1975), p. 244. On Marx and Engels' rejection of 'Critical-utopian Socialism and Communism', see their 'Manifesto of the Communist Party', pp. 61–64.

Green and the materialists Marx and Engels, then. For example in relation to identity-formation, Marx and Engels allow greater autonomous force to non-economic relationships than many of their interpreters appreciate, while in no way does Green ignore the importance of economic relationships, as some critics have alleged. Nevertheless, Green does not believe that ultimately economics will override all other social influences, in the way that the others do.[108] For Marx and Engels, alienation and exploitation result from economic relationships, whereas for Green oppression results from a combination of the power of the rich plus the culture of servility in which the workers and peasants are raised. Green argues that society's norms and practices, including those in the economic field, are imperfect historically-conditioned manifestations of human nature, with the imperfections stemming from ignorance, selfishness and oppression. For Marx, the 'human essence is no abstraction inherent in each single individual. In its reality, it is the ensemble of the social relations'.[109] Yet, this does mean that Marx and Engels believe the individual is a blank slate on which anything can be written without distortion. In fact, for Marx and Engels at birth the individual has an abstract 'species-being' which she struggles to realise in her concrete personality.[110] She seeks to transform the world through her actions, to express herself freely, to make the external world the medium of her self-expression. In this way, Marx and Engels adopt a position that is at least closely akin to that of Green.

All three seek to make class distinctions meaningless. For Green, this can be achieved primarily through the removal of differences of status between different social roles, together with much greater social mobility and inclusion than is found in current capitalist societies. For Marx and Engels, on the other hand, the removal of class distinctions requires in the long-run the ending of all fixed social roles, or perhaps merely the ending of the processes whereby individuals are defined by their social and economic relationships.[111] For Green, relatively stable social roles will always be necessary if the individual is to possess a similarly stable self-image. In practical terms, Marx and Engels believe that class distinctions will disappear only once

---

108 Karl Marx, 'A Contribution to the Critique of Political Economy' [1859], in their *Selected Works*, vol. 1, pp. 368–69.

109 Karl Marx, 'Theses on Feuerbach' [1845], in their *Selected Works*, vol. 1, p. 15.

110 Karl Marx, 'The Economic and Philosophic Manuscripts' [1844], in his *Early Writings*, pp. 327–29, 350, and David McLellan, *Marx before Marxism* (London: MacMillan, 1970), p. 222.

111 Karl Marx, *The German Ideology: Introduction to a critique of political economy*, ed. C.J. Arthur, second edition (London: Lawrence and Wishart, 1974), pp. 54–55, and James Furner, 'Marx's Sketch of Communist Society in *The German Ideology* and Problems of Occupational Confinement and Occupational Identity', *Philosophy and Social Criticism*, 37 (2011), 189–215.

capitalism has been replaced with a communist society following a 'dictatorship of the proletariat' during which the revolutionary class uses the state to destroy the vestiges of capitalism in institutions, material relationships and individual consciousness.[112]

Nevertheless, Green sees free exchange as a core moment of a eudaimonically-enriching kingdom of ends. He holds the removal of capitalist oppression to be best achieved through greater social, political and economic inclusion, especially as a result of the extension of the franchise, decentralisation, trade union action, cooperatives and educational reform. Politically, Green places great significance on civic and political decentralisation, as do Marx and Engels although they hold that this move should be made only once class-based socio-economic relationships have been transcended and replaced by a communist society. For Marx and Engels, enfranchisement of the workers is worse than useless without prior economic change.[113] They hold that a truly free society is possible only once the state has withered away in the sense that its public functionaries come to administer production non-coercively and for the good of all, rather than using force to serve the good of the ruling class.[114] In contrast, Green holds that oppressive power relationships are always present in any possible world of practice, and that consequently there will always be a need for a coercive body which can counter the oppression that is endemic within society.[115] Ideally for Green this would be a democratic state based on the universal suffrage of all conscientious adult citizens.

In terms of tactics, Green, Marx and Engels agree that oppressive conditions can be removed through social and political reform under certain circumstances. Nevertheless, Marx and Engels believe that under most conditions violent revolution is required if one is to lay the foundation for a lasting free society. While Green holds violent revolution to be the citizen's duty under certain circumstances, he believes that generally in advanced European societies an enriching kingdom of ends can be best promoted through a process of gradual reform. Indeed as has been noted above, Green wishes to see poor relief replaced with concessions won from employers, because he believes that only through mass conscientious trade union action will the poor take control of their own fate and become self-directed and self-realising human beings. Ultimately, however, even taking account of the significance of their many differences, Green, Marx and Engels all look forward to a time in which 'In place of the old bourgeois society, with its

---

[112] Marx *et al.*, 'Manifesto of the Communist Party', pp. 52–54.
[113] Karl Marx, 'On the Jewish Question' [1844], in his *Early Writings*, pp. 211–41.
[114] Frederick Engels, 'Socialism: Utopian and scientific', in Marx *et al.*, *Selected Works*, vol. 2, pp. 150–52, 155.
[115] PPO, for example 87–88.

classes and class antagonisms, we shall have an association, in which the free development of each is the condition of the free development of all'.[116]

d. William Morris (1834–96)

In a similar vein, it is interesting to contrast Green's liberal socialism with the mixture of Ruskinianism and Marxism that was expounded shortly after Green's death, in the writings of William Morris.[117] Fostering the conditions for the free development of the individual became a central concern for Morris in the 1880s and 1890s. Echoing Marx, Morris sees that capitalist civilisation as a necessary but temporary stage of human development, a stage that must be overthrown as a precondition of true human development. In his 1887 address, 'The Society of the Future', Morris argues that 'Free men, I am sure, must lead simple lives and have simple pleasures', something that requires us to break free of the 'complexity of dependence' in which we have 'wrapped our lives'; Morris holds that this would destroy the web of self-imposed oppression that makes us 'feeble and helpless' beings.[118] Reflecting his debts to Ruskin, Morris argues that only through this radical change could the individual enjoy 'Free and full life and the consciousness of life'.[119] In Morris's socialist society, there would be no social hierarchy, and no automatic right to hold private property; both the division of labour and all unpleasant jobs are either to be abolished or to be performed by machines, overcrowded cities will dissipate, and education is to be geared towards real human needs, rather than to the needs of business as at present. Only in this way can one remove the appalling social conditions that tend to dull the workers' senses and finally to send them insane.

Both Green and Morris build their respective socialisms on elements of the romantic tradition (MSF §2.III). Hence, Morris calls for the abolition of luxury, arguing that excessive wealth tend to destroy the environment and prevent most people from being able to enjoy Nature. Yet, Morris differs from Green in his more straightforwardly naturalistic conception of human nature. Hence, he condemns capitalism's denial of the enjoyment of 'a free and unfettered animal life' for everyone.[120] Most fundamentally, Morris argues that 'If we feel the least degradation in being amorous, or merry, or hungry, or sleepy, we are so far bad animals, and therefore miserable

---

[116] Marx *et al.*, 'Manifesto of the Communist Party', p. 127.

[117] One of the best studies of Morris' thought is Ruth Kinna, *William Morris: The art of socialism* (Cardiff: University of Wales Press, 2000).

[118] William Morris, *Political Writings*, edited by A.L. Morton (London: Lawrence and Wishart, 1973), p. 194.

[119] He continued: 'Or, if you will, the pleasurable exercise of our energies, and the enjoyment of the rest which that exercise or expenditure of energy makes necessary to us.' Morris, *Political Writings*, p. 191.

[120] Morris, *Political Writings*, p. 192; see *ibid.*, p. 193.

men'.[121] This is something that Green could never accept, given his rejection of the claim that purely animal needs and drives possess any intrinsic value. This contrast with Morris highlights, once again, the immense significance to Green's liberal socialism of his theory of distinctively human action and the role played by sublimation in his thought (MSF, chapter 5).

e. Arnold Toynbee (1852–83), D.G. Ritchie (1853–1903), L.T. Hobhouse (1863–1929) and R.H. Tawney (1880–1962)

In the harsher economic conditions that followed Green's death, many of his pupils diverged significantly from his practical views. Arnold Toynbee, one of Green's most influential pupils, is far more sceptical than Green regarding the working of Adam Smith's 'invisible hand', whose efficiency forms a fundamental presupposition of non-Marxist classical economics.[122] David Ritchie, arguably Green's most faithful disciple in social and political theory, justifies greater state intervention by placing far greater emphasis upon the social nature of the productive process under capitalism and the implications for social justice.[123] Like those of Ritchie and Toynbee, many of L.T. Hobhouse's fundamental normative commitments coincide with those of Green, as does much of his analysis of capitalism. Nevertheless like Ritchie and Toynbee, Hobhouse is more willing than Green to countenance state action to correct the harms caused by capitalism, especially where cooperatives and trade union action are likely to be ineffective. Hobhouse highlights two main ways in which the state might intervene: 'One would consist in providing access to the means of production, the other in guaranteeing to the individual a certain share in the common stock.'[124] Echoing Green, Hobhouse points to the recent use of legislation 'reversing the process which divorced the English peasantry from the soil', a process of divorce that has historical roots rather than being an inevitable result of the workings of capitalism.[125] Specifically, Hobhouse advocates the nationalisation of land and the granting of land tenancies to peasants, he endorses the recent (in 1911) extension of state pensions and advocates the creation of a system of state employment and sickness benefits.[126] Nevertheless, it is easy to overstate Green's aversion to state action.[127] Moreover, it is vital to notice that the divergences from Green's practical positions that one finds in Hobhouse and

---

[121] Morris, *Political Writings*, p. 192.

[122] Toynbee, *Industrial Revolution*, pp. 11–26; see also *ibid.*, pp. 1–26, 155–221. See also Fraser, *Evolution*, pp. 161–62.

[123] See Colin Tyler, 'D.G. Ritchie on socialism, History and Locke', *Journal of Political Ideologies,* 17:3 (October 2012). Hobhouse did the same later.

[124] Hobhouse, *Liberalism*, p. 174.

[125] Hobhouse, *Liberalism*, p. 175.

[126] Hobhouse, *Liberalism*, pp. 177–79.

[127] Compare LLFC 201–04.

Ritchie reflect changed circumstances rather than the rejection of the fundamental principles of his political economy. Hence, Green could write the
following in his *Principles of Political Obligation*:

> 'The reason for not more generally applying the power of the state to prevent
> voluntary noxious employments, is not that there is no wrong in the death of
> the individual through the incidents an employment which he has voluntarily
> undertaken, *but that the wrong is more effectually prevented by training and trust-
> ing individuals to protect themselves than by the state protecting them.'*[128]

The clear implication is that were it to be shown that deaths at work are
'more effectually prevented' by state intervention in particular types of
employment (Green's example here is the mining industry), then the state
should take over the role. Hobhouse observes that, 'instead of redeeming the
destitute,... [one] should seek to render generally available the means of
avoiding destitution, though in doing so we should uniformly call on the
individual for a corresponding effort on his part'.[129] Certainly, circumstances
did change in the years following Green's death. Some changes were positive: for example, in 1911 Hobhouse welcomed the success of the temperance
movements in which Green had participated so fervently in the 1870s and
1880s, as ensuring that the workers' wages were less likely to be wasted on
alcohol.[130] Others were far more negative, including the increasing concentration of capital in fewer firms: 'The bulk of industry is, and probably will
be, more and more in the hands of large undertakings with which the individual workman could not compete whatever instruments were placed in his
hands.'[131] This recalls the earlier discussion of Galbraith's concerns regarding
the technostructure (§10.III).

In addition to inspiring later idealists such as Ritchie and Toynbee and
New Liberals such as Hobhouse, Green's argument that reforming capitalism is a precondition of achieving the free development of the human spirit
anticipates the social democracy of R.H. Tawney, who wrote in 1949,

> 'Even if the way of co-operation did not yield all the economic advantages
> expected from it, we should continue to choose it. Both the type of individual
> character and the style of social existence fostered by it are those which we
> prefer... Civilisation is a matter, not of quantity of possessions, but of quality
> of life. It is to be judged, not by the output of goods and services per head, but
> by the use made of them. A society which values public welfare above private
> display; which, though relatively poor, makes the first charge on its small

---

128 PPO 159, emphasis added.
129 Hobhouse, *Liberalism*, p. 178.
130 Hobhouse, *Liberalism*, pp. 180–81.
131 Hobhouse, *Liberalism*, pp. 177–78.

resources the establishment for all of the conditions of a vigorous and self-respecting existence [is our goal.]'[132]

Socialists such as Green, Hobhouse, Ritchie, Tawney and Toynbee emphasise the conception of politics as an irreducibly collective endeavour, geared up to the service of the good of the whole society, with each citizen bearing their part in that collective endeavour as a condition of receiving the benefits that come from citizenship. Crucially in the present context, the differences between their respective strategies and policy recommendations in relation to social economics reflect their different circumstances rather than differences regarding principles. That Green's own approach justifies these divergences has been noted above.

Whether one compares Green's political economy to that of Engels, Hobhouse, Marx, Morris, Owen, Ritchie, Tawney or Toynbee, it is clear that all of them adopt forms of socialism, and, with the exceptions of Engels, Marx, Morris and Owen, all of them adopt more specifically forms of liberal socialism. Nevertheless, throughout Green remains sceptical regarding the efficacy of extensive state intervention for the same reason that he is cautious regarding systems of poor relief. Both approaches tend to maintain the poor in an infantilised state, rather than encouraging them to assert themselves conscientiously and collectively so that no longer do they 'have that given to them as charity that they ought to demand as a right'.[133] The true state is a community of self-asserting citizens, each treating one another as equals. Such citizens do not defer to one another, nor do they seek to suppress debate where their personal judgement leads them to reach different conclusions regarding the best way to run and reform society. Green's ideal is a society in which the public conception of the common good arises from conflicts between virtuous, conscientious citizens (§3.VII).[134] He recognises something that many later socialists have underappreciated: charity organisations and state-run welfare schemes may be necessary at times, but they tend to be imperfect substitutes for the creation by the poor themselves of schemes of collective economic life, and the winning of concessions from employers and the state by the self-determined actions of collectively-organised self-assertive workers. Green's position on welfare reform is a core element in his wider radicalism. That Green's liberal socialism is diametrically opposed Fabian elitism is evident in its contrast to Beatrice Webb's patronising faith that 'the poor needed supervision and direction,

---

[132] R.H. Tawney, 'Social Democracy in Britain' [1949], reprinted in his *The Radical Tradition*, ed. R. Hinden (Harmondsworth: Pelican, 1964), pp. 174–75. On Tawney's relationship to British idealism, see Carter, *T.H. Green*. Carter understates Tawney's debts to Edward Caird.

[133] Green's speech to the Agricultural Labourers Union, 23 October 1874 (GW 5:240).

[134] PPO 251.

not just means, in order not to be poor'.[135] Moreover, it comes through clearly in the assessment of his friend and fellow idealist Edward Caird.

> '[Green had] a natural disregard for the outward differences of rank and position and even of culture, by which... [the] essentials ["of humanity", "the spiritual experiences in which all men are alike"] are invested and concealed, [and as a result] his sympathies were always with the many rather than the few. He was strongly inclined to the idea that there is an "instinct of reason" in the movement of popular sentiment, which is often wiser than the opinion of the so-called educated classes. The belief in the essential equality of men might, indeed, be said to be one of the things most deeply rooted in his character, though it showed itself not in any readiness to echo the common-places of Radicalism, but rather in an habitual direction of thought and inter-est to practical schemes for "levelling up" the inequalities of human lot, and giving to the many the opportunities of the few.'[136]

VI

Conclusion

This chapter has covered significant ground. §II examined Green's influence on the New Liberalism and his analysis of the rights to bequeath and to inherit. §III established that his writings on land reform anticipate J.K. Galbraith's analysis of the technostructure in unexpected and enlightening ways. §IV explored the practical implications of Green's economic theory via a comparison with Mazzini's republicanism. §V located Green's political economy in relation to socialists such as Friedrich Engels, L.T. Hobhouse, Robert Owen, Karl Marx, William Morris, David Ritchie, R.H. Tawney and Arnold Toynbee.

It was established that even though Green sees free exchange as cong-ruent with free conscientious action, Richter is unfair when he claims that 'Although his [Green's] mode of thought led him to apply the formulae to the more complex issues of state intervention in economic life [as he had done in the areas of "public health, education, and temperance"], he had no particular interest in, or knowledge of, the problems peculiar to capital-ism'.[137] It has been shown that Green is emphatic that any judgement about the best course of action (whether by the state or individuals) in the econ-omic system should be always subject to revision in the light of empirical investigations of the inner-workings of capitalism in practice. There is no telling how much more sceptical and socialistic Green would have become if he had lived to see capitalism develop in the ways that it did in the decades following his sudden death on 26 March 1882.

---

135 Martin, *Hard and Unreal Advice,* p. 77, as quoted in Fraser, *Evolution,* p. 11.

136 Edward Caird, 'Preface', in Andrew Seth and R.B. Haldane, eds., *Essays in Philos-ophical Criticism* (London: Longmans, Green, 1883), pp. 4–5.

137 Richter, *Politics of Conscience,* p. 363.

11

Conclusion

I

Introduction

Thomas Hill Green was one of the most important philosophers among academics in Britain and its empire for over thirty years following the post-humous publication of his magnum opus *Prolegomena to Ethics* in 1883. Together with his *Principles of Political Obligation* and various other shorter pieces, such as his 'Lecture on Liberal Legislation and Freedom of Contract', the *Prolegomena* was a recurring point of discussion in many of the leading journals and monographs. His academic reputation rose and eventually began to fall with the fortunes of his followers, something that in turn reflected the change of philosophical fashion that came with the rise of G.E. Moore and Bertrand Russell in the early years of the twentieth century. Yet, there is a paradox here. Nowadays, Green is read most widely by ethicists and political philosophers, yet his own writings never had the direct impact on practical politics that one might have expected. Certainly, he exerted an important influence on the New Liberalism, through David Ritchie and especially L.T. Hobhouse. Yet, for the most part Green's practical political influence seems to have been mediated through the teachings of his close friend the philosopher Edward Caird and those whom Caird taught such as H.H. Asquith and William Beveridge. Green's lack of direct political inf-luence is probably due in part to the obscurity of the majority of even his writings on political theory, and the fact that his political speeches remained largely unpublished until the appearance of the fifth volume of his works in 1997, under the editorship of Peter Nicholson.

Nevertheless, hopefully the preceding chapters have shown that theorists and more practically-minded political participants have much to gain from reading Green. Hopefully also, this book has gone some way to suggesting that Green's reputation as an otherworldly 'ivory tower' philosopher was greatly undeserved. In supporting this suggestion, this book has covered a great deal of ground. Consequently, in order to bring this long study to a close, it will helpful to summarise the stages of the argument presented in both *The Metaphysics of Self-realisation and Freedom* (2010) and the present book. These summaries will be followed by some closing thoughts on the continuing value of Green's political theory.

II

The Metaphysics of Self-realisation and Freedom

The Liberal Socialism of Thomas Hill Green began by considering L.T. Hobhouse's conception of liberal socialism. 'If… there be such a thing as a Liberal Socialism', wrote Hobhouse in his *Liberalism* (1911), 'it must clearly fulfil two conditions.'

> 'In the first place, it must be democratic. It must come from below, not from above. Or rather, it must emerge from the efforts of society as a whole to secure a fuller measure of justice, and a better organization of mutual aid. It must engage the efforts and respond to the genuine desires not of a handful of superior beings, but of great masses of men. And, secondly, and for that very reason, it must make its account with the human individual. It must give the average man free play in the personal life for which he really cares. It must be founded on liberty, and must make not for the suppression but for the development of personality.'[1]

This understanding of liberal socialism has informed my analysis of Green's system. At its centre, it places notions of personality and active citizenship. Nevertheless, it recognises the contextualised nature of the individual, and the importance of social action. It insists on the moral imperatives of justice and personal development. Throughout, it is imbued with a profoundly democratic spirit, and a firm rejection of paternalism even in the latter's most benevolent forms. As has been indicated by the length and complexity of this book and the one that preceded it, when conceived in this way liberal socialism is a complex arrangement of claims regarding ontology, ethics, social theory, political theory and political economy. Human capacities and civic life are just as important to this ideology as are political and economic institutions.

With this thought in mind, *The Metaphysics of Self-realisation and Freedom* began (chapter one) by setting the terms of the study, before examining what might be called Green's current philosophical and ideological reputations. It was argued that Green tends to be judged wrongly against liberal concerns by liberals, and to be judged just as wrongly against narrowly Marxist-inflected conceptions of 'socialism' by many on the left. Hobhouse's conception of liberal socialism was argued to articulate a rather more typically Brit-

---

1   Leonard T. Hobhouse, *Liberalism* (London: Williams and Norgate, n.d. [1911]), pp. 172–73. For the contrast between Green's liberal socialism and John Stuart Mill's elitist model, see Colin Tyler, 'Elitism and Anti-elitism in Nineteenth Century British Political Thought', *History of European Ideas*, 32 (August 2006), 345–55, especially 345–51.

ish form of socialism, one that fitted Green's thought much more accurately. Chapter two raised doubts regarding recent allegations that Green's assumptions and approach make his thought inapplicable to modern circumstances. It argued that scholars have overstated Hegel's influence on Green, while also neglecting classical, romantic and republican authors such as Aristotle, Thomas Carlyle, Johann Fichte, Immanuel Kant, R.H. Lotze, Giuseppe Mazzini, William Wordsworth and several others. The chapter closed with a defence of the systematic method employed in my subsequent reconstruction of Green's system.

Chapter three examined Green's conceptualisation of the role of consciousness in knowing. Particular emphasis was placed on explaining his often-neglected use of critical and speculative metaphysics, and especially his use of the orienting device of what was called here 'crystallisation', a term taken from Stendhal which recalls Aristotle's notion of the 'prime mover'. Green adapted certain elements of a Kantian metaphysics of knowledge, and emphasised the unifying power of consciousness. Immediately, the question arises, what materials are being unified? Green claims they are sensations. Yet, on his own terms, he cannot legitimately make such a 'guess about what is beyond experience'. Another alleged problem considered in this chapter was Green's attachment to the idea that 'categories of experience' must exist within the mind before they are determined by sensations (although they cannot be known prior to such determinations). Against this objection it was noted that if one rejects the idea of innate but presently inchoate categories, it becomes impossible to conceptualise the observable human capacity to unify otherwise disparate perceptions into a coherent world of experience.

Chapter four argued that one could dispense with the specifically religious aspects of the 'eternal consciousness'. Instead, the latter is better understood as a point of orientation for the individual's efforts to construct coherent interlinked worlds of experience and practice. The eternal consciousness represented, then, Green's version of Aristotle's prime mover just as much as it was his radical reconceptualization of a broadly Christian idea of God.

Chapter five turned to an even more problematic area of Green's liberal socialism: his theory of the will. For the most part, both *Metaphysics* and *Civil Society* work on the assumption that Green adopts a self-interventionist line of the will. On this reading, an agent is responsible for her actions because she can make a voluntary choice between several options for action. In these moods, Green holds the individual's options for action to be conditioned by the current state of her personality, which, in turn, is conditioned by her previous courses of action. Nevertheless, the individual retains the ability to decide whether to act or not, and if she does decide to act she also retains the ability to choose any of the options available to her. Yet, it was argued in this

chapter that, at times, Green presupposes an alternative, spiritual determinist line. On this generally-neglected view, an individual's actions are
simply 'automatic' expressions of interactions of her current personality
with her current circumstances. There is no possibility of voluntary choice,
and the agent could not have acted otherwise than in fact she did. It was
established that this alternative theory undermines radically any claim that
an individual is morally responsible for her actions, something that has profound implications for Green's theory of conscientious agency. It was argued
that adopting the self-intervention approach commits Green to explaining
how an essentially non-determined choice is logically possible, which he
cannot do and indeed which at other times he argues against vigorously. He
does not appear to recognise the tensions between these two lines, and, for
the most part, merely adopts the self-intervention line without comment in
his logically-subsequent writings on ethics and politics. This discussion led
to an analysis of Green's concept of 'distinctively human action', its difference from the 'animal' aspects of human life, and his much neglected integration of these apparently opposed elements via his theory of the unconscious, emanation and sublimation.

This analysis was developed in chapter six where Green's conceptions of
'formal', 'juristic' and 'true' or 'positive' freedom were analysed. The chapter
focused on true freedom, which the individual enjoys to the extent that (i)
she subjectively endorses (ii) meanings and values which are objectively and
intrinsically valuable, and (iii) which she recognises as being objectively and
intrinsically valuable. Individual character (or synonymously personality)
and uncoerced endorsement were shown to be central to this understanding
of freedom. Finally, the chapter considered the implications for Green's
thought both of self-interventionist and of spiritual determinist theories of
the will, with particular notice being taken of the problems caused for his
theory of moral responsibility. Chapter seven explored the differences
between Green's ethics of virtue and self-realisation on the one hand, and
utilitarianism on the other, something that chapter eight extended by
considering the deeply misplaced allegation that Green neglects aesthetic
values, such as would later be championed by the likes of G.E. Moore and
John Skorupski.

III

Civil Society, Capitalism and the State

Chapter one of the present book began by highlighting Green's insistence on
the mutual interrelation of theory and practice. It noted also the ignorance of
critics such as Richard Crossman who have alleged that Green was too aloof
to bother himself with worldly problems. The chapter then summarised the
argument of the *Metaphysics of Self-realisation and Freedom*, before looking for-

ward to the remaining chapters of the present book. Having recapped the analysis of Green's true good that was presented in *Metaphysics,* chapter two of *Civil Society* reconstructed his relational social theory, as well as highlighting his scepticism regarding organic metaphors of the type that have been applied posthumously to his thought. It was established that, for Green, society exists only in the most fundamental meanings and values that are instantiated in and through the practice-structured activities of its individual concrete members. Yet, these participants are able to create coherence among what would be their otherwise disparate activities and identities, only to the extent that they are able to relate their practices to conceptions of a true good and a wider social whole of which those practices form parts. In this way, the agent conceives of herself as constituting a self-realising participant in society. She understands herself to be part of a group which is neither an individualistic aggregate of its members, nor something which exists 'beyond' its members. By conceiving of herself as participating in practices in this way, the individual tends to arrive at a clearer, more coherent and therefore more stable and satisfying understanding not only of the personalities of other people, but of her own personality as well.[2]

The attitudes that the individual believes other people hold about her form the basis of her attitudes regarding her own nature as a person. In some instances, she will endorse these perceived attitudes and beliefs, while in others she will react against them. To the extent that she judges the resulting intersubjective norms should be obeyed independently of her private wishes, they embody the categorical nature of moral imperatives. In that sense, such attitudes and social norms constitute 'objective' features of her world of practice.[3] To the extent that these attitudes and norms affirm her sense of personal identity and worth, the individual's self-conception and sense of self-respect will be reinforced and validated; to the extent that they do the contrary, her self-conception and self-respect will be undermined. Having established all of this, the chapter analyses Green's contention that while each of us believes innately that ultimately true meanings and values will form a harmonious system, he recognises that such a harmony must always escape our understanding. Consequently, human beings have to accept the irreducible moral pluralism of every world about which they can think and in which they can decide how to act.

Chapter three builds on the analysis of the preceding chapter, by examining Green's justification of his claim that the individual's true good lies in

---

2   This fact is emphasised by many contemporary philosophers, including Alasdair MacIntyre, *Dependent Rational Animals: Why human beings need the virtues* (London: Duckworth, 1999), chapters 8 and 9.

3   'Kant' 126. Raymond Geuss, *History and Illusion in Politics* (Cambridge: Cambridge University Press, 2001), pp. 133–35 is illuminating in this connection.

serving a common good, an examination that considered his adaptation of arguments from Aristotle, Rousseau and Kant. It was shown that Green's common good is inherently non-competitive, and that pursuing it does not require the individual to be completely selfless. Finally, the chapter examined Green's theory of social justice before highlighting the social fragmentation inherent in his perspectivalist conception of individual action and citizenship. Chapter four developed this thought, by analysing Green's theory of social criticism. It started from Green's contention that personal alienation is the motor of social reform, a claim which grounds his theory of conscientious citizenship. Next, the chapter turned to the difficult question of whether social service requires the individual to be motivated to help her fellow citizens, or whether it can happen as an unintended consequence of an agent's actions.

Taken together, chapters three and four established that the fact that sympathetic social structures are preconditions for individual self-realisation has significant consequences for Green's theory of conscientious agency. Firstly, it means that an individual tends to make that environment more hostile to every member of her society to the extent that she undermines the social structures within which they operate.[4] Through acting in an anti-social manner then, the agent tends to undermine everyone's practical capacity for agency including her own, by making their shared world harder to comprehend and live in.[5] The ways in which the agent conceives of herself as a spiritual being with objectively valuable capacities is conditioned by her analysis of the meanings, values and actions that she has internalised. The same holds true for the conception of an ideal personality that the individual projects during the crystallising phases of her efforts at self-understanding and self-improvement. Consequently, acting in ways that undermine social structures always tends to destabilise the individual's personality thereby tending to hinder her capacity for action.

It was shown, however, that this does not mean that the individual should suppress their concerns about conventional morality. Even though the individual can go only 'a certain distance, in the detail of conduct which [any ideal] requires, beyond the conditions of the given age',[6] her conventional stations and duties are authoritative only to the extent that she endorses them on the basis of her own judgement of their inherent spiritual value. Where she does not do so, conventional duties 'present themselves to the man as imposed from without'.[7] Hence the second and often more sig-

---

4   PE 234.
5   See Bernard Bosanquet, *The Principle of Individuality and Value* (London: MacMillan, 1912), pp. 180–81.
6   PE 268.
7   DSF 24.

nificant consequence of unconventional behaviour is its tendency to benefit both the individual and the wider society. Short-term destabilisation is a precondition of many long-term improvements in the individual's ability to act in a distinctively human manner.[8] Green accepts the attendant vagueness of philosophical prescriptions as an inevitable consequence of abstract theorising. Definite and well-founded moral judgements can be made only in actual situations and never in the abstract. Essentially the same response is given in chapter eight to the charge that Green's theory of civil disobedience and revolution offers little guidance to the political reformer.

Via a comparison of Green's thought with that of Mazzini, chapter five established that Green does not believe that moral progress can happen anywhere other than in the lives of individual people, nor does he believe such progress to be inevitable. Nevertheless, he does hold that, as a matter of fact, modern civilised societies are more advanced morally than those of antiquity. This is not to say that the strength of the desire to act well is stronger in modern societies: 'according to his lights the Greek might be as conscientious as any of us.'[9] Instead, Green argues that progress has taken the form of the widening of the sphere of one's moral community and greater subtlety in identifying the demands of virtue, morality and justice. The chapter concluded by considering progress from the perspective of Green's spiritual determinism, before arguing that, contrary to the claims of some scholars, Green does provide workable criteria by which to identify human development.

Chapter six examined Green's theory of moral rights and duties, as well as introducing his theory of legal rights and obligations. It was shown that, for Green, some moral claims should be accorded the status of moral rights and duties, and possibly even legal rights and obligations. He recognises that many are not accorded such status because currently they do not receive the social recognition required to transform them into claims that are generally valued by their fellow citizens. Similarly, Green insists that some current rights (moral claims currently recognised as rights) should not be so recognised. In short, our current systems of moral rights and duties are not perfect and should be corrected where possible. The same holds for some of our current legal rights and obligations. As part of this argument, various misunderstandings of Green's theory of recognition were addressed. It was also established that Green's fundamental value (self-realisation) precludes non-human animals, the severely mentally disabled and the severely and irredeemably insane from the sphere of rights. These exclusions are the most objectionable implications of his ethical position. Finally, the chapter analysed Green theory of punishment, showing it to be a unified theory of

---

8   PE 184, 199.
9   PE 206; see also PE 271.

retribution, deterrence and annulment. Importantly, the chapter established that Green rejects completely the claim that the state should punish 'wickedness'; apart from any other considerations, the difficulties of judging a person's character and motive make it impossible to do so in practice.[10]

Chapter seven examined Green's conceptions of sovereignty, the sovereign and the state. It argued that, as with the associated systems of legal rights and obligations, ultimately the authority of the sovereign and the state for which it claims to speak can be grounded only in the beliefs and attitudes of the community's determinate members and their respective concrete capacities for agency. The practical applicability of his theory was considered, paying particular attention to his educational theory. A central point in this chapter was the fact that the difficulties inherent in trying to discover what another agent's conscience tells her on any particular issue, and whether or not she is following it, provide Green with strong grounds to accord greater authority to the individual's judgement over the judgement of the community or the state. More fundamentally, Green insists that it is impossible for an external agency — the state, say, or another individual or group — to force the individual to become truly free or to live a life she judges to be truly good. Mere performance of an outward act which coincides with her duty is not in itself a moral or truly free action. For the action to be so, it must be performed from a good motive, and importantly no one can successfully command that motivation of another being. True freedom comes only from following one's own conscience. Consequently, Green's theory cannot justify attempts to force the individual to become more compliant through the application of external constraints.

From this basis, chapter eight explored the complexities of Green's theory of political obligation by considering his theories of democratic participation and conscientious citizenship. His defence of decentralised mass political participation was explored and interpreted within the context of his fervent but not unlimited support for the extension of the franchise both in the run-up to the 1867 Reform Act and beyond. His theory of the state was shown to be compatible with certain familiar types of contemporary cultural pluralism. Next, the chapter analysed Green's theory of dissent, starting from an extension of the earlier discussion (in chapter four) of the significance of his claim that any social practice, institution or even government enjoying popular support should be presumed to be operating in accordance with the fundamental principles of the wider society. Counterfactually: generally, 'it must be on the presence of a strong and intelligent popular sentiment in favour of resistance that the chance of avoiding anarchy, of replacing the existing government by another effectual for its purpose, must chiefly

---

[10] PPO 196.

depend'.[11] Yet, Green insists that one should never forget that 'the worst governments' are most apt to destroy public virtue and hence 'public spirit'. Under those conditions, for Green, 'there may be a duty of resistance in the public interest, though there is no hope of the resistance finding efficient popular support'.[12] It is interesting that here Green cites the 'Mazzinian outbreaks in Italy' to exemplify precisely this circumstance of recurring resistance by what is, initially at least, 'a hopeless minority'. Green argues that its 'repeated renewal and repeated failure may afford the only prospect of ultimately arousing the public spirit which is necessary for the maintenance of a government in the public interest'.[13] In other words, there are times when the individual has a duty to follow her conscience even when that means violating the beliefs endorsed by the remainder of her society.

The final two substantive chapters demonstrated that Green's political economics continues to offer a valuable way to conceptualise the economic realm in normative terms. Chapter nine examined the principles of Green's political economics, distinguishing his appeal to the primary value of self-realisation from a utilitarian appeal to considerations of maximising aggregate pleasure. It established also that Green values systems of private property rights because they tend to enable individuals to express their respective conscientious wills through their property holdings. Importantly, it was established that Green values any particular system of private property rights only to the extent that, in practice, it tends to enable everyone to exercise such a will. That the poor tended to be denied such opportunities in his own society, led him to advocate intervention to moderate the workings of capitalism. Chapter ten explored the ways in which Green used this approach to launch a radical critique of existing economic relationships. The chapter began by introducing Green's concerns regarding European capitalism, as well as introducing his method of responding to such problems via a brief consideration of his critical discussion of the rights of bequest and inheritance. Next, parallels were drawn between Green's calls for land reform and Galbraith's analysis of the technostructure. Green's defence of the collective self-assertion of the poor and marginalised through active and conscientious trade union and cooperative movements threw new light on his grudging acceptance of the current need for a system of poor relief. Finally, Green's practical socialism was compared to the socialisms of a range of his contemporaries and near-contemporaries: specifically, Friedrich Engels, L.T. Hobhouse, Robert Owen, Karl Marx, William Morris, David Ritchie, R.H. Tawney and Arnold Toynbee.

---

[11] PPO 108.
[12] PPO 108.
[13] PPO 108.

IV
Final Thoughts

Hopefully, it is clear from these two books that there is much to be gained from a return to the serious study of Green's writings. Stuart Hampshire was clearly incorrect when he stated that Green 'left no legacy of convincing argument or insight'.[14] The claim that Green addressed issues which 'no longer command our attention' is similarly misguided, as is the claim that his thought is irrelevant in the modern age because 'much of liberalism has been shaped by aspirations and beliefs which have ceased to command our allegiance'.[15] In reality, Green's thought articulates a plausible vision of the interrelationship between human life as it is and as it could be. Obviously, this is a very important conclusion to reach. As Ernest Barker has observed: 'If [Green's] principles are true, then each age can progressively interpret their meaning to suit its own needs.'[16]

Green's relational society theory and his theory of rights are particularly important here, highlighting as they do the fact that morally enriching societies are more than mere collections of individuals trying to get through their daily lives without hurting each other. People need communities – groups with which to identify themselves in a deep sense – groups to which they recognise themselves as belonging. This remains a potent idea for many people in modern societies. Where this feeling of belonging is absent, Green's analysis highlights the importance of the common good. Where people question the basis of their duties, Green's analysis highlights the importance of reciprocity in normative judgements. In these ways and many others, his thought helps to clarify what sort of beings we truly are. Green's ideal of a eudaimonically-enriching kingdom of ends is an ideal which is needed in the present age. Certainly, the social and political environment has changed markedly since Green's time.[17] Yet, far from invalidating Green's philosophical system, these changes serve to heighten its critical edge.

For these reasons, this study closes with the words of Alan Milne: 'I do not suggest that [Green] has said the last word on any topic. But I am suggesting that, if we are interested in developing a social philosophy for our-

---

14   Stuart Hampshire, 'Oxford Virtue', *New Statesman,* 7 August 1964, p. 184.

15   Andrew Vincent and Raymond Plant, *Philosophy, Politics and Citizenship: The life and thought of the British idealists* (Oxford: Basil Blackwell, 1984), p. 183, quoting Stefan Collini, *Liberalism and Sociology: L.T. Hobhouse and political argument in England 1880–1914* (Cambridge: Cambridge University Press, 1979), p. 253. Richard Bellamy, 'Introduction', in Richard Bellamy, ed., *Victorian Liberalism: Nineteenth century political thought and practice* (London: Routledge, 1990), p. 12.

16   Ernest Barker, *Political Thought in England from Herbert Spencer to the Present Day* (London: William and Norgate, 1915), p. 58.

17   Bellamy, 'Introduction', 12.

selves, it is by carrying further the work he has already begun that we shall make most progress.'[18] In this spirit, we should try to build Green's ideal of a society of self-confident and self-assertive citizens, each of whom treats all others as equals and each of whom expects her fellows to do the same. Greater trust and resources should be given to groups of ordinary citizens to identify and address the problems affecting them, a process that will often require much greater social and political decentralisation. Rather than relying almost exclusively on systems of welfare that help to maintain existing patterns of inequality and dominance, the marginalised should be given the resources and security required to assert themselves collectively and directly through forms of cooperative organisation and trade union action. Yet throughout, it is vital to remember that there are many circumstances in which state intervention is required to address entrenched and large-scale abuses, as well as to counter the massive organisations that commit them. These organisational developments, when combined with a greater practical recognition of the limits of a commercial mentality and the need for a clearer emphasis on deeper human needs, will help to build contemporary versions of the truly free society of the type that was analysed and actively promoted in the mid-Victorian period by the liberal socialist Thomas Hill Green.

---

[18] A.J.M. Milne, *The Social Philosophy of English Idealism* (London: Allen Unwin, 1962), p. 164.

Bibliography

Abbreviations: The key to the abbreviated references is given at the beginning of this book. They relate mainly to Green's own writings.

A
T.H. Green's Writings

'Special Report on Birmingham Free School, and General Report on the Counties of Stafford and Warwick', in Schools Inquiry Commission, vol. viii: *General Reports by Assistant Commissioners: Midland Counties and Northumberland*. London: HMSO, 1868, pp. 91–253.

'County of Buckingham' and 'County of Northampton', in Schools Inquiry Commission, vol. xii: *Special Reports of Assistant Commissioners, and Digests of Information Received: South Midlands Division*. London: HMSO, 1868, pp. 175–93, 313–79.

'County of Stafford' and 'County of Warwick', in Schools Inquiry Commission, vol. xv: *Special Reports of Assistant Commissioners, and Digests of Information Received: West Midlands Division*. London: HMSO, 1869, pp. 365–485, 669–752.

'County of Leicester', in Schools Inquiry Commission, vol. xvi: *Special Reports of Assistant Commissioners, and Digests of Information Received: North Midlands Division*. London: HMSO, 1868, pp. 17–90.

'Mr. Herbert Spencer & Mr. G.H. Lewes: Their Application of the Doctrine of Evolution to Thought (Part I)', *Contemporary Review*, 31 (1877–78), 25–53.

'Mr. Herbert Spencer & Mr. G.H. Lewes: Their Application of the Doctrine of Evolution to Thought (Part II)', *Contemporary Review*, 32 (1877–78), 745–69.

'Can there be a natural science of man? [Part I]', *Mind*, 7:25 os (January 1882), 1–29.

'Can there be a natural science of man? [Part II]', *Mind*, 7:26 os (April 1882), 161–85.

'Can there be a natural science of man? [Part III]', *Mind*, 7:27 os (July 1882), 321–48.

Prolegomena to Ethics, fifth edition, ed. A.C. Bradley. Oxford: Clarendon, 1906 [1883].

Works, 5 vols., ed. R.L. Nettleship and P.P. Nicholson. Bristol: Thoemmes, 1997.

'Part 1: Thomas Hill Green', in Colin Tyler, ed., *Unpublished Manuscripts in British Idealism: Political philosophy, theology and social thought*, 2 vols..

Bristol: Thoemmes Continuum, 2005; Exeter and Charlottesville, VA: Imprint Academic, 2008, vol. 1, pp. 1–188.

Lectures on the Principles of Political Obligation, and other writings, ed. P. Harris and J. Morrow. Cambridge: Cambridge University Press, 1986.

B

Archival Sources Used

Benjamin Jowett Papers, Balliol College, Oxford.

T.H. Green Papers, Balliol College, Oxford.

Bryce Papers, Bodleian Library, Oxford.

C

Secondary Literature Used

Abbott, Evelyn and Lewis Campbell, eds., *The Life and Letters of Benjamin Jowett, M.A.*, 2 vols. London: John Murray, 1897.

Anderson, Olive, 'The Feminism of T.H. Green: A late-Victorian success story?', *History of Political Thought*, 12:4 (1991): 671–93.

Aristotle, *Metaphysics, X–XIV, Oeconomica, Magna Moralia*, trans. Hugh Tredennick and G. Cyril Armstrong. Cambridge, MA, and London: Loeb, 1935.

Aristotle, *Politics*, trans. T.A. Sinclair, rev. T.J. Saunders. Harmondworth: Penguin, 1957.

Aristotle, *Ethics*, trans. J.A.K. Thomson, rev. Hugh Tredennick. Harmondsworth: Penguin, 1976.

Austin, John, *The Province of Jurisprudence Determined and the Uses of the Study of Jurisprudence*. London: Weidenfeld and Nicolson, 1954.

Ayer, Alfred J., *Metaphysics and Common Sense*. London: MacMillan, 1969.

Barbour, G.F., 'Green and Sidgwick on the Community of the Good', *Philosophical Review*, 17 (1908): 149–66.

Barbour, G.F., *A Philosophical Study of Christian Ethics*. Edinburgh and London: William Blackwood, 1911.

Barker, Ernest, *Political Thought in England from Herbert Spencer to the Present Day*. London: Williams and Norgate, 1915.

Barry, Brian, *Justice as Impartiality*. Oxford: Clarendon Press, 1995.

Barry, Brian, *Political Argument*. London: Routledge and Kegan Paul, 1965.

Beiser, Frederick C., 'Kant's Intellectual Development: 1746–1781', in Paul Guyer, ed., *The Cambridge Companion to Kant*. Cambridge: Cambridge University Press, 1992, pp. 26–61.

Bellamy, Richard, 'A Green Revolution? Idealism, liberalism and the welfare state', *Bulletin of the Hegel Society of Great Britain*, 10 (1984): 34–39.

Bellamy, Richard, 'Introduction', in Richard Bellamy, ed., *Victorian Liberalism: Nineteenth century political thought and practice.* London: Routledge, 1990, pp. 1–14.

Bellamy, Richard, 'T.H. Green and the Morality of Victorian Liberalism', in Richard Bellamy, ed., *Victorian Liberalism: Nineteenth century political thought and practice,* London: Routledge, 1990, pp. 131–51.

Bellamy, Richard, 'T.H. Green, J.S. Mill, and Isaiah Berlin on the Nature of Liberty and Liberalism', in H. Gross and R. Harrison, eds., *Jurisprudence: Cambridge Essays,* Oxford: Clarendon Press, 1992, pp. 257–85.

Bellamy, Richard, *Liberalism and Modern Society: An historical argument.* Oxford: Polity, 1992.

Benn, S.I. and R.S. Peters, *Social Principles and the Democratic State.* London: George Allen and Unwin, 1959.

Bentham, Jeremy, *Introduction to the Principles of Morals and Legislation*, ed. J.H. Burns and H.L.A. Hart. Oxford: Clarendon Press, 1996.

Berlin, Isaiah, *Four Essays on Liberty.* Oxford: Oxford University Press, 1969.

Beveridge, William, *Power and Influence.* London: Hodder and Stoughton, 1953.

Bevir, Mark, 'Welfarism, Socialism and Religion: On T.H. Green and others', *Review of Politics,* 55 (1993): 639–62.

Bevir, Mark, *The Making of British Socialism* (Princeton and Oxford: Princeton University Press, 2011).

Biersteker, Thomas J. and Cynthia Weber, eds., *State Sovereignty as Social Construct.* Cambridge: Cambridge University Press, 1996.

Bosanquet, Bernard, *Science and Philosophy, and other essays,* ed. J.H. Muirhead and R.C. Bosanquet. London: George Allen and Unwin, 1927.

Bosanquet, Bernard, *Some Suggestions in Ethics.* London: MacMillan, 1918.

Bosanquet, Bernard, *The Philosophical Theory of the State*, fourth edition. London: MacMillan, 1923.

Bosanquet, Bernard, *The Principle of Individuality and Value.* London: MacMillan, 1912.

Boucher, David, *The Limits of Ethics in International Relations: Natural law, natural rights, and human rights in transition.* Oxford: Oxford University Press, 2009.

Boucher, David and Andrew Vincent, *British Idealism and Political Theory.* Edinburgh: Edinburgh University Press, 2000.

Bowle, John, *Politics and Opinion in the Nineteenth Century: An historical introduction.* Oxford: Arden, 1954.

Bradley, Andrew C., *Oxford Lectures on Poetry.* London: MacMillan, 1965.

Bradley, Francis H., *Ethical Studies*, second edition. Oxford: Clarendon Press, 1927 [1876].

Bradley, Ian, *The Optimists: Themes and personalities in Victorian Liberalism.* London: Faber and Faber, 1980.

Bright, John, *Speeches on Questions of Public Policy*, 2 vols., ed. J.E.T. Rogers. London: MacMillan, 1869.

Brink, David O., *Perfectionism and the Common Good: Themes in the philosophy of T.H. Green*. Oxford: Clarendon Press, 2003.

Brinton, Crane, *English Political Thought in the Nineteenth Century*. New York: Harper and Brothers, 1962.

Brodrick, George C., 'The Law and Custom of Primogeniture', in J.W. Probyn, ed., *Systems of Land Tenure in Various Countries*. London: Cassell, Petter, Galpin, 1876, pp. 93–168.

Brodrick, George C., *English Land and English Landlords: An Enquiry into the Origin and Characters of the English Land System, with Proposals for its Reform*. London: Cassell, Petter, Galpin, 1881.

Brooks, Thom, 'Hegel and the Unified Theory of Punishment', in Thom Brooks, ed., *Hegel's Philosophy of Right*. Oxford: Wiley-Blackwell, 2012, pp. 103–23.

Brooks, Thom, 'T.H. Green's Theory of Punishment', *History of Political Thought*, 24:4 (Winter 2003): 685–701.

Brooks, Thom, 'Was Green a Utilitarian in Practice?', *Collingwood and British Idealism Studies*, 14:1 (2008): 5–15.

Brooks, Thom, Review of Colin Tyler, *Thomas Hill Green (1836–1882)...*, *Bulletin of the Hegel Society of Great Britain*, 51–52 (2005): 141–44.

Bryce, James, *Studies in Contemporary Biography*. New York: MacMillan, 1903.

Bull, Hedley and Adam Watson, *The Expansion of International Society*. Oxford: Oxford University Press, 1984.

Cacoullos, Ann R., *Thomas Hill Green: Philosopher of rights*. New York: Twayne, 1974.

Caird, Edward, 'Preface', in Andrew Seth and R.B. Haldane, eds., *Essays in Philosophical Criticism*. London: Longmans, Green, 1883, pp. 1–7.

Caird, Edward, *Collected Works*, 12 vols., ed. Colin Tyler. Bristol: Thoemmes, 1998.

Caird, Edward, *The Evolution of Religion*, 2 vols. Glasgow: James MacLehose, 1893.

Caird, Edward, *The Present State of the Controversy between Individualism and Socialism*. Glasgow: James MacLehose, 1897.

Calderwood, Henry, 'Another View of Green's Last Work', *Mind*, 10 os (1885): 73–81.

Carlyle, Thomas, *Past and Present*. London: Chapman and Hall, 1843.

Carpenter, S.C., *Church and People 1789–1889*. London: SPCK, 1959 [1933].

Carritt, E.F., *Ethical and Political Thinking*. Oxford: Clarendon Press, 1947.

Carritt, E.F., *Morals and Politics: Theories of their relation from Hobbes and Spinoza to Marx and Bosanquet*. Oxford: Clarendon Press, 1935.

Carritt, E.F., *The Theory of Morals: An introduction to ethical philosophy*. London: Oxford University Press, 1928.

Carter, Matt, *T.H. Green and the Development of Ethical Socialism*. Exeter and Charlottesville, VA: Imprint Academic, 2003.

Chin, Y.L., *The Political Theory of Thomas Hill Green*. New York: W. Dray, 1920.

Clarke, Peter, *Liberals and Social Democrats*. Cambridge: Cambridge University Press, 1978.

Coates, Ken, *Work-ins, Sit-ins and Industrial Democracy*. Nottingham: Spokesman, 1981.

Coker, Francis, *Recent Political Thought*. New York: Appleton-Century-Crofts, 1934.

Collingwood, Robin G., *Essays on Political Philosophy*, ed. D. Boucher. Oxford: Clarendon Press, 1989.

Collini, Stefan, *Liberalism and Sociology: L.T. Hobhouse and political argument in England 1880–1914*. Cambridge: Cambridge University Press, 1979.

Connelly, James, *Metaphysics, Method and Politics: The political philosophy of R.G. Collingwood*. Exeter and Charlottesville, VA: Imprint Academic, 2003.

Conybeare, F.C., 'On Professor Green's Political Philosophy', *National Review*, 13 (1889): 771–87.

Copleston, Frederick, *A History of Philosophy: Volume VIII, Bentham to Russell*. London: Burns and Oates, 1966.

Cowling, Maurice, 'The Use of Political Philosophy in Mill, Green and Bentham', *Historical Studies*, 5 (1965): 141–52.

Crossley, David, 'T.H. Green on Property and Moral Responsibility', *Logical Analysis and History of Philosophy*, 6 (2003): 193–217.

Crossman, Richard H.S., *Government and the Governed: A history of political ideas and political practice*. London: Christophers, 1958 [1939].

Cummiskey, David, *Kantian Consequentialism* (New York and Oxford: Oxford University Press, 1996).

Darby, Derrick, *Rights, Race, and Recognition*. Cambridge: Cambridge University Press, 2009.

de Burgh, W.G., *From Morality to Religion*. London: MacDonald and Evans, 1938.

de Sanctis, Alberto, *The 'Puritan' Democracy of Thomas Hill Green, with some unpublished writings*. Exeter and Charlottesville, VA: Imprint Academic, 2005.

de Spinoza, Benedict, *Political Writings*, ed. A.G. Wernham. Oxford: Clarendon Press, 1958.

Diggs, Bernard J., ed., *State, Justice and Common Good: An introduction to social and political philosophy*. Glenview, IL: Foresman, 1974.

Dimova-Cookson, Maria, *T.H. Green's Moral and Political Philosophy: A phenomenological perspective*. Houndsmill: Palgrave, 2001.

Dworkin, Ronald, *Sovereign Virtue: The theory and practice of equality*. Cambridge, MA: Harvard University Press, 2000.

Eliot, George, *Works*, 20 vols. New York: Jensen Society, 1910.

Engels, Friedrich, *The Condition of the Working Class in England*, trans. F. Kelley Wischnewetzky. London: Swan Sonnenschein, 1892 [1845].

Faber, Geoffrey, *Jowett: A portrait with background*. London: Faber and Faber, 1957.

Fairbrother, W.H., *The Philosophy of Thomas Hill Green*. London: Methuen, 1896.

Fichte, Johann G., *The Foundations of Natural Right,* ed. F. Neuhouser, trans. M. Baur. Cambridge: Cambridge University Press, 2000.

Fichte, Johann G., *The System of Ethics*, trans. Daniel Breazeale and Guenter Zöller. Cambridge: Cambridge University Press, 2005.

Fraser, Derek, *The Evolution of the Welfare State*, fourth edition. Houndsmill: Palgrave MacMillan, 2009.

Freeden, Michael, *The New Liberalism: An ideology of social reform.* Reprinted with corrections. Oxford: Clarendon Press, 1986 [1978].

Furner, James, 'Marx's Sketch of Communist Society in *The German Ideology* and Problems of Occupational Confinement and Occupational Identity', *Philosophy and Social Criticism*, 37 (2011): 189–215.

Galbraith, John K., *Economics and the Public Purpose*. Boston, MA: Houghton Mifflin, 1973.

Galbraith, John K., *The Good Society: The humane agenda*. London: Sinclair-Stevenson, 1996.

Gaus, Gerald, 'T.H. Green, Bernard Bosanquet and the Philosophy of Coherence', in C.L. Ten, ed., *Routledge History of Philosophy, Volume VII, The Nineteenth Century*. London: Routledge, 1994, pp. 408–36.

Gaus, Gerald, *The Modern Liberal Theory of Man*. Beckenham: Croom Helm, 1983.

Gaus, Gerald, 'The Rights Recognition Thesis: Defending and extending Green', in Maria Dimova-Cookson and W.J. Mander, eds., *T.H. Green: Ethics, metaphysics and political philosophy*. Oxford: Clarendon Press, 2006, pp. 209–35.

Germino, Dante, *Machiavelli to Marx: Modern western political thought*. Chicago, IL, and London: University of Chicago Press, 1972.

Geuss, Raymond, *History and Illusion in Politics*. Cambridge: Cambridge University Press, 2001.

Gilbert, Paul, *The Philosophy of Nationalism*. Boulder, CO: Westview, 1998.

Gordon, Peter and John White, *Philosophers as Educational Reformers: The influence of idealism on British educational thought and practice*. London: Routledge and Kegan Paul, 1979.

Gosse, Edmund, *The Life of Algernon Charles Swinburne*. London: MacMillan, 1917.

Grant, R.A.D., 'Defenders of the State', in G.H.R. Parkinson, ed., *An Encyclopaedia of Philosophy*. London: Routledge, 1988, pp. 690–712.

Gray, John, 'On Negative and Positive Liberty', in Z.A. Pelczynski and John Gray, eds., *Conceptions of Liberty in Political Philosophy.* London: Athlone Press, 1984, pp. 321–48.

Greaves, Harold R.G., *The Foundations of Political Theory*, second edition. London: G. Bell, 1966 [1958].

Greengarten, I.M., *Thomas Hill Green and the Development of Liberal-Democratic Thought.* Toronto: University of Toronto Press, 1981.

Greenleaf, W.H., *The British Political Tradition, Volume Two: The ideological heritage.* London: Methuen, 1983.

Hallowell, John H., *Main Currents in Modern Political Thought.* New York: Holt, Rinehart and Winston, 1950.

Hammond, T.C., *Perfect Freedom: An introduction to Christian ethics.* London: Inter-Varsity Fellowship, n.d.

Hampshire, Stuart, 'Oxford Virtue', *New Statesman,* 7 August 1964, p. 184.

Hansen, Phillip, 'T.H. Green and the Moralization of the Market', *Canadian Journal of Political and Social Theory*, 1:1 (1977): 91–117.

Hansen, Phillip, 'T.H. Green and the Limits of Liberalism: A response to Professor Lawless', *Canadian Journal of Political and Social Theory*, 2:2 (1978): 156–58.

Harris, J.W., *Property and Justice.* Oxford: Oxford University Press, 2002.

Harris, José, *William Beveridge: A biography.* Oxford: Clarendon Press, 1977.

Harris, Paul, 'Green's Theory of Political Obligation and Obedience', in Andrew Vincent, ed., *The Philosophy of T.H. Green.* Aldershot: Gower, 1986, pp. 127–42.

Harris, Paul, 'Moral Progress and Politics: The theory of T.H. Green', *Polity*, 21 (1988–89): 538–62.

Harris, Paul and John Morrow, 'Did Nettleship Corrupt Green's Lectures? A comment on Smith', *History of Political Thought*, 4:3 (1985): 643–46.

Harrison, Brian, *Drink and the Victorians: The temperance question in England 1815–1872.* London: Faber and Faber, 1971.

Harrison, Wilfred, *Conflict and Compromise: The history of British political thought.* New York: Free Press, 1965.

Hart, H.L.A., *Punishment and Responsibility: Essays in the philosophy of law.* Oxford: Clarendon Press, 1968.

Harvie, Christopher, *The Lights of Liberalism: University liberals and the challenge of liberal democracy 1860–86.* London: Allen Lane, 1976.

Hegel, Georg W.F., *Philosophical Propaedeutic*, trans. A.V. Miller, ed. Michael George and Andrew Vincent. Oxford: Basil Blackwell, 1986.

Hegel, Georg W.F., *The Philosophy of History,* trans. J. Sibree. New York: Dover, 1959 [1858].

Hegel, Georg W.F., *The Philosophy of Mind: Part Three of the Encyclopaedia of the Philosophical Sciences (1830)*, trans. William Wallace and A.V. Miller. Oxford: Clarendon Press, 1970.

Hegel, Georg W.F., *Elements of the Philosophy of Right*, ed. Allen W. Wood, trans. H.B. Nisbet. Cambridge: Cambridge University Press, 1991.

Himmelfarb, Gertrude, *Poverty and Compassion: The moral imagination of the late Victorians*. New York: Alfred A. Knopf, 1991.

Hinton, Timothy, 'The Perfectionist Liberalism of T.H. Green', *Social Theory and Practice*, 27:3 (July 2001): 473–99.

Hobbes, Thomas, *Leviathan*, ed. Richard Tuck. Cambridge: Cambridge University Press, 1991.

Hobhouse, Leonard T., *Liberalism*. London: Williams and Norgate, n.d. [1911].

Hobhouse, Leonard T., *The Metaphysical Theory of the State: A criticism*. London: George Allen and Unwin, 1918.

Holloway, Harry, 'Mill and Green on the Modern Welfare State', *Western Political Quarterly*, 13 (1960): 389–405.

Holyoake, George Jacob, *The Cooperative Movement To-day*. London: Methuen, 1891.

Hoover, Kenneth R., 'Liberalism and the Idealist Philosophy of Thomas Hill Green', *Western Political Quarterly*, 26 (1973): 550–65.

Horton, John, *Political Obligation*. London: MacMillan, 1992.

Hoskins, C. Wren, 'The Land Laws of England', in J.W. Probyn, ed., *Systems of Land Tenure in Various Countries*. London: Cassell, Petter, Galpin, 1876, pp. 169–212.

Hume, David, *A Treatise of Human Nature*, ed. L.A. Selby-Bigge, second edition, rev. P.H. Nidditch. Oxford: Clarendon, 1978 [1888].

Hurka, Thomas, *Perfectionism*. Oxford: Oxford University Press, 1993.

Hurren, E.T., *Protesting against Pauperism: Politics and poor relief in late Victorian England, 1870–1900*. London: Royal Historical Society, 2007.

Inglis, Fred, *Radical Earnestness: English social theory 1880–1980*. Oxford: Martin Robertson, 1982.

Irwin, Terence H., 'Eminent Victorians and Greek Ethics: Sidgwick, Green and Aristotle', in Bart Schultz, ed., *Essays on Henry Sidgwick*. Cambridge: Cambridge University Press, 1992, pp. 279–310.

Jackson, Robert, *Quasi-states: Sovereignty, international relations and the Third World*. Cambridge: Cambridge University Press, 1990.

Jay, Elizabeth and Richard Jay, eds., *Critics of Capitalism: Victorian reactions to 'political economy'*. Cambridge: Cambridge University Press, 1992.

Jenks, Craig, 'T.H. Green, the Oxford Philosophy of Duty and the English Middle Class', *British Journal of Sociology*, 28:4 (1977): 481–97.

Joachim, Harold H., *The Nature of Truth*. Oxford: Clarendon Press, 1906.

Jones, Henry, 'The Social Organism', in Andrew Seth and R.B. Haldane, eds., *Essays in Philosophical Criticism*, with a preface by Edward Caird. London: Longmans, Green and Co., 1883, pp. 187–213.

Jones, Sir Henry and John H. Muirhead, *The Life and Philosophy of Edward Caird, LL.D., D.C.L.*. Glasgow: MacLehose, Jackson, 1921.

Kadish, Alon, *The Oxford Economists in the Late Nineteenth Century*. Oxford: Clarendon Press, 1982.

Kadish, Alon, *Apostle Arnold: The life and death of Arnold Toynbee, 1852–83*. Notre Dame, IA: Duke University Press, 1987.

Kainz, Howard, *Democracy East and West: A philosophical overview*. London: MacMillan, 1984.

Kant, Immanuel, *Critique of Pure Reason*, trans. Norman Kemp Smith. London: MacMillan, 1929.

Kant, Immanuel, *Critique of Judgement*, trans. J.C. Meredith. Oxford: Clarendon Press, 1952 [originally published 1790].

Kant, Immanuel, *The Metaphysics of Morals*, trans. Mary Gregor. Cambridge: Cambridge University Press, 1991.

Kant, Immanuel, *Political Writings*, second edition, ed. Hans Reiss. Cambridge: Cambridge University Press, 1991.

Kant, Immanuel, *Practical Philosophy*, trans. and ed. Mary J. Gregor. Cambridge: Cambridge University Press, 1996.

Kant, Immanuel, *Theoretical Philosophy after 1781*, ed. H. Allison and P. Heath, trans. Peter Heath. Cambridge: Cambridge University Press, 2001.

Katz, Jerrold J., 'Semantic Theory and the Meaning of "Good"', *Journal of Philosophy*, 61:23 (10 December 1964): 739–66.

Kemp, J., 'T.H. Green and the Ethics of Self-realisation', in G.N.A. Vesey, ed., *Reason and Reality: Royal Institute of Philosophy Lectures, Volume Five, 1970–71*. London: MacMillan, 1972, pp. 222–40.

Kierkegaard, Søren, *Fear and Trembling*, trans. Alastair Hannay. London: Penguin, 2005 [originally published 1843].

Kierkegaard, Søren, *Philosophical Fragments or A Fragment of Philosophy*, second edition. Princeton, NJ: Princeton University Press, 1962 [1932] [originally published 1844].

King, Bolton, *Mazzini*. London: J.M. Dent, 1902.

Kinna, Ruth, *William Morris: The art of socialism*. Cardiff: University of Wales Press, 2000.

Kloppenberg, James T., *Uncertain Victory: Social democracy and progressivism in European and American thought, 1870–1920*. New York and Oxford: Oxford University Press, 1986.

Knapp, Vincent J., 'T.H. Green on the Exorability of Property', *Agora*, 1 (1969): 57–65.

Knight, William Angus, *Memoir of John Nichol, Professor of English Literature in the University of Glasgow*. Glasgow: James MacLehose, 1896.

Lamont, W.D., *An Introduction to Green's Moral Philosophy*. London: George Allen and Unwin, 1934.

Lancaster, Lane W., *The Masters of Political Thought: Volume Three, Hegel to Dewey*. London: George G. Harrap, 1959.

Laski, Harold J., 'Leaders of Collectivist Thought', in H. Grisewood, ed., *Ideas and Beliefs of the Victorians: An historic reevaluation of the Victorian age*. London: Sylvan, 1949, pp. 417–22.

Lawless, Andrew, 'T.H. Green and the British Liberal Tradition', *Canadian Journal of Political and Social Theory*, 2:2 (1978): 142–55.

Leighton, Denys P., *The Greenian Moment: T.H. Green, religion and political argument in Victorian Britain*. Exeter and Charlottesville, VA: Imprint Academic, 2004.

Lewis, H.D., *Freedom and History*. London: George Allen and Unwin, 1962.

Lindsay, A.D., 'Introduction', in T.H. Green, *Lectures on the Principles of Political Obligation*. London: Longmans, 1941, pp. vii–xix.

Locke, John, *Two Treatise of Government*, ed. Peter Laslett. Cambridge: Cambridge University Press, 1988.

Locke, John, *A Letter Concerning Toleration*, ed. John Horton and Susan Mendus. London and New York: Routledge, 1991.

Longfield, M., 'The Tenure of Land in Ireland', in J.W. Probyn, ed., *Systems of Land Tenure in Various Countries*. London: Cassell, Petter, Galpin, 1876, pp. 1–92.

Mabbott, J.D., *The State and the Citizen: An introduction to political philosophy*, second edition. London: Hutchinson University Library, 1967 [1948].

MacCallum, Gerald G., jnr, 'Berlin on the Compatibility of Values, Ideals, and "Ends"', *Ethics*, 77 (1966–67): 139–45.

MacCunn, John, *Six Radical Thinkers: Bentham. J.S. Mill, Cobden, Carlyle, Mazzini, T.H. Green*. London: Edward Arnold, 1907.

MacIntyre, Alasdair, *A Short History of Ethics*. London: Routledge, 1967.

MacIntyre, Alasdair, *Dependent Rational Animals: Why human beings need the virtues*. London: Duckworth, 1999.

MacKenzie, John S., *A Manual of Ethics*. London: University Tutorial Press, 1929 [1883].

MacKillop, Ian D., *The British Ethical Societies*. Cambridge: Cambridge University Press, 1986.

MacPherson, C.B., *Political Theory of Possessive Individualism: Hobbes to Locke*. Oxford: Oxford University Press, 1962.

MacPherson, C.B., *Democratic Theory: Essays in retrieval*. Oxford: Clarendon Press, 1973.

MacPherson, C.B., *The Rise and Fall of Economic Justice*. Oxford: Oxford University Press, 1978.

Maine, Sir Henry, *Ancient Law: Its connections with the early history of society and its relation to modern ideas*, with introduction and notes by Sir Frederick Pollock. London: John Murray, 1920 [1861].

Mander, W.J., *British Idealism: A history*. Oxford: Oxford University Press, 2011.

Marcuse, Herbert, *Reason and Revolution: Hegel and the rise of social theory*, second edition. London: Routledge and Kegan Paul 1963 [1954].

Martin, Kathleen C., *Hard and Unreal Advice: Mothers, science and Victorian poverty experts*. Houndsmill: Palgrave MacMillan, 2007.

Martin, Rex, 'Green on Natural Rights in Hobbes, Spinoza and Locke', in Andrew Vincent, ed., *The Philosophy of T.H. Green*. Aldershot: Gower, 1986, pp. 104–26.

Martin, Rex, 'T.H. Green on individual rights and the common good', in Avital Simhony and David Weinstein, eds., *The New Liberalism: Reconciling liberty and community*. Cambridge: Cambridge University Press, 2001, pp. 49–68.

Marx, Karl and Friedrich Engels, *Selected Works*, 2 vols.. Moscow: Foreign Languages Publishing House, 1962.

Marx, Karl, *The German Ideology: Introduction to a critique of political economy*, ed. C.J. Arthur, second edition. London: Lawrence and Wishart, 1974.

Marx, Karl, *Early Writings*, trans. Rodney Livingston and Gregor Benton. Harmondsworth: Penguin, 1975.

Mayer, J.P., in co-operation with R.H.S. Crossman, P. Kecskemeti, C.J.S. Sprigge and E. Kohn-Bramstedt, *Political Thought: The European tradition*. London: J.M. Dent, 1939.

Mayhew, Henry, *London Labour and the London Poor*, 4 vols.. London: privately printed, 1851–61.

Mazzini, Giuseppe, *The Life and Writings,* ed. Emilie Ashurst, 6 vols., second edition. London: Smith, Elder, 1891.

McCloskey, H.J., 'The State as an Organism, as a Person, and as an End in Itself', *Philosophical Review*, 72 (1963): 306–26.

McLellan, David, *Marx before Marxism*. London: MacMillan, 1970.

Mehta, Vrajendra R., 'T.H. Green and the Problem of Political Obligation', *Indian Political Science Review*, 7 (1973): 115–24.

Mehta, Vrajendra R., 'T.H. Green and the Revision of English Liberal Theory', *Indian Journal of Political Science*, 35 (1974): 37–49.

Mendus, Susan, *Impartiality in Moral and Political Philosophy*. Oxford: Oxford University Press, 2002.

Metz, Rudolf, *A Hundred Years of British Philosophy*. London: George Allen and Unwin, 1938.

Mill, John Stuart, *Collected Works, Volume III – The Principles of Political Economy with Some of Their Applications to Social Philosophy (Books III–V and Appendices)*, ed. John M. Robson, Introduction by V.W. Bladen. Toronto: University of Toronto Press; London: Routledge and Kegan Paul, 1965.

Milne, A.J.M., *The Social Philosophy of English Idealism*. London: Allen and Unwin, 1962.

Milne, A.J.M., 'The Idealist Criticism of Utilitarian Social Philosophy', *Archives Européenes de Sociologie*, 8 (1967): 319–31.

Milne, A.J.M., 'The Common Good and Rights in T.H. Green's Ethical and Political Thought', in Andrew Vincent, ed., *The Philosophy of T.H. Green*. Aldershot: Gower, 1986, pp. 62–75.

Monro, D.H., 'Green, Rousseau, and the Culture Pattern', *Philosophy*, 26:99 (1951): 347–57.

Morris, William, *Political Writings*, ed. A.L. Morton. London: Lawrence and Wishart, 1973.

Morrow, John, 'Property and Personal Development: An interpretation of T.H. Green's political philosophy', *Politics: Journal of the Australasian Political Science Association*, 18 (1981): 84–92.

Morrow, John, 'Review article: Ancestors, Legacies and Traditions: British idealism in the history of political thought', *History of Political Thought*, 6 (1985): 491–515.

Morrow, John, 'Private Property, Liberal Subjects and the State', in David Weinstein and Avital Simhony, eds., *The New Liberalism: Reconciling liberty and community*. Cambridge: Cambridge University Press, 2001, pp. 92–114.

Mouffe, Chantal, *Return of the Political*. London and New York: Verso, 1993.

Muirhead, John H., 'Recent Criticism of the Idealist Theory of the General Will', *Mind*, 33 (1924): no. 130, 166–75, no. 131, 233–41, no. 132, 361–68.

Muirhead, John H., *The Service of the State: Four lectures on the political teaching of T.H. Green*. London: John Murray, 1908.

Mukhopadhyay, Amal K., *The Ethics of Obedience: A study of the philosophy of T.H. Green*. Calcutta: World Press Private, 1967.

Nettleship, Richard Lewis, 'Professor T.H. Green. In memoriam', *Contemporary Review*, 61 (January–June 1882): 857–77.

Nevinson, Henry W., *Visions and Memories*, ed. Evelyn Sharp. London: Oxford University Press, 1944.

Nicholson, Peter P., 'Philosophical idealism and International Politics: A reply to Dr Savigear', *British Journal of International Studies*, 2 (1976): 76–83.

Nicholson, Peter P., 'A Moral View of Politics: T.H. Green and the British idealists', *Political Studies*, 35 (1987): 116–22.

Nicholson, Peter P., 'T.H. Green and State Action: Liquor legislation', *History of Political Thought*, 6 (1987): 517–50.

Nicholson, Peter P., *The Political Philosophy of the British Idealists: Selected studies*. Cambridge: Cambridge University Press, 1990.

Nicholson, Peter P., 'T.H. Green's Doubts about Hegel's Political Philosophy', *Bulletin of the Hegel Society of Great Britain*, 31 (1995): 61–72.

Nicholson, Peter P., 'Green's "Eternal Consciousness"', in Maria Dimova-Cookson and W.J. Mander, eds., *T.H. Green: Ethics, metaphysics and political philosophy*. Oxford: Clarendon Press, 2006, pp. 139–59.

Nomer, Nedim, 'Fichte and the Idea of Liberal Socialism', *Journal of Political Philosophy*, 13:1 (2005): 139–59.

Nomer, Nedim, 'Fichte and the relationship between self-positing and rights', *Journal of History of Philosophy*, 48:4 (2010): 469–490.

Norrie, Alan W., *Law, Ideology and Punishment: Retrieval and critique of the liberal idea of criminal justice*. London: Kluwer, 1991.

O'Sullivan, Noël, *The Problem of Political Obligation*. New York: Garland, 1987.

Owen, Robert, *A New View of Society, and other writings*. London: J.M. Dent, 1927.

Packe, Michael St John, *The Life of John Stuart Mill*. London: Secker and Warburg, 1954.

Pant, Nalini, *Theory of Rights: Green, Bosanquet, Spencer and Laski*. Varanasi: Vishwavidyalaya Prakashan, 1977.

Parekh, Bhikhu, 'A Misconceived Discourse on Political Obligation', *Political Studies,* 41:2 (June 1993): 236–51.

Parekh, Bhikhu, 'Cultural Diversity and Liberal Democracy', in David Beetham, ed., *Defining and Measuring Democracy*. London: Sage, 1994, pp. 199–221.

Pettit, Philip, *Republicanism: A theory of freedom and government*. Oxford: Oxford University Press, 1997.

Phillips, D.C., 'Organicism in the Late Nineteenth and Earlier Twentieth Centuries', *Journal of the History of Ideas*, 31 (1970): 413–32.

Phillips, Michael J., 'Thomas Hill Green, Positive Freedom and the United States Supreme Court', *Emory Law Journal*, 25 (1976): 63–114.

Pinkard, Terry, *German Philosophy, 1760 to 1860: The legacy of idealism*. Cambridge: Cambridge University Press, 2002.

Plamenatz, John, *Consent, Freedom, and Political Obligation*. London: Oxford University Press, 1938.

Poulton, Edward Bagnall, *John Viriamu Jones and other Oxford Memories*. London: Longmans, 1911.

Prest, John, ed., *Balliol College Annual Record 1998*. Privately printed, 1998.

Prichard, Harold A., *Moral Obligation: Essays and lectures*. Oxford: Clarendon Press, 1949.

Proudhon, Pierre-Joseph, *What is Property? An inquiry into the principle of right and of government,* trans. Benjamin R. Tucker. New York: Dover, 1970 [first French edition 1840].

Rashdall, Hastings, *The Theory of Good and Evil*, 2 vols.. London: Oxford University Press, 1924.

Rawls, John, *A Theory of Justice*, revised edition. Oxford: Oxford University Press, 1999.

Raz, Joseph, *The Morality of Freedom*. Oxford: Clarendon Press, 1986.

Reeve, Andrew, *Property*. London: MacMillan, 1986.

Reid, Alastair J., *United We Stand: A history of Britain's trade unions*. Harmondsworth: Penguin, 2005.

Rich, Paul, 'T.H. Green, Lord Scarman and the Issue of Ethnic Minority Rights in English Liberal Thought', *Ethnic and Racial Studies*, 10:2 (1987): 149–68.

Richards, E.F., ed., *Mazzini's Letters to an English Family 1861–72*, 3 vols. London: John Lane, n.d.

Richter, Melvin, *The Politics of Conscience: T.H. Green and his age*. London: Weidenfeld and Nicolson, 1964.

Richter, Melvin, 'Intellectual and Class Alienation: Oxford idealist diagnoses and prescriptions', *Archives Européenes de Sociologie*, 7 (1966): 1–26.

Ritchie, David George, *Darwinism and Hegel, and other philosophical studies*. London: Swan Sonnenschein, 1893.

Ritchie, David G., *The Principles of State Interference: Four essays on the political philosophy of Mr. Herbert Spencer, J.S. Mill, and T.H. Green*, third edition. London Swan Sonnenschein, 1902 [1891].

Ritchie, David George, 'The Rights of Animals', *International Journal of Ethics*, 10 (1899/1900): 387–89.

Ritchie, David George, *Natural Rights: A criticism of political and ethical conceptions*, second edition. London: George Allen, 1903.

Robbins, Peter, *The British Hegelians 1875–1925*. New York: Garland, 1982.

Rodman, John, ed., *The Political Theory of T.H. Green: Selected writings*. New York: Appleton-Century-Crofts, 1964.

Rodman, John, 'What is Living and What is Dead in the Political Philosophy of T.H. Green', *Western Political Quarterly*, 26:3 (1973): 566–86.

Rogers, Arthur K., *English and American Philosophy Since 1800: A critical survey*. New York: MacMillan, 1922.

Rousseau, Jean-Jacques, *The Social Contract*, trans. Maurice Cranston. London: Penguin, 1968.

Ruskin, John, *Unto This Last: Four essays on the first principles of political economy*. London: George Allen, 1900 [1862].

Sabine, George H., 'The Social Origin of Absolute Idealism', *Journal of Philosophy, Psychology and Scientific Methods*, 12:7 (1915): 169–77.

Sabine, George H., *A History of Political Theory*, rev. T.L. Thorson. Hindsale: Dryden, 1973.

Sampson, Geoffrey, 'Good', *Linguistic Inquiry*, 1:2 (April 1970): 257–60.

Sankhdher, M.M., 'T.H. Green: The forerunner of the welfare state', *Indian Journal of Political Science*, 30 (1969): 148–64.

Sankhdher, M.M., 'T.H. Green's Concept of the Welfare State', *Journal of Political Studies*, 3 (1970): 1–21.

Schneewind, Jerome B., *Sidgwick's Ethics and Victorian Moral Philosophy*. Oxford: Clarendon Press, 1977.

Scruton, Roger, *Palgrave MacMillan Dictionary of Political Thought*, third edition. London: Palgrave MacMillan, 2007.

Sherover, Charles M., ed., *The Development of the Democratic Idea: Readings from Pericles to the present*. New York: Mentor, 1974 [1968].

Sherover, Charles M., *Time, Freedom, and the Common Good: An essay in public philosophy*. Albany, NY: State University of New York Press, 1989.

Shionoya, Yuichi, 'The Oxford Approach to the Philosophical Foundations of the Welfare State', in Roger E. Backhouse and Tamotsu Nishizawa, eds., *No Wealth But Life: Welfare economics and the welfare state, 1880–1945*. Cambridge: Cambridge University Press, 2010, pp. 91–113.

Sidgwick, Henry, *Lectures on the Ethics of T.H. Green, Mr. Herbert Spencer, and J. Martineau*, ed. E.E. Constance Jones. London: MacMillan, 1907.

Sidgwick, Henry, *Outlines of the History of Ethics for English Readers,* fifth edition. London: MacMillan, 1902.

Simhony, Avital, 'Idealist Organicism: Beyond holism and individualism', *History of Political Thought*, 10:3 (1989): 515–35.

Simhony, Avital, 'On Forcing Individuals to be Free: T.H. Green's liberal theory of positive freedom', *Political Studies*, 49 (1991): 303–20.

Simhony, Avital, 'T.H. Green: The common good society', *History of Political Thought*, 14:3 (1993): 225–47.

Simhony, Avital, Review of Colin Tyler, *Thomas Hill Green…*, *Bradley Studies*, 5:1 (Spring 1999): 87–106.

Simhony, Avital, 'T.H. Green's Complex Liberalism: Between liberalism and communitarianism', in Avital Simhony and David Weinstein, eds., *The New Liberalism: Reconciling liberty and community*. Cambridge: Cambridge University Press, 2001, pp. 69–91.

Simhony, Avital, 'Rights that Bind: T.H. Green on rights and community', in Maria Dimova-Cookson and W.J. Mander, eds., *T.H. Green: Ethics, metaphysics and political philosophy*. Oxford: Clarendon Press, 2006, pp. 236–61.

Simmons, A. John, *Moral Principles and Political Obligation*. Princeton, NJ: Princeton University Press, 1979.

Smith, Craig A., 'The Individual and Society in T.H. Green's Theory of Virtue', *History of Political Thought*, 2:1 (1981): 187–201.

Smith, Denis Mack, *Mazzini*. New Haven, CT, and London: Yale University Press, 1994.

Smyth, Newman, *Christian Ethics*, second edition. Edinburgh: T. and T. Clark, 1893.

Squires, Judith, 'Culture, Equality and Diversity', in Paul Kelly, ed., *Multiculturalism Reconsidered: Culture and Equality and its critics*. Cambridge: Polity, 2002, pp. 114–32.

Stendhal, *Love*, trans. G. Sale and S. Sale. Harmondsworth: Penguin, 1975.

Sturt, Henry, *Idoli Theatri: A criticism of Oxford thought and practice from the standpoint of personal idealism*. London: MacMillan, 1906.

Symonds, John Addington, *Letters*, 3 vols., eds., Herbert M. Schueller and Robert L. Peters. Detroit, MI: Wayne State University Press, 1968–69.

Talmon, Jacob, *The Origins of Totalitarian Democracy*. London: Secker and Warburg, 1952.

Tawney, R.H., *The Radical Tradition*, ed. R. Hinden. Harmondsworth: Pelican, 1964.

Thakurdas, Frank, *The English Utilitarians and the Idealists: An introductory study of the development of English political theory in the eighteenth and nineteenth centuries*. Delhi: Vishal, 1978.

Thomas, Geoffrey, *The Moral Philosophy of T.H. Green*. Oxford: Clarendon, 1987.

Thomson, David, 'Conclusion: The Idea of Equality', in David Thomson, ed., *Political Ideas*. Harmondsworth: Penguin, 1969, pp. 196–200.

Tönnies, Ferdinand, *Community and Association*, trans. Charles P. Loomis. London: Routledge and Kegan Paul, 1955.

Toynbee, Arnold, *Industrial Revolution*. Newton Abbot: David and Charles Reprints, 1969 [1884].

Tyler, Colin, 'The Implications of Parekh's Cultural Pluralism', *Politics*, 16:3 (September 1996): 151–57.

Tyler, Colin, *Thomas Hill Green (1836–1882) and the Philosophical Foundations of Politics: An internal critique*. Lampeter and Lewiston, NY: Edwin Mellen, 1997.

Tyler, Colin, 'Cultural Pluralism: A response to Seglow's reply', *Politics*, 18:2 (May 1998): 107–10.

Tyler, Colin, '"This Dangerous Drug of Violence": Making sense of Bernard Bosanquet's theory of punishment', *Collingwood and British Idealism Studies*, 7 (2000): 116–40.

Tyler, Colin, 'Strangers and Compatriots: The political theory of cultural diversity', in John Rex and Gurharpal Singh, eds., *Governance in Multicultural Societies*. Aldershot: Ashgate, 2004, pp. 19–35.

Tyler, Colin, 'Contesting the Common Good: T.H. Green and contemporary republicanism', in M. Dimova-Cookson and W.J. Mander, eds., *T.H. Green: Ethics, metaphysics and political philosophy*. Oxford: Clarendon, 2006, pp. 262–91.

Tyler, Colin, 'Elitism and Anti-elitism in Nineteenth Century British Political Thought', *History of European Ideas*, 32 (August 2006): 345–55.

Tyler, Colin, *Idealist Political Philosophy: Pluralism and conflict in the absolute idealist tradition*. London and New York: Continuum, 2006.

Tyler, Colin, '"History's Actors"?: Insights into the "war on terror" from international relations theory', in Maurice Mullard and Bankole A. Cole, eds., *Globalisation, Citizenship and the War on Terror*. Cheltenham: Edward Elgar, 2007, pp. 32–54.

Tyler, Colin, 'Performativity and the Intellectual Historian's Re-enactment of Written Works', *Journal of the Philosophy of History*, 3:2 (2009), 167–186.

Tyler, Colin, 'The Liberal Hegelianism of Edward Caird: Or, how to transcend the social economics of Kant and the romantics', *International Journal of Social Economics*, 37:11 (November 2010): 852–866.

Tyler, Colin, 'Power, alienation and performativity in capitalist societies', *European Journal of Social Theory* 14:2 (May 2011): 161–80.

Tyler, Colin, 'D.G. Ritchie on socialism, History and Locke', *Journal of Political Ideologies*, 17:3 (October 2012).

Tyler, Colin, ed., *Unpublished Manuscripts in British Idealism: Political philosophy, theology and social thought*, 2 vols. London and New York: Thoemmes, 2005; Exeter and Charlottesville, VA: Imprint Academic, 2008.

Tyler, Colin, ed., 'Recollections Regarding Thomas Hill Green', *Collingwood and British Idealism Studies*, 14:2 (2008): 5–78.

Ulam, Adam B., *The Philosophical Foundations of English Socialism*. Cambridge, MA: Harvard University Press, 1951.

Vaughan, Charles Edwyn, *Studies in the History of Political Philosophy before and after Rousseau*, 2 vols.. Manchester: University of Manchester Press, 1925.

Vincent, Andrew, 'The State and Social Purpose in Idealist Political Philosophy', *History of European Ideas*, 8:3 (1987): 333–47.

Vincent, Andrew and Raymond Plant, *Philosophy, Politics and Citizenship: The life and thought of the British idealists*. Oxford: Basil Blackwell, 1984.

Walzer, Michael, *Interpretation and Social Criticism*. Cambridge, MA: Harvard University Press, 1985.

Weber, Max, *The Methodology of the Social Sciences*, ed. and trans. Edward A. Shils and Henry A. Finch. New York: Simon and Schuster, Free Press, 1949 [1904].

Weinstein, David, 'Between Kantianism and Consequentialism in T.H. Green's Moral Philosophy', *Political Studies*, 41:4 (1993), 618–35.

Wempe, Ben, *Beyond Equality: A study of T.H. Green's theory of positive freedom*. Leiden: Eburon, 1986.

Wempe, Ben, *T.H. Green's Theory of Positive Freedom: From metaphysics to positive freedom*. Exeter and Charlottesville, VA: Imprint Academic, 2004.

Williams, Robert R., *Hegel's Ethics of Recognition*. Berkeley and Los Angeles, CA: University of California Press, 1997.

Wintrop, Norman, 'Liberal-Democratic Theory: The New Liberalism', in Norman Wintrop, ed., *Liberal Democratic Theory and its Critics*. London: Croom Helm, 1983, pp. 83–132.

Index

Comprehensive entries on such terms as 'citizenship', 'community', 'enrichment', 'good', 'freedom' and 'the state' would be far too long to appear in this index. Consequently, readers should refer also to the table of contents given on pages vii to x.